Economics

Walter J. Wessels

Associate Professor of Economics
Department of Economics and Business
North Carolina State University

BARRON'S
New York • London • Toronto • Sydney

All inquiries should be addressed to:
Barron's Educational Series, Inc.
250 Wireless Boulevard
Hauppauge, New York 11788

International Standard Book No. 0-8120-3560-7

Library of Congress Cataloging No. 86-22203

Library of Congress Cataloging-in-Publication Data
Wessels, Walter J.
  Economics.

  (Business review series)
  Includes index.
  1. Economics.   I. Title.   II. Series.
HB171.5.W43 1986   330   86-22203
ISBN 0-8120-3560-7

CONTENTS

MACROECONOMICS: AGGREGATE SUPPLY AND DEMAND

MICROECONOMICS: CONSUMER AND COST

INTERNATIONAL TRADE

APPENDIX

PREFACE

This book provides a clear and concise introduction to economics. It focuses on the essentials needed to understand our economy, and it illustrates discussions with many problems (and explained answers) to test and reinforce this understanding. Students taking economics who want to do better in their courses, as well as business professionals who seek a fuller understanding of economics to make better business decisions, will benefit from this text. In addition, anyone seeking to understand the causes and effects of inflation, trade deficits, government deficits, and the business cycle will find the central insights of economists clearly explained. Keynesian, monetarist, and rational-expectation economics are all explained in detail. This study guide extensively shows the application of economics to business decisions.

Throughout this guide, you will find it easy to learn the essentials of economics, especially if you follow the procedure outlined:

1. *Learn the Definitions and Main Points.* Each chapter begins with *Key Terms* discussed throughout that unit. This is followed by *You Should Remember*, which summarizes main points taught.

2. *Work Each Example and Graph.* As you read the chapters, be sure you work out each example. In addition, because using graphs is essential to understanding economics, be sure you understand each graph before going on to new material. One way to assure this, is to redraw each graph and see how it matches the explanation given in the text.

3. *Do All Problems. Do You Know the Basics* tests your understanding of the basic concepts of economics. *Practical Application* tests your ability to apply the economic tools you've learned. Answers are provided for both. Don't skip either of these sections!

4. *Understand the Assumptions Being Made.* Economists use economic models to understand the world. Once you understand an economic model's *assumptions,* the *results* will follow logically. In this text, the assumptions of Keynesian, monetarist, and rational-expectations models are presented in separate chapters so that you can focus on each and thus understand how and why each model works the way it does.

An understanding of economics is essential for understanding the economic events that affect us all. Carefully studying this book in the way that I've outlined will help you gain that understanding.

Walter J. Wessels

LIST OF ABBREVIATIONS

%Δ	the percent change in	MRS	marginal rate of subs
AD	aggregate demand, aggregate demand curve	MS	money supply
		MSB	marginal social benefit
AFC	average fixed cost	MSC	marginal social cost
APC	average propensity to consume	MU	marginal utility
		MVP	value of marginal product
AS	aggregate supply, aggregate supply curve	NI	national income
		NNP	net national product
ATC	average total cost	NX	net export spending (foreign)
AVC	average variable cost		
C	consumption spending (household)	P	price level
		PC	Phillips curve
COLA	cost of living adjustments	P^d	demand price
CPI	consumer price index	PMC	private marginal cost
DI	disposable income	PPI	producer price index
DOL	Department of Labor	PQ	price × output, or nominal GNP
FOMC	federal open market committee		
		P^s	supply price
G	government spending	PV	present value
GNP	gross national product	Q	output, total income and spending, real GNP
$GNP	nominal GNP		
I	investment spending	QD	quantity demand
i	interest rate	R	required reserve ratio
M	nominal money supply	S	savings
MB	marginal benefit	SMC	social marginal cost
MC	marginal cost	S-Long Run	long-run aggregate supply curve
MD	nominal money demand		
MFC	marginal factor cost	T	taxes
M/P	real money supply	TC	total cost
MPC	marginal propensity to consume	TFC	total fixed cost
		TR	total revenue
MPP	marginal physical product	TVC	total variable cost
MPS	marginal propensity to save	V	velocity (or $GNP/MD)
MR	marginal revenue	VMP	value of marginal product
MRP	marginal revenue product		

1

WHAT IS ECONOMICS ALL ABOUT?

KEY TERMS

economics study of how people choose among alternative uses of their scarce resources.

marginal analysis solving for the most profitable level of a variable (such as output) by evaluating the effect of an additional unit of the variable on benefits and costs. If the addition to benefits (marginal benefit) exceeds or equals marginal cost, the unit is added.

opportunity cost value of the best alternative that had to be forgone in order to undertake a given course of action.

production possibility curve (or frontier) a graph showing combinations of goods that an individual, a firm, or an economy is capable of producing.

scarcity a condition that exists when current resources are inadequate to provide for all of people's wants.

THE BASIS FOR ECONOMICS

Economics is the study of how people choose to allocate their scarce resources. In this chapter, we investigate the meaning of scarcity, how scarcity results in costs, and how people can make the most of their scarce resources by using marginal analysis. *These three concepts—scarcity, cost, and marginal analysis—form the base upon which economics is built.*

SCARCITY

Most people want far more than their current resources allow them to have.

1

This is **scarcity**: people wanting more than can be satisfied with available resources.

Don't confuse scarcity with poverty: Even the rich want more! And remember, the fact that there is only a small quantity of a good (such as castor oil cola) does *not* make it scarce: It must also be desirable.

Test for Determining Scarcity of a Good: If having more units of a good makes someone better off, the good is scarce. If not, it is a **free good.** For example, air and sand in a desert are free goods.

• *CHOICE*

Scarcity forces people to make choices. When a good is scarce, people are forced to choose between which uses will be fulfilled and which will not be fulfilled. As a consequence, people face a **trade-off**: To satisfy *more* of one need means satisfying *less* of another. For example, when people save their money by putting it into a savings account, they are trading off spending that money today in order to have more to spend in the future.

OPPORTUNITY COST

When a good is scarce, choosing to use the good in one way means giving up some other use. The value of the use people give up is the **opportunity cost** of this choice. Opportunity costs can also be defined as the "value of the best foregone alternative use." This emphasizes that had people *not* made the choice they did, they would have then chosen the next best alternative.

Example: How Opportunity Costs Are Measured

PROBLEM An owner of a small firm needs to hire some managers. Assume that each manager has time to do only one task. Task A is worth $100,000 to the owner, Task B is worth $75,000, and Task C is worth $50,000. The owner hires only two managers, having one do Task A and the other do Task B. What is the opportunity cost of Task B?

SOLUTION The opportunity cost of Task B is the value of the foregone task that otherwise would have been accomplished, which in this case is Task C. So the opportunity cost of Task B is $50,000. Note that the opportunity cost of Task A is also $50,000 since, with two managers, Task C is forgone given up to do Task A.

Example: How the Value of a Good Is Measured

PROBLEM   In the above problem, assume the firm still has only two managers. Assume further that each manager can do the other's task with the same efficiency. What is the value of the second manager (i.e., what would the firm lose if it fired [and did not replace] the second manager)? What is the value of the first manager (when the second is still employed)?

SOLUTION   If the second manager is let go (and not replaced), Task B will not be done. So the second manager's value is $70,000. If the first manager is let go but the second remains, the second manager will take over Task A, leaving task B undone. So the first manager is also worth $70,000.

This illustrates a basic principle of rationality: When the units of a good or resource are *interchangeable,* people value each and every unit of the good by the good's least valued use (of its current uses). In economic terms, this is the good's marginal value: the value of the good's least important use, which people would forgo if they had one less unit.

YOU SHOULD REMEMBER

1. *Scarcity* occurs whenever people desire more of a good than exists. When a good is scarce, people have to choose among its uses. Scarcity is the source of all choice.

2. A good is a *free good* if it is not scarce. More units of a free good would *not* make anyone better off.

3. *Opportunity cost* is the highest-valued alternative people have to sacrifice because of the decisions they make. The concept of opportunity costs implies making trade-offs. Getting more of one thing means getting less of another.

4. When the units of a good are interchangeable, each unit should be valued by the good's *marginal value*—the value of the use that would be foregone if there were one less unit of the good.

• *PRODUCTION POSSIBILITY CURVE*

To illustrate the trade-offs faced by a person, firm, or economy, economists use **production possibility curves**. These curves show the *trade-offs* (or *opportunity costs*) people face because of the scarcity of resources. Table 1-1 shows the trade-offs a worker might face when the worker has only four hours in total to produce two goods: chairs and benches. In this example, time (the four hours) is the source of scarcity. The more time the worker spends making chairs, the less time can be spent making benches. Table 1-1 shows this trade-off as the worker spends more time making chairs.

Table 1-1. Determining Trade-Offs Because of Resource Scarcity

CHAIRS		BENCHES	
Time Spent (in hours)	Product Made	Time Spent (in hours)	Product Made
0	0	4	20
1	4	3	18
2	7	2	14
3	9	1	8
4	10	0	0

Figure 1-1 shows the production possibility curve derived from these numbers. If the worker devotes all four hours to making benches, 20 benches and no chairs will be produced (at Point *A*). One hour spent making chairs (and one *less* hour spent making benches) results in 4 chairs and 18 benches being produced (at Point *B*). Two hours on each results in 7 chairs and 14 benches (at Point *C*).

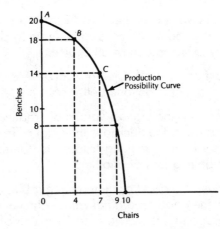

Figure 1-1 Law of Increasing Relative Cost Shown by Production Possibility Curve

Given this information, how do we measure opportunity cost?

Note: If you have trouble with graphs such as that in Figure 1-1, turn to Chapter 2.

Key Procedure for Calculating Opportunity Cost Per Unit for a Production Possibility Curve

1. Start with any *increase* in production of one good, and let this be the *gain.*

2. Measure the *loss* (the decrease in the other good's production necessary to get the gain).

3. Opportunity cost per unit of the good gained is the *loss* divided by the *gain.*

For example, a third hour added to chair-making has a gain of 2 chairs (from 7 to 9) and a loss of 6 benches (from 14 to 8), so the opportunity cost per chair over this range is 3 benches per chair (6/2).

Example: Measuring Opportunity Cost

PROBLEM   The worker is currently spending one hour making chairs and three hours making benches. What is the opportunity cost per chair of spending a second hour in chair-making (assuming the worker is still limited to four hours)? What is the dollar value of this opportunity cost if benches sell for $12? If chairs sell for $25, how many hours should be spent making chairs?

SOLUTION   The opportunity cost per chair during the second hour added to chair-making is four-thirds of a bench, or one and one-third benches. In dollar terms, this is $16 (4/3 × $12). That is, in the second hour, for every chair made, the worker gives up making four-thirds of a bench (or $16). The dollar opportunity cost per chair of the third hour added to chair-making is $24 (2 × $12) and for the fourth hour added to chair-making, $96 (8 × $12). The worker should spend three hours making chairs; up to and including the third hour, each chair adds more ($25) than is given up (where what is given up is measured by the dollar opportunity cost). But the fourth hour's opportunity cost per chair ($96) exceeds the $25 value of a chair.

LAW OF INCREASING RELATIVE COSTS

In our example, each additional hour spent in chair-making had a higher opportunity cost per chair than did the preceding hour. (The first hour's cost per chair was one-half a bench, the second hour's cost was one and one-third benches, the third hour's cost was two benches, and the fourth hour's cost was eight benches.) This *increase* in opportunity cost is shown by the production possibility curve becoming *steeper* as we move right in Figure 1-1.

This example illustrates **the law of increasing relative costs**: As more of a good is produced, its opportunity cost rises. Note that the law refers to "relative cost." In this example, relative cost is the good's opportunity cost. When individuals, firms, or economies face increasing relative costs, their production possibility curves are *bowed out* as in Figure 1-1.

Reasons for Increasing Relative Costs

1. *Diminishing returns,* a condition that occurs when each additional unit of input adds less and less to total output. For example, the worker produced four chairs in the first hour of chair-making, but the second hour added only three more chairs, and the third hour, only two more. Increasing relative costs result when all goods have diminishing returns.

2. *Differing Suitability of inputs,* which occurs when some workers are better at producing Good A, others Good B. Economically, the first set of resources an economy should devote to producing Good A will be those best-suited for A's efficient production. As more and more of Good A is produced, it is likely that resources less and less suited to its efficient production will eventually be used, and the result will be an increase in the relative cost of Good A. A major reason why inputs may differ in suitability is specialization (e.g., a worker who specializes in producing Good A may not know how to produce Good B).

YOU SHOULD REMEMBER

1. The trade-offs and opportunity costs caused by scarcity are illustrated with the *production possibility curve*. It shows a menu of possible outputs of goods (usually of two goods) that can be produced.

2. The *slope* of the production possibility curve shows the opportunity cost. For example, in Figure 1-1, a slope of -2 means that one more chair costs two benches. (See Chapter 2 for the definition of "slope.")

3. The *law of increasing relative cost* is shown by the slope of the production possibility curve becoming steeper as one moves along it to the right. This can be due to diminishing returns or to differences in suitability of inputs.

EFFICIENCY

The production possibility curve is drawn assuming that (1) the economy has a fixed amount of resources (including labor, materials, and capital) and (2) the economy is using these resources efficiently.

Figure 1-2 shows different combinations of consumption goods (such as food and toothpaste) and investment goods (such as factories and machinery). At Point A, the economy is *not* using its resources efficiently, since it could have more of both goods. An economy could be at Point A because of excessively high unemployment or because of laws and taxes that discourage efficiency. Only when an economy is at a point on its production possibility curve is it using its resources efficiently (one such point is Point B).

The Test for Efficiency: To produce more of one good, must the economy produce less of the other? If the answer is yes, then the economy is producing efficiently and is on its production possibility curve.

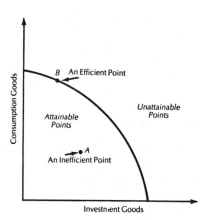

Figure 1-2   Test of Efficiency Shown by Production Possibility Curve

ECONOMIC GROWTH

The production possibility curve can also be used to show the causes and effects of economic growth. Figure 1-3 begins by reproducing Figure 1-2. A society that is at Point B produces 80 units of investment goods and 200 units of consumption goods. Investment goods, such as new plants and equipment, give workers more and better tools to work with so they will be more productive in following years.

So next year, the society faces a new production possibility curve (*CC'*). People can have more of both consumption and investment goods (e.g., 100 units of investment goods and 250 units of consumption goods). This upward and outward shift of the production possibility curve illustrates the impact of economic growth.

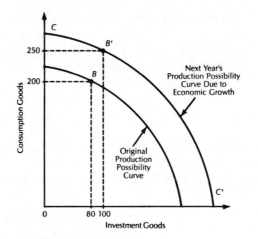

Figure 1-3 Impact of Economic Growth Shown by Production Possibility Curve

Factors That Cause Economic Growth

1. *Increase in investment,* since more investment goods make workers more productive. In order to invest more, people have to reduce their current consumption and save more so that their savings are available for investment.

2. *Innovation,* which occurs when someone discovers a way to produce more output from the same amount of inputs. Innovations in technology, in management, and in marketing can all contribute to economic growth.

3. *Increased division of labor,* which over the past two centuries has allowed workers to become more productive in their areas of specialization. Increased division of labor also means that workers are producing not for themselves but for other people. Thus, specialization and trade go together.

4. *Increase in inputs,* e.g., more workers, more machines, and more land. An increase in the number of inputs leads to more output and to economic growth.

YOU SHOULD REMEMBER

1. Only when an economy is on its production possibility curve is it being efficient. If the only way to produce more of one good is to produce less of another, then the economy is producing efficiently.

2. Growth allows an economy to have more of everything. The main ways to have growth are to invest more, innovate, increase specialization, and increase inputs.

3. The points inside the production possibility curve are attainable by society but are inefficient, since with its resources the economy could have more of both goods. The points outside the production possibility curve are unattainable.

MARGINAL ANALYSIS

How should people allocate their scarce resources to get the most value? To answer this question, economists use **marginal analysis**: the analysis of the benefits and costs of the marginal unit of a good or input. This technique is widely used in business decision-making and ties together much of economic thought.

In any situation, people want to maximize net benefits:

$$\text{Net Benefits} = \text{Total Benefits} - \text{Total Costs}$$

To do this, they can change a variable, such as the quantity of a good they buy or the quantity of output they produce. This variable is the *control variable*.

Marginal analysis focuses upon whether the control variable should be increased by one more unit.

Key Procedure for Using Marginal Analysis

1. Identify the control variable.

2. Determine what the increase in total benefits would be if one more unit of the control variable were added. This is the **marginal benefit** of the added unit.

3. Determine what the increase in total costs would be if one more unit of the control variable were added. This is the **marginal cost** of the added unit.

4. If the unit's marginal benefit *exceeds* (or equals) its marginal cost, it *should be added*.

Remember to look only at the *changes* in total benefits and total costs. If a particular cost or benefit does not change, ignore it.

Why does this work?

Because: Marginal Benefit = Increase in Total Benefits
 Marginal Cost = Increase in Total Cost
So: Change in Net Benefits = Marginal Benefit − Marginal Cost

When marginal benefits exceed marginal cost, net benefits go up. So the marginal unit of the control variable should be added.

Example: Should a Firm Produce More?

A firm's net benefit of being in business is its profits. The following formula illustrates how profits are calculated:

$$\text{Profits} = \text{Total Revenue} - \text{Total Cost}$$

(Note that total revenue is the same thing as total sales; don't confuse "revenue." with "profit.")

The firm's control variable is the output it produces.

PROBLEM International Widget is producing fifty widgets at a cost of $50,000 and is selling them for $60,000. If it produces a fifty-first unit, its total sales will be $62,000 and its total cost will be $51,500. Should the firm produce the fifty-first unit?

SOLUTION Yes. The fifty-first unit's marginal benefit is $2,000 and its marginal cost is $1,500. It should be produced. It adds $500 to profit ($2,000 − $1,500).

Example: Should a Better Worker Be Hired?

The following problem emphasizes the importance of looking only at the change in total benefits and costs.

PROBLEM Acme Manufacturing has trained Worker A at a cost of $30,000, and Worker A is worth $70,000 to Acme. Later, Acme has the opportunity to hire Worker B. Worker B would cost $30,000 to train but would be worth $90,000. However, to hire Worker B, Acme must fire Worker A. Should Acme hire Worker B?

SOLUTION No. Hiring Worker B and getting rid of Worker A adds $20,000 in increased worth (so the marginal benefit of this decision would be $20,000). The marginal cost of doing this is $30,000 in added costs for training Worker B. Since the marginal cost exceeds marginal benefit, Acme should not hire Worker B.

What about Worker A's $30,000 training cost? We ignore it, because firing A and hiring B neither increases nor reduces this cost, since it has already been incurred.

YOU SHOULD REMEMBER

Marginal analysis forms the basis of economic reasoning. To aid in decision-making, marginal analysis looks at the effects of a small change in the control variable. Each small change produces some good (its marginal benefit) and some bad (its marginal cost). As long as there is more "good" than "bad," the control variable should be increased (since net benefits will then be increased).

KNOW THE CONCEPTS

DO YOU KNOW THE BASICS?

1. How do scarcity and poverty differ?
2. Why can't opportunity costs exist without scarcity?
3. Does an economy that is inside its production possibilities curve face any trade-offs?
4. How can a good be costly yet not scarce?
5. What factors cause the production possibilities curve to be bowed out? And when the curve is bowed out, how does the opportunity cost of each good change if more of the good is produced?
6. What will cause an economy's production possibility curve to shift out and to the right?
7. How are trade and the division of labor related?
8. If the marginal cost of an action exceeds its marginal benefit, why will net benefits fall?
9. Why do people value each unit of a good by its marginal value?
10. Why is the opportunity cost of an option equal to the value of the best of all the alternatives that had to be forgone?

TERMS FOR STUDY

control variable	marginal cost
division of labor	net benefits
efficiency	opportunity cost
growth	production possibility curve
investment	scarcity
marginal analysis	specialization
marginal benefit	trade-off

PRACTICAL APPLICATION

1. The following shows the production possibilities for a plant that can man-
   ufacture iron or steel. Columns A–D show the number of tons of each
   metal that can be produced for each alternative.

POSSIBLE ALTERNATIVES

	A	B	C	D
Steel	0	6	10	12
Iron	18	12	6	0

   a. Draw the production possibility curve for this plant. Label the curve
      EE'. Does the curve show constant costs, or increasing costs?
   b. Suppose the firm increases steel production from Alternative B to
      Alternative C. What is the opportunity cost of each ton of steel in terms
      of iron? Suppose iron sold for $50 a ton. What would be the dollar
      opportunity cost of a ton of steel? Is this the minimum or maximum
      price the firm would have to charge in order to produce steel?
   c. Suppose new technology allows the firm to produce twice as much
      steel as shown above but does not affect its iron production. Draw the
      new production possibility curve and label it FF'. Will this raise or
      lower the opportunity cost of producing twelve tons of steel?

2. Studies have shown that females put a lot of time into raising children.
   How would the increase in female wages that has occurred over the last
   three decades affect the cost of raising children?

3. You have ten workers who are all equally skilled and who can do each
   other worker's job with the same efficiency. The first worker does a task
   worth $100, the second, $90, the third, $80, and so on until the last, whose
   task is worth $10. Worker number one comes to you, demands a raise,
   and threatens to quit if the raise is not forthcoming. How much at most
   should you be willing to pay worker number one?

4. Use the principle of opportunity cost to explain why firms might spend
   more time training workers when there is a recession in their industries
   (assuming the firms expect to retain the workers and the recession to
   eventually end).

5. What is wrong (from an economic point of view) with the following argument? "Marketing is vitally important. After all, without marketing, we
   wouldn't sell anything and our firm would be bankrupt. Therefore, our
   firm should spend more on marketing."

6. If a firm faces the following costs and benefits, how many plants should it build? Use marginal analysis.

Plants	Total Revenues	Total Costs
1	$10,000,000	$ 5,000,000
2	18,000,000	12,000,000
3	24,000,000	20,000,000

7. Currently, our military is voluntary; the armed forces sets its wages and benefits so it can attract an adequate and presumably skilled body of soldiers. In the past, our nation has used the draft, forcing people into military service at low pay. If we were to return to a draft, how would the opportunity cost of maintaining our military be affected?

8. How will the following events affect the production possibility curve of an economy?
    Event A: A large fraction of the work force becomes unemployed.
    Event B: The productivity of all workers doubles.
    Event C: The government requires dairy farmers to destroy part of their herds.

9. An economy is producing two goods, A and B. Then there is technological progress, but in Good A only. Can the economy then consume more of *both* goods?

10. Acme Manufacturing has spent $100,000 on safety equipment. If it spends an additional $20,000, its losses from accidents will fall from $160,000 to $130,000. Should it spend the additional $20,000?

ANSWERS

KNOW THE CONCEPTS

1. Poverty is having few goods. Scarcity is having more wants than goods with which to satisfy them, even if one has many goods.
2. Without scarcity, there are no alternatives that have to be given up, and thus there are no opportunity costs.
3. No. It can have more of all goods.
4. If a costly good is not desirable, it will not be scarce.
5. Diminishing returns and the fact that some inputs are more suitable than others for producing certain goods cause the bowing out of the production possibility curve. When the curve is bowed out, as more of any good is produced its opportunity cost goes up.

6. More investment. Innovation. Increased division of labor. Additional inputs.

7. The division of labor means that workers specialize. They must then trade what they produce to get the goods they want to consume.

8. When marginal costs exceed marginal benefits, more is being added to total costs than to total benefits, so net benefits must fall.

9. People value a unit of a good by what would be lost if they didn't have the unit. By interchanging units of the good, a person would have to lose only the least-valued use a unit of the good is being put to, i.e., its marginal value.

10. The opportunity cost of a decision is the value of what the person would have done otherwise. If the person is rational, they would otherwise have chosen the most valuable of the alternative options.

PRACTICAL APPLICATION

1. **a.** The curve is shown below. The curve shows increasing costs.
   b. Going from Alternative *B* to Alternative *C*, represented on the graph by Points *B* and *C*, Acme gets 4 more units of steel but 6 less units of iron. So the opportunity cost per ton of steel is 6/4, or 1.5 tons of iron per ton of steel. In dollars, this iron could sell for $75 (1.5 × $50), so the firm would want $75 at a minimum for a ton of steel (in this range of production) to cover its opportunity costs.
   c. The new production possibility curve will show that the opportunity cost of steel has gone down, while the opportunity cost of iron has gone up. Before, 12 tons of steel required giving up 18 tons of iron; now 12 tons require giving up only 6 tons of iron.

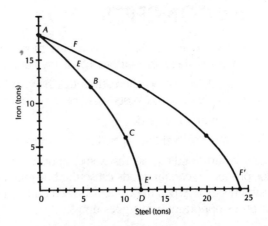

2. One of the main costs of raising children is the opportunity cost of female time. Because female wages have been rising, the effect has been to significantly increase the cost of raising children. Many economists believe that this may partly explain the drop in the number of children per household that has occurred in recent times.

3. If worker number one quit, the other workers could be reassigned tasks and you would be worse off by only $10. So worker one should be paid no more than $10.

4. The opportunity cost of training a worker is the value of what the worker would have been doing otherwise. Most likely, this would be producing goods for the firm to sell. But during a recession, this foregone cost is likely to be lower (since the firm has to sell its output at a lower cost or perhaps can't sell it at all). So this is the cheapest time to train workers.

5. This argument tries to measure the value of an additional expenditure on marketing not by its *marginal* contribution, but rather by the total value of *all* marketing. The correct way to evaluate the issue is to ask if the additional money spent on marketing is matched or exceeded by its additional or marginal benefit.

6. The firm should build two plants. The third plant's marginal cost is $8 million, while its marginal benefit is only $6 million. Therefore, the third plant should not be built.

7. The cost of maintaining our military forces is the opportunity cost of what the people in the military would have been doing otherwise. With a pay system, only those people whose opportunity cost falls below what the armed forces pay will join. But with a draft, persons with higher opportunity costs will likely be forced into service. Thus, the total opportunity cost of a draft will be higher.

8. *Event A:* This event has no effect. Rather, it would be illustrated by a movement to inside the production possibility curve (such as Point *A* in Figure 1-2). Recall that all inputs are fully employed when the economy is on its production possibility curve.
   Event B: This event moves the curve up and to the right so that more of all goods can be produced.
   Event C: This event shifts the curve down and to the left.

9. Yes. To produce the "old" amounts of Goods A and B takes less inputs; the leftover inputs can then be used to produce more A and B. The old and new production possibility curves look like the answer to Practical Application, Question 1, where steel is Good A.

10. The control variable is safety. More safety has a marginal cost of $20,000. Its marginal benefit is the reduction in accident losses: $30,000 ($160,000 − $130,000). So the firm should spend the additional $20,000.

2

HOW TO USE GRAPHS IN ECONOMICS

READING GRAPHS

A **graph** tells a story. The story a graph tells us is how two variables are related to each other. One of the variables is measured along the bottom of the graph, and it increases in value as we move from left to right. The other variable is measured along the left side of the graph, and it increases in value as we move from bottom to top. For example, Figure 2-1 shows the profits of a firm at different levels of output. Output is measured along the bottom, and as we move from 0 to the right, output is increasing. The bottom line is the **horizontal axis**. Profits are measured along the side, and they increase as we move up from 0. The side line is the **vertical axis**.

Graphs are read like a page, *from left to right.* Usually, we think of the variable on the horizontal axis as the *cause* of the changes that occur in the variable on the vertical axis.

In Figure 2-1, we begin to read the graph at its left. When output is 0, profits are equal to 0. As output increases, we follow the graph and see that profits are increasing. For example, at output level A, profits reach Point D. As output continues to increase, profits continue to climb, until we reach output level B. As the graph illustrates, we have reached the "top of the hill." Profits have reached their highest level (E) at output level B. Increasing output beyond B causes profits to fall, until they reach 0 at output level C.

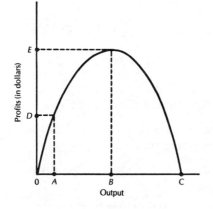

Figure 2-1 Determining Profits Based Upon Different Levels of Output

HOW TWO VARIABLES ARE RELATED

Figure 2-2 shows four different ways two variables, *X* and *Y*, can be related:

1. *Panel A* shows that *X* and *Y* are **positively related**. When *X* goes up, *Y* goes up, and when *X* goes down, *Y* goes down. For example, *X* could be workers hired and *Y*, output.

2. *Panel B* shows that *X* and *Y* are **negatively (or inversely) related**. When *X* goes up, *Y* goes down, and when *X* goes down, *Y* goes up. For example, *X* could be the amount of safety equipment a firm installs and *Y* could be the firm's accident rate.

3. *Panel C* shows that *X* has no effect on *Y*. No matter how large or small *X* is, *Y* remains the same. *Y* could be the size of the moon and *X*, pencil production.

4. *Panel D* shows that *Y* has no effect on *X*. No matter how large or small *Y* is, *X* remains the same. *Y* could be the price of a dead artist's paintings and *X* could be the world supply of the artist's paintings.

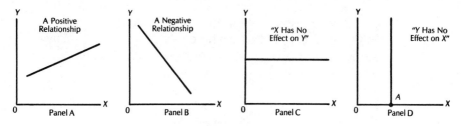

Figure 2-2 Determining Variable Relationships

YOU SHOULD REMEMBER

1. Read graphs from left to right.

2. Think of the variable on the horizontal axis as "causing" the other variable (on the vertical axis) to change.

3. Two variables are positively related to each other if they move together (both going up or both going down).

4. Two variables are negatively related if when one increases, the other decreases.

PLOTTING GRAPHS

To plot a graph, for each value of the variable on the horizontal axis, plot above it the value of the variable on the vertical axis that corresponds to it.

Example: Plotting a Budget Constraint

One type of graph used in economics is the "budget constraint," which shows the different combinations of goods a person could buy on a fixed budget.

PROBLEM   Susan has a weekly budget of $10 and can buy sodas at $1 each or hamburgers at $2 each. Plot a graph showing what she could buy over the week, assuming she spends all of the $10. Put hamburgers on the horizontal (or bottom) axis.

SOLUTION   If Susan buys no hamburgers then she can buy ten sodas. So we plot this as Point A in Figure 2-3. If she buys one hamburger, she can buy eight sodas. This is Point B. We continue until she buys five hamburgers and no sodas (Point C). We connect these points with a smooth line to have the budget constraint shown in Figure 2-3. Note that we have plotted a negative relationship: As Susan buys more hamburgers, she has less money to buy sodas.

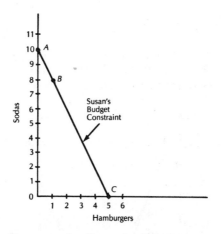

Figure 2-3 Measuring the Slope of a Straight Line

MEASURING THE SLOPE

Slope is a measure of how two variables are related. Let X be the variable on the horizontal axis and Y be the variable on the vertical axis.

Key Procedure for Measuring Slopes

1. Along the horizontal axis, pick a beginning value for X (which we will call X-old) and then move to the right a short distance to a new (higher) value of X (which is X-new). Let the increase be "the change in X" (which equals X-new minus X-old), or the "run."

2. Determine the values of Y from the graph that correspond to X-old and X-new.

3. Measure the change between the new and beginning values of Y (Y-new minus Y-old). Let this be "the change in Y." IF Y increases, this change is positive; if Y decreases, this change is negative. This change in Y is called the "rise" (even if Y decreases).

4. The slope is "rise over run" or the change in Y divided by the change in X.

In Figure 2-3, the slope is -2. (Note: for every added hamburger, Susan has to buy two fewer sodas.)

A positive slope (as in Panel A of Figure 2-2) shows a positive relationship. A negative slope (as in Panel B of Figure 2-2) shows a negative relationship. A zero slope (as in Panel C) shows no relationship.

A straight line has the same slope at every point on the line. But the slope of a curved line constantly changes as one moves along the curved line. To find the slope of a curved line at one of its points, just draw a tangent line through that point. A **tangent line** is a straight line that matches the direction of curve at that point and "touches" the curve just once. Line *BC* in Figure 2-4 is such a tangent line: It measures the slope of the curve at Point *A*. From the figures supplied, you should verify that the slope is −5/2 (or −2.5). At Point *E*, the curve has a slope of 2/1 (or +2). At Point *D*, the curve has slope of 0.

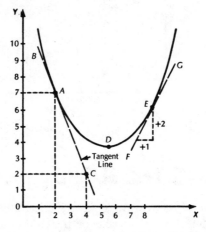

Figure 2-4 Measuring the Slope of a Curved Line

YOU SHOULD REMEMBER

1. To calculate the *slope of a straight line*, divide the "rise" by the "run," or the change in Y by the change in X, where X is the variable on the horizontal axis.

2. The *slope of a curved line* at a particular point is the slope of the tangent line through that point.

KNOW THE CONCEPTS

DO YOU KNOW THE BASICS?

1. In Figure 2-1, what is the slope of the curve at output level *A*? Between levels *A* and *C*? At output level *B*?

2. What are the four possible relationships two variables can have?

3. If X and Y are positively related, when X decreases, what will happen to Y? (In these questions, X is the variable on the horizontal axis.)

4. What do Points A and C represent in Figure 2-3?

5. What is true about all points along Line AC in Figure 2-3? What about all points to the left and inside?

6. If X and Y are negatively related, when X decreases, what will happen to Y?

7. If the slope of Y with respect to X is -3 over a given range, what will happen to Y if X increases from 7 to 9?

8. Answer question 7 when the slope is $+5$.

9. If a curve smoothly increases, levels out, and then decreases, what is its slope at its highest point?

   Hint: See Figure 2-1.

10. When X goes from 10 to 15, Y decreases from 20 to 10. What is the slope of this relationship over this range (assuming that it's a straight-line relationship)?

TERMS FOR STUDY

horizontal axis	slope
negative relationship	tangent line
positive relationship	vertical axis

PRACTICAL APPLICATION

1. Indicate which panel in Figure 2-2 best represents the relationships below. Assume that the first term is the X variable on the horizontal axis (such that X is the cause and Y is the effect).
   a. Population of a city and the cost of a home.
   b. The amount of wheat grown on a small farm and the world price of wheat (i.e., how will the world price of wheat change when the small farm grows more wheat).
   c. The fine for speeding and the fraction of the population that speeds.
   d. The pay for teachers and the number of people who want to become teachers.

2. Plot the following production possibility schedule:

Combinations	Houses	Food
A	0	16
B	4	12
C	7	8
D	9	4
E	10	0

Put houses on the horizontal axis. Give the slope between A and B, B and C, and so forth. What does the slope represent? Is this cost increasing or decreasing?

Hint: The slope shows an opportunity cost.

3. Plot the following table, with the number of workers on the horizontal axis. The table shows the output of a small chair workshop as workers are added.

Output	0	5	9	12	14	15	15	13	10
Workers	0	1	2	3	4	5	6	7	8

Give the slope for each worker added. What is the meaning of the slope in this case?

4. Draw a line that starts at the origin (at 0) and begins to rise with a slope of 1. What does this line mark off?

5. Draw a curve relating the tax rate (from 0 to 100%) to the total tax revenues that are collected. Put the tax rate on the horizontal axis. The curve should describe the following statement: "At a tax rate of zero, no taxes are collected. As the tax rate increases, total tax revenues rise. But once the tax rate becomes high enough, total tax revenues begin to fall as taxpayers take advantage of more loopholes in the tax law or work less because with taxes so high, the reward for working becomes too low. At a 100% tax rate, everyone evades taxes or leaves the country, so no tax revenues are collected."

6. Draw a curve that describes the following situation. Place safety spending on the horizontal axis and total costs on the vertical axis. "When a firm spends nothing on safety, total costs are very high due to high accident losses. As it increases its safety spending, its accident losses drop dramatically and so its total costs fall. But beyond some level in safety costs,

the reduction in accident losses fails to offset the costs of higher safety spending, and total costs begin to rise."

7. Draw a curve showing the following relationship: "As a foreman spends more hours supervising workers, the total output of the workers being supervised goes up. But each additional hour of supervision increases total output less than the previous hour." Plot hours of supervision on the horizontal axis. Does this statement describe a positive or negative relationship? What is happening to the slope as hours of supervision increase?

8. Assume that the foreman from Question 7 takes a course that improves his skill in dealing with workers. As a result, for any given number of hours of supervision, workers are more productive than before. But otherwise, the relationship described above is the same. How will the new curve compare with that in Question 7?

9. A firm finds that when it produces 100 widgets, its cost per widget is $10. When it produces 120 widgets, its cost per widget is $14. If the relationship between the number of widgets produced and per-unit cost is a straight line over this range (so the slope is the same between all points), what is the per-unit cost when 110 widgets are produced?

Hint: Change in Y = Slope × Change in X. In this case, let X be the number of widgets produced and Y be the unit cost.

10. When a firm produces fifty widgets, its total cost is $1,000. At fifty-one widgets, its total cost is $1,020. What is the marginal cost of the fifty-first widget? What is the slope of the total cost curve over this range (plotting widgets produced on the horizontal axis and increasing widget production from fifty to fifty-one)?

ANSWERS

KNOW THE CONCEPTS

1. Positive. Negative. Zero.
2. Figure 2-2 shows the four possible relationships.
3. Y will decrease.
4. Point A represents Susan's consumption if she consumes only sodas. Point C: only hamburgers.
5. Along Line AC, Susan is spending all of her budget ($10). At all points to the left and inside her budget constraint AC, she is spending less than $10.

6. *Y* will increase.
7. *Y* will decrease by 6 ($-6 = -3 \times$ Change in *X*, which is 2).
8. *Y* will increase by 10 ($10 = 5 \times 2$).
9. Zero.
10. -2 ($-2 = -10/5$).

PRACTICAL APPLICATION

1. **a.** Panel A. (Houses usually cost more in large cities.)
   b. Panel C. (One small farm will have no discernible effect on world wheat prices.)
   c. Panel B. (Higher fines discourage speeding.)
   d. Panel A. (Higher wages attract more people into teaching.)

2. At zero houses, the curve begins at 16 units of food and then falls until, at 10 houses, there is no food. The slope between *A* and *B* is -1, between *B* and *C* is $-4/3$ or -1.333, between *C* and *D* is -2, and between *D* and *E* is -4. Stated as a positive number, this is the opportunity cost of each home (in terms of sacrificed food). The opportunity cost of homes is increasing. See figure below.

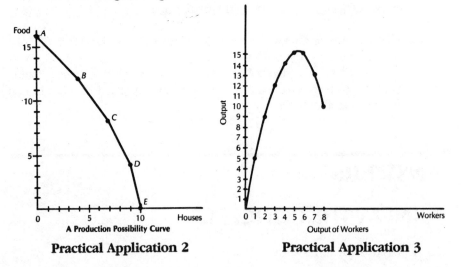

Practical Application 2

Practical Application 3

3. See the Figure above. Going from 0 to 1 worker, the slope is 5, from 1 to 2, it's 4, and then it's 3, then 2, then 1, and between 5 and 6 it's 0, then -2, and finally, -3. The slope represents how much each additional worker added to total output.

4. It marks off points where the variables on each axis have equal values (where $X = Y$). See figure on next page.

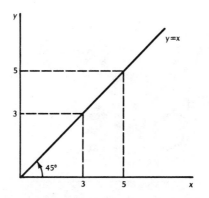

5. This is the famous Laffer Curve and looks like Figure 2-1 with the tax rate on the horizontal axis. At Point 0 and Point C (which represents the 100% tax rate), no taxes are collected. Maximum tax revenues are collected at tax rate B.

6. This will look like Figure 4-4. Total costs start rising again at D. If the firm wants the lowest total cost, D is its preferred level of safety spending.

7. The curve should show a positive relationship and therefore have a positive slope. As hours of supervision increase, the positive slope should become smaller. Mathematically, this curve is described as "increasing at a decreasing rate." See figure below.

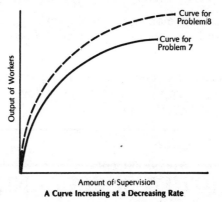

A Curve Increasing at a Decreasing Rate

8. The new curve will be above the old one and will have the same general shape. See above figure.

9. The slope of this relationship is .2 ($\$.20 = \$4/20$). So each additional widget adds 20¢ to the per-unit cost. Increasing widget production from 100 to 110, an increase of 10, increases the per-unit cost by $2.00 ($\$.20 \times 10$). So the unit cost at 110 units will be $12 ($\$10 + \$2$).

10. Marginal cost is $20. The slope is $20. Marginal cost is the slope of the total cost curve.

3
SUPPLY AND DEMAND: PART ONE

HOW TO STUDY SUPPLY AND DEMAND

To better understand supply and demand, you should remember:

1. *Supply and demand is about trade.* Buyers purchase goods with money, and sellers get money for selling goods. But behind this exchange of monies is the exchange of goods: Buyers are in effect trading what they make (and sell) for the goods they buy.

2. *Suppliers and demanders are different.* It is important to separate the **buyers** (**demanders**) from the **sellers** (**suppliers**) of a good. This is because they

react in different ways to changes in the price as well as to changes in other variables. For example, a higher price reduces the quantity of the good that demanders want to buy but increases the quantity sellers want to sell. It is important, therefore, to understand which variables each group reacts to, and how it reacts.

3. *Events that are caused by price changes are different from those that cause price changes.* Events that are caused by price changes are covered in this chapter, and events that cause price changes are addressed in Chapter 4 Events *caused* by price changes are shown by a demand or supply curve· events that *cause* the price to change are shown by a *shift* from an old to a new demand or supply curve.

4. *Demand and supply applies to all types of markets.* If in doubt, make a demand and supply diagram to answer a question. Such a diagram can apply to goods, labor, crime, marriage, and many other areas.

PRICE

The pertinent price of a good is its **relative price**: its price relative to the price of other goods. The relative price of Good A tells how much of Good B must be given to get one more unit of Good A.

Example: Calculating Relative Prices from Money Prices

PROBLEM   If a TV's price is $200 and a personal computer's is $2,000, what is the relative price of the TV? Of the computer?

SOLUTION   Divide the price of the good in question by the price of the good given up. The relative price of one TV is one-tenth of a computer, and the relative price of one computer is ten TVs.

When economists say that supply and demand responds to price changes, they are talking about changes in *relative* prices. But what if *all* prices doubled (including wages and income)? Then relative prices would be unchanged: Neither demand nor supply would change.

YOU SHOULD REMEMBER

The relevant price is the *relative* price of a good. The relative price of Good A is the quantity of the other good(s) sacrificed to get one more unit of Good A. It is calculated by dividing the price of Good A by the price of the other good(s).

DEMAND AND THE LAW OF DEMAND

At any given price, the **quantity demanded** is the maximum quantity buyers are willing and able to buy. The quantity demanded is what buyers *intend* to buy at that particular price, *not* what they can actually buy. Millions of Americans would want to buy a Mercedes-Benz if its price were only $100, but Mercedes-Benz would not be willing to sell any of its cars at this price.

The quantity demanded also depends upon other factors, such as income and tastes. We'll call these other factors the **non-price determinants of demand**.

The **law of demand** states that *when price increases, the quantity demanded decreases—assuming the non-price determinants of demand don't change*. We say that the quantity demanded and price have an *inverse* (or *negative*) relationship: When price goes up, quantity demanded goes down, and when price goes down, quantity demanded goes up.

Why the Law of Demand Holds

1. The *added buyer effect.* A lower price attracts new buyers.

2. The *income effect* of a lower price. A lower price allows buyers to buy the same number of goods with less money. The money left over is like having more income. Some of this income may go for buying more units of the good.

3. The *substitution effect* of a lower price. A lower relative price means that the consumer gives up less of other goods to buy the good for which the price has decreased. This encourages buyers to "substitute towards" the good.

YOU SHOULD REMEMBER

1. The *quantity demanded* is the maximum quantity buyers want to buy at a given price. It need not equal the amount actually bought at the price: Less, but not more, could be bought.

2. The *law of demand* works because of the added buyer effect, the income effect, and the substitution effect.

THE DEMAND CURVE

The **demand curve** shows the quantity demanded of a good at various prices, assuming that the non-price determinants of demand, such as consumers' income, don't change. Table 3-1 shows a demand schedule for wheat. At 90¢, buyers will buy up to forty-five bushels but no more. When the price is reduced to 85¢, they will buy up to sixty-five bushels. We say that "the quantity demanded has increased" by ten bushels as a result of this price change. We do *not* say "demand has gone up" by twenty bushels, because "demand" (i.e., the demand curve) hasn't changed.

Table 3-1. Determining Demand Based Upon Price

The Demand for Wheat*

Price (cents per bushel)	Quantity Demanded (bushels per month)	Point on Figure 3-1
90	45	A
85	65	B
80	85	C
75	105	D
70	125	E

*Hypothetical Data

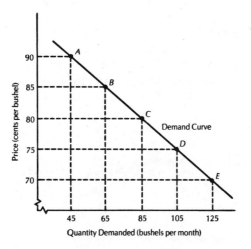

Figure 3-1 Law of Demand Shown by Demand Curve

Key Procedure for Plotting Demand Curves

1. Start at any price on Table 3-1. Locate the price on the vertical axis of Figure 3-1. Go horizontally to the right until the quantity on the horizontal axis agrees with the price quantity in Table 3-1. Mark that point.

2. Do this for each price.

3. Connect the points with a smooth line or curve.

YOU SHOULD REMEMBER

The demand curve shows the effect of price on the quantity buyers want to and are able to buy (with the non-price determinants of demand being held constant so that the focus is on the effects of changing the price). As we move down along the demand curve, the *quantity demanded* goes up as the price goes down. But *demand* (i.e., the demand curve) is unchanged.

SUPPLY AND THE LAW OF SUPPLY

The **quantity supplied** at any given price is the maximum amount sellers are willing and able to supply at that price. The quantity supplied is the maximum amount sellers *intend* to sell at that price—not necessarily the actual amount they will sell. For example, at a price of $1 million per car, General Motors would be glad to sell hundreds of millions of cars, but few would actually be sold. Like the demand curve, the supply curve shows intentions.

The **law of supply** states that the *quantity supplied will increase when the price is raised and will decrease when the price is reduced.* Price and the quantity supplied have a direct (or positive) relationship: When one goes up, the other goes up also, and when one goes down, so does the other. For any supply curve, the non-price determinants of supply, such as technology and wages of workers, are held constant.

A higher market price usually elicits a greater quantity supplied, for two reasons:

1. The higher price increases the profits of existing sellers, causing them to want to sell more; and

2. The higher price attracts new suppliers.

YOU SHOULD REMEMBER

1. The *quantity supplied* is the maximum amount sellers want to sell at a given price. It need not be the actual amount they do sell at that price: Less but not more could be sold.

2. The *law of supply* states that the quantity supplied goes up when the price goes up and goes down when the price goes down.

THE SUPPLY CURVE

The **supply curve** shows the quantity supplied at various prices, holding the non-price determinants of supply constant. Table 3-2 shows a supply schedule for wheat. At 80¢, sellers at most want to sell eighty-five units. But at 85¢, they will want to produce fifteen additional units. We say the "quantity supplied has increased" by fifteen bushels. We do not say "supply has increased," because supply (i.e., the supply curve) hasn't changed.

Table 3-2. Determining Quantity Supplied Based Upon Price

The Supply of Wheat		
Price (cents per bushel)	Quantity Supplied (bushels per month)	Point on Figure 3-2
90	115	A
85	100	B
80	85	C
75	60	D
70	55	E

*Hypothetical Data

Figure 3-2 shows the graph of the supply schedule shown in Table 3-2. At Figure 3-2, plot the supply curve by following the same procedure used for plotting the demand curve at Figure 3-1.

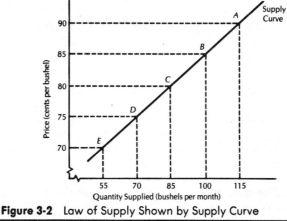

Figure 3-2 Law of Supply Shown by Supply Curve

YOU SHOULD REMEMBER

The *supply curve* shows the effect of price on the quantity sellers want to supply. The non-price determinants are held constant so the effects of price changes alone are shown. When the price goes up, the quantity supplied goes up. But supply (i.e., the supply curve) is unchanged.

MARKET EQUILIBRIUM

Equilibrium describes a state in which there is no tendency to change. A market is in equilibrium when neither buyers nor sellers see any need to change the quantity and price of the good they are buying or selling. This occurs at the price at which the quantity demanded equals the quantity supplied. Note that market equilibrium does *not* mean that "people get all they want" or that "everybody gets some." For example, due to the equilibrium price for Rolls Royces, few people own one, although many would want one if they were free.

Table 3-3 shows how markets get to equilibrium. The numbers in Table 3-3 are from Tables 3-1 and 3-2.

Table 3-3. How Markets Get to Equilibrium

DEMAND AND SUPPLY OF WHEAT				
Price (cents per bushel)	Quantity Demanded (bushels per month)	Quantity Supplied (bushels per month)	State of Market	Tendency for Price Change
90	45	115	Surplus of 70 units	Decreases
85	65	100	Surplus of 35 units	Decreases
80	85	85	Equilibrium	Stays Same
75	105	70	Shortage of 35 units	Increases
70	125	55	Shortage of 70 units	Increases

The **market equilibrium price** is 80¢. The quantity demanded (eighty-five) equals the quantity supplied (eighty-five) at that price.

At any price *higher* than the equilibrium price, there will be a **surplus**: Sellers will want to supply more goods than buyers want to buy. At 90¢, the surplus is seventy units (70 = 115 − 45). The market is not in equilibrium because the sellers who can't sell all they want will seek buyers by lowering the price.

At any price *lower* than the equilibrium price, there will be a **shortage**: Buyers will want to buy more goods than sellers want to sell. At 75¢, there is a shortage of thirty-five units (35 = 105 − 70). The market is not in equilibrium: Buyers who cannot purchase all they want will seek to induce sellers to supply more by bidding the price up.

At 80¢, the market **clears**: Buyers are actually buying the most they intend to at that price and sellers are actually selling the most they intend to at that price. The quantity demanded equals the quantity supplied. Since everyone is actually buying or selling what they want to at 80¢, no one has any incentive to change the price. So at 80¢, the market is in *equilibrium.*

Figure 3-3 uses the numbers from Table 3-3 to plot the supply and demand curves.

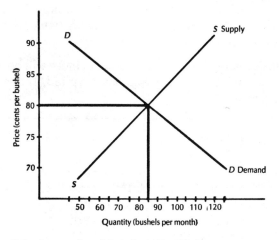

Figure 3-3 Demand and Supply in Equilibrium

The supply curve is labeled *SS*, and the demand curve is *DD*. The equilibrium price of 80¢ and the equilibrium quantity of eighty-five bushels of wheat are drawn in with a dark line. Equilibrium occurs when the two curves cross.

Key Procedure for Reading Supply and Demand Diagrams

1. At any given price, draw a line horizontally across the graph.

2. The point at which this line intersects the supply curve is the quantity supplied at that price. The point at which it intersects the demand curve is the quantity demanded at that price.

3. When the quantity supplied exceeds the quantity demanded, the excess supply shows the *surplus.* For example, at 85¢, there is a surplus of thirty-five units.

4. When the quantity demanded exceeds the quantity supplied, the excess demand shows the *shortage.* For example, at 75¢, there is a shortage of thirty-five units.

5. When quantity demanded equals quantity supplied, the market is in *equilibrium.*

YOU SHOULD REMEMBER

1. Market equilibrium occurs at the price at which the quantity supplied equals the quantity demanded. There is no tendency for the price to change (as long as the non-price determinants of demand and supply remain unchanged).

2. If the price is above the market equilibrium price, there will be a *surplus*. Quantity supplied exceeds quantity demanded. The market price will tend to fall.

3. If the price is below the equilibrium price, there will be a *shortage*. Quantity demanded exceeds quantity supplied. The market price will tend to rise.

PRICE FLOORS

A **price floor** is a restriction imposed by the government that prohibits the price from falling below a certain level. If the price floor is below the market equilibrium price, the floor has no effect. But if the price floor is above the market price, it causes a *shortage*: At least some sellers will not be able to find buyers for all they want to sell.

Figure 3-4 shows the effect of a particular floor: a minimum wage that must be paid for the labor of teenagers.

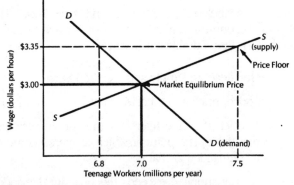

Figure 3-4   Determining the Effect of a Price Floor

DD is the demand curve for teenage employment. At the lower wage shown on the graph, employers are willing to hire more teenagers. *SS* shows the supply curve. At the higher wage, more teenagers are willing to work.

The market clearing wage is $3.00, and the market clearing quantity employed is 7 million. If the government imposes a minimum wage of $3.35, employers are willing to employ only 6.8 million teenagers, while 7.5 million want to work. There will be a surplus of 0.7 million teenagers (0.7 = 7.5 − 6.8). Of the 0.7

million, 0.2 million will come from reduced demand (from lost jobs), and 0.5 million will come from increased supply (as more teenagers want to work).

PRICE CEILINGS

A **price ceiling** is a restriction imposed by the government that prohibits a price from going above a certain level. If the price ceiling is below the equilibrium price, shortages are created. Shortages are not just the scarcity of goods; all goods are scarce but only those with price ceilings have chronic shortages.

Figure 3-5 shows the effect of a price ceiling on gasoline. With a ceiling price of 60¢ per gallon, there is a shortage of 40 million gallons. The gasoline shortages in the 1970s, for example, were caused by our government's price ceiling on the price of gas. OPEC made gasoline more scarce, but it didn't create the shortages.

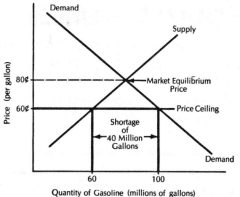

Figure 3-5   Determining the Effect of a Price Ceiling

EFFECTS OF PRICE CEILINGS AND FLOORS

When lawmakers try to force the price away from its equilibrium level, some of the results are:

1. *Non-Price Rationing:* This is any method of equating supply and demand other than price. Two main methods of rationing without prices are:
   a. *Waiting lines,* such as the high unemployment caused by the minimum wage law or the waiting lines of customers at gas stations caused by the ceiling on gas prices; and
   b. *Discrimination,* for example, the discrimination caused by the minimum wage law. The law resulted in a surplus of applicants, so employers can be selective as to whom they hire. In the past, faced with surplus of applicants, employers have hired mainly whites: The result is that black teenagers have had at least twice the unemployment rate of whites.

2. *Changes in Quality:* With a price *ceiling*, sellers, to save on costs, will cut back on quality. For example, the rent controls in New York City have produced some of the most run-down apartments and unresponsive landlords in the country.

With a price *floor*, sellers try to attract buyers by offering better quality (since they can't lower the price). For example, when there was a ceiling on the interest rate that banks could pay savers, banks typically gave "free" toasters and other appliances to those opening accounts.

3. *Black Markets and Violation of the Law:* To get around a price ceiling, the buyers who cannot buy what they want at the ceiling price will seek out sellers who are willing to sell at illegal prices (which usually are higher then the market equilibrium price).

YOU SHOULD REMEMBER

1. A price *ceiling* set *below* the equilibrium price results in a *shortage* of the good. A price *floor* set *above* the equilibrium price results in a *surplus*.

2. Price controls (either ceilings or floors) lead to non-price rationing (including waiting lines and discrimination), changes in quality, and black markets.

ON THE NATURE OF THE PRICE SYSTEM

The creation of money and the price system stands with the invention of language and the alphabet as one of the great social inventions of mankind. Like language, the price system summarizes and communicates information. For example, people do not need to know that a mine cave-in in Chile has reduced the world's supply of copper; they need only know that copper wire has gone up in price so that they will have to cut back on its use. Thus, the price system saves on information costs. With prices, no one has to tell businesses which goods consumers want them to produce nor tell consumers which goods are too expensive to consume.

In competitive markets, the demand curve for a good is also the good's *marginal benefit schedule*, and the supply curve is the good's *marginal cost schedule*. This is because at any given level of output, (1) the price that demanders are willing to pay reflects the marginal benefit they derive from the last unit of the good and (2) the price at which suppliers are willing to sell reflects their marginal cost. Marginal analysis tells us that a good's supply should be increased as long as its marginal benefit exceeds its marginal cost. Doing this maximizes net benefits. So when sellers sell until the quantity demanded equals the quantity supplied ("where demand equals supply"), society is achieving its maximum net benefit.

KNOW THE CONCEPTS

DO YOU KNOW THE BASICS?

1. Is the quantity demanded different from the quantity bought?
2. Is the quantity supplied different from the quantity sold?
3. What is the difference between scarcity and shortage?
4. Can there be a surplus of a scarce good?
5. How can a merchant tell whether his or her price is too low? Too high?
6. Does demand change when the price changes?
7. When there is a shortage, how will the price change? What will happen to the quantity demanded and supplied?
8. Why does an individual usually buy more of a good when its price falls? Give two reasons.
9. Is a market in equilibrium when the amount bought equals the amount sold?
10. If the price of TVs stays at $200 while inflation continues, what will happen to the demand for TVs according to the law of demand?

TERMS FOR STUDY

law of demand
law of supply
market clearing price
market equilibrium
non-price rationing
price floors and ceilings

quantity demanded
quantity supplied
relative price
shortage
surplus

PRACTICAL APPLICATION

1. In the table below, what will be the equilibrium price for hamburgers? At what price will the most hamburgers be sold? Indicate which prices will lead to a surplus of hamburgers and which to a shortage.

Price	Quantity of Hamburgers Demanded (per day)	Quantity Sold (per day)
$1.20	1,000	1,600
1.10	1,100	1,400
1.00	1,200	1,200
.90	1,300	1,000
.80	1,400	800

2. Is the following statement correct? "Home prices are so high there is a shortage of homes. Not everyone who wants a home will be able to buy one."

3. Suppose a rent control law forces rents below the market level of rents. How might owners of apartment buildings offset the effects of rent control laws on their profits?

4. Over a two-year period, the price of TVs went up 5% and the price of all other goods went up 12%. During the same period, more TVs were sold. Does this support or contradict the law of demand?

5. If each person demands one movie a month when one movie ticket costs $6, two movies a month when each costs $4, and three when each costs $2, what will the total demand be for 100 people for each price?

6. You have been asked to study the effect of price changes on the quantity of widgets demanded, using data from the last ten years. Which of the following variables would you use: (a) The price of widgets or (b) the price of widgets divided by the price level of other goods (for example, the Consumer Price Index, or CPI).

7. How would you expect a minimum wage (that is above the market clearing wage) to affect the working conditions and the on-the-job training supplied by employers?

8. Use the law of demand and the concept of relative price to explain why a higher percentage of the oranges sold in New York City are of better quality then oranges sold in Florida.

9. Suppose that employers dislike hiring blue-eyed workers and suffer a loss in their personal satisfaction equivalent to 50¢ an hour for each hour they employ a blue-eyed worker. How could a blue-eyed worker then get a job with an employer? In this case, what would be the effect of a minimum wage law that pushed blue-eyed workers' wages up by 50¢?

10. When John earned $10, he bought four hamburgers at $2 each and two sodas at $1 each. In the following month, he earned $20, but the price of hamburgers had risen to $3 and the price of sodas had risen to $4. So if John wanted to, he could still buy four hamburgers and two sodas. Will he?

Hint: What has happened to the relative price of sodas?

ANSWERS

KNOW THE CONCEPTS

1. Yes. For example, at a price of $1,000 per home, the quantity demanded would likely be very high, but the amount people would sell at this price would be zero. So the quantity demanded will not equal the quantity actually bought, except in equilibrium.

2. Yes.

3. Scarcity is when there are not enough units of a good to satisfy all of everyone's wants when the price of the good is zero. A shortage is when there are not enough units sold *at a given price* to satisfy what people want to buy *at that price.*

4. Yes; just impose a price floor above the equilibrium price.

5. If the price is too low, there is excess demand for the merchant's goods. If it is too high, there is excess supply.

6. No. The *quantity demanded* changes when the price changes.

7. The price will rise; the quantity demanded will decrease while the quantity supplied will increase.

8. Income effect and substitution effect.

9. No. The market is in equilibrium *only* when the quantity demanded equals the quantity supplied.

10. The *relative price* of TVs will fall, so the quantity demanded will increase.

PRACTICAL APPLICATION

1. The equilibrium price will be $1.00 (the price at which the quantity demanded equals the quantity supplied). Also at $1.00, the most hamburgers will be sold. At a higher price, less will be demanded, and at a lower price, less will be supplied. A shortage occurs at lower prices (90¢ and 80¢). A surplus occurs at higher prices ($1.10 and $1.20).

2. The statement is incorrect. At the equilibrium price, there will be no shortages, since all buyers who want homes at *prevailing* prices will get them. If there were a shortage of homes, the price would *rise* until the housing market reached equilibrium.

3. Rent controls create a shortage of apartments, so owners can cut back on maintenance and service without losing renters. Apartment owners also may seek ways to charge renters for "extra" services, even if these ways

are illegal. For example, some apartment owners have allegedly used these methods to reduce the adverse impact of rent controls: (1) "key money" for the key to the apartment, (2) kickbacks from rental brokers who get paid to find apartments for their clients, and (3) lower pay to the apartment's superintendent, who then collects "tips" from renters.

4. The *relative* price of TVs went down over the two-year period (by 7%) and more TVs were demanded. So this supports the law of demand.

5. The market demand is the sum of the individual's demand at each price. At $6 per movie ticket, 100 tickets will be sold. At $4, 200 tickets, and at $2, 300 tickets.

6. b. The relevant price is the *relative* price of widgets to other goods.

7. A minimum wage prevents employers from offering lower wages in exchange for training and good working conditions. As a consequence, employers faced with a minimum wage that is above what they'd otherwise pay will cut back on training (by hiring only experienced workers) and be less concerned with working conditions. One study found that minimum wages actually caused many workers to lose more, in training and working conditions, than they gained from higher wages.

8. The cost of transporting and selling oranges in NYC does not depend on their quality. Therefore, the *relative* price of high-quality oranges is less in NYC, so the law of demand predicts relatively more high-quality oranges will be demanded in NYC. For example, suppose a carton of low-quality oranges costs $10 in Florida, while high-quality oranges cost $15. If it costs $5 to ship a carton, the NYC prices will be $15 and $20 respectively. The relative price of high-quality oranges is 1.5 in Florida (1.5 = $15/$10) but only 1.33 in NYC (1.33 = $20/$15).

9. Blue-eyed workers can get a job with employers if they work for 50¢ less per hour than do other workers. This will compensate the employers for their dislike of blue-eyed workers. A minimum wage that prevents blue-eyed workers from accepting lower wages in order to get work will reduce their employment.

10. The relative price of sodas has gone up from one-half ($1/$2) to four-thirds ($4/$3) of a hamburger. The substitution effect predicts that John will substitute "away" from sodas "toward" hamburgers

4
SUPPLY AND DEMAND: PART TWO

KEY TERMS

complements two goods that go together (such as hammers and nails or lettuce and salad dressing). When the price of one goes up, the quantity demanded of the other goes down.

inferior good a good that people demand less of when their income increases.

normal good a good that people demand more of when their income increases.

shift in demand change in demand curve such that a different quantity is demanded at each price. Curves shift only when some variable *other than price* (i.e., a non-price determinant) changes. Also referred to as a "change in demand."

substitutes two goods that compete with each other (such as butter and margarine or Coke and Pepsi). When the price of one good goes up, the quantity demanded of the other also goes up.

THE DIFFERENCE BETWEEN ECONOMIC *SHIFTS* AND *MOVEMENTS*

One of the most important distinctions in economics is between:

1. Movements *along* the demand curve. This refers to moving along a given demand curve, tracing out the effects that different prices have on the quantity of goods people want to buy. (See Chapter 3.)

2. **Shifts *in* the demand curve.** This refers to changing the demand curve, i.e., shifting it left or right, because some variable other than price has changed. Again, note that some texts refer to a "shift in demand" as a "change in demand." This chapter focuses on shifts in demand and supply.

FACTORS SHIFTING DEMAND

When we constructed the demand curves in the previous chapter, we were holding the *non-price determinants of demand* constant. What will happen when they change?

Key Procedure for Shifting the Demand Curve

1. Draw a supply and demand diagram and indicate the equilibrium price and output by drawing a **price line** (a horizontal line drawn from the intersection of the demand and supply curves to the vertical axis: for example, Line *AF* in Figure 4-1) and **output line** (a vertical line drawn from the intersection to the horizontal axis: e.g., line *AG* in Figure 4-1).

2. Holding the price constant, ask yourself whether a specific event will increase or decrease the quantity people want to buy. If the event will increase the quantity demanded, draw a new demand curve to the *right* of the old one, as in Figure 4-1. If the event will decrease the quantity demanded, draw a new demand curve to the left, as in Figure 4-2.

3. Find the new intersection and indicate the new equilibrium price and output as in Step 1 (e.g., with Line *BH* and Line *BI* in Figure 4-1).

Table 4-1 lists the main factors that shift the demand curve and describes their effects. **Normal goods** are goods whose demand goes up when income goes up (most goods "normally" act this way). **Inferior goods** go down in demand when income goes up (low-quality products often fit this category). **Substitutes** are goods that compete with one another, such as Shell and Exxon gas. **Complements** are goods that go together, such as left and right shoes, or gas and cars. Note that consumers determine which goods are substitutes and which are complements. (For example, if all consumers wanted to wear right but not left shoes, they would not be complements.)

Table 4-1. The Main Factors That Shift Demand

Factor	Change In Factor	Effect On Demand
Consumer Income		
Normal Good	Income Up	Increase (Right)
	Income Down	Decrease (Left)
Inferior Good	Income Up	Decrease
	Income Down	Increase
Price of Substitutes		
(P-S)	P-S Up	Increase
	P-S Down	Decrease
Price of Complement		
(P-C)	P-C Up	Decrease
	P-C Down	Increase
Population		
(of Buyers)	Population Up	Increase
	Population Down	Decrease
Tastes		
	Towards Good	Increase
	Away From Good	Decrease

YOU SHOULD REMEMBER

To determine how an event shifts the demand curve, ask yourself how the event will change the quantity demanded if the price does *not* change. An event that *increases* demand shifts the demand curve to the *right*; an event that *decreases* demand shifts the curve to the *left*.

• *EFFECTS OF SHIFTS IN DEMAND*

Figure 4-1 shows the effect of an *increase in demand*. When demand increases, at any given price people want to buy more of the good. The demand curve shifts outward and to the right.

Figure 4-1 shows the demand and supply for cheese. Initially, the demand curve is *DD* and the supply curve is *SS*. The equilibrium price is $1.30 and the equilibrium quantity is 90 tons (at Point *A*). Now suppose some event causes people to buy more cheese at every price (e.g., people come to believe that cheese cures cancer). At $1.30, they previously demanded 90 tons of cheese, but now they want 120 tons at that price (at Point *C*). Similarly, at $1.50, they previously wanted 80 tons but now they want 110 tons. The new demand curve is *D'D'*.

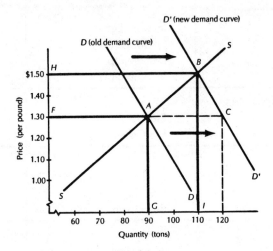

Figure 4-1 Effects of a Demand Increase

If after this event the price stays at $1.30, there will be a 30-ton shortage of cheese (with a quantity demanded of 120 tons and a quantity supplied of 90 tons). So the price will be bid up. The shortage will be eliminated at $1.50 The equilibrium output will have increased from 90 tons to 110 tons. The new equilibrium will be at Point *B*.

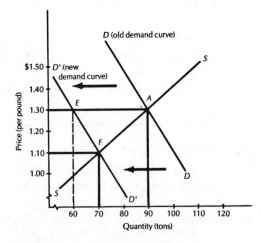

Figure 4-2 Effects of a Demand Decrease

Figure 4-2 shows the effects of a *decrease in demand*. When demand decreases, people buy less at each price. Beginning with the same equilibrium (90 tons of cheese and a price of $1.30), suppose some event decreases demand (e.g., people come to believe that cheese causes heart attacks). At each price, people want to buy less, so the demand curve shifts inward and to the left. At $1.30, for example, people want 30 fewer tons of cheese than before (from 90 to 60 tons, at Point *E*). If the price remained at $1.30, there would be a 30-ton surplus of cheese. So the price falls. The new equilibrium price is $1.10 and the new equilibrium output is 70 tons (corresponding to the new intersection of demand and supply at Point *F*).

Key Results of Shifts in Demand

1. If an event *increases* demand, the demand curve will shift outward and to the *right*. If the supply curve is not affected, the equilibrium *price* and *quantity* will *increase*.

2. If an event *decreases* demand, the demand curve will shift inward ana to the *left*. If the supply curve is not affected, the equilibrium *price* and *quantity* will *decrease*.

FACTORS SHIFTING SUPPLY

Supply is affected by a different set of factors than is demand. Basically, supply is affected by those factors that affect the unit cost of production. The effect of the main factors is shown in Table 4-2, when P = price, I = input, SP = substitute products, and JP = joint products. An **input** is something used to produce the good, such as labor or materials. A **substitute product** is one that could be produced with the same (or very similar) set of inputs. A substitute product to gasoline is heating oil and a substitute product to wheat is corn. When the price of a substitute product of a good goes up, the opportunity cost of producing the good goes up. **Joint products** are goods that are almost always produced together because it is difficult to produce them separately. Examples include leather and beef, or lumber and wood shavings.

Key Procedure for Shifting the Supply Curve

1. Draw the supply and demand curves as they appear before the event, and draw in the price and output lines from the intersection of demand and supply.

2. Holding price constant, ask yourself if the event would increase or decrease the quantity supplied at the price level in Step 1. If the event would increase the quantity supplied, draw the new supply curve to the right of the old, as in Figure 4-3. If the event would decrease the quantity supplied, draw the new curve to the left, as in Figure 4-4.

Sometimes, it makes more sense to hold the quantity constant and ask if the supply price will go up or down. If it will go up, draw the new supply curve to the left of the old; if it will go down, draw the new curve to the right.

3. Identify the new intersection of demand and supply by drawing in the new price and output lines.

Table 4-2. The Main Factors That Shift Supply

Factor	Change in Factor	Effect on Supply
Technology		
	Greater Efficiency	Increase
	Less Efficiency	Decrease
Price of Inputs (*P-I*)		
	P-I Up	Decrease
	P-I Down	Increase
Number of Firms		
	Number Up	Increase
	Number Down	Decrease
Price of Substitute Products (*P-SP*)		
	P-SP Up	Decrease
	P-SP Down	Increase
Price of Joint Products (*P-JP*)		
	P-JP Up	Increase
	P-JP Down	Decrease

YOU SHOULD REMEMBER

To determine how an event will affect supply, ask yourself how the quantity supplied will change if the price is held constant. Alternatively, holding output constant, ask yourself if the supply price will go up or down. If it will go down, supply will increase; if it will go up, supply will decrease. An event that *increases* supply shifts the supply curve to the *right*. An event that *decreases* supply shifts the curve to the *left*.

• *EFFECTS OF SHIFTS IN SUPPLY*

Figure 4-3 shows the effects of an *increase in supply.* Initially, equilibrium is at Point *A,* where the price is $1.30 and output is 90 tons of cheese. Then some event increases the supply of cheese (e.g., the wage of cheese workers falls). The new supply curve is *S'S'.* At $1.30, for example, suppliers are willing to supply 110 tons (at Point *G*), 20 more tons than previously. If the price were to remain unchanged, there would be a surplus. So the price will fall. The new equilibrium will be at Point *H,* with a new equilibrium price of $1.10 and output of 100 tons.

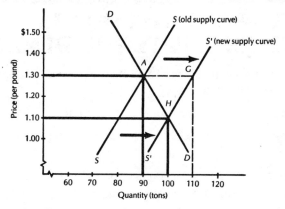

Figure 4-3 Effects of a Supply Increase

Figure 4-4 shows the effect of a *decrease in supply.* The initial equilibrium is at Point *A.* Then some event decreases supply, shifting the supply curve left from *SS* to *S'S'.* At $1.30, suppliers now will supply only 70 tons, compared to the 90 they would have supplied before the event. If the price remained at $1.30, there would be a shortage. So the price rises. The new equilibrium is at Point *I,* with a price of $1.50 and an output of 80 tons.

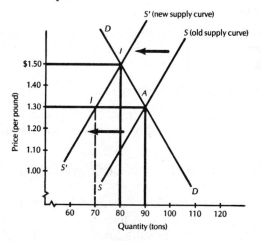

Figure 4-4 Effects of a Supply Decrease

Key Results of Shifts in Supply

1. An event that *increases* supply causes the supply curve to shift outward and to the *right*. If the demand curve is not affected, then the equilibrium *price* will *decrease* and the equilibrium *quantity* will go *up*.

2. An event that *decreases* supply causes the supply curve to shift inward and to the *left*. If the demand curve is not affected, the equilibrium *price* will *increase* and the equilibrium *quantity* will go *down*.

HOW TO AVOID MISTAKES IN ANALYZING SUPPLY AND DEMAND

Using the following logical sequence will help you avoid mistakes in analyzing how events affect demand and supply.

Key Procedure for Analyzing Supply and Demand

1. *Initial Equilibrium.* Draw the supply and demand diagram. Label the initial equilibrium price and output.

2. *Event and Shift.* Some event occurs. Ask yourself how demand and supply would change if the price did *not* change from its initial level. Draw in the new demand or supply curve.

3. *Shortage or Surplus?* If the initial price did not change, would there be a shortage or a surplus?

4. *Change in Price.* If there is a shortage, the price will rise. If there is a surplus, the price will fall. This change in price does not shift the (new) demand and supply curves. Rather, the change in price *causes* the quantity demanded and the quantity supplied to change *along* the new demand and supply curves.

5. *New Equilibrium.* The new equilibrium price will be the point at which demand intersects supply. The change in price in Step 4 is what brings the market into equilibrium.

Example: Effect of Higher Consumer Income

PROBLEM   How will the price and quantity of new cars be affected if the income of consumers goes up? Remember that cars are a "normal" good.

SOLUTION   1. *Initial Equilibrium.* We begin with the car market being in equilibrium.

2. *Event and Shift.* Then consumer income goes up. If the price were unchanged, consumers would buy more cars. So we draw the new demand curve to the right of the old one, as in Figure 4-1.

3. *Shortage or Surplus?* If car prices were to remain at their initial level, there would be a shortage of new cars.
4. *Change in Price.* So the price of cars will rise.
5. *New Equilibrium.* As shown in Figure 4-1, at the new equilibrium, the price and quantity of cars will increase.

By drawing the demand and supply curves, an added insight you'll have is that if *both* the demand and supply curve shift, you cannot tell how *both* output and price will change. You can only tell how one will change. See Practical Application, Question 3.

KNOW THE CONCEPTS
DO YOU KNOW THE BASICS?

1. Why do we hold price constant when we talk about increasing or decreasing demand?

2. Is it the same when people are willing to (1) buy more at each price and (2) pay a higher price for each quantity?

3. If consumers buy fewer burner covers for their stoves when their income goes up, are burner covers a normal good, or an inferior good?

4. When the price of a good's complement goes up, what happens to the demand for the good?

5. Is it the same thing when suppliers are willing to (1) supply more at each price and (2) charge a lower supply price at each quantity?

6. What is the *sequence* of events for describing how an event affects price and quantity?

7. Does an increase in both price and output violate the law of demand?

8. If the cost of production goes up, does the supply curve shift to the left, or to the right?

9. What is the only factor that changes the quantity demanded (and supplied) but not demand (and supply)?

10. If world demand for wheat goes up and at the same time farmers find a cheaper way to grow wheat, what will happen to wheat prices and output?

TERMS FOR STUDY

complements	joint products
increase and decrease in demand	normal goods
increase and decrease in supply	shift in demand and supply
inferior goods	substitute products
inputs	substitutes

PRACTICAL APPLICATION

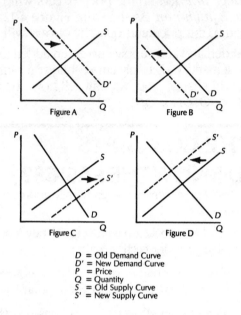

Figure A   Figure B

Figure C   Figure D

D = Old Demand Curve
D' = New Demand Curve
P = Price
Q = Quantity
S = Old Supply Curve
S' = New Supply Curve

1. Refer to Figures A, B, C, and D above. Select the figure that best reflects the likely effect of the following events. The dotted lines represent the shifts caused by the events.

   Event A: Steel, a major input for the automobile industry, goes up in price. Which figure illustrates the effect on the car market?

   Event B: National income grows as the economy comes out of a recession. Which figure illustrates the effect on the lettuce market? (Lettuce is a normal good.)

   Event C: The price of margarine falls. Which figure illustrates the effect on the butter market? (Butter is a substitute for margarine.)

   Event D: The price of heating oil goes up. Which figure illustrates the effect on the gasoline market? (Gasoline is a substitute product for heating oil, since oil refiners can make one or the other.)

   Event E: The consumption of fish is found to prevent heart attacks. Which figure illustrates the effect on the fish market?

   Event F: The price of bacon goes up. Which figure illustrates the effect on the egg market? (Eggs are a complement to bacon.)

2. Beside each of the events below, place a plus or minus sign or a zero to indicate the change in the respective variable. Here *D* stands for shifts in demand, *S* for shifts in supply, *P* for change in price, and *Q* for change in quantity.

Event A: Consumer income rises. Effect on Age-Old Wine (an inferior good)? S__D__P__Q__

Event B: The automobile union negotiates for lower wages. Effect on car market? S__D__P__Q__

Event C: Technological progress allows calculators to be produced at lower cost. Effect on calculator industry? S__D__P__Q__

Event D: The price of lumber goes up. Effect on the wood shavings market (a joint product of lumber)? S__D__P__Q__

Event E: National income goes down. Effect on "canned meals" (inferior goods)? S__D__P__Q__

3. Fill in the following table with +, −, 0, and ? to describe the effect of the combination of events. The + sign is for increase, − for decrease, 0 for no change, and ? for uncertain. For example, in the first row and the first column, indicate how price and quantity will change if both demand and supply increase.

	Supply +	Supply −	Supply 0
Demand +	P__Q__	P__Q__	P__Q__
Demand −	P__Q__	P__Q__	P__Q__
Demand 0	P__Q__	P__Q__	P__Q__

4. In 1970, electronic calculators cost over $100. Today, calculators with the same capacity cost under $10. Yet more are sold today than in 1970. Does this violate the law of supply?

5. Draw a supply and demand diagram for Good A, a free good, and Good B, a good that is too costly to produce.

6. There is currently a trend toward "natural clothing." This trend has increased the demand for clothing made out of cotton. How will this trend affect the price of cotton sheets?

7. As an application of Table 4-1, consider the plight of the U.S. automobile industry in the late 1970s. Choose the correct answer from the *italicized choices:*

   a. Due to a recession, consumer income was down, so the demand curve for U.S. cars shifted [*left or right*].

   b. The price of foreign cars (a substitute for U.S. cars) had fallen, shifting the demand curve for U.S. cars [*left or right*].

   c. The price of gasoline, a complement to automobiles, was rising. The demand curve for cars shifted [*left or right*].

   d. The effect of events a–c was to [*increase or decrease*] the quantity of U.S. cars sold and to [*increase or decrease*] the price of U.S. cars.

e. In addition, auto workers demanded and got higher wages. This event shifted the [*demand or supply*] curve to the [*left or right*].

f. Combined with the above events, these events would have [*increased, decreased, or had an uncertain effect*] on car production and would have [*increased, decreased, or had an uncertain effect*] on car prices.

8. As an application of Table 4-2, consider the effect of a freeze that reduces the suply of corn. Choose the correct italicized choices:

a. Because of the freeze, the price of corn will go [*up or down*].

b. Because corn is an input in cattle raising (since the cows are fed corn), there will be [*an increase or a decrease*] in the supply of cows once cattle farmers adjust their herds.

c. The price of beef will go [*up or down*].

d. If corn prices are expected to remain high, wheat farmers may convert some of their land to corn. Corn and wheat are substitute products and the price of wheat will go [*up or down*] as its supply is [*increased or reduced*].

e. If there is a sudden fad to wear leather boots, increasing both the demand for leather and the price of leather, beef (a joint product of leather) prices will go [*up or down*].

9. In Yorkville, rent controls have created a shortage of apartments. If rent controls (which impose a price floor on rents) were removed, what would happen to the quantity of apartments demanded? To the quantity supplied? To the number of apartments rented?

10. The third and fourth sentences of the following statement are wrong. Why? "Consumer demand for cars has increased because of higher consumer income. As a consequence, the price of cars has risen. We know that when the price of cars goes up, the demand will go down. So fewer cars will be bought when consumer income goes up."

ANSWERS

KNOW THE CONCEPTS

1. We hold price constant to avoid confusing an event that *causes* a shift in demand while holding price constant with the events *resulting* from price changes.

2. Yes: Both show an increase in demand.

3. An inferior good.

4 It shifts to the left and down.

5. Yes: Both show an increase in supply.

6. Equilibrium, event and shift, shortage or surplus at old equilibrium price, movement to new equilibrium price, new equilibrium.

7. No. This event occurs when demand shifts to the right.

8. To the left.

9. Price.

10. Wheat prices: effect is uncertain.
   Wheat output: up.

PRACTICAL APPLICATION

1. *Event A:* D
   Event B: A
   Event C: B
   Event D: D
   Event E: A
   Event F: B

2. *Event A:* 0, −, −, −
   Event B: +, 0, −, +
   Event C: +, 0, −, +
   Event D: +, 0, −, +
   Event E: 0, +, +, +

3. *First Row:* Column 1: ?, +. Column 2: +, ?. Column 3: +, +.
   Second Row: Column 1: −, ?. Column 2: ?, −. Column 3: −, −.
   Third Row: Column 1: −, +. Column 2: +, −. Column 3: 0, 0.

4. No. The event describes the effects of an outward shift in the supply curve, not a movement *along* the supply curve as in Figure C in Practical Application, Question 1.

5.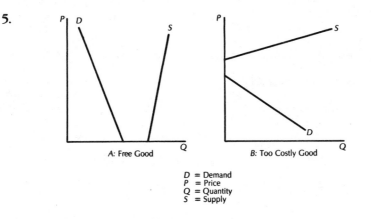

A: Free Good

B: Too Costly Good

D = Demand
P = Price
Q = Quantity
S = Supply

6. Because of the increase in demand for cotton, the price of cotton will rise (as in Figure A in Practical Application, Question 1). This higher cost will reduce the supply of sheets, raising the price (as in Figure D).

7. a. Left.
   b. Left.
   c. Left.
   d. Decrease; Decrease.
   e. Supply; Left.
   f. Decreased; Had an uncertain effect.

8. a. Up.
   b. Decrease.
   c. Up.
   d. Up; Reduced.
   e. Down.

9. As rents rise, the quantity demanded will go down while the quantity supplied will go up. This will remove the shortage. The number of apartments rented will go up.

10. What we "know" is that when the price goes up, the quantity demanded goes down, but "demand" and the demand curve remain unchanged. The price goes up because if it did not, there would be a shortage of cars. As the price goes up, the quantity demanded on the *new* curve goes down, but on *net* the quantity demanded will go up because of the shift in demand. Also, the higher price causes the quantity supplied on the *old* supply curve to go up. This gets rid of the shortage. More cars will be bought and sold at the higher price.

5
MEASURING NATIONAL OUTPUT

KEY TERMS

capital stock of plants, equipment, inventory, and other resources of production.

depreciation decline in the value of an asset over a given time, usually a year.

final good a good that is produced for final use and not for resale.

gross national product (GNP) total money value of all final goods and services produced by an economy within a given time, usually a year.

net investment addition to capital stock of nation (over a year). Gross investment is the year's production of capital goods. Net investment equals gross investment minus depreciation.

nominal GNP GNP derived by valuing goods and services at the prices they were sold at and then summing up their values (also called "GNP in current dollars" because the prices used to value goods are concurrent with the period during which the goods were sold).

real GNP GNP derived by valuing goods and services at the prices they were sold at in a certain year. At the present time, 1972 prices are used. (Also called "GNP in constant dollars" because the prices used to value goods are constant and don't change.) Real GNP corrects for the effects of inflation.

BASIC PREMISES

In order to find out how our economy is doing, our government uses *national income accounting* to measure *national output*. To understand what national income is and how it is measured, it is first necessary to understand two basic identities (e.g., 2 + 2 = 4 is an identity; an identity is a relationship, not a premise or an argument).

> *Identity 1:* A dollar spent is also a dollar received. Every dollar spent is received by someone as income. So total spending equals total income.

> *Identity 2:* Each good produced is a good bought (since even goods produced but not sold are counted as being purchased for inventory by the firm producing them). So total output equals total sales.

To make sure these identities work, economists count only final goods and services in measuring our nation's national output. A **final good** is one that is produced but not resold within the year. So if a farmer sells wheat for $1.00 to a miller, who mills the wheat into flour and sells it for $2.50 to a baker, who then sells it as a cake to a consumer for $5.00, *only* the final sale of $5.00 is counted as part of national income. To add in the other sales ($1 and $2.50) in addition to the $5.00 final sale would be double-counting, since the other sales are already counted in the $5.00.

Economists want to measure **nominal GNP**: the total money value of all the final goods and services produced by an economy in a year. To do this, they in effect take each final good and service, value it at the price it was sold, and then add them all together to get nominal *GNP*.

Nominal *GNP* can change from year to year because (1) the prices of the goods and services change and (2) the quantity of goods and services produced changes. So that changes in *GNP* better reflect changes in output and *not* changes in prices, economists value all goods and services using prices from a given base year: this is the economy's **real GNP**. Currently, 1972 prices are used. For example, suppose a simple economy produces and consumes only wheat. In 1980, it produced fifty tons of wheat that sold for $40 a ton. The economy's nominal *GNP* was $2,000. If the 1972 price of wheat was $20 a ton, the economy's real *GNP* for 1980 was $1,000. If in 1981 it still produced fifty tons of wheat but the price had risen to $50 a ton, nominal *GNP* went up to $2,500 but real *GNP* was unchanged (at $1,000).

THE CIRCULAR FLOW OF INCOME

The two basic "identities"—income and spending, or the monetary flows, and income and output, or the flows of goods and services—are illustrated in Figure

5-1, which shows the **circular flow of income**. *Households* are defined as the owners of all factors of production in the economy. Households provide the factor services of labor, land, capital, and ownership to businesses. This is Flow A. In return, households get paid wages, rent, interest, and profits. This flow of factor payments is Flow B. *Businesses* provide goods and services to households; this is Flow C. In return, households buy the goods and services; their spending is Flow D.

The identity of income and spending is represented by the equality of Flow B (factor payments) with Flow D (spending). These are the monetary flows in the economy. The identity of income and output is represented by Flow A (factor services) and Flow C (goods and services): These are the flows of goods and services in the economy.

Figure 5-1 The Circular Flow of Income

MEASURING GNP

There are two basic ways to measure national income. The first is to measure total spending on goods and services (Flow D). This is the **expenditures approach**. The second method is to measure total income (Flow B); this is the **incomes approach**.

Two Ways to Measure *GNP*

1. The Expenditures Approach
One way to measure *GNP* is to add up the spending on goods and services by households, businesses, governments, and foreigners. The following formula can be used:

$$GNP = C + I + G + NX$$

where C = Household Consumption Spending
It *includes* all household spending on final goods and services. However, it *excludes* the purchase of new homes (because such a purchase is counted as an investment) and the purchase of used cars (because only current output is included in *GNP*).

I = Business Investment Spending
It *includes* all private domestic investment spending: (1) business investment in new plant and equipment, (2) additions to the inventories of goods businesses hold, and (3) residential construction (or new homes). However, it *excludes* machines sold to foreign nations (because they are counted as exports). The purchase and sale of stocks and bonds are excluded from *GNP* because they represent the trading of property rights in existing capital and not the production of new capital.

I is gross investment, the total amount of capital goods produced in a year. *Capital* is a nation's stock of productive resources, including plants, equipment, and inventories. Each year, a certain amount of a nation's capital stock *depreciates*, or wears out and becomes obsolete. Gross investment minus depreciation equals net investment. Net investment is how much on net is added to a nation's capital stock.

G = Government Spending
Because government goods and services are not directly bought and sold in the open market, the government's output is valued at its cost. Note that G does not include **transfer payments**, which are payments other than those for factor services. For example, Social Security payments and food stamp payments are transfer payments.

NX = Foreign Net Export Spending: Exports Minus Imports
Adding up what U.S. citizens sell to other nations and then subtracting what they buy from other nations results in net sales to other nations. This measures what our nation has produced, whether the products are sold here or abroad.

2. The Incomes Approach
    Method One: Sum of Factor Payments
One way to measure total income is to sum the incomes of each type of factor. To do this, though, two adjustments must be made.
   a. First, *depreciation* is subtracted from *GNP* to take account of the fact that our capital stock wears out a little each year. (Depreciation is also called the *capital consumption allowance*.)
   b. Next, *indirect business taxes,* which include sales taxes and any other taxes not based on income, are subtracted.

This yields the formula:

GNP − Depreciation − Indirect Business Taxes = National Income

where National Income = Wages + Rent + Interest + Profits.

> It *includes* wages (compensation of employees), rent (rental income), interest (net interest), and profits (corporate profits plus proprietors' income). These are payments to the *factors* of production (land, labor, capital) plus profits. It *excludes* interest payments made by households or the government, because it is assumed that only interest payments by businesses are based upon the production of goods and services. Proprietors' income is the income of the self-employed.

Note: The terms in parentheses are the official *national income accounting* names.

Method Two: Sum of Values

This method adds the income created by each business, i.e., the **value added** by each business. Value added is the value of a business's output minus its purchases from other businesses.
For each firm, we have:

Factor Payments = Wages + Rents + Interest Payments

and

$$\text{Profits} = \text{Value of Output} - \text{Factor Payments} - \text{Purchases from Other Firms}$$

But since

Value Added = Value of Output − Purchases from Other Firms

it follows from the definition of profits that:

Value Added = Factor Payments + Profits

For the nation as a whole, then, we have:

$$\text{Sum of Value Added} = \text{National Income} = \text{Sum of Factor Payments} + \text{Profits}$$

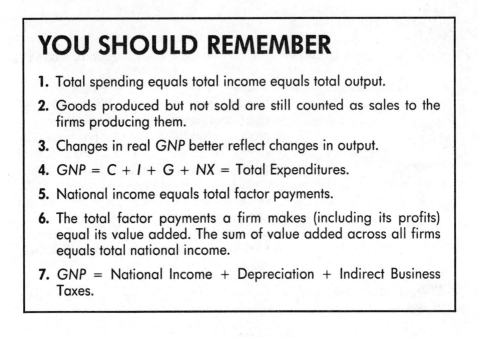

YOU SHOULD REMEMBER

1. Total spending equals total income equals total output.

2. Goods produced but not sold are still counted as sales to the firms producing them.

3. Changes in real *GNP* better reflect changes in output.

4. $GNP = C + I + G + NX =$ Total Expenditures.

5. National income equals total factor payments.

6. The total factor payments a firm makes (including its profits) equal its value added. The sum of value added across all firms equals total national income.

7. $GNP =$ National Income + Depreciation + Indirect Business Taxes.

GNP AND NATIONAL WELFARE

GNP should not be confused with national well-being, although it is closely related. Some of *GNP*'s limitations are:

1. GNP *ignores many nonmarket transactions,* such as the value of a person who works in the home but is not paid by his or her spouse. Also, unreported income earned in the "underground economy" is ignored (e.g., some waiters may not fully report their tip income and some plumbers may not report their cash sales).

2. GNP *ignores the value of leisure.* If everyone were forced to work sixteen hours a day, *GNP* would go up, but national welfare would not.

3. GNP *ignores ecological costs* of producing output (including the costs of pollution).

4. GNP *focuses on output, but it is consumption that affects our nation's welfare.* For example, if other nations sell us more goods than we sell them, our nation will likely be better off because it can then consume more. But this will reduce *GNP,* since net exports will then be negative. Focusing only on output thus gives a distorted view of national welfare.

5. *Government spending is valued at cost, not at its value.* Worthwhile projects are thus undervalued and worthless projects overvalued.

NATIONAL INCOME ACCOUNTING FORMULAS

The specifics of national income accounting briefly, are as follows.

Basic Formulas

1. Gross National Product (GNP) $= C +$ Gross Investment $+ G + NX$

2. Net National Product (NNP)
   (a) $NNP = GNP -$ Depreciation
   (b) $NNP = C +$ Net Investment $+ G + NX$

3. Net Investment $=$ Gross Investment $-$ Depreciation

4. National Income (NI)
   (a) $NI = NNP -$ Indirect Business Taxes
   (b) $NI =$ Sum of Factor Payments

5. Personal Income (PI)
   (a) $PI = NI -$ Social Security Contributions $-$ Corporate Income Taxes $-$ Undistributed Corporate Profits $+$ Transfer Payments
   (b) $PI =$ Household Income

6. Personal Disposable Income (DI)
   (a) $DI = PI -$ Personal Taxes
   (b) $DI =$ After-Tax Household Income
   (c) $DI =$ Consumption Expenditures $+$ Personal Savings $+$ Interest Payments to Businesses
   (d) $DI = NI -$ Corporate Profits $-$ Taxes (personal, corporate, and Social Security) $+$ Personal Dividend Receipts $+$ Interest Paid by Government $+$ Transfer Payments by Government and Businesses to Households

   where $C =$ household consumption spending
   $DI =$ disposable income
   $G =$ government spending
   $GNP =$ gross national product
   $NI =$ national income
   $NNP =$ net national product
   $NX =$ foreign net export spending

Note: Depreciation is the same as Capital Consumption Allowance

APPLYING THE NATIONAL INCOME PREMISES

National income equals total income, but because each dollar received as income is also a dollar spent, national income also equals total spending. If we look at national income as total spending, we have:

$$\text{National Income} = C + I + G + NX.$$

But if we look at national income in terms of how it is *allocated,* it is either consumed, saved, or taxed:

$$\text{National Income} = C + \text{Savings} + (\text{Taxes} - \text{Transfer Payments}).^*$$

Now, if we equate the two expressions above, for national income we have:

$$C + I + G + NX = C + \text{Savings} + (\text{Taxes} - \text{Transfer Payments})$$
$$I + G + NX = \text{Savings} + (\text{Taxes} - \text{Transfer Payments})$$

In an economy without a government and without world trade, we'd simply have:

$$I = \text{Savings}$$

Actual investment (including increased inventories) always equals savings if (*and only if*) there is no government sector or foreign trade.

Example: Identity of Savings and Investment

PROBLEM   In an economy with no government sector or foreign trade, suppose businesses produce $1,000 and thus pay $1,000 in income. But households consume $800 and buy $150 in investment goods, throwing the remaining $50 of income into a jar. Will savings equal investment in this case?

SOLUTION   Yes. Savings are $200 ($1,000 − $800). Investment equals $200: $150 is for investment goods and $50 is in increased inventory (since firms produce $1,000 worth of goods and only sell $950 of it, the unsold $50 of goods goes into inventory). Note that counting additions to inventory as "sales" assures that total income equals total spending.

---

*(*Taxes* − *Transfer Payments*) is in parentheses because this is the *net taxes* the public pays the government. **Savings** is that part of disposable income that is not consumed. Thus:

$$\text{Disposable Income } (DI) = C + \text{Savings}.$$

In turn,

$$\text{Disposable income } (DI) = \text{National Income} - (\text{Taxes} - \text{Transfers}).$$

Adding the government sector, we have

$$I + G = \text{Savings} + (\text{Taxes} - \text{Tr. Payments})$$
$$I + (G + \text{Tr. Payments} - \text{Taxes}) = \text{Savings,}$$
$$I + \text{Government Deficit} = \text{Savings.}$$

Note: Tr. = Transfer

Note: The difference between total government expenditures (G + Transfer Payments) and taxes is the **government deficit**.

So this equation says that savings will go towards financing investment or the government's deficit.

YOU SHOULD REMEMBER

1. GNP measures national output and not necessarily national welfare.

2. Total Spending is on Consumption, Investment (I), Government Spending (G), or Net Exports (NX). Total Income is allocated either to Consumption, Savings, or Taxes.

3. Since

Total Income = Total Spending,

it is also true that

I + G + NX = Savings + (Taxes − Transfer Payments).

KNOW THE CONCEPTS

DO YOU KNOW THE BASICS?

1. Why are only final goods and services counted in *GNP*?
2. Why do changes in real *GNP* better reflect how total output is changing than changes in nominal *GNP*?
3. What are the two basic national income identities, and how are they pictured in the circular flow of income?
4. What makes *GNP* gross and *NNP* net?
5. Which national income account best reflects total factor payments?

6. Which national income account best reflects the income households receive? The after-tax income that households receive?

7. How do households dispose of disposable income?

8. In a simple economy without international trade for a government, how are investment (I) and savings related?

9. With a government sector, how do businesses and the government in a sense compete for savings?

10. Does *GNP* measure national welfare?

TERMS FOR STUDY

businesses	households
circular flow of income	incomes approach
depreciation	investment, gross and net
expenditures approach	net exports
final goods	savings
GNP, NNP, NI, PI, DI	transfer payments
government deficit	value added

PRACTICAL APPLICATION

1. Which of the following are counted in *GNP*?
   a. Purchase of $2,000 of IBM stock.
   b. $3,000 payment to a lawyer to sue a neighbor to keep his dog quiet.
   c. $500 in unemployment compensation collected by an unemployed worker.
   d. $600 paid by a student for a used car.
   e. The purchase of a bottle of French wine.
   f. $5,000 earned by an American in Paris.
   g. $5 million worth of new computers produced by AT&T that AT&T can't sell.

2. Suppose *GNP* = $3,000, C = $2,400, G = $100 and *NX* = $80.
   a. What is I?
   b. If exports equal $350, what are imports?
   c. If depreciation is $150, what is *NNP*?
   d. If taxes equal $200 and transfer payments equal $120, what is the deficit equal to? What are savings equal to?
   e. If indirect business taxes equal $70, what is national income?

3. What are net exports equal to when *GNP* = $1,000, I = $100, C = $600,

and G = $150? If taxes = $100 and there are no transfer payments, what do savings equal? And if imports equal $80, what do exports equal?

4. Indicate how the following will affect measured *GNP* and the national welfare:
   a. An oil spill occurs and is cleaned up at a cost of $2 million.
   b. The government requires all house persons be paid for their work.
   c. The Army Corps of Engineers builds a dam at a cost of $5 billion that is worth only $2 billion.
   d. A teenager quits work and goes back to school, which she regards as much more worthwhile.

5. Should a welfare recipient's payments from the government be included in *GNP*?

6. Suppose that savings are fixed at 15% of *GNP*. Also assume that net exports are zero. If the government's deficit equals 5% of *GNP*, what percentage of *GNP* is investment?

7. A farmer grows corn, which she sells for $10; a miller buys the corn, grinds it, and sells it as corn meal for $15; a baker buys the corn meal and sells it as corn muffins for $22. How much was contributed to *GNP* in these transactions? What was the value added of each person?

8. An economy produces $15 billion in investment goods and $100 billion in consumption goods. All investment goods were sold, but only $90 billion of the consumption goods were sold. There is no government or international trade. What was *GNP*? What was consumption and investment?

9. There are only two firms in an economy. Firm A buys from Firm B and vice versa. What is the value added for each firm? What is *GNP*? Show that total factor income equals *GNP*.

	Firm A	Firm B
Total sales	$1,000	$3,400
Wages, rent, and interest	$ 800	$1,600
Purchases from other firm	$ 100	$1,000
Output	$1,100	$3,400

10. In an economy, households consume $600 and save $400. The government spends $200 and taxes $150. There are no transfer payments or foreign trade. What is *I*? What is *GNP*?

ANSWERS

KNOW THE CONCEPTS

1. Because all other sales (of intermediate products that are resold within the year) are reflected in the price of final goods.
2. Changes in real *GNP* reflect changes in real output only. Nominal *GNP* changes when prices and/or output changes.
3. A dollar spent is a dollar received: Flow D equals Flow B. A good sold is a good bought: Flow A equals Flow D.
4. "Net" refers to subtracting depreciation. "Gross" includes depreciation.
5. *NI:* National Income.
6. *PI:* Personal Income. *DI:* Personal Disposable Income.
7. They consume or save it.
8. I = Savings.
9. When we added the government sector, we had

$$\text{Investment} + \text{Government Deficit} = \text{Savings}$$

Businesses borrow to finance their investment spending, and the government borrows to finance its deficit. Thus, to the degree that savings are fixed in size, the more the government borrows, the less businesses can borrow for investment.
10. No. It is a measure of output and spending.

PRACTICAL APPLICATION

1. Only b, f, and g are included in *GNP.* The other transactions do not reflect the production of goods and services by U.S.-owned factors in the current year.
2. a. I = $420.
   b. Imports = $270.
   c. *NNP* = $2,850.
   d. The deficit = $20, and savings = $520.
   e. National income is $2,780.
3. Net exports = $150, savings = $300, and exports = $230.
4. a. Increases *GNP,* reduces national welfare.
   b. Increases *GNP,* has no effect on national welfare.

   c. Increases *GNP,* reduces national welfare.

   d. Decreases *GNP,* increases national welfare.

5. No. The welfare recipient is not producing any goods or services for the welfare payment. The welfare payment is a transfer payment.

6. Investment plus the government's deficit equals savings. So investment equals 10% of *GNP.*

7. The final good sold for $22; this is the contribution to *GNP.* It also equals the sum of the value added: $10 for the farmer, $5 for the miller, and $7 for the baker.

8. *GNP* was $115 billion, the sum of output produced. Consumption was $90 billion (the amount households spent), while investment was $25 billion. $15 billion was for the investment goods produced. The other $10 billion of investment was the increased inventory due to the unsold consumption goods.

9. The value added is the firm's output (recall that unsold output is treated as a sale to the firm) less its purchases from other firms. Firm A's value added is $1,000 and B's is $2,400. So *GNP* equals $3,400. Firm A's profits are $200 (once again, the value of its output is counted as its revenue even if it's not sold). Firm B's profits are $800. So wages, rent, and interest total $2,400 and profits total $1,000, giving us a national income of $3,400.

10. With no foreign trade or transfer payments, we have:

$$I + G - \text{Taxes} = \text{Savings. So } I = \$350.$$
$$GNP = C + I + G = \$1,150.$$

6
INFLATION AND UNEMPLOYMENT

MEASURING INFLATION

To measure how much prices have risen, economists use price indexes. **Price indexes** measure how prices today compare with those in some selected year (called the **base year**): they express today's cost of a market basket of goods as a percentage of the basket's cost in the base year. For example, the 1984 Consumer Price Index (CPI) was 316. Thus, the market basket of 256 goods in the CPI in 1984 costs 316% of what it did in 1967 (the base year for the CPI). Prices have risen 216% since 1967. (The percentage increase in prices since the base year is the index's value minus 100).

Key Procedure for Constructing a Price Index

1. For a base year, determine what goods people bought and how much of each they bought. Calculate the cost of this basket of goods for the base year.

2. Calculate the cost of the basket for Year "T."

3. The price index for Year T is shown by the following formula:

$$\frac{\text{Cost of Basket in Year T}}{\text{Cost of Basket in Base Year}} \times 100.$$

For example, if the basket costs $6,000 in the base year and $9,000 in 1975, the 1975 price index is 150. Prices have gone up 50%. The price index for the base year is always 100.

Example: Calculating a Price Index

PROBLEM   In 1980, Joe, in a typical week, bought ten bottles of wine (at $4 each) and twenty pizzas (at $6 each). In 1985, wine cost $6 and pizza cost $8. What is Joe's 1985 price index, using 1980 as the base year?

SOLUTION   137.5. The 1980 basket cost $160 in 1980 ($4 × 10 + $6 × 20) and would have cost $220 in 1985 ($6 × 10 + $8 × 20). $220/$160 times 100 equals 137.5.

THE THREE MAIN PRICE INDEXES

- *The Consumer Price Index (CPI).* The CPI measures the cost of a market basket of consumer goods and services. Currently, these are goods and services in the amounts that consumers bought in 1972–1973.

- *The Producer Price Index (PPI).* The PPI measures a basket of wholesale goods, bought by producers early in the production process. This index is often an early indicator of inflation.

- *The GNP Deflator.* The GNP Deflator measures the price of all goods and services produced in the United States. This basket is constantly being updated to reflect current spending patterns (unlike the CPI, whose basket is based on 1972 spending patterns). Economists use the GNP Deflator to measure inflation. It covers more goods than either the CPI or the PPI and is more up-to-date.

PROBLEMS WITH PRICE INDEXES

Price indexes often do not accurately measure the change in prices, because of two major problems:

1. *Price indexes do not fully account for changes in quality.* To the degree that price indexes do not take account of improvements in quality, they *overstate* how much prices have risen. For example, suppose 1988 prices were 10% higher than 1987 prices but 1988 goods were 10% better. While consumers in 1988 were paying 10% more in higher prices, they were also getting (in terms of better quality) 10% more, so the true cost of living had not changed. A price index showing a 10% increase in prices would overstate the increase in the cost of living.

2. *The major price indexes (such as the CPI) ignore changes in consumption patterns.* Due to the law of demand, consumers buy less of those goods whose prices have gone up more. In this way, consumers partially offset some of the impact of higher prices on their cost of living. Because the CPI ignores this, it overstates the increase in the cost of living. This problem is called "the index number problem." See Practical Application, Question 7.

THE MEANING OF INFLATION

Inflation is a rise in the general price level of goods and services. The **inflation rate** is the percent change in the general price level over a year.

Key Procedure for Measuring the Inflation Rate

1. Let *P (Year T)* be Year T's price index and *P (Year T-1)* be the prior year's price index.

2. The *rate of inflation in Year T is:*

$$\frac{P\ (Year\ T)\ -\ P\ (Year\ T\text{-}1)}{P\ (Year\ T\text{-}1)} \times 100$$

YOU SHOULD REMEMBER

1. *Price indexes* measure the cost of a market basket of goods, expressed as a percent of its cost in some base year. Price indexes overstate the rise in prices when they ignore improvements in quality and shifts in spending away from goods whose prices have increased more.

> **2.** The *measured inflation rate* is the percent increase in the price index in a year.

HOW INFLATION AFFECTS REAL INCOME

To fully understand the effect of inflation, it is necessary to understand two key concepts. The first is *nominal*: it refers to the actual money amount. For example, the **nominal interest rate** is the money paid on loans, expressed as a percent per year. The nominal hourly wage is the money one earns per hour of work. The second concept is *real*: it refers to the goods and services one can buy with what one gets paid. The **real interest rate** is the increase in goods and services savers receive for lending money, expressed as a percent per year. Real hourly wages are the goods and services one can buy with the pay for an hour of work.

In most years, workers get raises. But are the workers really better off? To answer these questions, economists use price indexes to convert nominal amounts into real amounts.

Key Procedure for Using Price Indexes to Calculate Real Values

1. Convert the price index from its percent form to a decimal form by moving its decimal point two places to the left.

2. Divide the nominal amount by the price index to derive its real value.

Example: Using the CPI to Calculate Changes in Real Wages

PROBLEM   In 1970, average hourly earnings in manufacturing were $3.35. In 1980, they were $7.27. In 1970, the CPI was 116.3, and in 1980, 246.8. What was the real wage in both years and how much had it changed between 1970 and 1980?

SOLUTION   The real wage in 1970 was $2.88 ($3.35/1.163). In 1980, it was $2.95 ($7.27/2.468). So between 1970 and 1980, real hourly wages had increased by about 2.4%.

To show how inflation affects real income, assume for the moment that workers consume only bread. If they are paid $4 an hour and can buy a loaf of bread for 50¢, their nominal wage is $4 and their real wage is eight loaves of bread. But suppose the price of bread rises to $1. Their real wage will fall by 50% to four loaves. They will be worse off because they didn't anticipate the rise in prices. But suppose both employers and workers alike anticipate that prices will double. Since the price of what workers produce has doubled, the dollar value of each hour of work will double from $4 to $8. So employers will be willing to pay a wage of $8. Similarly, workers will demand a wage of $8, which will give them the same real wage (eight loaves) as before. In this case, the wage will rise to $8 and workers will not suffer any loss in real income. Inflation harms people mainly when they do not anticipate and adjust to it.

THE ECONOMIC COSTS OF INFLATION

Now let us consider the costs of inflation to an economy before and after people come to anticipate inflation.

• *UNANTICIPATED INFLATION*

It has often taken years for people to fully anticipate and adjust to inflation. During the period before people fully adjust, inflation's main effect is to harm those with long-term contracts that pay them a fixed dollar amount over several years. For example, savers who bought a twenty-year bond that pays them a fixed amount of money each year for twenty years will find that inflation erodes the real value of their returns.

But just as there are losers from inflation, there are winners: those with long-term contracts that have to pay out fixed amounts of money per year. Winners include employers with long-term contracts paying fixed money wages to workers and borrowers paying back fixed interest payments on loans. These winners benefit from lower real costs.

• *ANTICIPATED* STEADY *INFLATION*

Even if inflation comes to be fully anticipated and persists year after year at a constant rate, it still has costs. But once anticipated, there usually is not the redistribution of wealth as described above. For example, unions will seek to protect workers by putting cost-of-living adjustments (called COLAs) into their contracts. And nominal interest rates will likely rise to offset the loss in purchasing power. In particular:

Nominal Interest Rate = Real Interest Rate + Expected Rate of Inflation

For example, if savers want a real return of 4% and expect a 10% rate of inflation, they will want a 14% nominal interest rate.

The Two Main Costs of Steady *Anticipated* Inflation

1. *Excessive Cash Management.* Inflation acts like a tax on money holdings. For example, suppose your money holdings equal $1,000. An inflation rate of 10% will reduce the value of your holdings. In order to maintain the real value of your money holdings, you will have to increase your holdings by 10%, or in this case $100. This $100 in added cost is like a 10% tax on money holdings. The higher the rate of inflation, the more expensive it becomes to maintain the real value of one's money holdings. The result is that *inflation causes people to reduce their real money holdings.*

   But smaller real money holdings result in inconveniences for people. For example, if people carry less cash in their pocket, they may have to go to the bank more often to get cash. The added cost of more frequent financial transactions due to inflation is called the "shoe leather cost" of inflation (the "shoe leather cost" being the wearing out of one's shoes due to the more frequent trips to the bank). In this way and others, inflation raises the cost of cash management.

2. *More Frequent Posting of Prices.* The greater the rate of inflation, the more often businesses have to post new prices. Menus have to be changed, advertising increased, and catalogs revised.

• *VARYING INFLATION WHOSE AVERAGE RATE IS ANTICIPATED*

Suppose people have come to correctly anticipate the average rate of inflation, but inflation varies, sometimes being above and other times below its average rate.

The Two Main Costs of Anticipated but Varying Inflation

1. *Compensating for Uncertainty.* Suppose workers' nominal wages are set by a long-term contract to increase with the average rate of inflation. On average, then, their real wages will be unchanged. But as inflation goes above and then below its average level, their real wages will go below and then above its anticipated average level. Because of the uncertainty as to what their actual real wages will be, workers who sign long-term contracts will demand extra compensation. Real wages will increase. The result will be higher real wages and a fall in employment. Some economists estimate that the increased fluctuations in the inflation rate our nation has experienced since 1979 have raised the real rate of interest by at about one percentage point.

2. *Destroyed Information.* When inflation varies, it becomes difficult to know what a good price is or to shop wisely. It is like the Twilight Zone episode in which a man finds that the meaning of words is constantly changing. Just to converse, he must constantly relearn his language. Similarly, varying inflation forces people to constantly relearn prices.

YOU SHOULD REMEMBER

1. The *nominal* value of a payment is its dollar amount; its *real* value is expressed in terms of the goods and services it can buy.

2. Unanticipated inflation hurts lenders and those on fixed incomes. It helps borrowers and those whose costs are fixed in nominal terms.

3. When inflation is fully anticipated and steady, it still costs the economy in added cash management costs and in more frequent posting of prices.

4. When inflation's average rate is anticipated but it varies around that rate, it brings the added costs of greater uncertainty and a higher cost due to destroyed information.

5. Nominal interest rates equal the real rate *plus* the expected rate of inflation (as compensation for lost purchasing power).

MEASURING UNEMPLOYMENT

Every month, the Department of Labor (DOL) interviews 60,000 households that have been randomly selected to represent the whole U.S. population. Based upon their answers, all people aged 16 or older are put into one of the following three categories.

Labor-Force Categories

1. *Employed.* A person is employed if the person (1) has done any work in the week prior to the interview, or (2) has a job but is absent because of illness, a strike, or vacation.

2. *Unemployed.* A person is **unemployed** if the person (1) did not work in the previous week, but has made specific efforts to find a job in the last four weeks, (2) has been laid-off and is waiting to be recalled in the next thirty days, or (3) is waiting to report to a new job in the next thirty days.

3. *Not in the Labor Force.* The **labor force** is all those who are employed or unemployed; the rest of the population is not in the labor force. This includes people who are full-time students, nonworking spouses, or retired. It also includes **"discouraged workers,"** persons who want to work but have given up looking for employment.

The **rate of unemployment** is the percent of the *labor force* that is unemployed. So if there are 100 million employed persons and 20 million unemployed persons, the unemployment rate will be 16.7% (20/120 × 100).

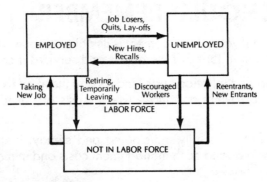

Figure 6-1 Labor Force Flows

Figure 6-1 shows the flows in the labor market. People leave unemployment either by finding jobs or by becoming discouraged and leaving the labor force. On average, half leave each way. After a few months, most discouraged workers will reenter the labor force. Of those entering unemployment, 50% are job-losers (having either been fired or being put on indefinite layoff), 25% are reentrants, and the rest are evenly divided between job-leavers (quitting to seek better work) and new entrants.

THE EFFECT OF RECESSION

The economy is in a **recession** when total output falls. A recession increases the unemployment rate in two main ways. First, there is an increase in the number of workers losing their jobs: This increases the "flow" into unemployment. Second, it takes longer to find a job during a recession: This reduces the "flow" out of unemployment. The number unemployed thus swells during a recession.

THE TYPES AND COSTS OF UNEMPLOYMENT

The Three Types of Unemployment

1. *Frictional unemployment* is due to the normal workings of an economy. Frictional unemployment occurs because (a) workers quit to find better jobs, (b) employers fire workers and look for better ones to replace them, (c) consumers change the goods they buy, thereby reducing jobs previously available in producing the goods they no longer want but increasing jobs elsewhere, and (d) technological progress makes the skills of some workers obsolete.

2. *Structural unemployment* occurs if cause (c) or (d) above seriously affects certain industries, occupations, or areas of the country so that only with very high costs can workers relocate and/or retrain for new careers.

3. *Cyclical unemployment* is due to downturns in the economy. When economists say the economy is at **full employment**, they mean that there is no cyclical unemployment. However, both frictional and structural employment can and do exist when the economy is fully employed. The unemployment rate at full employment is about 5% to 6%.

Frictional unemployment, while costly to those losing their jobs, benefits the economy. Because it exists, the economy can better match workers with the employers and can shift output toward those goods consumers want. *Structural unemployment* has a net social cost if the benefits of retraining (and/or relocating) the unemployed workers exceed the cost. *Cyclical unemployment* is costly mainly because it is associated with the cost of lost output. This cost is the difference between the value of the output and the opportunity cost of producing it. So if output falls by $100 billion and this output would have cost $40 billion to produce, the social loss is $60 billion.

Unemployment is linked to real *GNP* by what is called "Okun's Law." The law states that for every 2% that real *GNP* is below its potential full employment level over a year's time, the unemployment rate will increase by 1%. (Some studies put this ratio at 2.5 to 1 rather than 2 to 1.) Since potential full-employment *GNP* usually grows at 3% a year, if real *GNP* grows at 3%, the unemployment rate should remain unchanged. If it grows at 5% over a year, the unemployment rate should fall by 1 percentage point (e.g., from 5% to 4%). And if real *GNP* does not grow at all, the unemployment rate should rise 1.5% (e.g., from 5% to 6.5%).

Be careful to note that Okun's Law is an observed regularity of how changes in *GNP* affect unemployment. It does not say that decreasing unemployment (e.g., by a government program to train the unemployed) will cause *GNP* to rise.

The official unemployment rate does not necessarily capture the full extent of the misery caused by a recession. It fails to count (1) discouraged workers who have dropped out of the labor force because they can't find a job, and (2) the **underemployed**, part-time workers who want to work full-time.

YOU SHOULD REMEMBER

1. The unemployment rate is the percentage of the labor force that is unemployed.

2. Unemployment goes up in a recession because more people lose jobs and find that it takes longer to find new jobs.

3. Okun's Law states that every 2% increase in the real GNP growth rate above its potential level, if sustained for a year, results in a 1% decrease in the unemployment rate.

4. Cyclical unemployment is costly because of the lost output associated with it.

5. At full employment, both frictional and structural unemployment will be present; only cyclical unemployment will be zero.

KNOW THE CONCEPTS

DO YOU KNOW THE BASICS?

1. How does inflation hurt those on fixed incomes?
2. How can savers protect themselves from inflation?
3. Why do interest rates eventually go up during a period of inflation?
4. When inflation causes greater uncertainty in the economy, workers often demand higher real wages as compensation for the higher uncertainty. How does this hurt the economy?
5. If real *GNP* is constant while the *GNP* Deflator increases, what will happen to nominal *GNP*?
6. What does a price index of 180 mean? How much have prices risen since the base year?
7. Why does an improvement in quality cause a price index to overstate how much prices have gone up?
8. What are the different ways someone can become unemployed?
9. If the unemployment rate is 10% and 90 million workers are employed, how many are unemployed?
10. What is the main cost associated with cyclical unemployment?

TERMS FOR STUDY

discouraged worker
employed, unemployed
frictional, structural, and
    cyclical unemployment
inflation
inflation rate
labor force
Okun's Law

real interest rate,
    nominal interest rate
real, nominal
real wages, nominal wages
steady inflation and varying inflation
unanticipated inflation and
    anticipated inflation

PRACTICAL APPLICATION

1. The ABC Corporation had a nominal profit of $300,000 in 1980 and a nominal profit of $330,000 in 1982. The CPI was 246.8 in 1980 and 289.1 in 1982. How much did ABC's real profits change?

2. Fill in the missing numbers in this table. The price index used is the *GNP* Deflator.

Year	Real GNP	Price Index	Nominal GNP
1970	1,085.6	91.45	------
1972	------	100.00	1,185.9
1974	1,246.3	------	1,434.2
1976	------	132.34	1,718.0

Hint: Real *GNP* equals nominal *GNP* divided by *GNP* Deflator, stated as a decimal number.

3. If inflation continues for twenty years at a 6% rate, by how much will prices increase?

4. From the following figures, calculate the price index for this worker, using 1980 as the base year. How much did prices go up? What is the real income in each year? (Assume that the worker spent all of his or her income in each year.)

Item	Price and Quantity			
	1980		1985	
Food	$1	2,000	$2	2,000
Housing	$500	4	$1,500	3
Clothing	$50	40	$80	50

5. In 1981, the news media was alarmed over high interest rates when the Treasury Bill rate equaled 14%. But many economists said that interest rates were not high. Use the concepts of real and nominal interest rates to explain this apparent paradox.

6. Indicate the labor-force status of the following persons:
   a. A doctor who is too sick to work.
   b. A mechanic who couldn't find a job needing his skills and is waiting for the economy to improve before he looks for work again.
   c. A full-time student.
   d. A laid-off steel worker waiting to return to work.
   e. A laid-off executive who is making ends meet by working at a car wash.
   f. An executive given a year off to have a baby.

7. This example illustrates the index number problem. Suppose John consumes only bread. In Year 0, John buys four loaves of white bread and four of dark bread, all at $1 each. John likes both equally. In Year 1, white

bread costs $2 but dark bread still costs $1. So John switches to dark bread.

   a. What has happened to John's cost of living?

   b. What will the values be for a price index using Year 0 as the base year? Does it overstate or understate the true increase in John's cost of living?

8. In 1982–83, real *GNP* was below its potential (full-employment) level by about 4% each year. According to Okun's Law, how much should the unemployment rate have changed?

9. This problem illustrates what is called "bracket creep": the increase in income taxes through inflation. Suppose the first $5,000 earned is tax-free, the next $5,000 is taxed at 10%, and the next $5,000 at 20%.

   a. A worker earned $7,000 in 1980. Calculate the worker's taxes, average tax rate (taxes/income), and after-tax income.

   b. Now suppose that over the next five years, all prices and earnings doubled (so the worker earned $14,000). The tax system is still the same. Calculate the worker's taxes, average tax rate, after-tax income, *and* real after-tax income (using 1980 as the base year).

10. This problem illustrates how inflation combined with our tax code increases the tax rate on profits. (A related fact is that stock prices and inflation have been negatively related in recent years.) In Year 0, the XYZ Corporation buys a $100,000 machine, which will have to be replaced every five years. So it writes off a fifth of the value of the machine each year as depreciation. The following table illustrates its profits in Year 4, assuming there is no inflation.

Sales	$40,000
− Factor Costs	$10,000
− *Depreciation*	*$20,000*
Profits	$10,000
− Taxes (50%)	5,000
After-Tax Profits	$ 5,000

Now suppose there is inflation, so all prices double (including the replacement cost of the machine, sales, and costs). But the government allows depreciation to be written off at only historical cost (i.e., $20,000). What is the new profit statement in Year 4? What is the effective tax on profits?

ANSWERS

KNOW THE CONCEPTS

1. It reduces their *real* income.

2. They can demand a higher nominal interest rate. Recently, some savers

have been demanding a variable interest rate based upon short-term interest rates, which usually reflect current inflation rates.

3. As savers come to expect higher rates of inflation, they demand higher nominal interest rates to compensate them for their loss in purchasing power.

4. Applying the laws of demand and supply to labor, this event causes the supply curve of labor to shift left. As a result, employment falls. With less employment, output and *GNP* fall.

5. Nominal *GNP* will increase.

6. The cost of a basket of goods is 180% of its base-year cost. Prices have risen 80% since the base year.

7. An improvement in quality gives the consumer more value per dollar, so that even if the price of the item is unchanged, its cost-per-unit value is reduced.

8. A person can quit, be fired, or be laid off. Also, a person can be an entrant or reentrant into the labor force.

9. 10 million.

10. The loss due to decreased output.

PRACTICAL APPLICATION

1. ABC's real profits in 1980 were $121,556 ($300,000/2.468), and in 1982, $114,147 ($330,000/2.891). Real profits went down by $7,409.

2. 992.8 for 1970, 1,185.9 for 1972, 115.08 for 1974, and 1,298.2 for 1976.

3. If the price level starts at 1, then at the end of one year, it will be at 1.06. Then prices will grow 6% more, or 1.06 times 1.06, to 1.1236 by the end of the second year. By the end of twenty years, the price level will grow to 1.06 times itself twenty times, or to 3.21. Prices will have risen 221%.

4. The price index using 1980 as the base year is 100 in 1980 and 220 in 1985. The cost of the 1980 basket was $6,000 in 1980, and the same basket (the *1980* quantities) cost $13,200 at 1985 prices. So 220 is from $13,200/$6,000 times 100. Prices went up by 120%.

   Using the 1980-based index, real income in 1980 was $6,000 ($6,000/1.00) and in 1985, $5,000 ($11,000/2.20).

5. Nominal (or "the newspaper") interest rates were very high in 1981. But what matters to the economy is the *real* rate, which equals the nominal rate minus the rate of inflation. The rate of inflation was 10% in 1981, so

the real rate of interest was only 4% (and probably lower since many people were expecting higher rates of inflation).

6. **a.** The doctor is employed.
   b. The mechanic is not in the labor force (and is a discouraged worker).
   c. The student is not in the labor force.
   d. The steel worker is unemployed.
   e. The laid-off executive is employed.
   f. The executive having a baby is not in the labor force.

7. **a.** John's cost of living remains unchanged since John has avoided the price rise by changing his consumption pattern.
   b. The calculated price index will be 100 in Year 0 and 150 in Year 1, showing a 50% increase in the general level of prices. So the rise in the calculated price index overstates the true increase in the cost of living (which in this case didn't go up at all).

8. The unemployment rate should have increased by two percentage points each year, or by four percentage points over the two-year period. It actually increased from 7.5% to 10.4%, an increase of about 3%.

9. **a.** In 1980, the worker paid $200 in taxes (10% of the income exceeded $5,000), an average tax rate of 2.86%, and had an after-tax income of $6,800.
   b. In 1985, the worker paid $1,300 in taxes, an average tax rate of 9.29%, and had an after-tax income of $12,700. The worker's real after-tax income is $6,350 ($12,700/2.00, where 2.00 reflects the doubling of prices since 1980). Even though the worker earns the same real before-tax income, the worker's after-tax income has gone down due to inflation pushing the worker into a higher tax bracket.

10. According to the government, this firm's profits will be $40,000 ($80,000 in sales minus $20,000 in factor costs and $20,000 in depreciation). So the government will impose a tax of $20,000. But the firm s *true* profits (taking into account the fact that depreciation has gone up to $40,000 because the machine is now more costly to replace) will be only $20,000. The firm's after-tax profits are calculated as follows:

Sales	$80,000
− Factor Costs	$20,000
− *Depreciation*	*$40,000*
Profits	$20,000
− *Taxes*	*$20,000*
After-tax Profits	$0

The effective tax rate went from 50% to 100%. In 1979, some economists estimated that the high inflation in that year raised the effective tax rate on corporate profits to as high as 95%.

7

AGGREGATE DEMAND AND SUPPLY: THE KEY TO MACRO-ECONOMICS

Macroeconomics is the study of the economy as a whole, including the causes of the business cycle, unemployment, and inflation. In order to focus on the main factors affecting inflation and unemployment, macroeconomics *aggregates* output (into *GNP*) and prices (into a price index, such as the *GNP* Deflator). Macroeconomics ignores the demand and supply for individual goods and instead looks at the demand and supply for *all* goods.

AGGREGATE DEMAND AND SUPPLY

The main tool of macroeconomics is the *aggregate* demand and supply diagram shown in Figure 7-1. This looks just like the demand and supply diagram for an individual good such as those in Chapters 3 and 4, but the quantity on the horizontal axis is the total real output of the whole economy (or real *GNP*), which we label Q. And instead of price (i.e., relative price) on the vertical axis, we have the price level P (which is the *GNP* Deflator).

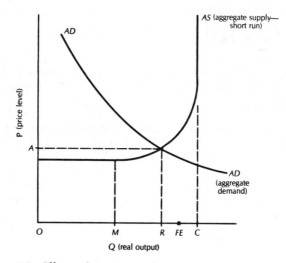

Figure 7-1   Effects of Aggregate Demand and Supply

AD is the aggregate demand curve. **Aggregate demand** is the total output demanded in an economy at a given price level (over a given period of time). It is the total amount of goods people *want* to buy, so it does *not* include the unwanted output that firms produce but cannot sell. (This is in contrast to the practice in national income accounting of counting this unwanted output as part of "sales.") Aggregate demand equals the sum of the consumption, investment, government, and net export expenditures that people want to make. The **aggregate demand curve** shows that aggregate demand goes up when the price level falls.

AS is the short-run aggregate supply curve. **Aggregate supply** is the total output produced in an economy at a given price level. The **short run** is that period of time over which nominal factor costs don't change (due, perhaps, to workers having long-term contracts that are not easy to change). Nominal factor costs include the dollar wages that workers are paid, the dollar cost of machinery and plants, and the dollar interest payments that firms have to pay on their borrowings to buy plant and equipment. The **short-run aggregate supply curve** shows that aggregate supply rises when the price level rises.

In Figure 7-1, the economy will produce where aggregate demand intersects aggregate supply at price level *A* and output level *R*. At a *higher* price level, aggregate supply exceeds aggregate demand: Firms will not be able to sell all the goods they produce (and will experience a resulting increase in their inventories). Firms will respond by decreasing their output and lowering their price. At a *lower* price level than the equilibrium price level *A*, aggregate demand exceeds aggregate supply: Firms will find their inventories running low and will respond by raising prices and output. Only at price level *A* and output level *R* will the economy be in equilibrium.

YOU SHOULD REMEMBER

1. *Aggregate demand*—the aggregate quantity of output demanded—increases when the price level falls and decreases when the price level rises.

2. In the *short run, aggregate supply* increases when the price level rises and decreases when the price level falls. The short run is the period over which nominal factor costs don't change.

3. Equilibrium results when firms produce the quantity of goods people want to buy; i.e., when aggregate supply equals aggregate demand.

AGGREGATE DEMAND

The aggregate demand curve shows that as the price level falls, total real demand increases. This result seems to follow from the law of demand, but in fact it does not. Recall that the law of demand states that the quantity of a good demanded goes up when the good's *relative* price falls. But when the price level falls, such that all prices fall by the same percentage amount, the relative price of all goods is *unchanged*! So why does a lower price *level* result in an increase in aggregate demand?

The reason is that some assets (in particular, money and most bonds), are nominally fixed in value. When prices fall, these assets are worth more in real terms because they can buy more. This makes people richer, and so they increase their real spending. This increase in aggregate demand due to a lower price level is called the **real wealth effect** or the **real balance effect**. To go back to our "bread only" example (where a consumer consumes only bread), if the consumer holds $200 in money and the price of bread is $1, the consumer's real money holdings are worth 200 loaves of bread. But if the price of bread falls to 50¢, the $200 is now worth 400 loaves in real terms. So the consumer is now richer and will spend more, thereby increasing aggregate demand.

AGGREGATE SUPPLY (SHORT RUN)

Factor costs (such as wages and machine costs) are often slow to adjust to changing price levels. Economists say that costs tend to be "sticky." Wages, for example, are often fixed by long-term contracts and take time to change. The short run is the period of time when nominal (or dollar) factor costs do *not* change.

In the short run then, a higher price level means more profits for firms, profits that firms pursue by increasing output. So the **aggregate supply curve** has a positive slope in the short run.

The aggregate supply curve is drawn as a horizontal line over a range of output that is far below the economy's capacity output (this range going from 0 to *M* in Figure 7-1). Over this range, there is no shortage of inputs and firms can increase output without any increase in **unit costs** (the cost of each unit of output). But as the economy begins to approach the capacity of what its plants and equipment can produce, it becomes harder and harder to produce extra output, and so unit costs start to rise. The aggregate supply curve then begins to rise as well, and it rises faster as the economy approaches its capacity (moving from *M* to *CP*). When the economy reaches its capacity output (*CP* in Figure 7-1), the aggregate supply curve becomes vertical since it is impossible to produce any more goods, no matter how high the price level. Because at full employment there is still unemployment, an economy's capacity output level (*CP*) is *above* the full employment output level (*FE*).

YOU SHOULD REMEMBER

1. Aggregate demand goes up at lower prices because people holding money and bonds are then richer and so buy more.

2. In the short run, dollar factor costs are defined to be constant. So higher prices mean more profits and more output. But as the economy approaches its capacity, unit costs rise and so it takes higher and higher prices to induce firms to produce more.

THE EFFECTS OF SHIFTS IN AGGREGATE DEMAND AND SUPPLY

• *SHIFTS IN AGGREGATE DEMAND*

The effects of an *increase in aggregate demand* (from *AD* to *AD'*) are shown in Figure 7-2. Aggregate demand increases when, holding the price level constant, people want to buy more (i.e., the aggregate demand curve shifts right). For example, business firms may want to spend more on capital goods. Equilibrium goes from Point *E* to Point *F*. The output level increases from *R* to *S* and the price level increases from *A* to *B*. So prices and output will rise. How much prices and output will rise depends upon where the economy was initially on the aggregate supply curve. The closer the economy is to its capacity, the more prices will rise and the less output will rise for any given increase in aggregate demand.

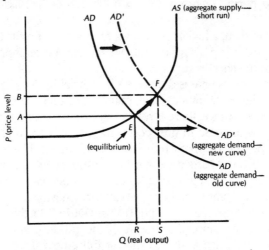

Figure 7-2 Effects of an Increase in Aggregate Demand

The effects of a *decrease in aggregate demand* are shown in Figure 7-3. Aggregate demand decreases (i.e., the aggregate demand curve shifts left) when, holding the price level constant, total real spending falls. For example, consumers may decide to buy fewer goods. As a consequence, equilibrium goes from Point *E* to Point *G*. The price level falls to *C* and the output level falls to *T*. Note that prices and output both fall as a result of a decrease in aggregate demand. For example, from 1929 to 1933, prices fell about 20%, while output fell 30%.

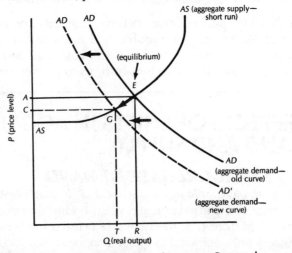

Figure 7-3 Effects of a Decrease in Aggregate Demand

• *SHIFTS IN AGGREGATE SUPPLY*

The effects of an *increase in short-run aggregate supply* are shown in Figure 7-4. The price level falls from A to D while the output level increases from R to U. Equilibrium shifts from Point E to Point K. Output increases and the price falls.

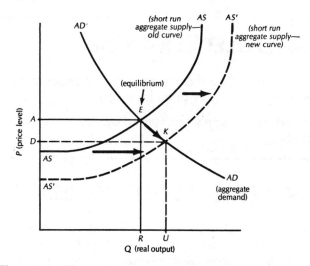

Figure 7-4 Effects of an Increase in *Short Run* Aggregate Supply

Aggregate supply will increase (i.e., the aggregate supply curve will shift right) when (1) factor costs fall, (2) a decrease in taxes reduces production costs, or (3) improvements in technology reduce costs.

The effects of a *decrease in short-run aggregate supply* are shown in Figure 7-5. Aggregate supply decreases when, holding prices constant, firms produce less. The aggregate supply curve shifts left. Equilibrium shifts from Point E to

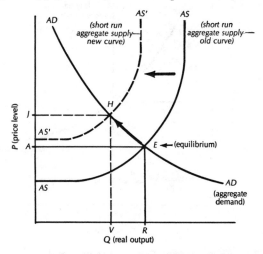

Figure 7-5 Effects of a Decrease in *Short Run* Aggregate Supply

Point *H*, the price level rises from *A* to *J*, and the output level falls from *R* to *V*. Price rises and output falls. This undesirable mix of price increases and economic contraction is called **stagflation**. For example, in 1974–75, real output fell by 5%, while inflation soared above 12%.

YOU SHOULD REMEMBER

1. Shifts in aggregate demand are caused by changes in aggregate real spending, holding the price level constant.

2. Shifts in aggregate supply are caused by changes in factor costs and technology.

AGGREGATE SUPPLY (LONG RUN)

The **long run** is the period of time over which input costs, such as wages, are free to adjust. *Long run* (in macroeconomics) refers to the time it takes the economy to come to a complete full-employment equilibrium. In the long run, all contracts (such as those between employers and workers) can be rewritten so that contracted-for wages reflect the actual price level and so that any false expectations (about price level) that cause unemployment are eliminated. In the long run, workers will set their wages such that they will be fully employed. Thus, output will be at its full-employment level. In Figure 7-6, long-run output

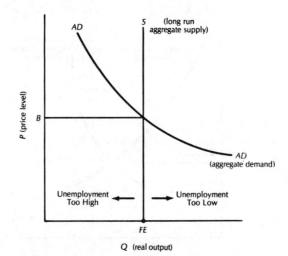

Figure 7-6 Effects of *Long Run* Aggregate Supply

will be at *FE* (Full Employment) no matter what the price level. So we draw the **long-run aggregate supply curve** as a vertical line at *FE*.

The long-run price level will be determined by where the aggregate demand curve intersects the long-run aggregate supply curve (here, at price level *B*). At this price level, the economy will be at full employment. The level of unemployment that exists at full employment is called the **natural rate of unemployment**. If unemployment is above its natural rate, wages (and thus costs and prices) tend to fall. And if unemployment is below its natural rate, wages (and thus costs and prices) tend to rise. Only at price level *B* (where *AD* intersects the long-run aggregate supply curve) will the economy be in a *long-run equilibrium*. Chapter 9 shows how the economy reaches full employment in the long run.

YOU SHOULD REMEMBER

In the long run, factor costs can change. Factor costs change so full employment is achieved. As a consequence, the long-run aggregate supply curve is a vertical line at the full-employment level of output.

HOW TO APPLY AGGREGATE DEMAND AND SUPPLY

When the aggregate demand and supply diagram shows prices falling (as in Figures 7-3 and 7-4), it is predicting that prices will be lower than they otherwise would have been. For inflationary times, this means it is predicting that the rate of inflation will fall (say from 10% to 4% a year). This is called **disinflation**. If the price level actually falls, it is called **deflation**. And when prices are shown to increase (as in Figures 7-2 and 7-5), it is predicting that the rate of inflation will increase (say from 4% to 8% a year).

Similarly, when output is shown to increase (as in Figures 7-2 and 7-4), it is predicting that the growth rate of output will increase (say from 2% to 4% a year). And a decrease in output (as in Figures 7-3 and 7-5) predicts a decrease in the growth rate of output. A drop in the growth rate of output below its usual 3% growth rate is called a **growth recession** (e.g., if output grew at only 1% per year). But when output falls for two consecutive quarters, it is called a **recession**. When output falls steeply for a prolonged period, the economy is in a **depression**.

YOU SHOULD REMEMBER

1. Aggregate demand and supply analysis predicts *changes* in the *rate* of price growth (i.e., in inflation) and in the *rate* of output growth.

2. Inflation is an increase in the price level. Disinflation is a decrease in the rate of inflation. Deflation is a fall in the price level.

3. A growth recession is when output grows at less than its potential (which is about 3% per year). A recession is when output falls for two consecutive quarters.

KNOW THE CONCEPTS

DO YOU KNOW THE BASICS?

1. On the aggregate demand and supply diagram (Figure 7-1), what do output and price represent?

2. How can the price level go up and yet the "price" of each good remain unchanged?

3. How does a lower price level increase the aggregate output demanded?

4. When prices are lower, total dollar spending may fall. Does this contradict the fact that lower prices increase aggregate demand?

5. Does output always go up when prices go up?

6. In the Great Depression, prices and output fell. What shift in aggregate demand and supply would best describe the cause of this event?

7. What changes in wages will cause the short-run aggregate supply curve to shift to the left?

8. How should the government shift the aggregate demand curve if it wants to raise output? What will happen to the price level?

9. How should the government shift the aggregate demand curve to reduce inflation? What will happen to output?

10. How will wages and other input costs tend to change when unemployment is above its natural rate?

TERMS FOR STUDY

aggregate demand
aggregate supply (long run)
aggregate supply (short run)
disinflation, deflation

natural rate of unemployment
recession, growth recession, depression
stagflation

PRACTICAL APPLICATION

1. Select from Figures 7-2 through 7-5 the figure that best reflects the following events:

   Event A: The vigorous growth in the economy is marred by rising inflation.

   Event B: Recent shortages have led to greater inflation combined with reduced output.

   Event C: The growth of output has gone from 3% to 1% while inflation has gone from 12% to 6%.

   Event D: An improved business environment has led to higher growth rates and less inflation.

2. Chapter 5 stated that total spending always equals total output in national income accounting. So how can aggregate demand be different from aggregate supply in this chapter?

3. Use the table below to answer the following questions.
   a. What is the equilibrium output and price level?
   b. Why won't the economy be in equilibrium at a price level of 160?
   c. Why won't the economy be in equilibrium at a price level of 100?
   d. Suppose money wages are fixed at $10 an hour. What is the real wage at each price level? How does this explain why aggregate supply increases in the short run when the price level is higher?

Price Level	Aggregate Demand	Aggregate Supply (Short Run)
80	2,400	1,500
100	2,200	1,750
120	2,000	2,000
140	1,800	2,200
160	1,600	2,300
180	1,400	2,350

4. An economy produces bread and clothing. In 1980, bread cost $2 a loaf and clothing cost $20 a unit. In the same year, the economy produced

20,000 loaves of bread and 5,000 units of clothing. In 1981, bread cost $1 and clothing $10.

    a. If in 1981, the same quantities of goods were produced, what happened to nominal income? To real income (letting 1980 be the base year)? To relative prices?

    b. Was output the same in 1981 as it was in 1980 (assuming aggregate demand equaled aggregate supply in 1980)?

5. According to some economists, the government can stimulate output growth with tax cuts. If this is the case, what will happen to the price level?

6. A recent headline read "Renewed Growth Will Fuel More Inflation." This headline reflects a common notion in the press that a high growth rate in *GNP* causes higher inflation rates. Use the aggregate demand and supply diagram to show when this is incorrect.

7. If aggregate supply shifts to the right each year due to technological progress, then what must the government do to maintain a stable price level?

8. Many economic commentators state that "recessions cause prices to fall." If they mean that reduced output (i.e., reduced aggregate supply) *causes* lower prices, are they correct?

9. When will reduced output be accompanied by lower prices?

10. What will happen if, at the same time, workers demand and get higher wages and consumers decide to increase their real consumption spending?

ANSWERS

KNOW THE CONCEPTS

1. Output is real *GNP* and the price level is the *GNP* Deflator.

2. An increase in the price level that raises all prices an equal percentage amount will leave the *relative* price of all goods unchanged.

3. A lower price level increases the purchasing power of money, bonds, and other nominally fixed assets. This increase in wealth causes people to buy more goods.

4. Aggregate demand refers to total desired *real* spending. So it is possible for total dollar spending to fall, but if prices fall even more, real spending (i.e., the real quantity of goods bought) will go up.

5. No. If aggregate supply decreases, output can fall when prices rise.

6. A decrease in aggregate demand.

7. An increase in wages.

8. The government should increase aggregate demand so that the curve shifts right. Prices will rise.

9. To reduce inflation, the government should decrease aggregate demand so that the curve shifts left. Output will fall.

10. Wages and other factor costs will fall.

PRACTICAL APPLICATION

1. *Event A:* Figure 7-2
   Event B: Figure 7-5
   Event C: Figure 7-3
   Event D: Figure 7-4

2. In national income accounting, unsold output is counted as a "sale" to the firm producing it. But aggregate demand reflects the true quantity demanded and so excludes unsold and unwanted output.

3. a. Equilibrium output is 2,000, and price level 120.
   b. At 160, aggregate supply exceeds aggregate demand. Unsold output will cause firms to cut back on production and also to reduce prices in order to boost sales.
   c. At 100, aggregate demand exceeds aggregate supply. Inventories will be drawn down. Firms will increase output and raise prices.
   d. Real wages equal money wages/P where P is the price index stated as a decimal. Starting at 80 ($P = .8$) and going down, real wages will be $12.50, $10.00, $8.33, $7.14, $6.25, and $5.56. As real wages fall, the real cost of producing output falls, so firms produce more at higher price levels.

4. a. In 1980, nominal income was $140,000. With the same output, 1981's nominal income was $70,000 but its real income was still $140,000 ($70,000/.050, where 0.50 is the 1981 price level since prices are one-half of what they were in 1980). Relative prices did not change. For example, the relative price of a loaf of bread was one-tenth of a unit of clothing in both 1980 and 1981.
   b. The lower price level in 1981 increased the real value of people's nominal assets, causing people to demand more. The economy will move down and to the right along its aggregate demand curve.

5. The price level will fall as in Figure 7-4.

6. As Figure 7-4 shows, an increase in output (growth) will cause inflation to decrease, not increase. So if the output growth is caused by an increase in aggregate supply, the headline is wrong. But if the output growth is caused by an increase in aggregate demand (as in Figure 7-2), the higher output will be accompanied by higher inflation, and the headline will be correct. So it is important to know whether output is going up because of an increase in aggregate demand or in aggregate supply. This is a distinction that many economic commentators ignore.

7. If the government does nothing, then prices will fall when output grows (as in Figure 7-4). To keep prices stable, aggregate demand must be increased along with aggregate output (so both shift right by the same amount). (For more information on what the government can do to increase aggregate demand, see Chapters 10 through 14.)

8. No. Reduced aggregate supply will increase the price level (as in Figure 7-5).

9. When aggregate demand is reduced (as in Figure 7-3). Contrasting this answer with that to Question 8, the reduced output in this case is a *result* of a *decrease in aggregate demand,* not a *cause* of the *reduced output.*

10. The price level will rise. The effect on output cannot be predicted without more information as to how much aggregate demand and supply shift.

8
AGGREGATE DEMAND IN THE PRIVATE SECTOR: THE KEYNESIAN MODEL

KEY TERMS

actual or realized investment total investment spending, including unsold output put into inventory.

consumption household spending on consumption goods and services.

desired or planned investment total investment spending that businesses *want* to make. It does *not* include unwanted inventory accumulation.

equilibrium in aggregate demand when spending equals income.

marginal propensity to consume (MPC) additional consumption spending caused by one dollar being added to disposable income.

savings the unconsumed portion of disposable income.

spending multiplier the number by which an initial increase in spending must be multiplied to get the resulting change in total spending.

This chapter presents the basic Keynesian model. Keynesian economics is based upon the writings of John Maynard Keynes and emphasizes the importance of total spending in determining national income. We make the following assumptions to simplify matters. (Be sure to read assumption 4!)

1. The government and the rest of the world do not exist. So government spending, taxes, transfer payments, and net exports are all zero.

2. All savings are personal savings (i.e., there is no business saving). There is no depreciation.

   Note: Assumptions 1 and 2 imply that $GNP = NNP = NI = PI = DI$.

3. Output is far below capacity such that it is on the horizontal section of the aggregate supply curve (see Figure 7-1, 0 to M). Thus, when aggregate demand goes up, the price level stays unchanged. As a consequence, all changes in spending and income are *changes in real income and spending*.

4. "Spending," "desired spending," and "planned spending" all refer to the same thing: the spending people *want* to do. Unlike national income accounting, we will *not* count unwanted and unsold output (that goes into inventories) as part of spending. Thus, while national income accounting defines spending so that spending always equals income, we will now define spending as desired spending. Thus, with this new definition, it is no longer true that spending will always equal income.

THE BASIC KEYNESIAN MODEL

CONSUMPTION FUNCTION

Consumption is the spending on consumer goods over a given period (usually a year). **Consumer goods** are goods and services that are consumed or used up within the year, such as food and electricity. (In practice, however, many goods counted as consumption goods last longer than a year, such as dresses, cars, and toasters.)

John Maynard Keynes made two key assumptions about what determines consumption spending:

Keynes' Assumptions on Consumption Spending

• *Assumption 1:* People base their consumption spending mainly on their *current* take-home pay (i.e., on disposable income, or *DI*).

• *Assumption 2:* When people get additional income, they don't spend it all.

An example of a Keynesian consumption function is shown in Table 8-1. The **consumption function** shows the level of consumption at different levels of disposable income, holding constant the other determinants of consumption (discussed later in this chapter). In the **Keynesian consumption function,** consumption goes up as *DI* goes up but not all of the additional income is consumed. In this example, each additional $1,000 in income adds $800 to consumption. The added consumption due to $1 more of income is the **marginal propensity to consume (*MPC*).** *MPC* equals the addition to consumption *divided* by the addition to disposable income that caused consumption to go up. In this case, *MPC* equals 0.8 ($800/$1,000).

Table 8-1. The Keynesian Consumption Function

Disposable Income (DI)	Consumption (C)	Savings (S)
$ 3,000	$3,400	−$ 400
4,000	4,200	− 200
5,000	5,000	0
6,000	5,800	200
7,000	6,600	400
8,000	7,400	600
9,000	8,200	800
10,000	9,000	1,000

Savings is unconsumed income (disposable income minus consumption). At the "breakeven" income of $5,000, savings are zero. Below $5,000, there is dissaving (or negative savings). To **dissave**—to consume more than is earned—people can borrow money or draw down their bank accounts. Above $5,000, savings are positive. Every $1,000 added to income adds $200 to savings. The **marginal propensity to save (*MPS*)** is the added savings *divided* by the added disposable income that caused saving to go up. In Table 8-1, *MPS* = 0.2 ($200/$1,000).

Since every added dollar of income is consumed or saved, we have:

$$MPC + MPS = 1.$$

Note that the **average propensity to consume (*APC*),** which is consumption divided by disposable income, doesn't have to equal the marginal propensity to consume. At *DI* = $10,000, for example, *C/DI* = 0.9 while *MPC* = 0.8.

Example: Using MPC

PROBLEM   If *MPC* = 0.75, how much will consumption increase when disposable income goes up by $10,000? What will happen to savings?

SOLUTION   Consumption will go up $7,500 (0.75 × $10,000) and savings will go up $2,500 (0.25 × $10,000).

Figure 8-1 shows both the consumption and savings curves from Table 8-1.

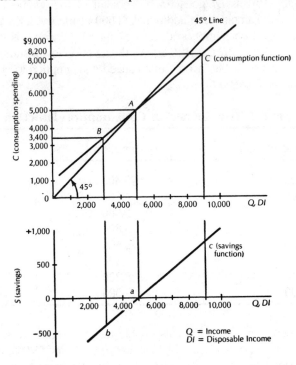

Figure 8-1   The Relationship of Consumption and Savings

The **45° line** in Figure 8-1 serves as a valuable reference line. All points on this line have the same value on the vertical and horizontal axes. So at Point *A*, consumption equals income (of $5,000). Since disposable income (*DI*) is on the horizontal axis, for any given level of disposable income, the 45° line tells us how far we have to go up vertically to find the same disposable income. For example, Point *B* is above the 45° line, so consumption ($3,400) is above income ($3,000). Point *C* is below this line, so consumption ($8,200) is below income ($9,000).

The savings curve is shown on the bottom graph. "Savings" is defined as the difference between income and consumption, or the difference between the 45° line and consumption.

The slope of the consumption curve is the *MPC* and the slope of the savings curve is the *MPS*.

YOU SHOULD REMEMBER

1. In the Keynesian Consumption Function, consumption is mainly determined by disposable income and the MPC is less than one.

2. Every dollar of disposable income is either consumed or saved: MPC + MPS = 1.

3. The 45° line tells us whether consumption at each level of income is above, at, or below income.

INVESTMENT FUNCTION

Desired investment spending is the total investment spending on such items as new plants and equipment that businesses *want* to make. It does *not* include the unwanted additions to inventory that result when firms can't sell all their output. **Actual realized investment** is the total investment spending (including unwanted inventory accumulation) and is the investment reported in the national income accounts. When we refer to "investment" below, we mean *desired* investment spending. Since we've assumed that businesses do not save, they must borrow from households the money they need to invest (e.g., by issuing bonds).

Keynes' Assumption on Investment Spending

• **Assumption:** While savings decisions are made by households, the decision to invest those savings is made independently by businesses such that there is no guarantee that businesses will automatically invest what households want to save.

Investment is usually considered by Keynesians to be fixed, no matter what the level of income (as at the left of Figure 8-2) or as increasing very little when income goes up (as at the right of Figure 8-2). In the top graph, when income increases from *Y1* to *Y2*, investment stays unchanged at *I0*. In the bottom graph, an increase in income from *Y1* to *Y2* increases investment spending from *I1* to *I2*.

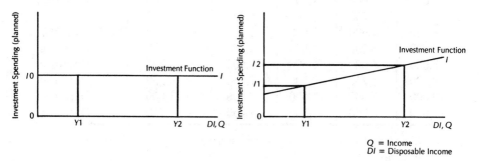

Figure 8-2 Effects of Increased Income on the Investment Function

Normally, economists assume that businesses produce what consumers want; e.g., if consumers want more toothbrushes, more toothbrushes will be produced. But this is not the case for the Keynesian investment function. When people save more, they are in effect demanding businesses to invest more since savings represent a demand for greater consumption in the future, and investment is the way businesses produce the supply for this future demand. But in the Keynesian investment function, businesses do not invest more when people save more.

EQUILIBRIUM IN AGGREGATE DEMAND

The spending side of the economy will be in **equilibrium** when income equals desired spending. And since we are assuming that the economy is on the flat section of the aggregate supply curve, changes in dollar spending will equal changes in *real* spending *and* output.

Table 8-2 presents the Keynesian consumption and investment functions for a simple economy. Disposable income (*DI*) (or simply income [*Q*] when there are no taxes) is in the first column. Consumption (*C*) is shown to be increasing with an *MPC* of 0.75. Investment (*I*) is "autonomous," i.e., it isn't affected by income. The investment spending we are talking about here is the desired or planned investment spending firms really want to make. It does not include unwanted changes in inventories. Total desired spending (*D*) is in the next column. The change in inventories (output − sales) is next. How producers will change their output given their current sales is shown in the last column.

Table 8-2. Reaching Equilibrium in Aggregate Demand

Q or DI Income	C	I	D (C + I)	Change in Inventories (Q − D)	Output Response by Businesses
$ 1,000	$ 750	$1,500	$2,250	−$1,250	Increase
2,000	1,500	1,500	3,000	− 1,000	Increase
3,000	2,250	1,500	3,750	− 750	Increase
4,000	3,000	1,500	4,500	− 500	Increase
5,000	3,750	1,500	5,250	− 250	Increase
6,000	4,500	1,500	6,000	0	NO CHANGE
7,000	5,250	1,500	6,750	+ 250	Decrease
8,000	6,000	1,500	7,500	+ 500	Decrease
9,000	6,750	1,500	8,250	+ 750	Decrease
10,000	7,500	1,500	9,000	+ 1,000	Decrease
11,000	8,250	1,500	9,750	+ 1,250	Decrease

C = Consumption   I = Investment
D = Spending   Q = Income
DI = Disposable Income

When income is below $6,000, spending exceeds output and businesses find their inventories falling. They will respond by increasing output. At an income of $2,000, for example, $2,000 is produced but $3,000 is spent. Businesses will respond by producing more. Note that realized investment (equal to $1,500 plus the change in inventory of − $1,000) equals savings ($500), but that desired (or planned) investment ($1,500) exceeds savings ($500).

When income is above $6,000, output exceeds spending and businesses find their inventories rising. They will respond by decreasing their output. For example, when $Q = \$10,000$, spending equals $9,000. Realized investment ($2,500) equals savings, but in this case businesses want to invest less ($1,500) than what households want to save ($2,500).

When income equals $6,000, the economy is in equilibrium. Spending ($6,000) equals income. Only in equilibrium does savings equal desired investment (in this case, each equals $1,500).

Figure 8-3 illustrates Table 8-2. Figure 8-3 is referred to as the **income-expenditure diagram** (or the output-expenditure diagram). Curve D is the **total spending curve**; it shows the total spending (consumption plus investment) at each level of income. This curve is derived by adding the consumption and investment spending at each level of income.

Equilibrium occurs when total spending equals income *or* where the total spending curve D intersects the 45° line (at Point E). (Recall that the 45° line tells us how far up we must go to have the same number that is on the horizontal axis. So when D crosses the 45° line at Point E, income equals spending.) To the right of Point E, the economy has inadequate demand to support its income; to the left of Point E, there is excess demand.

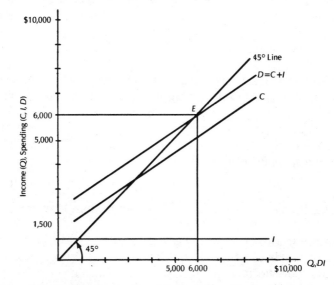

Figure 8-3 Income-Expenditure Diagram Showing Equilibrium: Spending Equaling Income

YOU SHOULD REMEMBER

1. When desired spending exceeds income, inventories fall and firms respond by producing more. When income exceeds spending, inventories rise and firms cut back on output. Only when income equals spending will output remain unchanged (i.e., equilibrium will be reached).

2. At all income levels, savings always equals realized investment. Only at equilibrium does savings equal planned or desired investment.

3. In the income-expenditure diagram, equilibrium occurs where the total spending curve crosses the 45° line (where spending equals income).

APPLYING THE KEYNESIAN MODEL

SHIFTS IN INVESTMENT

To show the effect of an increase in investment spending, go back to Table 8-2 and increase investment spending to $2,500 at each level of income. How will this affect *equilibrium* income? First, we can see that at each level of income, total spending (*D*) goes up $1,000. Now, *equilibrium* total spending will equal income at $10,000 (Be sure you verify this by rewriting the *D* column.) So an increase in investment spending of $1,000 increases income and total spending by $4,000. This illustrates the **spending multiplier** effect. In this case, the spending multiplier is 4: it equals the amount by which the initial increase in spending ($1,000) has to be multiplied to get the increase in income and spending ($4,000). Figure 8-4 illustrates this case. As investment shifts up by $1,000 from *I* to *I'*, total spending at each level of income also shifts up by the same amount (from *D* to *D'*). But the equilibrium shifts from Point *E* to Point *F*, increasing equilibrium income *and* spending from $6,000 to $10,000.

Hints For Understanding the Income-Expenditure Diagram

1. Be sure that you compare Table 8-2 with Figure 8-4. This will give you the *I, C,* and *D* lines. Then add $1,000 to the *I* and *D* lines to get *I'* and *D'*.

2. Focus your attention on where the total spending curve *D* crosses the 45° line. This represents equilibrium (where spending equals income). Note how this point shifts from *E* to *F* along the 45° line when *D* shifts up to *D'*.

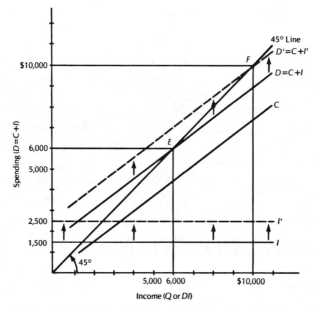

Figure 8-4   The Spending Multiplier Effect Showing the Outcome of
Increased Investment

Why does this multiplier effect occur? The initial added spending is received
as someone else's income. This person in turn spends more, which again means
income to someone else, and so forth. If everyone has the same *MPC*, then each
added dollar of spending will eventually result in an increase in total spending
according to this formula:

$$\text{Spending Multiplier} = 1/(1 - MPC)$$

Table 8-3. The Spending Multiplier Effect

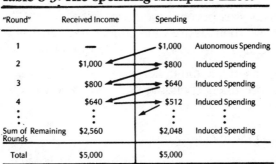

"Round"	Received Income	Spending	
1	—	$1,000	Autonomous Spending
2	$1,000	$800	Induced Spending
3	$800	$640	Induced Spending
4	$640	$512	Induced Spending
⋮	⋮	⋮	⋮
Sum of Remaining Rounds	$2,560	$2,048	Induced Spending
Total	$5,000	$5,000	

Table 8-3 illustrates the case for an *MPC* of 0.8. The multiplier is 5 (1/.2) so an
increase in investment spending of $1,000 results in an eventual increase in total
spending of $5,000. In the first round, $1,000 is spent. In the second round, 80%
of the $1,000 in added income is spent, so $800 is spent and then received as
income. Then $560 is spent and earned, and so forth. The sum of the infinite

series of $1,000 times $(1 + .8 + .8^2 + \ldots)$ is $1,000/(1 - .8)$ (which equals $1,000/.2$, or $5,000$).

A major source of confusion usually arises at this point. It involves the failure to distinguish between (1) the initial shift in spending that occurs at a given level of income (which economists call the **change in autonomous spending**) and (2) the secondary consumption responding caused by the change in autonomous spending (which economists call the **induced change in spending**). In the multiplier formula, the total change in spending is divided by the change in autonomous spending (i.e., $5,000 is divided by $1,000). In general, we have for any increase in autonomous spending:

$$\text{Change in National Income} = \frac{\text{Spending}}{\text{Multiplier}} \times \frac{\text{Increase in Autonomous}}{\text{Spending}}$$

YOU SHOULD REMEMBER

1. An increase in autonomous spending is the increase in spending (holding income constant).

2. An increase in autonomous spending increases equilibrium income by some multiple of itself. This multiplier process occurs because the initial addition to spending becomes income, part of which is spent and earned and then spent again, and so forth.

3. The spending multiplier equals the total change in spending (or income) divided by the change in autonomous spending. In our simple case, it equals $1/(1 - MPC)$.

Example: Calculating the Effects of Changes in Investment Spending

PROBLEM   Businesses become more optimistic about the future and increase their desired investment spending by $5 billion. If the *MPC* is 0.9, by how much will equilibrium income increase?

SOLUTION   The spending multiplier is 10 (1/0.1). So the $5 billion increase in investment spending increases national equilibrium income by $50 billion (10 × $5 billion).

Example: Using the Spending Multiplier

PROBLEM   The economy is in equilibrium at an income of $200 billion. At this level of income, households suddenly decide to increase their consumption spending by $10 billion. If the *MPC* is 0.8, how much will equilibrium national income increase? What is the change in autonomous consumption? What is the induced increase in consumption spending?

SOLUTION The increase in autonomous consumption spending is $10 billion. Since the spending multiplier is 5 (1/0.2), equilibrium national income will increase by $50 billion. Since investment spending in this example doesn't change, spending and thus total consumption spending goes up $50 billion. The induced increase in consumption spending (caused by the multiplier process) is $40 billion (change in induced consumption = *MPC* × change in equilibrium income, or 0.8 × $50 billion).

LEAKAGES AND INJECTIONS

Figure 8-5 illustrates the circular flow in a simple economy, where total spending (and income and output) is represented by the level of water in a bathtub. Savings forms a leakage away from total spending. A **leakage** is any allocation of income that is not directly spent. Investment spending (i.e., desired or planned investment) is an injection into the spending pool. **Injections** are any form of spending other than consumption. When more is going into the bathtub than out (i.e., when injections exceed leakages), the water level rises. When more flows out than in (when leakages exceed injections), the water level falls. Only when inflows equal outflows, when injections equal leakages, will the water level remain unchanged. This occurs when (planned) *investment equals savings*.

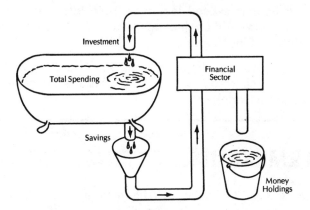

Figure 8-5 The Circular Flow of Consumption and Investment, Showing Leakages and Injections

Be sure you remember that *investment* is the production of *new* capital. It does not include buying stocks and bonds, unless these stocks and bonds are newly issued with their funds going to build new capital equipment. Similarly, *savings* is the foregone consumption for this year. Suppose you earn $10,000 and consume $9,000 of it. You put the $1,000 difference into your savings account, increasing it from $15,000 to $16,000. What is your savings? In our terms, your savings equals $1,000—the amount you add to your savings account. So *savings* is "new savings" just as *investment* is "new capital."

What happens when leakages exceed injections? Savings then exceeds investment. So where does the excess savings go? It goes into the money bucket shown in Figure 8-5 (i.e., into the money holdings of households). The rest of savings is invested (in newly issued stocks and bonds and in loans to businesses through the banking system). Income exceeds spending since not all of savings is invested. The result will be a lower level of aggregate demand.

What happens when injections exceed leakages? Investment exceeds savings. To finance the amount by which investment exceeds savings, money must be drawn from the money bucket (i.e., people have to reduce their cash holdings). Keynes assumed that people would be willing to do this. But if people do not want to reduce their money holdings, the whole multiplier process is stopped. (See Practical Application, Question 10.)

YOU SHOULD REMEMBER

1. *Injections* are inflows into the spending stream (other than consumption spending). *Leakages* are outflows from the spending stream.

2. When injections exceed leakages, both total spending and income increase. When leakages exceed injections, both total spending and income fall.

3. Equilibrium occurs when injections equal leakages. This occurs when investment equals savings (if there is no government or international trade).

DETERMINANTS OF CONSUMPTION

The following is a list of variables (other than disposable income) that affect the level of consumption spending at any given income level.

1. *Wealth:* **Wealth** is the net value of all the assets that a person owns (including the value of the person's skills, i.e., the value of all future earnings). When income is held constant, wealthier persons consume more. All of the determinants below affect consumption because they affect wealth.

2. *Price Level:* A lower price level makes people wealthier because their *real* money holdings are now worth more, and so they consume more. A major confusion occurs at this point between real consumption (which increases

when the price level falls) and nominal or dollar consumption spending (which falls at a lower price level). The income-expenditure diagram, the consumption function, and the total spending curve are all in *real terms.* So a lower price level shifts them *up,* with a resulting increase in output and real spending.

3. *Future Income Prospects:* When people expect to earn more in the future, they are likely to consume more in the present. This is the fundamental idea behind the **permanent-income hypothesis. Permanent income** is one's expected average future earnings, and the permanent-income hypothesis assumes that a person's consumption spending will be a constant fraction of the person's permanent income. The **lifecycle model of consumption** modifies this basic idea by taking into account people's ages, when they expect to retire, and how many retirement years they expect to have. For example, older workers nearing retirement typically save more of their income.

  A major implication of the permanent-income hypothesis is that consumption will increase very little (if at all) when an increase in income is expected to last only a short time. Thus, it would follow that a one-year tax rebate, for example, could not stimulate consumption spending very much (as in fact it did not in 1975).

DETERMINANTS OF INVESTMENT

Some of the main variables that affect investment spending are:

1. *Future Expected Profits:* When businesses expect future profits to be higher, they are willing to invest more.

2. *The Real Interest Rate:* Businesses usually borrow to finance their investment spending. The real interest rate reflects the real cost of this borrowing. The higher the real borrowing cost, the lower investment spending will be.

3. *Optimism About Future:* When businesses are optimistic about the future, they speed up their investment spending. And when they are pessimistic, they postpone investments.

4. *The Accelerator Effect:* Capital produces goods and services (Q). So the demand for *new* capital depends upon *new* Q, i.e., the increase in Q. Therefore, changes in output can increase investment. This is termed the **accelerator effect.** (See Practical Application, Question 8.)

5. *The State of the Capital Stock:* During a recession, capital improvements and additions are postponed. Once the recession is over, they are speeded up. Thus the state of the capital stock can affect how much new investment will be needed.

FACTORS SHIFTING THE TOTAL SPENDING CURVE

Any factor that increases spending at a given level of income will shift the total spending curve, which in turn will increase equilibrium spending and income. Table 8-4 summarizes these factors.

Table 8-4. Factors Shifting The Total Spending Curve

Factor	Change in Factor	Shift in Total Spending Curve
Affecting Consumption		
Wealth	Up	Up
	Down	Down
Price Level	Up	Down
	Down	Up
Permanent	Up	Up
Income	Down	Down
Affecting Investment		
Future	Up	Up
Profits	Down	Down
Real	Up	Down
Interest	Down	Up
Rate		
Optimism	Up	Up
	Down	Down

PLOTTING AGGREGATE DEMAND

The income-expenditure diagram (Figure 8-6) can be used to derive the aggregate demand curve (which relates the price level to aggregate demand) in five steps:

Step 1: Start out with Price Level -0 and show the initial equilibrium in the income-expenditure diagram. The left panel of Figure 8-6 shows that the economy initially is in equilibrium at Price Level -0, with the total spending curve D (Price Level -0) crossing the 45° line at Point E and output level Q.

Step 2: Plot the equilibrium output Q and Price Level -0 as Point E in the right panel. This is a point on the aggregate demand curve.

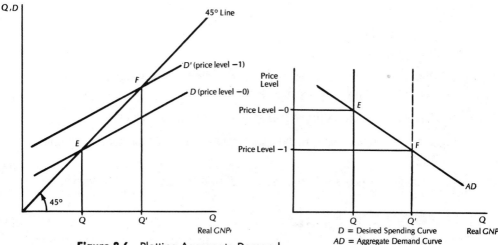

Figure 8-6 Plotting Aggregate Demand

Step 3: Show the effects of *a lower price level* in the income-expenditure diagram. Let the price level fall to Price Level −*1* (exactly why the price level is falling doesn't matter at this point). Due to the real balance effect, the total spending curve will shift upward as shown in the panel on the left as the total spending curve *D* (Price Level −*1*). The new equilibrium is at Point *F* with output at level *Q'*.

Step 4: Plot the new Price Level −*1* and output *Q'*, in the panel on the right as Point *F* This gives us a second point on the aggregate demand curve.

Step 5: Continue changing the price level, which in turn changes the total spending curve, which in turn changes the equilibrium level of output. This output, when plotted with the price level, gives the aggregate demand curve *AD*. Thus, along the *AD* curve, income equals spending.

KNOW THE CONCEPTS

DO YOU KNOW THE BASICS?

1. In the Keynesian Consumption Function, if people receive $1,000 in additional income, will they increase their consumption spending by $1,000, more than $1,000, or less than $1,000?

2. When the economy is in equilibrium, how are spending and income related? Investment and savings?

3. What does the 45° line represent? How does it help you find equilibrium?

4. What is the difference between a change in autonomous spending and an induced change in spending?

5. How can spending go up if the price level falls?

6. What is the leakage from the economy described in this chapter? What is the injection?

7. What is the main variable that changes in the Keynesian model to ensure that the economy reaches equilibrium?

8. How will an increase in wealth shift the total spending curve?

9. How will an increase in the real interest rate shift the total spending curve?

10. How will an increase in the price level shift the total spending curve?

TERMS FOR STUDY

consumption function
desired investment, actual investment
equilibrium
autonomous changes in spending
induced changes in spending
injections, leakages
inventory changes

marginal propensity to consume, to save
permanent income
savings
spending multiplier
wealth

PRACTICAL APPLICATION

1. Use the following table to answer these questions.
   a. What is the marginal propensity to consume? To save?
   b. What is the equilibrium level of income?
   c. At $5,000, what will happen to inventories? How is actual investment related to desired investment and savings?
   d. Answer (c) again, using $9,000.
   e. If investment spending goes up by $400, how much will equilibrium income go up? What is the multiplier?
   f. If consumption spending at each level of income goes up by $400, how much will equilibrium income go up? How much will consumption go up? What is the multiplier?

Income (Q)	Consumption (C)	Investment (I)
$5,000	$3,400	$2,000
6,000	4,200	2,000
7,000	5,000	2,000
8,000	5,800	2,000
9,000	6,600	2,000
10,000	7,200	2,000

2. Fill the blanks in the following table.

MPC	Multiplier	Change in Q Caused by Autonomous Increase of Spending by $1,000
0.9	————	————
0.8	————	————
0.75	————	————
0.6	————	————
0.5	————	————
0.25	————	————

3. If (desired) investment is $1,000 no matter what output is, what will savings be when the economy is in equilibrium? How will income be affected if people want to save more?

4. How will the following events affect *real* consumption spending?
Event A: A rise in the general price level.
Event B: The real values of homes increase.
Event C: Taxes are increased

5. Other things being equal, in which case would investment spending be highest?

Case	Nominal Interest Rate	Expected Rate of Inflation
A	5	0
B	10	8
C	9	3
D	20	15

6. Suppose the *MPC* is 0.6. If at each level of income, people want to consume $2,000 more, how will income change? How will consumption change (break *C*'s change into its initial autonomous increase and the induced secondary consumption respending)? Assume *I* is fixed.

7. Suppose the *MPC* is 0.75. By how much must investment spending increase for *GNP* to go up $50 billion?

8. This question illustrates the accelerator effect. Let *WQ* equal the number of widgets consumed in a year. Every 1,000 widgets requires a widget-making machine to produce them. Let *WMMQ* be the number of machines. These machines are well-built and last forever. Fill in the following table and explain how the table illustrates the accelerator effect.

Year	WQ	WMMQ	New Machines Built
1	20,000	20	0
2	22,000	22	2
3	25,000		
4	29,000		
5	30,000		
6	30,000		

9. Assume the following: (1) When the price level P falls from 2.00 to 1.00, real consumption spending at each level of Q increases by $2,000. (2) $MPC = 0.8$. (3) At $P = 2$, equilibrium Q is $20,000.
   a. At $P = 2.00$, what is real income? Nominal income?
   b. At $P = 1.50$, what is real income? Nominal income?

10. Keynes assumed that people didn't care whether their savings were invested (and earning interest) or kept in cash. This problem illustrates what happens if this isn't true. Suppose an economy is in equilibrium at $Q = \$10,000$. At this income, people want to hold $1,000 in cash, no more and no less. $MPC = 0.8$. What will happen if planned investment spending increases by $100?

ANSWERS
KNOW THE CONCEPTS

1. Less than $1,000, since $MPC < 1$.

2. Spending = Income and Investment = Savings.

3. The set of points at which the values on the vertical and horizontal axes are equal. Since income is on the horizontal axis and spending is on the vertical axis, it crosses the point on the total spending curve at which spending equals income.

4. Change in autonomous spending is the change in spending *if* income does not change. Induced changes in spending occur because income changes.

5. When the price level falls, the real balance effect causes an increase in *real* spending. So even if nominal spending falls (such that fewer dollars are spent), more real dollars will be spent.

6. Savings is a leakage, and desired investment spending is an injection.

7. Income (and output). Keynes assumed that businesses facing inadequate

demand would reduce their output and employment (and thus reduce the income they pay out) instead of reducing their prices.

8. The total spending curve will shift up and to the left.

9. Investment spending will fall: The total spending curve will shift down and to the right.

10. The real balance effect will reduce real consumption spending. The total spending curve will shift down and to the right.

PRACTICAL APPLICATION

1. **a.** $MPC = 0.8; MPS = 0.2$
   b. $7,000
   c. Inventories fall by $400 ($5,000 output minus $5,400 sales). Actual investment equals $2,000 of desired investment (I) plus the change in inventories (which is $-$400), or $1,600. Savings equals actual investment ($1,600) but is less than desired investment ($2,000).
   d. Inventories rise by $400 ($9,000 output less $8,600 sales). I is $2,000 but actual investment is $2,400, which is also savings ($O - C$).
   e. Equilibrium income will increase by $7,000 to $9,000 (where $I + C$ now equals Q). The multiplier is 5 (from either $2000/$400 or $1/(1-0.8)$.
   f. Equilibrium income will increase to $9,000, as in e above, with a multiplier of 5. Consumption will increase by $2,000.

2.

MPC	Multiplier	Change in Q caused by Autonomous Increase in Spending of $1,000
0.90	10	$10,000
0.80	5	5,000
0.75	4	4,000
0.60	2.5	2,500
0.50	2	2,000
0.25	1.333	1,333

Notice that when the *MPC* is higher, more is respent in each round of the multiplier process, making the total increase in spending and the multiplier higher.

3. Savings will be $1,000 when the economy is in equilibrium. This is the only level of savings consistent with spending equaling income. If people want to save a larger share of their income, income will *fall* in order to reduce their savings back to $1,000.

4. *Event A:* Decreases consumption spending by reducing the real value of money holdings.

   Event B: Increases consumption spending by increasing wealth.

   Event C: Decreases consumption spending by decreasing disposable income.

5. Case B, where the real interest rate (i.e., the real borrowing cost) is lowest (only 2%).

6. The multiplier is 1/0.4 (or 2.5), so income goes up by $5,000. Total consumption goes up by $5,000. This is the sum of the $2,000 initial autonomous increase and the induced $3,000 consumption respending (*MPC* times increase in income).

7. The multiplier is 4 (1/0.25). So 4 times the increase in *I* should equal $50 billion. The increase in *I* needed is $12.5 billion.

8.

Year	WQ	WMMQ	New Machines Built
1	20,000	20	0
2	22,000	22	2
3	25,000	25	3
4	29,000	29	4
5	30,000	30	1
6	30,000	30	0

The demand for *new* machines (i.e., investment demand) depends on the *change* in widget demand, not the level of widget demand. So even though widget demand does not decline, the demand for new widget-making machines falls when widget demand levels off. For the economy, the accelerator effect states that investment spending goes up when consumption spending accelerates and falls when consumption spending decelerates and levels off.

9. a. Real income = $20,000. Nominal income ($P \times Q$) = $40,000.

   b. Real income = $30,000 (increase in Q = spending multiplier times autonomous increase in C). Nominal income equals $30,000. Note that even though nominal income went down, real income went up!

10. We answer this question by asking how businesses can get the $100 when income is still equal to $10,000. Since the economy is at equilibrium, all savings are invested. The only source of cash is from money holdings, but by assumption, people won't reduce (or lend out) these holdings. So businesses will be trying to borrow more than people want to lend them. The interest rate will go up, causing businesses to reduce their planned investment spending back to its original level. The actual multiplier is 0, not 5 as it would be in the Keynesian model.

9

AGGREGATE SUPPLY AND GETTING TO FULL EMPLOYMENT

KEY TERMS

full-employment level of output the level of output at which the demand and supply for labor (and other factors) are equal, there being neither a shortage nor a surplus of workers. Also termed "potential output."

GNP gap gap between actual output and full-employment output. When output is above its full-employment level, there is an "inflationary" or "expansionary" gap; when it's below, there is a "recessionary" or "contractionary" gap.

self-correcting mechanism the means by which an economy gets to full employment without governmental intervention.

Chapter 8 showed you how to construct the *aggregate demand curve*. Now we will construct the *aggregate supply curve* to show how the economy gets to full employment. First, a short review.

1. *Aggregate demand* is the total output demanded. Along the aggregate demand curve, spending equals income. Aggregate demand is higher at lower price levels.

2. *Aggregate supply* is the total output supplied. In the short run, factor costs (especially wages) are fixed in money terms. A higher price level causes firms to produce more: The short-run aggregate supply is larger at higher prices. In the long run, factor costs adjust freely until the economy is at full employment.

CONSTRUCTING THE AGGREGATE SUPPLY CURVE TO GET TO FULL EMPLOYMENT

FULL-EMPLOYMENT EQUILIBRIUM

Figure 9-1 shows the economy at its **full-employment equilibrium**. This is where the economy, left undisturbed, will eventually go.

First look at the top panel. Equilibrium is at Point E, with output at FE (its full-employment level). The short-run aggregate supply curve (AS), the long-run aggregate supply curve (S-Long Run) and the aggregate demand curve (AD) all intersect at Point E. The AS curve is drawn with costs fixed at the level consistent with price level A.

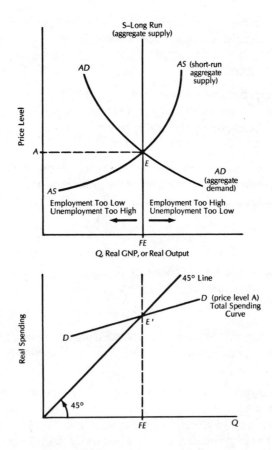

Figure 9-1 An Economy at Full Employment

The bottom panel shows the spending side of the economy (from Chapter 8). The total spending curve (D) is constructed assuming the price level is at A (in the top panel). Total spending equals income at point E' on the 45° line at the full-employment level of output. E' plots into the top panel as Point E' on the AD curve.

Three Conditions for Full-Employment Equilibrium

1. *Spending equals income.* This is shown in the bottom panel, where D, the total spending curve, crosses the 45° line at point E'. *All* points on the aggregate demand curve (AD) satisfy this condition.

2. *All output is bought.* This is shown in the top panel by the intersection of the short-run aggregate supply curve (AS) and the aggregate demand curve (AD).

3. There is *full employment.* Workers are fully employed, unemployment being neither too high nor too low but instead at the natural level of unemployment. The economy is at the point at which AS and AD curves intersect. That the economy is at full employment is shown in the upper panel by the AS and AD curves intersecting at full employment on the long-run aggregate supply curve (S-Long Run).

Study Hint
1. Redraw Figure 9-1, and determine why and where all three conditions are met.
2. Go back to Chapter 8 and see how the AD line in the bottom panel of Figure 9-1 was derived.

YOU SHOULD REMEMBER

1. The economy will be where the AD curve intersects the AS curve. This is where all output is sold with no unwanted changes in inventories.

2. In the long run, the economy will always be at full employment. This is where all workers wanting work at current wages can get work. Unemployment is neither too high nor low at *FE.*

FROM RECESSION TO FULL EMPLOYMENT

What happens when AD and AS curves intersect at a level of output other than the full-employment level? Basically, because Condition 3 is *not* satisfied, wages and other factor costs change to shift the AS curve towards full employment.

Suppose the economy is in a recession. How can the economy get back to full employment? Figure 9-2 shows an economy in a recession. The economy will always be where the *AD* curve intersects the *AS* curve: at Point *F*, with prices at level *B* and output level *R*. At price level *B*, aggregate demand equals *R*, as shown in both the top and bottom panels.

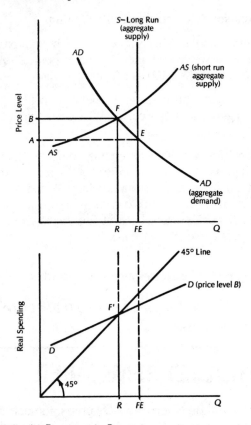

Figure 9-2 An Economy in Recession

Conditions 1 and 2 are satisfied at Point *F*. But output is below the full-employment level. Unemployment is too high, and condition (3) is *not* satisfied. The economy has a **recessionary gap** of *FE − R*.

The Sequence from Recession to Full Employment

1. *Unemployment is too high.* Output (*R*) is below its full-employment level in Figure 9-3.

2. *Nominal wages will fall.* The surplus of workers causes wages to fall. (*Note:* Saying there is a surplus of workers is the same as saying the unemployment rate is too high.)

3. *Aggregate supply will shift right.* Lower wages (and other factor costs) plus competition between firms causes prices to fall, shifting the aggregate supply curve down and outward from *AS* to *AS'* in Figure 9-3.

4. *Lower prices stimulate aggregate demand.* The lower price level makes consumers richer, since their money holdings now buy more. The bottom panel shows the lower price level shifting up the whole total spending curve from D to D'. The top panel shows total real spending increasing as the economy shifts *along* the aggregate demand line (*AD*) from Point *F* to Point *E*.

5. *The economy moves to full employment.* Wages and prices fall until workers are fully employed at *FE*. The *AS* curve shifts and slides down along the *AD* curve until the economy reaches full employment.

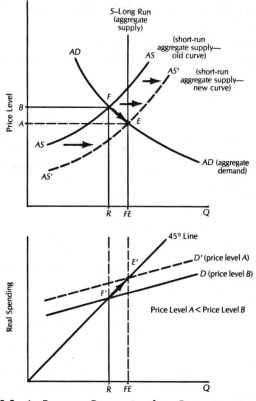

Figure 9-3 An Economy Recovering from Recession

How long will it take an economy, once in a recession, to return to full employment? Keynesian economists typically feel that an economy's **self-correcting mechanism**, the means by which it reaches *FE* without government intervention, is too slow (and usually recommend governmental action to increase aggregate demand).

Study Hint
1. Redraw the Figure 9-3 graph yourself. First draw the *AS* and *AD* curves so that they intersect at less than full employment.
2. Next, visualize the *AS* curve slowly falling as wages and prices fall. Trace how its intersection with *AD* moves the economy toward full employment. Once full employment is reached, prices stop falling and the economy is in equilibrium.

FROM TOO LITTLE UNEMPLOYMENT TO FULL EMPLOYMENT

Too little unemployment sounds like having too much money—most of us could live with it. But too little unemployment is the same thing as too much work. Workers find themselves working too long for too little as firms push output beyond its full-employment level.

Figure 9-4 shows such an "overemployed" economy. The economy is at Point *G*, with output at level *V* and price at level *C*. It has an **expansionary gap** of *V − FE*.

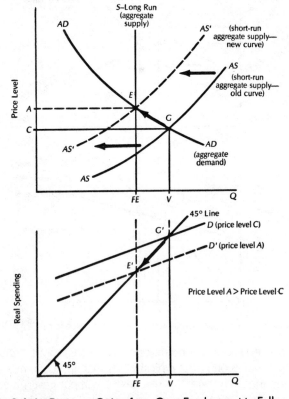

Figure 9-4 An Economy Going from Over Employment to Full Employment

The Sequence from Too Little Employment to Full Employment

1. *Unemployment is too low,* since output (*V*) exceeds its full-employment level (*FE*).

2. *Wages will rise* since there is a shortage of workers.

3. *The aggregate supply curve will shift left* as costs are pushed up from *AS* to *AS'* in Figure 9-4.

4. *Aggregate demand is dampened* by the rise in prices. In the bottom panel, the total spending curve shifts down from *D* to *D'*, and in the upper panel the *AS* curve shifts up *along* the *AD* curve from *G* to *E*.

5. *The economy reaches full employment* at output level *FE*.

YOU SHOULD REMEMBER

1. The aggregate supply (AS) curve shifts so as to bring the economy to full employment.

2. When output is less than its full-employment level, wages and prices fall until the AS curve shifts down along the aggregate demand curve (AD) enough for output to reach its full-employment level.

3. When output exceeds its full-employment level, wages and prices rise until the AS curve shifts up and along the AD curve enough for output to reach its full-employment level.

THE EFFECTS OF EMPLOYMENT ON THE SPENDING MULTIPLIER

In Chapter 8, the effect of more spending was to increase total output by some multiple of itself. But we assumed that the economy was producing at far below its capacity, so that the price level wasn't increased when aggregate demand went up. As a consequence, increases in aggregate demand caused equal increases in real income. But what happens if the economy is close to capacity? As you will see, the spending multiplier will be smaller than that suggested in Chapter 8.

The economy begins at its long-run full-employment equilibrium in Figure 9-5. The solid lines (*AS, AD,* and *S*-Long Run) show where the economy starts out. They intersect at Point *E,* at price level *A* and output level *FE.*

Now suppose investment spending at each level of output goes up $1,000 and that the marginal propensity to consume (*MPC*) is .8. According to the spending multiplier, total spending will increase by $5,000. So the horizontal shift in ag-

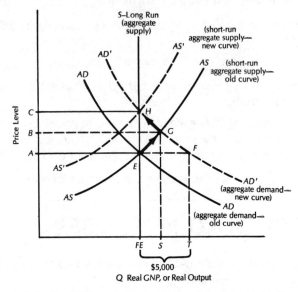

Figure 9-5 The Effects of Output on the Spending Multiplier

gregate demand from Point *E* to Point *F* will be $5,000. This would also be the increase in output if prices remained unchanged. But prices *do* rise as output expands. In the short run, the economy goes from Point *E* to Point *G*. (The solid *AS* curve still holds, since costs have not changed, but *AD'* is the new aggregate demand curve.) So the short-run increase in output (from level *FE* to level *S*) is smaller than the increase suggested by the multiplier (from level *FE* to level *T*).

In the long run, the economy will return to full employment as the *AS* curve shifts up to *AS'*. The long-run multiplier will be zero, since output is unchanged. (Note, however, that this is true only when we start at level *FE*; at less than *FE*, increased spending *can* increase output in the long run.)

KNOW THE CONCEPTS
DO YOU KNOW THE BASICS?

1. Along the aggregate demand curve (*AD*), what is true about spending and income?

2. Why does the *AD* curve have a negative slope?

3. Can there be too much employment?

4. Where will output always be in the long run?

5. If an economy is producing less than its full-employment level of output, what will happen to wages and prices? How will this bring the economy back to full employment?

6. If an economy is producing more than its full-employment level of output, what will happen to wages and prices? How will this bring the economy back to full employment?

7. How will prices change when the economy is underemployed?

8. *(Assume in this question as well as in questions 9 and 10 that the economy is at full employment and then the following event occurs, and that the government doesn't aid the economy's return to full employment.)*
   In 1981–82, the U.S. government took steps that shifted the aggregate demand curve inward and to the left. Describe what happened and how the economy recovered.

9. In the 1960s, the U.S. government shifted the aggregate demand curve outward and to the right. Describe what happened and how the economy recovered.

10. In the mid-1970s, high oil prices shifted the aggregate supply curve to the left. Describe what happened and how the economy recovered.

TERMS FOR STUDY

aggregate demand, aggregate
  demand curve
aggregate supply, aggregate supply
  curve (short and long run)
full employment

overemployment
self-correcting mechanism
underemployment
unemployment

PRACTICAL APPLICATION

1. Use the table below to answer the following questions. The table shows short-run aggregate supply schedule (AS) for various nominal wages. Each entry shows the real level of output (Q) firms will produce. Note how higher wages reduce AS at each price level. The last column shows aggregate demand at each price level.
   a. What is the short-run equilibrium price level and wage when the nominal wage (W) is $10? $14? $18?
   b. Suppose full employment occurs at the real output level of 2,000. What happens when initially W = $10? W = $18?

Price Level (P)	AS if W = $10	AS if W = $14	AS if W = $18	AD
80	1,800	1,200	700	2,400
100	2,200	1,700	1,100	2,200
120	2,400	2,000	1,500	2,000
160	2,500	2,300	1,800	1,800
180	2,500	2,500	2,100	1,600

2. During the Great Depression, Herbert Hoover and other prominent leaders urged businesses not to cut wages, asserting that cutting wages would reduce spending. Was this good advice?

3. Suppose the economy is initially in a long-run full-employment equilibrium. The aggregate demand increases, shifting the *AD* curve to the right.
   a. What will happen in the short run to employment? To real wages?
   b. What will happen in the long run?

4. Over the last decade, more unions have been putting cost-of-living adjustment clauses into their contracts, so that their wages go up or down with the price level. How will this affect the time it takes for the economy to reach full employment if it is in a recession?

5. How will an economy's recovery time be affected if workers become more militant, such that they will go on strike if the firm tries to negotiate lower wages?

6. State and local planners often claim that a plant being located in their area has a "multiplier" effect. The area's residents will benefit, it is claimed, by the spending and employment the new plant adds to the community. Will this be true if the state's resources are fully employed?

7. In the following table, what is the multiplier, holding the price level constant? (Note: I = investment spending.) What is the multiplier once price increases are taken into account? Each entry shows the real aggregate output (Q) demanded or supplied.

Price Level (P)	AD $I = 130$	AD $I = 140$	AS
100	2,210	2,310	2,110
110	2,205	2,305	2,155
120	2,200	2,300	2,200
130	2,195	2,295	2,245
140	2,190	2,290	2,290
150	2,185	2,285	2,335

8. Assume that at full employment, the demand for workers equals supply at a real wage of $10.00; the quantity demanded and supplied is 100 million. The money wage is fixed in the short run at $10 and the price level at full employment is 100. The solid lines in the following graph show this. The graph shows that as *real wages* go down, firms demand more workers but fewer workers want to work. Assume that employment equals the employers' demand for workers in the short run because the workers are under contract to work the hours the employers demand. Where will the economy be on the graph if the price level falls to 80? Rises to 120?

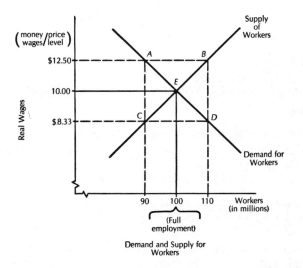

Demand and Supply for
Workers

9. Using the same set of circumstances used in Question 8, label the price levels for the aggregate supply curve when the real money wage is $10. Assume that 90 million workers produce a *GNP* of $500 billion, 100 million produce a real *GNP* of $600 billion, and 110 million produce a real *GNP* of $650 billion, all three amounts being in real dollars.

10. If workers in Question 8 had expected a price level of 120, what nominal money wage would they have demanded? Draw the short-run aggregate supply curve for this wage in the graph for Question 9.

Hint: The *AS* curve there is drawn for an expected price level of 100.

ANSWERS

KNOW THE CONCEPTS

1. They are equal.

2. A lower price level increases the real value of nominal assets, which in turn causes people to increase real spending.

3. Yes, when a shortage of workers forces wages and prices up.

4. At its full-employment level (*FE*).

5. Wages and prices will fall, shifting the *AS* curve to the right.

6. Wages and prices will rise, shifting the *AS* curve to the left.

7. Prices will fall.

8. In the short run, output and prices fell.
   In the long run, output returned to its full-employment level as prices fell further.

9. In the short run, output and prices rose.
   In the long run, output fell back to its full-employment level as prices rose further.

10. In the short run, prices rose and output fell.
    In the long run, output rose back to its full-employment level as prices fell back to their original level.

PRACTICAL APPLICATION

1. a. At $W = \$10$, equilibrium Q is 2,200 at $P = 100$. At $W = \$14$, 2,000 and 120. At $W = \$18$, 1,800 and 140.
   b. In the long run, $W = \$14$, $P = 12$, and equilibrium $Q = 2,000$. At $W = \$10$, the economy is overemployed at $Q = 2,200$. Wages will rise, shifting the AS schedule "up" to the second column. At $W = \$18$, the economy is underemployed, so wages will fall. AS schedule shifts "down" to the middle column.

2. It was the worst thing to advise. Lower wages would have shifted the AS curve out and to the right, increasing output and employment. It is true that lower wages (and lower other factor costs) will reduce *nominal* income and spending. But *real* spending will be increased as the lower prices make money holdings more valuable.

3. a. Output will increase and prices will rise. Since money wages are constant in the short run, *real* wages will fall as prices go up. Employment will increase as employees find their real costs reduced. Workers will not like working for lower real wages, but they may be locked in to a long-term contract.
   b. Workers will demand and get higher real wages. Employment will fall back to its full-employment level. Output will fall. Prices will rise even further than in the short run.

4. Wages will adjust faster to changing prices, speeding the economy's return to recovery. For example, the recession in the early 1980s was shorter than would have had been predicted based upon prior wage-change patterns.

5. In a recession, this will slow the time it takes to reduce wages. Recovery will take longer.

6. No. At full employment, the resources used by the plant (including land and labor) must come from other uses. To get these resources, the plant (and its employees) must bid them away from others in the area by

offering higher prices for them. The effect will be higher prices and a lower real income for those not directly benefited by the plant. The area as a whole will benefit only to the degree the plant *on net* adds resources to the area.

7. At a given price level, an increase in investment spending of $10 increases aggregate demand by $100. So the spending multiplier is 10. But at $I = 130$, $AD = AS$ at $P = 120$ and $Q = 2,200$. Increasing I to 140, $AD = AS$ at $P = 140$ and $Q = 2,290$. An increase in I of $10 increases Q by $90 once price increases are taken into account, giving a smaller multiplier of 9.

8. At a price level of 80, real wages rise to $12.50 ($10/0.8). The economy will be at Point A and employment will be at 90 million workers. The economy will have less than full employment.

   At a price level of 120, real wages fall to $8.33 ($10/1.20). Employment rises to 110 million as the economy will be at Point D. The economy will have more than full employment.

9. To answer this question, you have to find the price level that converts the nominal wage of $10 into the real wages at each level of employment in Question 8. The real wage of $12.50 is associated in Question 8 with an employment level of 90 million and thus an output level of 650 million: The price level must be 80 (real wage is $12.50 = $10/0.80). 100 is the price level associated with 100 million employed and output 600 billion, with a real wage of $10. 120 is the price level associated with output of 500 billion (and a real wage of $12.50). This corresponds respectively to underemployment (Point A in the graph for Question 8 and A' here), full employment (Points E and E'), and overemployment (Points D and D'). As real wages fall, employment expands.

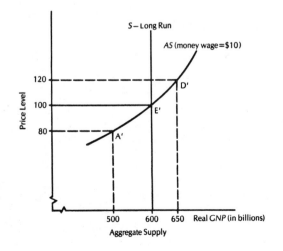

10. Workers, to be fully employed, will demand a nominal wage of $12, giving them the real full-employment wage of $10 ($12/1.20). The new aggregate supply curve (for a nominal wage of $12) will be *above* the *AS* curve for Question 9 and will intersect the full-employment long-run supply curve at price level 120.

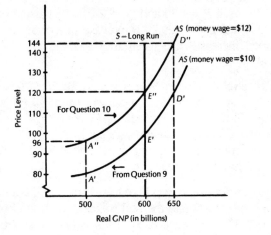

10
FISCAL POLICY: GOVERNMENT SPENDING AND TAXATION

KEY TERMS

built-in stabilizers government spending and taxation, which automatically change to offset undesirable changes in *GNP*, thereby reducing the multiplier effects of spending changes. Also called *automatic stabilizers*.

government debt the total amount the government owes.

government deficit excess of government spending over taxes collected (for a year).

government surplus the excess of taxes over government spending.

marginal tax rate amount of taxes paid on the last dollar of income earned.

tax multiplier number that a tax change must be multiplied by to get the resulting change in *GNP*. A tax multiplier of −5 implies that a $200 increase in taxes will reduce *GNP* by $1,000.

In Chapter 9, we saw that an economy can get out of a recession by itself. But many economists consider this process to be too slow and thus recommend that the government stimulate the economy by increasing aggregate demand. This chapter discusses how the government may do this (according to the Keynesian Model) through its **fiscal policy**, which involves changing government spending and taxation.

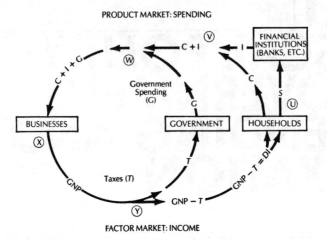

PRODUCT MARKET: SPENDING

FACTOR MARKET: INCOME

Figure 10-1   The Circular Flow of an Economy — with Government

Figure 10-1 shows the circular flows in an economy with a governmental sector. Beginning at Point U, households either consume (C) or save (S) their disposable income. Savings go into the financial system (eg., into bank accounts, mutual funds, or pension plans) and come back into the spending stream as investment spending at Point V. Then at Point W, we add government spending (G). Total spending (and GNP) equals $C + I + G$. Businesses pay out as total income the GNP at Point X. The government collects taxes (T) at Point Y, leaving disposable income (DI) equal to $GNP - T$.

Note: We are ignoring transfer payments from the government to households.

WHAT FISCAL POLICY IS

THE EFFECT OF SPENDING

Government *adds* spending but it *takes away* dollars from the economy in the tax revenues it collects. We'll examine the effect of spending first, holding tax revenues constant. Then, we'll examine the effect of changing taxes, holding government spending constant. To get the combined effect, we just add these two effects together.

Returning to the Keynesian Model of aggregate demand as described in Chapter 8, we assume that the economy is on the horizontal section of the AS (aggregate supply) curve so that more output will not raise prices.

Government spending is just like investment spending and has identical effects. Table 10-1 shows the spending at various levels of real *GNP* (*Q*).

Table 10-1. Total Government Spending and the Effect on Economic Equilibrium

Q	C	I	G	D	Output Response
3,000	1,800	500	1,500	3,800	Increase
4,000	2,400	500	1,500	4,400	Increase
5,000	3,000	500	1,500	5,000	NO CHANGE
6,000	3,600	500	1,500	5,600	Decrease
7,000	4,200	500	1,500	6,200	Decrease

When output equals $5,000, total spending equals income and the economy is in equilibrium. Note that *Q*, real output, is also real income.

Figure 10-2 illustrates Table 10-1. Equilibrium occurs where spending equals income, or where the total spending curve (*D*) crosses the 45° line (at Point *E*). Note that *D* (total spending) is derived by adding *C, I,* and *G* at each level of output.

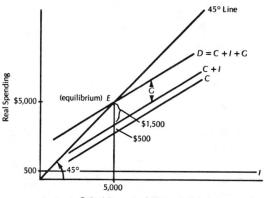

Figure 10-2 A Visual Look at Total Government Spending and the Effect on Economic Equilibrium

Since government spending is like investment spending, it has the same *spending multiplier*. A new dollar of government spending is spent and earned as income, *MPC* of it is respent and earned, and so forth. The total increase in equilibrium spending (and income) will be determined by:

$$\text{Spending Multiplier} = \frac{1}{1-MPC}.$$

Example: Effect of Government Spending

PROBLEM $MPC = 0.6$ and government spending (G) increases by $800. What will happen to equilibrium income?

SOLUTION   The spending multiplier is 2.5 (1/.4), so equilibrium income and spending will increase by $2,000.

YOU SHOULD REMEMBER

1. Without international trade, total spending equals C + I + G.

2. Every dollar increase in government spending increases GNP by the spending multiplier.

THE EFFECT OF TAXATION

Holding government spending constant, how will a change in taxes affect aggregate demand? Remember that taxes affect total spending *only through their effects on consumption spending*! If a person's taxes go up by $1, the person's disposable income is $1 lower. If *MPC* is 0.8, the person will then reduce consumption spending by $.80. This initial $.80 reduction in consumption *then* has a spending multiplier effect on the economy. The **tax multiplier** is thus:

$$\text{Tax Multiplier} = -MPC \times \text{Spending Multiplier.}$$

Example: Effect of Taxes

PROBLEM $MPC = 0.8$ and taxes go up by $1,000. What will happen to equilibrium income?

SOLUTION   Consumption initially falls by $800 (Change in $C = -MPC \times$ change in taxes). The spending multiplier is 5 (1/.2). So equilibrium income falls by $4,000 ($-5 \times$ $800). The tax multiplier is -4 ($-.8 \times 5$).

So far, we have treated taxes as if they were lump sum, such that they do not change when income changes. But in fact more taxes are paid as income goes up. When taxes go up with income, the spending multiplier will be smaller. To see why, recall the "rounds" of spending, earning, and respending that take place in the multiplier process. (See Table 8-3.) Because earnings are taxed, *less* disposable income is available for respending on each round. The result is that total secondary consumption respending will be smaller.

YOU SHOULD REMEMBER

1. The tax multiplier is $-MPC/(1 - MPC)$.

2. When taxes go up with income, the spending multiplier becomes smaller.

• *SUPPLY-SIDE ECONOMICS*

In recent years, supply-side economists have become more prominent, although their views do not yet represent the views of the majority of economists. **Supply-side economics** is based upon those four assumptions:

1. People supply less labor, capital, and other factors when taxes are increased.

2. The decision to supply more or less of a factor is determined by the **marginal tax rate** (the rate of taxes people pay on their last dollar earned).

3. When *marginal* tax rates go up, aggregate supply goes down. The *average* tax rate doesn't matter.

4. This shift in aggregate supply is more important for predicting what taxes will do than is the shift in aggregate demand.

Figure 10-3 illustrates these assumptions. When taxes are decreased, aggregate demand and aggregate supply increase, but according to the last assumption, the

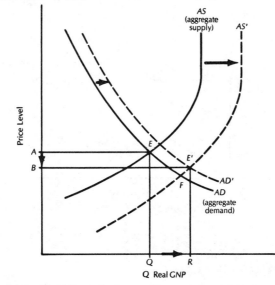

Figure 10-3   The Effect of a Tax Cut Shown by Supply-Side Economic Model

AS curve shifts out more. The economy goes from Point *E* to Point *E'*. Output increases (from level *Q* to level *R*) and prices fall (from level *A* to level *B*). In this case, it is possible to stimulate the economy out of a recession without higher rates of inflation.

In our progressive tax system, as people earn more, each addition to earnings is taxed at a progressively higher tax rate. By going to a less progressive tax structure, it is possible to collect the same average tax but have a lower marginal tax rate (at least for most people). Thus, if the government lowered the marginal tax rate but left the average tax rate the same, aggregate supply would shift out and right, but aggregate demand (which depends on total tax revenues) wouldn't shift. The economy would go from Point *E* to Point *F* in Figure 10-3. This is the theory behind 1986 tax reform.

A related part of supply-side economics is the **Laffer Curve,** which is illustrated in Figure 10-4. The tax rate is on the vertical axis. Total tax revenues are on the horizontal axis. At a tax rate of 0% or 100%, no taxes will be collected (at 100%, no one will work). These rates are represented by Points *A* and *B*, respectively. As the tax rate increases from 0%, total tax revenues go up but people begin to work and earn less, so *GNP* falls. At first, the tax rate goes up more than the amount by which the *GNP* falls. But at Point *C,* the rise in the tax rate is exactly offset by a fall in income (*GNP*), so *on net* tax revenues don't change. *T* is the most taxes the government can ever collect. At a higher tax rate, income (*GNP*) falls by more than the tax rate increases, so total tax revenues fall. Above the tax rate *C*, to increase tax revenues, the government should *reduce* the tax rate. Some studies suggest that a marginal tax rate above 40% reduces tax collections.

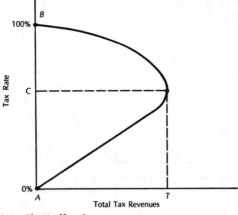

Figure 10-4 The Laffer Curve

THE OVERALL EFFECTS OF SPENDING AND TAXATION

When government spending (*G*) and taxes (*T*) both change, just add their separate effect together. One important combination occurs when *G* and *T* both increase by the same amount. The **balanced-budget multiplier** is the number the increase in G is multiplied by to get the increase in equilibrium income when T increases by *exactly* the same amount as G. One more dollar of G increases equilibrium income by $1/(1-MPC)$, while one more dollar of T decreases equilibrium income by $-MPC$ times $1/(1-MPC)$. Adding these two effects together, the balanced-budget multiplier is just 1:

$$\frac{1}{1\quad MPC} + \frac{-MPC}{1-MPC} = \frac{1-MPC}{1-MPC} = 1.$$

For example, if government spending and taxation both increase by $2,000, equilibrium income goes up by $2,000.

LIMITS OF AN ACTIVE FISCAL POLICY

While fiscal policy sounds easy, economists often don't know whether it's needed, or exactly when and how much it's going to affect the economy. As an analogy, suppose your car's gas pedal and brake worked with a variable time lag, sometimes working immediately, sometimes working thirty to sixty seconds after you press them. And suppose that for a given push, they resulted in varying degrees of acceleration or braking. Most likely your driving policy would be to hold a "steady course." So it is with fiscal policy when the timing and degree of its effects are uncertain.

YOU SHOULD REMEMBER

1. The balanced-budget multiplier equals 1.

2. The case for an active fiscal policy is weakened when its effects are uncertain in timing and degree.

THE EFFECT ON AGGREGATE SUPPLY AND DEMAND

Up to this point, we've assumed that fiscal policy does not affect prices. But near full employment, it will. To take this into account, we must return to the aggregate demand and supply analysis from Chapter 9 and Figure 9-5. Assume the economy is in equilibrium at price level A and full-employment output FE. Then government spending goes up $1,000 when the MPC is 0.8. Equilibrium income will go up $5,000 *if the price level does not change.* In Figure 9-5, this $5,000 increase is shown by the horizontal outward shift of the aggregate demand curve from Point *E* to Point *F*. If the price level did *not* change, output would also increase, from level *FE* to level *T*. But in the short run, the economy moves up the *AS* curve to *G*, where prices are higher (*B* > *A*) and output smaller (*S* < *T*). So the true short-run multiplier will be smaller than 5. In the long run, wages will increase, shifting the *AS* curve up and to the left. Prices will rise still more (from *B* to *C*) and output will fall back to its full-employment level. Thus, at full employment, more government spending and lower taxes raise prices, not output. The modified multiplier is zero.

DEFICITS: DO THEY MATTER?

Note: In this section, we discuss a theory that is in direct opposition to that taught in most textbooks. Nevertheless, the view presented here has a substantial body of evidence backing its claims and is thus worthy of attention.

Because the government deficit equals government spending minus taxes (*G* − *T*), we can also write:

$$G = T + \text{Deficit.}$$

That is, government spending is financed either by taxes *or* by the government borrowing money (by issuing government bonds) to cover its deficit.

Some economists believe that "deficits do not matter"; i.e., equilibrium income will be the same whether government spending is paid for with taxes or borrowings. In contrast to this is the Keynesian result derived above, which suggests that *lower* taxes (and thus higher deficits) will increase equilibrium income (assuming *G* is unchanged).

To see why deficits might not matter, assume that government spending is fixed. The only issue is how to pay for *G*: pay taxes now or run a deficit. But deficits are just delayed taxes that the public will have to pay later. If the public knows this, it may regard a $150 billion deficit the same as $150 billion more in taxes, since the money will eventually have to be paid anyway. (This theory is called the Ricardian Tax Equivalence Theorem, after David Ricardo, a famous nineteenth-century economist.)

If this is the case, then "deficits don't matter." What will happen? Suppose taxes go down by $1,000 (and *G* stays the same so the government has to borrow $1,000). Disposable income (*DI*) will go up by $1,000. Households, knowing they will have to pay the $1,000 eventually, save the $1,000 in added disposable income. Consumption spending (*C*) will be *unchanged*! Therefore, because *C* is unchanged (and so are *G* and *I*, investment spending), total spending (*C* + *G* + *I*) is unchanged. The deficit will *not* change equilibrium income.

There is a considerable body of evidence supporting this point of view. Economic data suggests that deficits do not affect output, interest rates, foreign exchange rates, and investment spending, *other things being equal.* Nevertheless, until recently, deficits have been so small that their effects may have been undetectable.

• *BUILT-IN STABILIZERS*

Fiscal policy involves (1) active programs designed to influence the economy (such as special spending programs and changes in the tax breaks) and (2) automatic programs, which respond to changes in the economy without explicit orders from our political officials. Programs that are automatic are called **built-in stabilizers.** They include (a) unemployment insurance and welfare programs and (b) our tax system. When *GNP* goes down and unemployment up, (a) increases transfer payments automatically while (b) reduces taxes (since people pay less taxes at lower incomes). This *reduces* the amount by which disposable income decreases when *GNP* goes down. In turn, this reduces the decrease in consumption spending when *GNP* falls. Built-in stabilizers thus "dampen" the multiplier process and the resulting change in *GNP.*

• *THE FULL-EMPLOYMENT DEFICIT*

How active is fiscal policy? To find out, many economists look at what the deficit *would be* if the economy were at full employment: the **full-employment deficit** (also called the "active" or "structural" deficit). By looking at the full-employment deficit instead of the actual deficit, the cyclical effects of the automatic stabilization programs are removed and only the *active* component of fiscal policy remains. The full-employment deficit (or surplus) tells economists how much fiscal policy is actively working to affect the economy: A higher full-employment deficit indicates a shift toward a great stimulation of the economy.

• *BURDEN OF THE DEBT*

The federal **government's debt** equals the government's total indebtedness and now exceeds $2.1 trillion (about 50% of *GNP*). Does this debt (and the deficits the government runs that add to this debt) represent a burden to our economy? Economists make the following conclusions:

1. A deficit that stimulates the economy out of a recession into full employment will be a benefit, not a burden.

2. If deficits do matter, then a deficit incurred when the economy is near full employment can be harmful. To see why, consider the injections = leakage equation when the government sector is added:

$$I + \text{Government Deficit} = S,$$

where the government deficit (government spending minus taxes, or $G - T$) is the government's net injection into the spending stream (where G is an injection and T is a leakage). If deficits *do* matter, an increase in the deficit causes government borrowing to compete with private investors for savings. More government borrowing will then reduce private investment borrowing. Less investment reduces future output and growth.

3. If deficits do not matter, then the increase in the deficit causes an equal increase in savings (since households know they'll need to add to their savings to meet the future taxes implicit in the deficit). In this case, investment spending will remain unchanged as will the future growth of the economy.

4. The part of the debt owed to Americans is less of a burden than that owed to foreigners. What we "owe ourselves" represents a transfer of resources between Americans. But what Americans owe foreigners represents a loss of resources from the U.S.

YOU SHOULD REMEMBER

1. Deficits help the economy if lower taxes cause GNP to expand.

2. Deficits harm the economy when they (a) do not stimulate the economy and (b) reduce private investment, thereby reducing growth.

KNOW THE CONCEPTS
DO YOU KNOW THE BASICS?

1. Why is government spending the same as investment or consumption spending?

2. Why does a decrease in taxes have a smaller multiplier effect than the same increase in government spending?

3. If the government wants to spend more *without* increasing equilibrium income, by how much must it increase taxes (as compared to the increase in government spending)?

4. How does the income tax affect the size of the spending multiplier?

5. Why isn't the actual deficit a good guide to how active the government's fiscal policy is?

6. If government borrowing reduces business borrowing, how does this affect our economy's growth?

7. If the public anticipates having to pay the future taxes implicit in any deficit, why won't a lower tax increase consumption spending (and aggregate demand)?

8. Why is government spending (G) an injection? Why are taxes (T) a leakage?

9. Will the multiplier effect of more government spending be larger or smaller when prices go up as output increases?

10. How do built-in stabilizers help stabilize the economy?

TERMS FOR STUDY

automatic fiscal policy

balanced-budget multiplier

built-in stabilizers

"deficits don't matter"

discretionary or active fiscal policy

full-employment deficit (and surplus)

spending multiplier

supply-side economics

tax multiplier

PRACTICAL APPLICATION

1. Fill in the following table and answer these questions based on:

$$MPC = 0.6, I = \$500, G = \$700, \text{ and } T = \$500$$

   a. What is the equilibrium income?
   b. What are the injections ($G + I$) and leakages ($S + T$) at this income?
   c. What will happen to equilibrium GNP if government spending goes up $400? If I goes up $400 instead?

Q	DI	C	D = C + I + G
$2,000	1,500	1,200	2,400
3,000	———	———	———
4,000	———	———	———
5,000	———	———	———
6,000	———	———	———

2. a. When $MPC = 0.75$, if G and T both increase by $1,000, what will happen to equilibrium income?
   b. By how much must T be increased (assuming G is increased by $1,000) so that equilibrium income does *not* increase?

3. If the government wants to increase equilibrium income by $4,000 when $MPC = 0.8$, by how much must it increase G?

4. If the government wants to increase equilibrium income by $4,000 when $MPC = 0.8$, by how much must it reduce T?

5. Suppose that in equilibrium, business firms want to invest more than households want to save. For this to be possible, what must be true about *G* and *T*?

6. Government spending goes up by $5,000 while taxes go up $3,000. What will happen to equilibrium income if the *MPC* = 0.6?

7. If the economy is at or near full employment, what will be the main impact of a reduction of government spending on real *GNP* and prices?

8. Households decide to save $10,000 more. By how much must the government increase *G* if it wants to maintain the same level of national income?

Hint: *C* is going down by $10,000.

9. If "deficits don't matter," what will happen to *DI, C,* and *S* when *T* goes down $5,000?

10. If *G* goes up $1,000 and equilibrium income goes up $4,000, what is the *MPC*?

ANSWERS

KNOW THE CONCEPTS

1. Because *C, G,* and *I* all directly enter the spending stream and are received as income.

2. Because a decrease in *T* initially increases *C* by a smaller amount (since *MPC* < 1). The resulting change in total spending is smaller.

3. It would have to increase *T* more than *G.*

4. It makes the spending multiplier smaller.

5. The size of the actual deficit in a recession will be larger because of the effects of the automatic stabilizers. To measure the active component of fiscal policy, these effects must be removed.

6. It reduces future growth.

7. Because households will regard less taxes now as *more* taxes later, they will save an amount equal to the delayed tax. *C* will be unchanged.

8. *G* adds to total spending, while *T* represents an allocation of income away from spending.

9. Smaller.

10. They reduce the multiplier effects of changes in autonomous spending.

PRACTICAL APPLICATION

1. **a.** $3,000
   b. Injections ($I + G$) equal $1,200. At $3,000, $S = $700 ($S = DI - C$). Leakages ($S + T$) equal $1,200.
   c. The spending multiplier is 2.5. Equilibrium income will increase by $1,000 in either case.

2. **a.** The balanced-budget multiplier is 1, so equilibrium income will go up $1,000.
   b. To not change equilibrium income the increase in taxes must reduce C by the amount G goes up so that total spending is unchanged. To decrease C by $1,000, DI must fall by $1,333.33: T must increase by $1,333.33. To get the $1,333.33 figure, solve the equation: Change in C equals $-MPC$ times increase in taxes. (In this case, the change in C is $-$1,000.)

3. G must increase by $800 (the spending multiplier is 5: 5 × 800 = $4,000).

4. T must be reduced by $1,000 (the tax multiplier is -4).

5. Injections must equal leakages in equilibrium, so $I + G$ must equal $S + T$. Rewriting this, $I - S = T - G$. Since I is greater than S, T must be greater than G. The government must be running a surplus. This surplus retires part of the government's debt, freeing these funds to support the excess of I over S.

6. The increase in G increases equilibrium income by $12,500 (2.5 × $5,000). The increase in T decreases it by $4,500 ($-1.5$ × $3,000). On net, equilibrium income will go up $8,000.

7. The AD curve will shift left by the change in G times the spending multiplier. In the short run, with the AS curve unchanged, prices will fall as output falls. Unemployment will go up. In the long run, wages (and thus prices) will fall, shifting the AS curve down and right, causing output to return to its full-employment level but pushing the price level down below its short-run level.

8. By $10,000.

9. DI goes up $5,000, savings go up $5,000, C remains unchanged ($C = DI - S$).

10. $MPC = .75$.

11
THE SUPPLY OF MONEY

KEY TERMS

asset physical property or intangible right (e.g., plant, equipment, patents, money, or bonds) that has economic value.

liquidity the ease with which an asset (such as a stock or bond) can be converted into cash. Cash is the most liquid asset. Bonds are relatively liquid, and land is usually illiquid.

money the medium of exchange; what people use to pay for goods and services.

WHAT IS MONEY?

An increase in the money supply can dramatically increase aggregate demand, as later chapters illustrate. This chapter, however, covers what causes the money supply to change.

Money is an asset with which people buy and sell goods. Hence, it is defined as the medium of exchange. Coins, currency (such as dollar bills), and checking accounts all serve as money.

Trade without money is **barter**. In barter, you have to find someone who (1) wants what you have and (2) has what you want. When such a person is found, it's called a **double coincidence of wants**, since both (1) *and* (2) have to be true for barter to occur.

With money, trade takes place just by having people (1) sell what they have for money and then (2) use the money to buy what they want. Money therefore does not require a double coincidence of wants, and thus expands the range of mutually advantageous trades people can make.

At times, gold and other goods served as **commodity money**, i.e., a widely traded good that was valued both for its use as a medium of exchange and for its intrinsic value. Currently, most monies of the world are **fiat money**, not backed by gold or any other valuable material. The dollar is a fiat money.

Unfortunately, the term "money" is commonly used in other ways that are confusing. Money is *not* "savings," "income," or "borrowings." These terms refer to real goods and services. (For example, income is the real goods and services a person earns.) They are not money. Just as a picture of a house is not the house, money is a measure of the value of goods and services; it is not the goods and services themselves.

The Functions of Money

1. *Separate sales from purchases:* Money allows people to avoid the double coincidence of wants.

2. *Unit of account:* Money allows people to put a price on all goods.

3. *Standard of deferred payment:* In almost all contracts, when people agree to be paid in the future, it's usually in money. (The alternative is to be paid in goods.)

4. *Store of value:* People "store" their savings by setting aside an amount of money (often in a bank account).

HOW MONEY IS MEASURED

The more easily and more quickly one can trade an asset for goods without taking a loss, the more **liquid** the asset. Money is the most liquid asset; a bond is less liquid, since it takes some time and effort to trade it for most goods. Land is illiquid.

There are many different measures of the money supply. What economists categorize as money depends on what assets they think are liquid enough to be considered money.

Classifications of Money Measurement

1. **M1**: *The most liquid measure of money is M1.* It counts only those assets commonly used for *transactions.* This includes currency (cash and coin) held by the public and checking accounts against which checks can be written.

2. **M2**: *The next most liquid measure of money is M2.* It adds savings accounts to M1 (including certain money market mutual funds that allow checks to be written on them).

3. **M3**: M3 adds large-denomination time deposits ($100,000 or more) to M2.

4. **L**: "L" adds to M3 U.S. savings bonds, short-term U.S. securities, banker's acceptances, commercial paper, and Eurodollar deposits (dollar deposits in Europe) held by Americans.

5. **D**: "D" includes the entire range of financial instruments, including bonds and mortgages.

Most economists use either M1 or M2.

YOU SHOULD REMEMBER

1. Money is the medium of exchange; using money for trade means people don't have to seek a double coincidence of wants.

2. Money serves as a unit of account, a means of deferred payment, and as a store of value. It serves all these functions because it separates sales from purchases.

3. Savings, income, and borrowing all are real physical goods and services; they are not money.

4. M1 is currency (held by the public) and checkable deposits. It represents transaction monies. M2 adds savings accounts and checkable money market accounts to M1.

BALANCE SHEETS AND BANKS: FEDERAL AND COMMERCIAL

Table 11-1 shows a partial balance sheet for the U.S. banking system for early 1986. **Assets** are what people own or what other people owe them. **Liabilities** are what people owe others.

The top panel shows the balance sheet for the **Federal Reserve System** (Fed). The Fed is the nation's banking regulatory agency. It controls the money supply. It also serves as a "lender of last resort" to banks needing funds (see 1 and 11 on the Balance Sheet). Referring to the Assets column, the Fed's assets include loans to banks, which it lends at an interest rate called the "discount rate" (1), government securities, which are part of the open market operations discussed below (2), and gold (3). Its liabilities include Federal Reserve notes, which in effect are all of the U.S. paper currency held either by the public or the banks (4) and deposits of commercial banks at the Fed (5).

The assets of all commercial banks (see bottom panel) include their deposits at the Fed (6A) and their vault cash, i.e., the cash and coin banks keep on hand to meet daily cash withdrawals (6B). Banks lend money either to the public (7) or the government (8). The funds needed to make these loans come from the

Table 11-1. Partial Balance Sheets of the U.S. Banking System

The Balance Sheet of the Federal Reserve Bank
(in billions of dollars)

Assets	Liabilities

1. Loans to banks ....$ 1
2. Government securities.......$180
3. Gold and other assets.......$ 26
	4. Federal Reserve notes
	   A. Currency held by the
	      public.....................................$154
	   B. Vault cash of banks..............$ 21
	5. Deposits of banks at Fed..........$ 25

The Balance Sheet of Combined Commercial Banks
(in billions of dollars)

Assets	Liabilities

6. Reserves
   A. Deposits at fed.........$ 25
   B. Vault cash..................$ 21
7. Loans to public..............$1,361
8. Government
   securities......................$ 267
	9. Checkable deposits..............$ 459
	10. Other deposits.....................$1,134
	11. Loans from Fed.....................$ 1

liability side of the commercial banks' balance sheet. The sources of funds include checkable deposits (9), other deposits, which are mainly time and savings deposits (10), and money borrowed from the Fed (11).

Note that 1 matches 11, 4B matches 6A, and 5 matches 11, these being the assets and liabilities that banks and the Fed owe each other.

M1 equals (4A), the currency held by the public plus (9), checkable deposits (so M1 = $613 billion). The Fed limits how much banks can loan by requiring them to place a certain fraction of their deposits at the Fed (this fraction is called the **required reserve ratio**); banks place (5) at the Fed and the Fed owes them (6A).

HOW MONEY IS CREATED

For the rest of the chapter, we'll define money as M1, or money = currency (held by the public) + checkable deposits. We will follow how money is created step by step. To simplify our analysis, assume that: (1) banks lend all their excess reserves and (2) the public redeposits all lent money into the banking system.

Steps by One Bank

Step 1: Suppose the Fed somehow causes $1,000 in new money to be deposited at a bank. The bank puts the $1,000 into reserves. Let us assume that the Fed has a required reserve ratio of 10%. So the bank puts $100 into deposits at the Fed (its required reserves) and puts its **excess reserves** (the reserves a bank holds over what the Fed requires of it) of $900 into its vault. Here's how the balance sheet looks:

Combined Commercial Banks' Balance Sheet

Assets	Liabilities

6. Reserves
  A. Deposits at Fed   +$100
  B. Vault cash   +$900
	9. Checkable deposits +$1,000

So far, the money supply has increased only by the $1,000 the Fed has added. Note that the currency held by the bank is defined to *not* be a part of the money supply.

Step 2: The bank lends out its excess reserves of $900. It does this by creating a new $900 checkable deposit in the borrower's name. So instead of +$1,000 in checkable deposits, there is +$1,900.

Combined Commercial Banks' Balance Sheet

Assets	Liabilities

6. Reserves
  A. Deposits at Fed   +$100
  B. Vault cash   +$900
7. Loans   +$900
	9. Checkable deposits +$1,900

Now the money supply has increased by $1,900! The right given to banks by the government to lend money it owes its depositors is called **fractional reserve banking**. It is this right that allowed this bank to create the added $900.

Steps by the Banking System

Step 3: The borrower of the $900 spends it, and the people getting the $900 deposit it *at another bank*. Nothing has changed from above, except that the other bank now holds the $900 as deposits at the Fed and as vault cash.

Step 4: The new bank getting the $900 will put 10% of it ($90) into required reserves and lend the remainder ($810) by putting $810 into some other borrower's checking account. Now the balance sheet will look like this:

Combined Commercial Banks' Balance Sheet

Assets	Liabilities
6. Reserves	9. Checkable deposits + $2,710
A. Deposits at Fed + $190	
B. Vault cash + $810	
7. Loans +$1,710	

By this step, the initial $1,000 deposit has increased the money supply by $2,710 (the increase in checkable deposits). As long as there are excess reserves and as long as banks lend these reserves out, this process will continue *until all of the initial cash is deposited at the Fed* as required reserves.

Step 5: When all of the $1,000 goes for meeting the 10% reserve requirement, banks will stop this process of lending and relending. The last balance sheet will look like this:

Combined Commercial Banks' Balance Sheet

Assets	Liabilities
6. Reserves	9. Checkable deposits +$10,000
A. Deposits at Fed +$1,000	
B. Vault cash + 0	
7. Loans +$9,000	

Now the $1,000 is all in required reserves; it equals 10% of total added deposits, $10,000. The money supply has increased by $10,000 (the added deposits). In general, if R is the required reserve ratio, we have:

$$\text{Increase in the Money Supply} = \frac{\text{Initial Cash Added}}{R}$$

$1/R$ is the money supply multiplier. It tells us by how much an added dollar in banks' reserves (no matter what the source) will increase the money supply. The higher the ratio, the smaller the multiplier.

Mathematically, let "f" be the fraction of each dollar deposited that is loaned out *and* redeposited. When a dollar is added to the banking system, it is lent and relent out such that the increase in the money supply is:

$$1 + f + f^2 + \ldots = 1/(1 - f)$$

In our simple case, $1 - f = R$, so the money multiplier is $1/R$.

The *actual* money multiplier is *smaller* than $1/R$, for two reasons: (1) banks like to keep some vault cash to meet their daily needs to cash checks and provide change; (2) the public doesn't redeposit all the money that's lent—it holds some fraction of it out as cash. When new money is introduced into the banking system, both of these factors *reduce* the amount redeposited in each step, resulting in a smaller f and a *smaller multiplier.* For example, the reserve ratio for checking accounts is 12%, which would imply a simple money multiplier for M1 of 8.33 (1/.12). But in fact, M1's actual money multiplier is currently near 2.7, a far smaller number.

YOU SHOULD REMEMBER

1. Banks mainly put their deposits and loans from the Fed into their reserves, loans to the public, and government securities.

2. Banks create money by lending out their excess reserves. They do this by increasing the borrower's checking account by the amount lent.

3. The simple money multiplier is 1/R, R being the required reserve ratio (the fraction of deposits that banks must deposit at the Fed). A dollar of new reserves will increase the money supply by, at most, 1/R dollars.

4. The actual money multiplier is less than 1/R, because banks don't lend all their excess reserves and the public doesn't redeposit all it borrows from banks.

HOW THE FED CONTROLS THE MONEY SUPPLY

The Fed has direct control over the **monetary base** (also called *high-powered money*). The monetary base is essentially all the cash in the economy: It is the sum of bank reserves and currency held by the public (in Table 11-1, 4 + 5). It represents the total cash the banking system *could* use as reserves (and *would* be used if the public deposited all its cash in banks).

The Fed can affect the *actual money multiplier.* The actual money multiplier takes into account the fact that banks do not lend out all their excess reserves and the public does not deposit all its money in banks. We have:

M1 = Actual Money Multiplier $\times$ Monetary Base

Table 11-2. Major Methods of Money Control

Method	Effect		
	on Monetary Base	on Money Multiplier	on Money Supply
1. Required Reserve Ratio			
Increase	None	Decrease	Decrease
Decrease	None	Increase	Increase
2. Open Market Operation			
Fed Buys Bonds	Increase	None	Increase
Fed Sells Bonds	Decrease	None	Decrease
3. Discount Rate			
Increase	Decrease	None*	Decrease
Decrease	Increase	None*	Increase

*Note: A higher discount rate will discourage banks from keeping excess reserves and therefore will reduce the money multiplier. A lower rate will increase the money multiplier. This effect is so small, though, that "none" is closer to reality as an answer.

How the Methods of Money Control Actually Work

Method 1: Change the reserve requirement. If our simple money multiplier $(1/R)$ held, then an increase in R from 10% to 15% (0.10 to 0.15) would decrease the money multiplier from 10 to 6.67. For a given monetary base of, say, $50 billion, this would decrease the money supply from $500 billion to $333.3 billion.

Method 2: Add or subtract new reserves by buying and selling government securities. This is called an **open market operation** and is carried out by the

Federal Open Market Committee (FOMC). This is the method the Fed uses most often to change the money supply.

If the FOMC buys securities from banks, it pays for the bank's government securities (8 in Table 11–1) by adding to the bank's reserves at the Fed (6A). This increases the monetary base and thus the money supply. By selling government securities, the Fed has the opposite effect: It reduces the monetary base and the money supply, by taking money in exchange for the bonds it sells.

Method 3: Add new reserves by lending to banks. When banks borrow from the Fed, the Fed charges banks a rate of interest called the **discount rate.** A reduced discount rate encourages banks to borrow. When banks borrow, the Fed increases 5 (and banks increase 11 and 6A). This increases the monetary base, and thus the money supply. Actually, banks borrow very little from the Fed, and thus changes in the discount rate have very little impact on the money supply. Nevertheless, the changes are widely watched, because they often signal changes in Fed policy.

Other Methods: The Fed also sets the minimum percentage of a stock purchase that must be paid for in cash (the **stock margin requirement**). The higher the margin, the harder it is to buy stocks on credit. Also, the Fed has at times restricted the credit conditions for home mortgages and consumer loans. By limiting credit, the Fed makes it harder for people to buy homes and expensive consumer goods. Neither of these methods directly impacts the money supply unless it reduces what banks lend. One last method the Fed uses is **moral suasion,** or "jawboning" to get banks to do what it wants (e.g., it may encourage or discourage banks to lend to foreign governments).

YOU SHOULD REMEMBER

1. The Fed *increases* the money supply by reducing the required reserve ratio (R), by buying government securities, and by lowering the discount rate.

2. The Fed *decreases* the money supply by raising R, by selling government securities, and by raising the discount rate.

3. The monetary base is at the base for all the loans that the banking system can make. It includes the currency held by the public plus all bank reserves.

4. M1 equals the actual money multiplier times the monetary base.

KNOW THE CONCEPTS

DO YOU KNOW THE BASICS?

1. How does money make it easier for people to trade?

2. Why is income not money?

3. What is it that is really "borrowed" when people borrow "money"?

4. Are credit cards money?

5. How does the lending of excess reserves by banks create money?

6. If the legal reserve requirement is 20%, what is the most the banking system can lend out if an individual deposits $1,000?

7. How does the Fed's buying government securities add to monetary base? How does this change the money supply?

8. Why does lowering of the discount rate add to the monetary base?

9. What factors make the actual money multiplier smaller than $1/R$?

10. How does increasing the monetary base change the money supply?

TERMS FOR STUDY

checkable deposits
commodity money
discount rate
double coincidence of wants
excess reserves
fiat money
liquidity

M1
M2
monetary base
money
open market operation
required reserve ratio (R)

PRACTICAL APPLICATION

1. In a barter economy, how would an economics professor survive?

2. Assume the required reserve ratio is 20%.
   a. If a single bank in the banking system has $10 million in excess reserves, how much new money, at most, could it create by itself?
   b. If the whole banking system has $10 million in excess reserves, how much new money, at most, could it create?

3. Fill in the following table. Assume that banks keep 20% of their deposits backed by reserves and that the public redeposits all the money it is lent. Show the effect of $1,000 in new reserves being deposited at Bank A, Bank A lending its excess reserves, the money from the loan being spent and deposited at Bank B, and so forth.

	Increase in Deposits	Increase in Loans	Increase in Reserves
Bank A	$1,000	$800	$200
Bank B	------	------	------
Bank C	------	------	------
. . . . .			
Total	------	------	------

4. Indicate whether the following events will increase or decrease the money supply.

   Event A: The Fed buys government securities from the public.

   Event B: Banks decide to hold more excess reserves.

   Event C: The public wants less cash because of an increased fear of being robbed.

   Event D: The Fed raises the discount rate.

   Event E: The Fed prints more currency.

   Event F: Interest rates rise.

5. Jane withdraws $1,000 from her checking account and puts it in a cookie jar. How much, at most, could the money supply fall if the required reserve ratio is 10%?

6. During Christmas time, the public's demand for cash goes up. How should the Fed react to this if it wants to keep the money supply constant? What will happen to the monetary base and the money multiplier?

7. If the public suddenly wanted to hold all its money in the form of cash (withdrawing all its money from checking and savings accounts), what would happen to the money supply?

8. If banks could not find anyone willing to borrow funds at the interest rate they charge, what would happen to the money supply?

9. One of the liabilities of the Federal Reserve is Federal Reserve notes (the dollar bill is an example). Since this is a liability, what does the Fed "owe" the public or banks that hold these dollars?

10. How can the public cause the money supply to shrink?

ANSWERS

KNOW THE CONCEPTS

1. With money, people don't have to sell their goods and services only to those who have goods and services they want.

2. Income is the goods and services one earns; money is only a measure of its value.

3. A borrower is actually borrowing real goods and services.

4. No. Credit cards are a means of spending money. Money is what people use to pay their credit card bills.

5. The lending of excess reserves creates money (1) instantly when the borrower's checkable deposit is increased (this is how banks give people loans), and (2) later, when the lent money is redeposited by the people from whom the borrower buys goods and services, and this is relent and so on.

6. $4,000.

7. This increases the monetary base, and through the money multiplier process, the money supply is increased even more.

8. A lower discount rate encourages banks to run down their excess reserves, since it is then cheaper to get some extra cash from the Fed when needed. Banks run down their excess reserves by lending them: This creates money.

9. The two main factors are (1) banks don't lend all their excess reserves and (2) the public does not redeposit all the funds it has been lent.

10. The bigger the monetary base, the more money that can be created through the money multiplier process.

PRACTICAL APPLICATION

1. The professor would have to find students that wanted economic lessons *and* had something the professor wanted (such as food, housing, and clothing). Obviously, there aren't too many professors of economics in barter economies. Indeed, there is very little specialization in barter economies, since most people produce only goods that are in common demand.

2. a. $8 million.
   b. $40 million (5 × $8 million).

3. Bank B: $800, $640, $160. Bank C: $640, $512, $128. Total: $5,000 (1/.2 × $1,000). $4,000 (80% of $5,000), and $1,000 (20% of $5,000 and the initial increase in reserves).

4. *Event A:* Increase.
   Event B: Decrease (smaller multiplier).
   Event C: Increase (larger multiplier because more of the money lent will be redeposited).
   Event D: Decrease (reduces the base when banks borrow less from the Fed).
   Event E: Increase.
   Event F: Increase (banks hold smaller excess reserves when they can make more on them by lending them out: This increases the multiplier.)

5. $9,000 (checking deposits will fall $10,000 but currency held by the public will go up $1,000).

6. The increased demand for cash reduces the actual multiplier (because less lent money is redeposited). So the Fed must increase the monetary base. Typically, it does this by buying government securities.

7. The money supply would shrink back down to the size of the monetary base.

8. The money supply would shrink, because banks could not lend and relend.

9. Our currency is a fiat currency. The Fed really doesn't owe anything.

10. By holding more in cash and less in checking and savings accounts.

12

MONEY AND AGGREGATE DEMAND: KEYNESIAN MODEL

This chapter shows how money affects aggregate demand in the Keynesian Model. This is the model presented in most texts, and it will be contrasted with the Monetarist Model in the next chapter. While both models believe that the same set of factors affects aggregate demand, they differ over which factors matter most.

THE KEYNESIAN MODEL

Basic Premises

1. *Savings can be put either into money holdings or into other assets that pay interest.* (The latter we'll lump together and call "bonds.") Bonds and money holdings are considered to be close substitutes.

2. The choice of where to put one's savings is determined by the *interest rate*

bonds pay. The lower the interest rate, the less attractive are bonds and the more attractive are money holdings.

3. Money has its main impact on aggregate demand through its impact on *investment spending.*

How the Money Supply Affects the Economy

Step 1: The money supply *(MS)* is increased (e.g., by the Fed buying government bonds in an open market operation). To maintain equilibrium, money demand must be increased. Because of premises 1 and 2 above, the quantity of money holdings that people demand is increased by reducing the interest rate.

Step 2: The lower interest rate *(i)* increases investment spending.

Step 3: Higher investment spending *(I)* increases aggregate demand *(AD)* for goods and services through the multiplier process.

Step 4: The shift in the aggregate demand curve *(AD)* to the right increases output and prices.

The basic steps, therefore, are:

$$MS \text{ up} \rightarrow i \text{ down} \rightarrow I \text{ up} \rightarrow AD \text{ up} \rightarrow \text{output and prices up}$$

HOW THE MONEY SUPPLY AFFECTS THE ECONOMY

STEP 1: MONEY DEMAND AND INTEREST RATES

To keep the analysis simple, let's make two assumptions:

1. There are only two financial assets that people put their savings into:
   - **Money,** which can be cash or checking accounts. (Assume that the accounts do not pay any interest.) Even though money does not pay interest, people have money holdings with which to buy and sell goods.
   - **Bonds,** which are IOUs issued by borrowers promising to pay fixed amounts of money on specified dates. For simplicity, assume that bonds pay a *fixed annual payment.* The interest rate a bond pays is:

$$\text{Interest Rate} = \frac{\text{Fixed Annual Payment}}{\text{Price of Bond}} \times 100$$

For example, a bond paying $500 a year, year after year, forever, that sells for $4,000, has an interest rate of 12.5%. Such a bond that pays interest forever is called a *consul* and is very rare. Most bonds pay an annual fixed payment for a stated number of years and then pay back their face value. We'll discuss the value of bonds later in this chapter but for now, we'll assume all bonds are consuls just to keep our analysis simple.

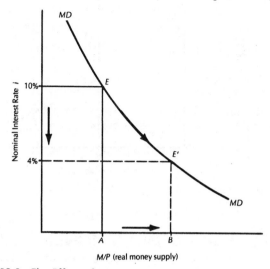

Figure 12-1   The Effect of Interest Rates on Money Demand

2. Businesses finance their investment spending by borrowing. They issue bonds that are sold to savers.

Bonds pay interest; money doesn't. So the opportunity cost (see chapter 1) of holding money is the interest people could have earned by holding bonds instead. The higher the interest rate bonds pay, the less money people want to hold. This is shown in Figure 12-1.

On the vertical axis is the **nominal interest rate** (the rate paid by bonds). On the horizontal axis is the quantity of **real money** (M/P, where P is the price level). We use the real quantity of money because money is demanded for its purchasing power (real value).

As the interest rate falls from 10% to 4%, the quantity of money demanded increases from A to B. As bonds pay less, people want to hold fewer bonds and more money.

In Figure 12-2, the real money supply (M/P) is shown by a vertical line. The nominal supply (M) is determined by the Fed. In this chapter, we assume that the price level doesn't change, so an increase in M also increases M/P. When the money supply equals A, the interest rate is 10%. Now suppose the Fed increases the money supply to B. At 10%, there is an *excess supply* of money. What do people do with their excess supply of money? They try to buy bonds. Bond prices are bid up and the interest rate falls. This continues until interest rates fall to 4%. At 4%, the quantity of money demanded has increased to equal the new higher money supply (at E').

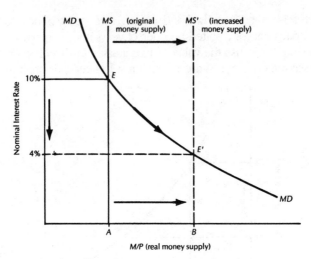

Figure 12-2 The Effect of an Excess Money Supply

MONEY: WHY PEOPLE DEMAND MONEY

- **Transaction Demand for Money:** People have money holdings because they allow people to buy and sell goods easily. (The alternative would be use bonds or try barter.)

- **Speculative Demand for Money:** People also have money holdings because they are safer than many other assets. Stocks, bonds, and real estate can all fluctuate widely in price. On the other hand, only inflation can erode the real value of money holdings.

  Keynes argued that if people expect bond prices to fall (or interest rates to rise), they will sell their bonds and put the proceeds into their money holdings. He thus thought the speculative demand for money to be very important.

- **Precautionary Demand for Money:** Larger money holdings allow people to meet unforeseen expenses. For example, the expense of an accident may be met more cheaply out of money holdings than by selling off other assets.

YOU SHOULD REMEMBER

1. In the Keynesian Model, savings can be added to bond holdings or money holdings.

---

2. When the price of bonds goes up, interest rates go down. And when bond prices go down, interest rates go up.

3. The opportunity cost of holding money is the interest rate that could have been earned by holding bonds instead. A lower interest rate increases the quantity of money people want to hold.

4. An increase in the money supply causes an excess supply of money. This excess money goes to buy bonds, thereby increasing bond prices and lowering the interest rate.

BONDS: INTEREST RATES AND PRICES

Bonds usually pay yearly or semiannual payments for a fixed number of years and then pay back their face value (usually $1,000) when they are retired. To calculate what you should pay for a bond, ask the question, "What would I have to save at the interest rate I earn on my other savings in order to get the same return?" The answer will be the bond's **present value.** Your current interest rate is the best rate you can earn on other assets of similar risk (and are willing to lend at). For example, suppose you can earn 10% on your savings. A dollar saved today would yield $1.10 a year from now. So what would you be willing to pay for a treasury bill (a short-term U.S. government bond) that pays back $1,000 in one year? You should be willing to pay $909.09 (or $1,000/1.10). By dividing by 1.10, you find out how many dollars you need to invest today to get $1,000 back in one year. If the treasury bill sells for more than this, don't buy it (as you can do better elsewhere at 10%). If it sells for less, buy it (because it's paying better than 10%). The **yield** on any bond is the interest rate that makes its actual price equal to its present value. For example, if the above treasury bill sold for $892.86, its yield would be 12%.

If you save a dollar for two years at 10% per year, the dollar will grow to $1.21 in two years. In one year, it's worth 10% more ($1.10) and in the next year, the $1.10 is worth 10% more, or $1.21 ($1.10 × 1.10). In the second year, not only does the original dollar earn interest, so does the interest (of $.10) earn interest. This phenomenon is called **compound interest.**

In general, in N years, $1.00 will be worth $(1 + i)^n$ dollars, where i is the interest rate stated as a decimal number. To find the present value *(PV)* of a bond, economists use the formula:

$$PV = \frac{C1}{(1 + i)} + \frac{C2}{(1 + i)^2} + \frac{C3}{(1 + i)^3} + \ldots + \frac{\text{Face Value}}{(1 + i)^n}$$

C1 is the coupon or payment in the first year, *C2*, the second year's payment, and so on. Each *C* is divided by what a dollar saved today would be worth at *i*% interest by the year that the *C* is paid. For example, *C2*/(1 + *i*)² is what one would have to save today at $i\%$ to get $C2$ in two years. So PV is what one would have to save today to get the same payments the bond makes.

If all the coupon payments are equal, a bond that pays C forever is worth:

$$PV = C/i.$$

A bond that pays C for N years and then stops (with no return of face value) is worth:

$$PV = C/i \times (1 - 1/(1 + i)^n)$$

When the bond pays back its face value, we just add the face value's present value to this term. Note that as N gets large, the value of the bond gets very close to C/i, its value when it pays C forever.

Example: Calculating Present Value

PROBLEM   When the interest rate is 10%, what is the present value of a ten-year bond paying $70 a year for ten years and in the tenth year, an additional $1,000?

SOLUTION $887.11. $80 a year for ten years is worth $491.57 (letting $N = 10$ in the equation above). $1,000 in ten years is worth $387.54 ($1,000 divided by 1.10 to the tenth power).

An important point to remember when investing in bonds is that the price of long-term bonds changes far more when interest rates change than does the price of short-term bonds. This point can be demonstrated by using the formulas above. Suppose the market interest rate is 10%. Bond A pays $1,100 in one year. Bond B pays $100 a year forever. According to our formulas, both have a present value of $1,000. This will also be the price at which they will sell. Now suppose the interest rate goes up to 20%. Bond A's price (and PV) will fall to $916.67, while Bond B's price will fall to $500. Thus, the price of the longer-term bond (Bond B) changes more when the interest rate changes. In general, the value of short-term bonds is far less volatile than that of long-term bonds, and thus short-term bonds are a safer investment; on the other hand, long-term bonds usually pay a higher interest rate to compensate bond buyers for the higher risk.

STEP 2: INTEREST RATES AND INVESTMENT

Businesses sell bonds to raise the funds necessary to finance their investment spending. Each business has a menu of projects that it is interested in undertaking, listing those paying a high rate of return to those that pay little. The menu of returns for these projects is shown by the **marginal efficiency of investment**

curve. This curve, also called the marginal efficiency of capital curve, is shown in Figure 12-3 as *II*.

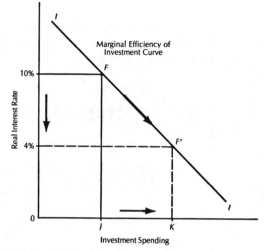

Figure 12-3 The Effect of *Real* Interest Rates on Investment
Spending

The total cost of the best projects paying 10% or more is *J* dollars. Thus, if the interest rate is 10%, investment spending will equal *J* dollars (the rate of return on the project investing the *Jth* dollar equaling 10%). (See Practical Application, Question 10.) But a lower interest rate of 4% makes all projects costing a total of *K* dollars profitable (the project involving the *Kth* dollar breaking even at 4%). A lower interest rate thus increases investment spending (by increasing the number of projects whose returns cover their cost).

The relevant interest rate for investment decisions is the **real interest rate,** since investment projects produce and yield real returns. (See Practical Application, Question 8.) Lower real interest rates also encourage people to borrow to buy homes (which is counted as part of investment spending) and consumer durables (such as cars and washing machines).

STEP 3: INVESTMENT SPENDING AND AGGREGATE DEMAND

A lower interest rate increases investment spending, increasing aggregate demand through the multiplier process. (Review Figure 8-4.)

Example: Effect of Interest Rate on Aggregate Demand

PROBLEM   Assume that (1) for every $20 billion increase in the money supply, interest rates fall 1%, (2) for every 1% fall in interest rates, investment spending increases $50 billion, (3) *MPC* =

0.6, and (4) the economy is on the horizontal section of its aggregate supply curve. How much will a $40 billion increase in the money supply increase aggregate demand?

SOLUTION $250 billion. The interest rate will fall 2%, increasing investment spending $100 billion. The spending multiplier is 2.5 (1/.4) so aggregate demand will go up $250 billion (2.5 × $100 billion).

STEP 4: AGGREGATE DEMAND AND SUPPLY

Suppose the economy is in equilibrium with an interest rate of 10%. Then the Fed increases the money supply enough to reduce the interest rate to 4% (as in Figure 12-2). Investment spending increases from J to K in Figure 12-3: Suppose this increase in I is $20 billion. If the MPC is 0.8, aggregate demand will increase $100 billion ($20 billion/.2).

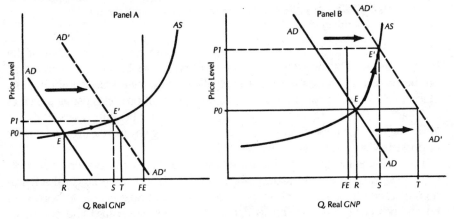

Figure 12-4   The Effect of Aggregate Demand and Supply on Output and Prices

In Figure 12-4, this is shown in both Panel A and Panel B by the horizontal shift in the AD curve from R to T (R to T being $100 billion). But the resulting increase in the price level will partially offset this increase. In Panel A, the economy starts out (at E) with high unemployment and an output below its full-employment level ($R < FE$). Thus, the price increase will be small (from PO to $P1$) so that the increase in real GNP (R to T) will be only slightly less than $100 billion.

But when the economy starts out at or above its full-employment level, as in Panel B ($R > FE$), the main result will be higher prices. The increase in real GNP (R to S) is smaller than it was in Panel A because the increase in prices is higher.

YOU SHOULD REMEMBER

1. Businesses borrow to invest. They invest only in those projects that pay a return greater than or equal to the interest rate.

2. A lower real interest rate increases investment spending.

3. An increase in investment spending increases aggregate demand. How much *AD* increases depends upon the spending multiplier.

4. If aggregate demand shifts to the right, the result will be higher output and prices. The steeper the aggregate supply curve, the more prices will increase and the less output will increase.

THE LONG-RUN EFFECT OF MONEY SUPPLY ON INTEREST RATES

What we have described in the section "How the Money Supply Affects the Economy" is the effect of an increase in the money supply when people do not expect an increase in inflation. When people do not expect higher inflation, an increase in the money supply has a **liquidity effect**: It reduces interest rates and increases investment spending as described above. But when the money supply persistently grows at a high rate, prices will persistently rise. Eventually, people will come to expect inflation. Therefore, persistent increases in the money supply will lead to *higher*, not lower, **nominal interest rates** (which equal the real interest rate *plus* the expected rate of inflation). This is called the **inflationary premium effect**. In this case, real interest rates and investment spending will *not* be affected by increases in the money supply.

YOU SHOULD REMEMBER

1. A faster-growing nominal money supply can cause higher rates of inflation.

2. If people expect higher inflation rates, the nominal interest rate will go up (by the increase in expected inflation).

3. A higher nominal money supply will lower interest rates only if people don't expect higher inflation rates.

THE SPENDING MULTIPLIER AND FISCAL POLICY

The spending multiplier (and thus fiscal policy's impact) is smaller when the effects of money demand are taken into account. Suppose government spending increases but the money supply is held constant. Further, assume prices don't change. Initially, total aggregate demand will increase according to the spending multiplier. *But* the corresponding increase in income will increase money demand. People with higher incomes typically want higher money balances (a 10% increase in real income increases real money demand by between 7% and 10%). The higher money demand creates an excess money demand, resulting in people trying to sell their bonds to get money. The price of bonds will fall, and interest rates will rise. Investment spending will fall. (Economists say that investment spending has been **crowded out** by government spending.) This decrease in investment spending will partially offset the impact of higher government spending. We will have:

G up $\rightarrow$ AD, GNP up $\rightarrow$ M demand up $\rightarrow$ i up $\rightarrow$ I down (offset G up)

For further information on how to solve for national output in the Keynesian model, see the Appendix, page 462.

KNOW THE CONCEPTS
DO YOU KNOW THE BASICS?

1. Why is the opportunity cost of holding money the interest rate that a bond pays?

2. Why does the quantity of money people want to hold go up when the interest rate falls.

3. How can a person reduce money holdings yet spend the same amount of money per period?

4. How does an excess supply of money lead to lower interest rates?

   Hint: What happens to the demand for bonds and bond prices?

5. How does a lower interest rate increase investment spending?

6. Why does aggregate demand go up when interest rates fall?

7. Is it the nominal interest rate or the real interest rate that affects money demand? Investment spending?

8. Why is the horizontal shift in aggregate demand greater than the equilibrium increase in real *GNP*?

9. When will an increase in the money supply cause higher, not lower, interest rates?

10. Why is the spending multiplier weaker when we consider the effects of higher real income on money demand?

TERMS FOR STUDY

bonds	liquidity effect
crowding out	precautionary demand for money
inflationary premium effect	speculative demand for money
interest rate	transaction demand for money

PRACTICAL APPLICATION

1. How will the following events affect interest rates, investment spending, and aggregate demand?
   Event A: The Fed buys government bonds in an open market operation.
   Event B: The Fed sells government bonds in an open market operation.
   Event C: Credit cards are outlawed: The public's demand for money goes up as a consequence.
   Event D: Banking by computers allows the public to more cheaply manage its money holdings: The public's desired money holdings go down.

2. A bond pays $100 a year forever. How much is the bond worth when the interest rate is 20%? 10%? 5%? and 1%?

3. A firm has the following menu of projects, listed in no particular order: project A, with a yield of 12% and a cost of $100,000; project B, with a yield of 8% and a cost of $200,000; project C, with a yield of 10% and a cost of $300,000; and project D, with a yield of 15% and a cost of $250,000. How much will this firm borrow and invest when the interest rate is 12%? 10%? 8%?

4. Describe the effect of a $40 billion increase in the money supply under these conditions: (a) a $40 billion increase in the money supply reduces the interest rate by 1%, (b) a 1% decrease in the interest rate increases investment spending by $60 billion, (c) the spending multiplier is 2.5, and (d) the economy is on the horizontal segment of its aggregate supply curve, so prices don't rise when aggregate demand increases.

5. If the Fed increases the money supply by $40 billion, will it have a bigger or smaller impact on *GNP* than in Question 4 above when we make the following changes? (Treat each change as if it is the only change in Question 4's conditions.) For each of the changes, calculate the increase in *GNP.*

    Change A: A $40 billion increase in the money supply reduces the interest rate by ½%.

    Change B: A 1% decrease in the interest rate increases investment spending by $80 billion.

    Change C: The spending multiplier is 2.0.

    Change D: Prices do rise when aggregate demand increases.

6. Select the correct term from the italicized choices. An increase in the money supply will increase real *GNP* more when:
    a. It decreases the interest rate [*more/less*].
    b. Investment spending responds [*more/less*] to changes in the interest rate.
    c. The multiplier is [*bigger/smaller*].
    d. The aggregate supply curve is [*flatter/steeper*].
    e. Money demand increases [*more/less*] when the interest rate changes.

7. If the quantity of money demanded exceeds its supply, what will happen to interest rates?

8. This problem analyzes why investment spending depends on the *real* interest rate, not the nominal interest rate. To show this, consider a very simple example.

    Case 1. There is no inflation. Axel Widget Company has to pay $10,000 in advance to buy a machine. Axel gets it one year later and produces 1,000 widgets with it, and then the machine falls apart and is worthless. Each widget sells for $11. What are the real and nominal rates of return on this machine?

    Case 2: There is a 20% rate of inflation expected over the year. Axel expects widgets to sell for 20% more ($13.20 each). What are the real and nominal rates of return on the machine?

9. In 1933, the interest rate on Aaa-rated corporate bonds was 4.49%. Consumer prices fell 5.1% in that year. In 1981, the bonds paid 14.16% and prices rose 10.4%. In which year would businesses have had to pay a lower real rate to borrow?

10. At a cost of $2,000, Widget, Inc., can buy a machine that will add $500 to its annual revenues. The annual operating and maintenance costs of the machine will total only $300. The machine (with maintenance) is expected to last forever. What is the highest interest rate at which Widget should be willing to borrow funds to buy this machine?

ANSWERS

KNOW THE CONCEPTS

1. Because instead of holding money, people could hold bonds, which pay interest.

2. At lower interest rates, bonds are less attractive, so people increase their money holdings.

3. The individual would have to hold more of other assets (such as money market funds, bonds, and stocks) and cash them in more frequently.

4. People with an excess supply of money will try to increase their bond holdings, thereby increasing the demand for bonds. Bond prices will go up and interest rates will go down.

5. A lower interest rate makes more investment projects profitable, so total investment spending will go up.

6. A lower interest rate increases investment spending, so aggregate demand will be higher.

7. The basic rule is: Nominal assets (such as money) are affected by the nominal interest rate, and real assets (such as investment in plant and equipment) are affected by real interest rates.

8. A shift to the right in aggregate demand causes prices to go up. So while total dollar spending has gone up, the higher price level means that real spending (and real *GNP*) have gone up less.

9. When people expect a higher growth rate of the money supply to produce higher rates of inflation.

10. Because people want to put some of their higher income into money holdings. This reduces the savings available for investment spending, and therefore investment spending will fall. In turn, this offsets to some degree the initial increase in aggregate demand.

PRACTICAL APPLICATION

1. *Event A:* Increases money supply, causes excess money supply. Bond prices rise, i falls, I rises, and AD goes up.

   Event B: Decreases money supply, causes excess money demand. Bond prices fall, i rises, I falls, and AD falls.

   Event C: Causes excess money demand. i rises, I falls, and AD falls.

   Event D: Causes excess money supply. i falls, I rises, and AD rises.

2. Ask yourself how much you would have to invest at these interest rates to get $100 a year in interest. At 20%, $500. At 10%, $1,000. At 5%, $2,000. At 1%, $10,000. Or in general, $100/$i$, where i is expressed as a decimal (with the decimal point in the percent term moved two places to the left).

3. At 12%, project A just covers its cost, and project D makes a 3% net rate of profit. The firm will invest $350,000. At 10%, it invests in projects A, C, and D, at a total cost of $650,000. At 8%, it invests in projects A, B, C, and D, at a total cost of $850,000.

4. *GNP* will be increased by $150 billion.

5. *Change A:* The increase in *GNP* will be smaller (a $75 billion increase as opposed to the $150 billion increase in Question 4).
   Change B: The increase in *GNP* is bigger: $200 billion.
   Change C: The increase in *GNP* smaller: $120 billion.
   Change D: The increase in *GNP* smaller: When prices go up, the increase in real *GNP* is smaller.

6. (a) more, (b) more, (c) bigger, (d) flatter, (e) less, (e) needs further explanation. When money demand is less sensitive to changes in the interest rate, then the money demand curve in Figure 12-2 is *steeper.* That means when the money supply goes up, interest rates must fall *more* to increase the quantity of money demanded to equal the new supply.

7. People will try to sell bonds to increase their money holdings. This attempt will cause bond prices to fall and interest rates to rise. As a consequence of the higher interest rates, the quantity of money demanded will fall until it equals the money supply.

8. In Case 1, the real and nominal rates of return are the same, since there is no inflation. The rate is 10%. An investment of $10,000 today grows in worth by 10% to $11,000 (the revenues from selling 1,000 widgets at $11).

   In Case 2, the nominal return is 32%. The real return is still 10%. (The real value of $13,200 in sales one year from now is $13,200/1.20, or $11,000. We divide by 1.20 since goods costing $1 today will cost $1.20 in one year.)

9. The relevant rate for businesses is the real rate of interest (= nominal rate − expected rate of inflation). If we assume that the expected rate of inflation is also the current rate of inflation, then the real rate of interest was higher in 1933 than in 1981. In 1933, the real rate of interest was 9.59% (= 4.49% − [−5.1%]; note that when prices fall, we have a *negative* rate of inflation). In 1981, the real rate of interest was only 3.76% (= 14.16% − 10.4%).

10. 10%. The machine's annual return is $200 ($500 − $300). At a 10% interest rate, the annual interest payments on the machine will be $200 (.10 × $2,000). Thus, at 10%, the machine's return just covers its interest cost. At any higher rate, it would prove unprofitable.

13

MONEY AND AGGREGATE DEMAND: MONETARIST MODEL

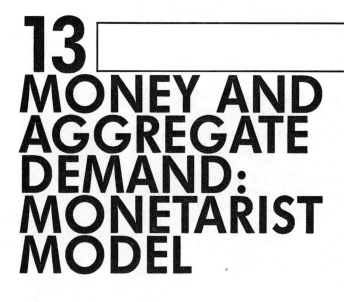

KEY TERMS

the equation of exchange $MV = PQ$, or money × velocity equals price × output.

long-run neutrality of money in the long run, a larger money supply has no effect on output or on relative prices.

quantity theory of money theory that uses the equation of exchange to make predictions by assuming that the annual change in velocity is small and predictable.

velocity the number of times an average dollar is used in a year to buy final goods and services. (Also called "income velocity.")

So far, we have been starting out at some "given" price level without explaining where the given price level came from. In fact, the simple Keynesian Model can't explain how the price level is determined in an economy. In addition, the shifts in the *AD* and *AS* curves that we have examined explain once-and-for-all changes in the price level and *not* persistent inflation. For example, more real government spending can cause prices to go up, say, 1%, but once prices have risen 1%, they will stop rising (unless *G* goes up again). To explain continuing inflation, we need to find a variable that will cause both the *AD* and *AS* curves to shift up *persistently*. This variable is the money supply *(MS)* and the theory that explains why persistent increases in the money supply cause inflation is the **Monetarist Model**.

THE MONETARIST MODEL

Basic Premises

1. *People hold money for different reasons than they save.* Bonds and money are *not* close substitutes.

2. The main factor affecting how much money people hold is their *income,* not the interest rate.

3. Money has its main impact on aggregate demand through its effects on *total spending.* An excess supply of money is spent on goods (and not only on bonds as in the Keynesian Model).

The basic steps of the Monetarist Model are:

MS up $\rightarrow$ Excess Money Supply $\rightarrow$ Spending Up $\rightarrow$ AD up $\rightarrow$ P and Q up

---

THE QUANTITY THEORY OF MONEY

The **quantity theory of money** holds that changes in aggregate demand are mainly explained by changes in the money supply. To see how, let us examine the demand and supply of money.

MONEY DEMAND (MD)

People demand money to make transactions and to meet emergencies. The basic insight of the quantity theory is that as people earn and spend more, they will also want to have larger money holdings. The quantity theory assumes that the money holdings people want will be a certain fraction *(k)* of their income. For the economy as a whole, then:

$$MD = k \times \$GNP = k \times P \times Q$$

where *$GNP* is nominal *GNP* (or total dollar spending, which in turn equals price times output: $\$GNP = P \times Q$).

The fraction k is called the **Cambridge k.** Suppose people want to hold 10% of their income in money holdings (so $k = MD/\$GNP$). If nominal *GNP* (*$GNP*) is $2,000, then they demand $200 in money holdings.

More often, economists refer to the **velocity** of money *(V)*: the number of times, on the average, that people want to spend each dollar each year. $V = \$GNP/MD = 1/k$. Thus, if $MD = \$200$, people would want to spend an average dollar 10 times (1/.10) to support $2,000 in spending.

We thus have:

$$MD = (1/V) \times \$GNP$$

MONEY SUPPLY (MS)

The money supply *(MS)* is determined by the Fed. We regard it as fixed in quantity unless the Fed acts to change it.

How money demand comes to equal the money supply is shown in Figure 13-1. *MS* is fixed by the Fed at *M0*. But the quantity of money demanded goes up as people spend more (i.e., as *$GNP* goes up as shown by the *MD* = (1/V) × *$GNP* line.

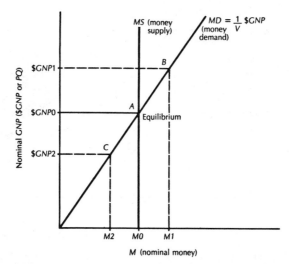

Figure 13-1 How Money Demand Equals Money Supply

Equilibrium occurs at Point *A*: Money demand *(MD)* equals the money supply *(MS)* at a nominal *GNP* of *$GNP0*.

At Point *B*, the economy has an excess demand for money *(MD>MS)* of *M1* − *M0*. People try to increase their money holdings by spending less. But while it is possible for one person to increase money holdings by spending less, it is not possible for everyone to do so. This is because the money supply is fixed. If some people hold more money, others must hold less. But everyone trying to get larger money holdings *instead* reduces spending *and* nominal income. This lowers *$GNP* until money demand returns to Point *A*.

At Point *C*, the economy has an excess supply of money *(MS>MD)* of *M0* − *M2*. People try to get rid of their excess supply of money by spending more, thereby increasing *$GNP*. Once again, the money supply doesn't change; instead, *$GNP* goes up. The higher dollar income increases money demand back to Point *A*.

When *MD* = *MS*, we have:

$$MS = (1/V) \, \$GNP$$
$$MS = (1/V) \, P \times Q$$
$$V \times MS = P \times Q$$
$$M \times V = P \times Q \text{ where } M \text{ is } MS$$

These are all forms of the *equation of exchange,* which forms the basis for the quantity theory of money. For example, if the money supply equals $400 and $V = 20$, total dollar spending (GNP) equals $8,000. If real output (Q) is 2,000 units, P is $4.00 ($8,000/2,000).

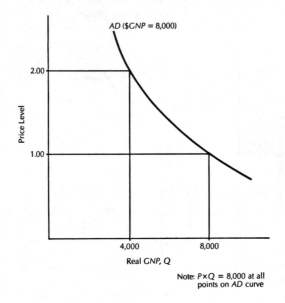

Figure 13-2   Real Spending Versus Dollar Spending

This $8,000 corresponds to the *AD* curve shown in Figure 13-2. At each point on the *AD* curve, price times output $(P \times Q)$ equals $8,000 ($GNP$). Note that aggregate demand refers to *real* spending (Q) while $8,000 is total dollar spending $(P \times Q)$.

THE LONG-RUN NEUTRALITY OF MONEY

In the long run, the economy is at full employment. If the money supply then doubles, what will happen? In the short run, before prices adjust, output will rise. But in the long run, output will return to its full-employment level. With Q and V the same in the long run, prices must have doubled. This result is called the **long-run neutrality of money:** In the long run, money does not affect anything real (it is "neutral").

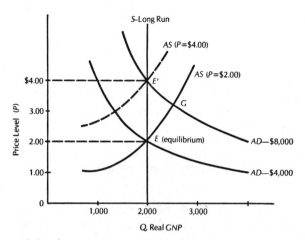

Figure 13-3 The Long-Run Neutrality of Money

Figure 13-3 illustrates this proposition. Suppose full-employment output is 2,000 units of output. This is shown by the long-run *AS* curve (*S*-Long Run). Assume also that people want to hold 10% of their income in money holdings so $V = 10$ (1/.10). Initially, the money supply is $400: *$GNP* must then be $4,000 (10 × $400), corresponding to *AD*-$4,000. If the economy is at full employment, the price level will be $2.00 (since $2.00 × 2,000 = $4,000).

Initially, the economy is at its long-run full-employment equilibrium at *E*. Its short-run *AS* curve corresponds to the price level $2.00. Now let the money supply double to $800. The new *AD* curve is *AD*-$8,000 ($8,000 = 10 × $800): Along this curve, $P × Q = $8,000. In the short run, output increases (to *G*). But prices rise and this will eventually shift the short-run *AS* curve up as workers' wages increase. The economy returns to its long-run full-employment equilibrium (at *E'*) when the price level is $4.00: At this price level, real aggregate demand (*$GNP/P*) equals 2,000 units—the full-employment level of output. The new short-run *AS* curve will be *AS* (*P* = $4.00). Wages will have doubled, all prices will have doubled, and nominal *GNP* will have doubled. But real wages and real output will be the same. Thus, the change in the money supply has had no impact on any real variable in the long run.

It is important to note that in the long run, the *real* money supply (*MS/P*, or $200) is unchanged. While the Fed can change the *nominal* money supply (*MS*), in the long run the public determines what the real supply of money will be by how much it spends (and by the resulting change in *P*). This is a very important point. In the last chapter, the increase in the money supply that reduced *real* interest rates and increased *real* aggregate demand was an increase in the *real money supply* (recall that we held the price level constant to get this result). But while the Fed can increase *MS*, it might *not* be able to increase the real money supply if the public responds to more *MS* by raising prices!

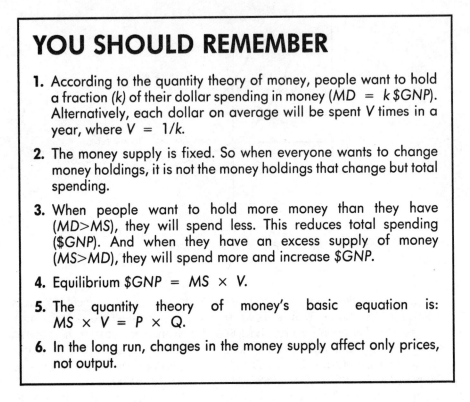

YOU SHOULD REMEMBER

1. According to the quantity theory of money, people want to hold a fraction (*k*) of their dollar spending in money ($MD = k\,\$GNP$). Alternatively, each dollar on average will be spent *V* times in a year, where $V = 1/k$.

2. The money supply is fixed. So when everyone wants to change money holdings, it is not the money holdings that change but total spending.

3. When people want to hold more money than they have ($MD > MS$), they will spend less. This reduces total spending ($\$GNP$). And when they have an excess supply of money ($MS > MD$), they will spend more and increase $\$GNP$.

4. Equilibrium $\$GNP = MS \times V$.

5. The quantity theory of money's basic equation is: $MS \times V = P \times Q$.

6. In the long run, changes in the money supply affect only prices, not output.

HOW TO APPLY THE QUANTITY THEORY OF MONEY

HOW TO PREDICT AGGREGATE DEMAND

1. *Increases in the money supply* shift the *AD* curve right. Suppose $V = 20$. If the money supply increases by $30 billion, $\$GNP$ will increase by $600 billion. So at any given price level, aggregate demand will be higher.

2. *Increases in velocity (V)* shift the *AD* curve right. For example, if *V* increases from 20 to 25 when the money supply is $100 billion, $\$GNP$ will increase from $2,000 to $2,500 billion. So at each price level, aggregate demand will be higher. The main reasons velocity increases are:
   • *Increases in Banking Efficiency:* Credit cards, automatic tellers, and many other recent banking innovations have made it easier to get cash. This has reduced *k* and increased *V*.

- *Increases in Nominal Interest Rates (and Inflation):* These increase the opportunity cost of holding money, causing k to fall and V to rise.
- *Increases in Real Income:* As people get richer, they find it easier to economize on their money holdings, reducing k and increasing V.

YOU SHOULD REMEMBER

1. An increase in V or MS shifts the AD curve to the right.

2. To predict what will happen to aggregate demand, ask how events will affect V and M.

3. Velocity increases when there is an increase in banking efficiency, nominal interest rates go up, or real income goes up.

HOW TO PREDICT INFLATION

To predict what inflation will be, economists put the quantity theory equation into its *percent change* form:

$$\%\Delta P = \%\Delta MS - \%\Delta Q + \%\Delta V$$

$\%\Delta$ stands for "the percent change in." The percent change in prices ($\%\Delta P$) is the inflation rate. $\%\Delta MS$ is the growth rate in the money supply. $\%\Delta Q$ is the growth rate of real *GNP*. For example, if the money supply grows at 10%, output at 3%, and V increases by 1%, inflation will be 8%.

We get the following predictions from this equation (each prediction holds the other variables unchanged):

1. The *rate of inflation will go up* when the money supply grows at a faster rate. If the monetary growth rate goes up 5%, the rate of inflation will go up 5%.

2. The *rate of inflation will go down* when output grows at a faster rate. For example, if output growth increases from 1% to 3%, the inflation rate will fall 2%.

3. Usually, Q and V change so little that high rates of inflation (of 6% or more) can be caused only by high growth rates in the money supply.

YOU SHOULD REMEMBER

1. Inflation will be higher (a) the faster the money supply grows, (b) the slower output grows, and (c) the faster V increases.

2. Inflation will be lower (a) the slower the money supply grows, (b) the faster output grows, and (c) the slower V increases.

THE DIFFERENCES BETWEEN KEYNESIAN AND MONETARIST VIEWS

Most texts list the disagreements between Keynesians and Monetarists. Typically on these lists are the following issues:

- *How fast will the economy recover on its own from a recession?* Monetarists generally believe that the economy will usually be at full employment unless the government acts to destabilize the economy. In addition, Monetarists believe in a faster recovery time than Keynesians.

- *What causes recessions?* Monetarists believe that most recessions have been caused by sharp decreases in the growth rate of the money supply. They point to the Great Depression (when the money supply was cut by one-third) and to the 1981–82 recession (when the money growth rate was cut by one-half). Keynesians believe that changes in investment spending (and consumer durable spending) have caused our recessions. They point to the dramatic decline in investment that has preceded most of our recessions.

- *Should the government actively try to keep the economy at full employment?* Economists have identified several key "lags" in using economy policy to actively affect the economy (which is called **discretionary economic policy**). Suppose the economy is in a recession. The first lag is the **recognition lag**: It takes time for the government to recognize that something is wrong with the economy. The second lag is the **implementation lag**: It takes time for the government to implement its policy and take action. The final lag is the **effectiveness lag**: It takes time for government action to affect the economy. If these lags are too long and if their length is uncertain, the effect of discretionary policy can be for the government to do the wrong thing at the wrong time. For example, a policy to dampen inflation may impact the economy later when it's in a recession, making the recession worse. Monetarists believe the government should steer a steady course by following a set of fixed rules (such as increasing the money supply at a steady 4%). Keynesians, on the other hand, more readily advocate discretionary policy action, although many now reject trying to "fine-tune" the economy with continual discretionary policy action.

- *How productive is government spending?* Keynesians believe that government spending can have a strong positive effect on our economy. Investments in basic research, in highways, and in related projects have produced very good results. Monetarists tend to doubt that most added government programs will be efficient.

- *How harmful are higher taxes?* Keynesians believe that if government spending is productive, then the higher taxes needed to support the government spending will not harm the economy. Supply-side economists and Monetarists believe that taxes reduce aggregate supply and slow the growth rate of output.

- *How steep is the aggregate supply curve and how fast does it shift up when prices go up?* Keynesians tend to believe the AS curve is flat (especially when the economy is in a recession) and is slow to shift up when prices increase. Monetarists tend to believe that the AS curve is steep and that it will shift up quickly when prices increase.

- *Is investment spending insensitive to changes in the interest rates?* Some texts set forth the position that investment spending is insensitive to changes in the interest rate as Keynesian, which it is, but some texts then ascribe the opposite belief to Monetarists. They state this in the context of the model in Chapter 12, where money supply affects aggregate demand only through changing the interest rate and investment spending. But Monetarists don't believe this is the main way monetary policy affects the economy (except perhaps in the short run). Monetarists believe that more money causes people to spend more *even if the interest rate doesn't change!*

So who is right? Over the years, Monetarists and Keynesians, by studying real-world data, have come closer in their beliefs about the economy. Almost all economists, for example, believe that very high rates of inflation can be caused only by high rates of monetary growth. Most Monetarists acknowledge that fiscal policy can affect the interest rate (and thus *V*) and that increases in government spending have stimulated the economy in the past. Finally, most economists will predict a recession when the money supply's growth rate is decreased dramatically.

KNOW THE CONCEPTS

DO YOU KNOW THE BASICS?

1. What variable affects money demand the most in the Monetarist Model? In the Keynesian Model?

2. What two variables determine aggregate demand in the quantity theory model?

3. How will inflation and the growth rate of output be related (when the growth rates of *MS* and *V* don't change)?

4. When we observe output growing faster, does it mean inflation will fall?

5. Why, in the long run, does a change in the money supply not affect anything real, including real output and the real money supply?

6. Why, in the long run, does a change in the money supply change all prices and nominal incomes by the same percent?

7. How does the public, not the government, determine what real money supply it wants to hold?

8. What causes a difference between desired spending and income in the Monetarist Model? In the Keynesian Model?

9. If people have an excess supply of money, how do they try to reduce their money holdings?

10. How does fiscal policy stimulate the economy in the quantity theory of money?

TERMS FOR STUDY

Cambridge *k*	quantity theory of money
equation of exchange	quantity theory of money (percent change form)
neutrality of money	rules versus discretion
nominal income	velocity

PRACTICAL APPLICATION

1. Using the quantity theory, how will the following events affect the money supply, *V,* and nominal income (or *$GNP*)?

Event A: Because of widespread bank failures, the public increases its cash holdings.

Event B: Credit cards become widely used.

Event C: The money supply is reduced.

Event D: The nominal interest rate rises.

2. If money demand equals 5% of income, the money supply is $60, and real *GNP* is 1,000 units of output, what will the price level be? What will the price level be if the money supply is $120? What happens to nominal income? To real money holdings?

3. An economic forecaster predicts that output will grow by 4% next year, the money supply will grow at 10%, and *V* will follow its historical pattern of growing at 3% per year. What will be the predicted rate of inflation?

4. A small country produces 5,000 units of output and has a money supply of $2,000. Its citizens want to hold 10% of their income in money ($k = 0.10$).
   a. What are V, GNP, P, and the real money supply (MS/P).
   b. If the money supply doubles to $4,000 but real output and V stay the same, what will GNP, P, and the real money supply be?

5. Suppose you believe that over the next thirty years V will increase by 2% annually, output will grow at 3% per year, and the money supply will grow at 9% per year. Would you invest in a thirty-year bond paying 10% if you want a real return of 6%?

6. Show with an *AD* and *AS* diagram how a decrease in the money supply can cause a recession and how the economy can recover on its own.

7. Assume that V is constant. Assume the money supply is growing at 10% and output at 3%. The real rate of interest is 5%. What is the nominal rate of interest? What will happen to interest rates, real and nominal, if the money-supply growth rate drops to 4% and the public has fully anticipated this event?

8. In a small country, $MS = \$300$, $V = 10$, and $Q = 1,500$.
   a. What is P?
   b. If MS falls to 250 and the price level does *not* change, what will happen to Q?
   c. If 1,500 is the full-employment level of output, what will P be in the long run?

9. In terms of the quantity theory, how could unions raise the rate of inflation? Could a 10% inflation rate be explained by union activity?

10. Can higher oil prices cause inflation?

ANSWERS

KNOW THE CONCEPTS

1. In the Monetarist Model, income. In the Keynesian model, interest rates.

2. The money supply (MS) and velocity (V).

3. Nominal income ($\$GNP$) grows at a rate equal to $\%\Delta MS + \%\Delta V$. This in turn equals $\%\Delta P + \%\Delta Q$ ($= \%\Delta\$GNP$). So when the growth rate of output ($\%\Delta Q$) increases 1%, inflation ($\%\Delta P$) falls 1%.

4. Holding aggregate demand (i.e, MS and V) constant, more output means lower prices. But output may be growing because aggregate demand is increasing. In this case, prices will increase.

5. In the long run, prices adjust to assure full employment. The full-employment level of output (Q') will be unchanged. The real money supply (MS/P) will also be unchanged if V is the same, since $MS/P = Q'/V$.

6. Since Q and V are constant in the long run, the real money supply will be the same. So when MS increases a certain percent, all prices will have to increase the same percent in order that people have the same real money supply.

7. If the public wants a certain real level of money holdings, it will change its spending and thus the price level until it gets the level of MS/P it wants.

8. In the Monetarist Model, a difference between desired spending and income is caused by either an excess demand for money ($MD>MS$) or an excess supply of money ($MS>MD$). An excess demand reduces desired spending, and an excess supply increases it. In the Keynesian Model, the difference is caused by changes in desired spending (particularly investment spending).

9. People will try to reduce their money holdings by increasing their spending. For one person, this will reduce the person's money holdings. But for all persons, the sum of all money holdings is fixed and equal to the money supply. By everyone's effort to reduce their money holdings, total spending and income will go up.

10. By increasing the interest rate and increasing V.

PRACTICAL APPLICATION

1. *Event A:* MS down, V down, $\$GNP$ down. (This happened in the Great Depression.) Note that the change in $\$GNP$ is also the change in aggregate demand.

Event B: MS unchanged, V up, $GNP up.
Event C: MS down, V unchanged, $GNP down.
Event D: MS unchanged, V up, $GNP up.

2. $P = MS/kQ$. k is 0.05 and $V = 20$. In the first case, P equals $1.20. In the second case, $2.40. $GNP equals V times MS, increasing from $1,200 to $2,400. Note that P also equals GNP/Q. The real money supply (MS/P) equals 5% of real income or $50 (in *real* dollars). In the first case, it's $60/1.20; in the second, $120/2.40.

3. 9% (10% + 3% − 4%).

4. a. $V = 10$. $GNP = $20,000. $P = $4.00. $MS/P = 500$.
   b. $GNP = $40,000. $P = $8.00. $MS/P = 500$.

5. You should believe that inflation will be 8%. The real rate of interest on the bond will only be 2%. You should not buy the bond.

6. A fall in the money supply reduces $GNP and shifts the *AD* curve left. In the short run, the short-run *AS* curve remains unchanged, so prices and output will fall as the economy sinks into a recession. In the long run, the *AS* curve will shift down as wages fall. This will reduce prices further and shift the economy to the right along the new *AD* curve to full employment. (See Practical Application, Question 8, for an illustration of these events.)

7. Inflation will be 7%. The nominal interest rate will be 12% (5% + 7%). If money supply growth falls to 4%, inflation will fall to 1%. The nominal interest rates will fall to 6% (5% + 1%). The real interest rate will still be 5%.

8. a. $P = $2.00.
   b. $Q = 1,250$ (i.e., the economy is in a recession).
   c. $P = $1.67 (when prices fall, the economy returns to full employment).

9. Unions do not affect the money supply or V. So they can affect inflation only by reducing output growth. To increase inflation by 1%, they must reduce output growth by 1%. To cause a 10% rate of inflation, they would have to reduce national output by 10%. Unions have never been observed causing output to fall this drastically: They cannot be a major cause of inflation.

10. Higher oil prices will not affect the money supply or V. So they affect inflation only by reducing output growth. Some economists estimated that output grew about 1% to 2% slower for several years because of the oil price increases in the '70s. Thus, higher oil prices added only 1% to 2% to the inflation rate. So why did our economy have such a high inflation rate (12%) when oil prices went up? Because the Fed dramatically increased the growth rate of the money supply. In Germany and Japan, the inflation rates were low and almost unaffected by the higher oil prices, because the money growth rate was kept low.

14
INFLATION AND UNEMPLOYMENT

KEY TERMS

accelerationist theory theory that unemployment cannot be permanently reduced through inflation.

natural rate of unemployment unemployment rate determined by demand and supply for workers such that employers and workers are paying and receiving the real wages they expected.

Phillips Curve (PC) curve showing trade-off between inflation and unemployment when the public's expected rate of inflation is unchanged.

We are now ready to use our models to explain the business cycle. So far, we've developed both the Keynesian and Monetarist models of aggregate demand. Now, we'll ask how increases in aggregate demand will affect prices and output. To get our answer, we need to know what causes the short-run aggregate supply curve to shift.

WHAT CAUSES SHIFTS IN THE SHORT-RUN AGGREGATE SUPPLY CURVE *(AS)*?

Along any given short-run *AS* curve, nominal wages *(W)* are held constant. But how are these wages set? In a competitive economy, real wages *(W/P)* will be set so the demand and supply for labor are equal. The labor market will then be in equilibrium and the economy at full employment. But workers must contract ahead of time to work for a money wage *(W)*. They will set *W* so that their expected real wage *(W/P)* will be consistent with full employment.

For example, suppose the labor market is in equilibrium when the real wage is $5.00. That is, at a real wage of $5.00, the demand for workers equals the supply of workers and the economy is, by definition, at full employment. If workers expect a price level of 200 (so $P = 2.00$), they will receive a nominal wage of $10.00 at full employment ($10/2.00 = $5.00). The short-run aggregate supply (AS) curve associated with a nominal wage of $10 is thereby also the AS curve associated with an expected price level of 200. Skipping ahead for the moment to Figure 14-2, if full-employment output is 4,000 units, and then AS-0 (in Panel A) is the AS curve associated with an expected price level of 200 since at full employment ($Q = 4,000$), the actual price level on this curve is 200. Similarly, AS-1 in Figure 14-2 is associated with the expected price level of 220.

To find the expected price level associated with each AS curve, find the price level at which it intersects the full-employment level of output.

YOU SHOULD REMEMBER

1. Wages are constant along each short-run AS curve.

2. Workers must estimate what the future price level will be and then contract for money wages. Money wages will be set so the expected real wage assures workers of being fully employed.

3. The expected price level for each AS curve is the price level at which it intersects the full-employment level of output.

4. An increase in the expected price level increases money wages and shifts the AS curve up.

THE RELATIONSHIP BETWEEN THE *AS* CURVE AND THE PHILLIPS CURVE

If the aggregate supply curve stays fixed, then a rightward shift in the *AD* curve will increase prices and output and reduce unemployment. To describe the resulting relationship between prices and unemployment, economists use the **Phillips Curve**. There is one Phillips Curve for each aggregate supply curve. It shows how prices and unemployment are inversely related when the *AD* curve shifts and the *AS* curve (and thus wages and the expected inflation rate) stays constant.

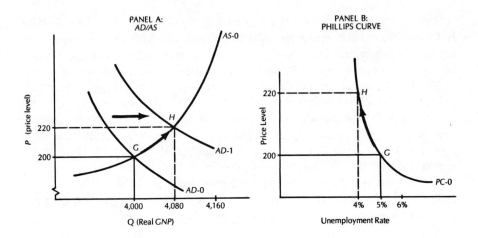

Figure 14-1   The Effect of Supply and Demand on the Phillips Curve

Figure 14-1 shows how we draw a Phillips Curve. In Panel A, we have aggregate supply curve AS-0. If aggregate demand is AD-0, the price level will be 200 and output will be 4,000 units. Assume this corresponds to a 5% unemployment rate. In Panel B, this is Point G. Now suppose AD shifts to AD-1. This increase in aggregate demand moves the economy from Point G to Point H. Output goes up 2% to 4,080 units. The price level is now 220. Suppose the 2% added output reduces unemployment by one percentage point to 4%. (This would correspond to Okun's Law.) We connect Points G and H to get the Phillips Curve PC-0 that is derived from AS-0. On the Phillips Curve, price and unemployment are inversely related: When one goes up, the other goes down.

Along the Phillips Curve, *higher* prices result in more output and *less* unemployment because when only AD shifts, prices and unemployment move in opposite directions. The rise in prices caused by a rightward shift in AD is called **demand-pull inflation**: the shift in AD "pulling" the economy up the AS curve.

Why does a higher price level result in more output and employment? Assume that workers contract with employers in the short run to work whenever the employers want them to at a certain nominal wage. Workers set this nominal wage based upon what they think the price level is. But if inflation is higher than expected, they will be "fooled" into working for a lower real wage. Employers will hire more workers at the lower real wage, increasing output and reducing unemployment. So, the more inflation and prices exceed expected levels, the higher will be the level of output and employment and the lower will be the rate of unemployment.

YOU SHOULD REMEMBER

1. The Phillips Curve describes how prices and unemployment are related when aggregate supply is unchanged.

2. When the aggregate supply curve has not changed, higher prices mean less unemployment.

HOW SHIFTS AFFECT THE *AS* CURVE AND THE PHILLIPS CURVE

An increase in costs will shift up the *AS* curve and the Phillips Curve. In Figure 14-2, *AS*-0 is the aggregate supply curve we had in Figure 14-1 (and *PC*-0 is its corresponding Phillips Curve).

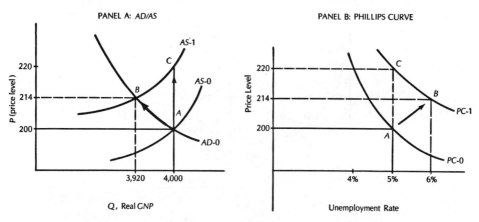

Figure 14-2 The Effect of Stagflation on the Phillips Curve

Let us start in Panel A with *AD*-0 at Point *A*. Suppose wages and other input costs go up such that aggregate supply shifts up to *AS*-1. To have firms produce 4,000 units of output with unemployment equaling 5%, prices now must rise to 220 to cover the higher costs. This is Point *C* on *AS*-1 and *PC*-1 (in Panels A and B respectively). But the economy will go to Point *B*. When output falls to 3,920 units, unemployment rises to 6%. So at Point *B* on the Phillips Curve, the price level is 214 and the unemployment rate is 6%.

When the *AS* curve shifts up, the economy goes from Point *A* to Point *B*: Prices go up, output goes down, and unemployment goes up. Prices and unemployment move up together: This is called *stagflation*. The increase in prices caused by the *AS* curve shifting up is called **cost-push inflation**.

YOU SHOULD REMEMBER

1. When nominal wages and other costs increase, the aggregate supply curve and the Phillips Curve shift up.

2. If aggregate demand doesn't change, a higher aggregate supply curve (and a higher Phillips curve) will result in higher prices, lower output, and more unemployment: This is called stagflation.

VISUALIZING THE BUSINESS CYCLE

• A RECESSION

The following describes a typical recession, starting at full employment.

Suppose workers have an expected price level of 220 and set their money wages accordingly: AS-0 is the AS curve associated with an expected price level of 220, and PC-0 is the Phillips Curve associated with an expected price level of 220. See Figure 14-3.

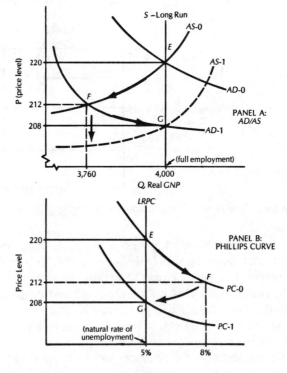

Figure 14-3   The Effect of Recession on the Phillips Curve

Assume the economy is at full employment with $Q = 4,000$ (shown by the Long-Run Aggregate Supply Curve, S-Long Run) and an unemployment rate of 5% with AD-0 and AS-0. The economy will be at E in both panels. Then the government reduces AD from AD-0 to AD-1. As a consequence, the economy goes from Point E to Point F in both panels. Prices have fallen to 212, real wages will go up, and employment will fall. Unemployment increases from 5% to 8%. Output falls 6% to 3,780 units. Note that the actual price level (212) is below the price level that workers were expecting (220). Workers will be getting a higher real wage than they had initially expected when contracting with employers for work. The result is that employers will hire fewer workers and the economy will produce less than its full-employment level of output.

Once workers realize the price level has fallen, they will reduce the money wages they're requesting. In addition, the higher unemployment will force wages down. The AS curve will then shift down from AS-0 until it reaches AS-1 (it may take some time to do this). AS-1 is the AS curve associated with an expected price level of 208. The economy will move from Point F to Point G. The Phillips Curve will shift from PC-0 to PC-1: PC-1 is the Phillips Curve associated with an expected price level of 208. Prices and unemployment will fall. Unemployment returns to its full-employment level of 5%. Output has returned to its full-employment level of 4,000 at a price level of 208.

YOU SHOULD REMEMBER

1. Recessions are caused mainly by decreases in aggregate demand.
2. The economy returns from a recession back to full employment as wages and prices fall.
3. It is the decline in people's expected price level that causes the Phillips Curve and the aggregate supply curve to shift down.

• *AN EXPANSION*

The following sequence of events describes a typical economic expansion starting at full employment.

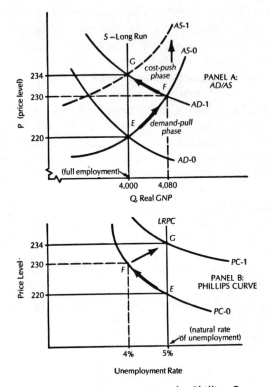

Figure 14-4   The Effect of Expansion on the Phillips Curve

Suppose workers expect the price level to be 220: This corresponds to AS-0 and AD-0 in Figure 14-4. Assuming the economy is in equilibrium at full employment, the initial price level is 220 and unemployment is 5%. Then suppose AD shifts to AD-1. In the short run, the economy shifts from Point E to Point F in both panels: Prices go up to 230, output goes up 2% to 4,080, and unemployment falls to 4%. Note that the expected price level (220) is below the actual price level (230), so workers are getting a lower real wage than expected. As a consequence of the lower real wage, employers will hire more workers. This is the demand-pull inflation phase of the business cycle (since it's caused by the shift in AD).

The higher price level and the tight labor market will cause workers to demand higher nominal wages. AS will shift up. Eventually it will reach AS-1. The Phillips Curve similarly shifts, from PC-0 to PC-1. The economy moves from Point F to Point G as prices rise to 234, output falls back to 4,000, and unemployment returns to its natural level of 5%. This is the cost-push phase of the business cycle (since it's caused by the shift in AS).

The first phase of the expansion (or recession) was demand-push; the second, cost-push. Note though that the cost-push phase is *caused* by the demand-push phase.

YOU SHOULD REMEMBER

1. An expansion in aggregate demand can push output above its full-employment level, but this higher output is not sustainable.

2. The economy returns from overemployment to full employment as prices and costs go up.

3. The increase in people's expected price level causes the aggregate supply curve to shift up.

INFLATION AND THE PHILLIPS CURVE

The Phillips Curve related price levels with unemployment. More often, the Phillips Curve is shown relating inflation to unemployment. To change the above Phillips Curves from price level on the vertical axis to the inflation rate, take the prior year's price level and calculate how much prices have increased. Thus, if the prior year's price level was 200 in Figure 14-1, Point *G* corresponds to a zero rate of inflation, Point *F* to a 5% rate of inflation, and Point *E*, to 10%. In Figure 14-3, if the prior year's price level was 200, Point *E* corresponds to a 10% rate of inflation, *F* to 6%, and *G* to 4%.

Figure 14-5 shows the Phillips Curve *PC*-A associated with Figure 14-4 (with corresponding points) when the prior year's price level was 200 and when the expected price level was 220 (so people were expecting a 10% rate of inflation). *PC*-A is associated with *AS*-0. If people initially expected a 17% rate of inflation, the Phillips Curve instead would have been *PC*-B.

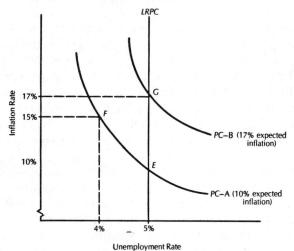

Figure 14-5 The Effect of Inflation on the Phillips Curve

Because the *AS* curve shifts up when workers expect higher wages, the *AD* and *AS* curves have to be *redrawn* each period when there is persistent and expected inflation. Fortunately, the standard Phillips Curve (with the inflation rate on its vertical axis) remains unchanged as long as the expected rate of inflation stays unchanged. But if workers come to expect higher rates of inflation, the *PC* shifts up.

• *THE ACCELERATIONIST THEORY*

The natural rate of unemployment is that level of unemployment at which the price level that workers and other suppliers have expected equals the actual price level. Thus, while there is frictional unemployment (from employers and workers adjusting to new information and changing economic conditions), there is no additional unemployment at the natural rate due to mistaken expectations about the general price level or other macroeconomic variables. In a free economy without governmental restraints or unions, the natural rate occurs when the economy is fully employed: when the demand and supply for labor are equal (but allowing for frictional unemployment). Unions and minimum wage laws will keep the demand for labor from equaling its supply, but studies have shown that their effect on total employment is small.

The **accelerationists** argue that there is no long-run trade-off between inflation and unemployment. They argue as follows. The government in effect can get less unemployment only by fooling workers as to what their real wages are. It does this by pushing prices up more than workers expected. This causes workers to get less in real wages than what they had expected. In turn, the lower real wages cause employers to hire more workers and reduce unemployment. But the government can't fool workers forever. As they catch on, wages will catch up; the economy will return to full employment. So to keep unemployment below its natural rate, the government has to keep the inflation rate ahead of what workers expect it to be. But like a dog chasing its tail, inflation keeps going up as workers' expectations keep chasing it: *Inflation must keep accelerating to keep unemployment below its natural level.* The story ends with a total collapse of the monetary system or the government giving up its attempt to reduce unemployment below its natural rate.

The accelerationists indicate that, with no permanent trade-off between unemployment and inflation, society faces a **long-run Phillips Curve** (labeled *LRPC* in Figures 14-3, 14-4, and 14-5) that is vertical at the natural rate of unemployment. This is the only rate of unemployment that can be sustained in the long run, and it is the rate the economy returns to in the long run.

YOU SHOULD REMEMBER

1. According to the accelerationists, only the natural rate of unemployment is sustainable in the long run. The long-run Phillips Curve is a vertical line at the natural rate of unemployment.

2. To lower unemployment below its natural rate, inflation must rise at an ever-accelerating rate.

THE BUSINESS CYCLE

CAN ECONOMIC RECOVERY BE MADE FASTER?

In the Great Depression, it took ten years (from 1929 to 1939) for the economy to return to its 1929 level of real *GNP*, and even this was not a full recovery since the economy would normally have grown 37% in ten years. It took over four years for the U.S. economy to fully recover from the 1981–82 recession. Is there anything our government can do to make recovery go faster?

If you review this chapter's section on "A Recession," you will see that the speed of recovery depends upon how fast the aggregate supply curve shifts down. That is, recovery is faster if wages and other costs fall faster. Four methods of lowering wages and other costs are:

1. *Wage and Price Controls:* The government explicitly tells firms and unions what prices and wages they can set. Milder forms of controls include "jawboning" ("encouraging" firms and unions to cooperate) and wage and price guidelines (with set ranges of price and wage increases).

In the past, wage and price controls generally have failed in that prices quickly shot up once the controls were removed. The drawbacks include (a) the shortages that result from price ceilings, (b) the impossibility of monitoring cheating in the hundreds of thousands of firms in our economy (see Practical Application, Question 9), and (c) the temptation for the government to increase aggregate demand (and thus the ultimate increase in prices) with the excuse that "price controls will control inflation." As an example of (c), during the wage-price freeze of 1971–1973, the growth rate of the money supply increased from 4.8% (in 1970) to 8.1% (in 1972).

2. *Tax-Based Income Policy (TIP):* In this untried plan, the government increases taxes on firms and workers who raise prices too much and reduces taxes for those who keep their prices within guidelines. The advantages of this policy are that it (a) rewards those that comply (thus assuring wider compliance) and (b) is more flexible than wage and price controls, allowing goods in demand to go up in price.

   The potential drawbacks of this program include (a) the possibility that higher taxes will shift the aggregate supply curve to the left and raise prices even more, and (b) the fact that changing demand will cause consumers to increase the prices of the goods they want more of and decrease the prices of the goods they want less of. The TIP plan thus taxes those goods people want more of and in effect subsidizes those goods people don't want. This is inefficient, though possibly not as inefficient as wage and price controls.

3. *Supply-Side Incentives for Increasing Output:* By reducing marginal taxes and cutting back on transfer programs, it is possible to shift aggregate supply to the right. This will reduce inflation and increase output. The magnitude of these changes is uncertain. For example, it would take a 5% increase in output to reduce inflation by 5%: We have rarely witnessed such high annual increases in output over long periods of time, and certainly have not seen them result from tax decreases.

4. *Removing Barriers to Lower Prices:* By abolishing minimum wage laws and by reducing the powers of monopolies (including the monopoly power of unions), it may be possible to shift prices down faster. But the political likelihood of such an approach is small.

YOU SHOULD REMEMBER

1. Various methods have been tried or proposed to speed the reduction in wages and prices that is necessary for an economy to recover from a recession.

2. Wage and price controls have been tried in the past, and worked temporarily, but ultimately did not reduce prices below what they would have been.

CAN INFLATION (AT FULL EMPLOYMENT) BE REDUCED?

Some of the above programs have been suggested to reduce inflation when the economy is at full employment. The issue is whether inflation can then be reduced *even if* aggregate demand is not reduced. Proponents of wage and price controls and TIPS argue that by reducing the expectation of higher prices, they will reduce how much the *AS* curve will shift up, and thus reduce inflation.

Opponents point out that if the *AD* curve does not *also* shift down, the expected price level cannot be permanently reduced: In the long run, people will expect prices to be where the *AD* curve intersects the long-run aggregate supply curve. So, if aggregate demand is unchanged, wage and price controls will not lower price expectations. Returning to our bathtub analogy (see Figure 8-5), wage and price controls would then be like trying to keep the bathtub from overflowing by hitting the top of the water. Instead, the tap needs to be turned off.

The real issue is whether the public has correctly anticipated what prices are going to be. If their expectations are too high, *then* wage and price controls might help reduce the public's price expectations.

The main way to reduce inflation when the economy is near or at full employment is to reduce aggregate demand. Doing this quickly is called going "**cold turkey.**" The idea is to break inflationary expectations quickly and abruptly. Reducing *AD* slowly is called **gradualism.** This, it is claimed, allows workers and other suppliers to work out new contracts and reduce wages and costs without the loss in output that has occurred in the past when our economy has gone cold turkey. Both policies depend upon the credibility of our government. If people don't believe the government is really going to reduce aggregate demand (either quickly or slowly), then a recession will result: It will be deep and short under the cold-turkey approach and shallow but long under the gradualist approach.

Finally, we come to those who claim that indexing can make it easier for our economy to live with inflation. All these methods involve *indexing*, whereby a monetary cost or payment is automatically adjusted whenever a specified price index (such as the CPI) changes. These methods include the following. [Note that (1) and (2) are already widespread, (3) is currently in effect, and (4) and (5) have been proposed.]

1. Indexing wages with cost-of-living adjustment (COLA) clauses.

2. Indexing interest rates on mortgages and bonds to change with short-term interest rates or with inflation.

3. Indexing the tax code to avoid bracket creep (so people with the same real income do not get pushed by inflation into a higher tax bracket).

4. Indexing the tax code so that inflationary premiums on interest and capital gains are not taxed (since they do not represent real added income).

5. Indexing depreciation costs so that firms can depreciate equipment at current costs and not at historic costs (which don't reflect inflation).

> # YOU SHOULD REMEMBER
>
> 1. Wage and price controls will reduce inflation only if they reduce a false impression by the public of where prices are going to be.
> 2. Some of the main issues are whether inflation should be reduced quickly ("going cold turkey") or slowly (gradualism) and whether people can learn to live with inflation through indexing.

KNOW THE CONCEPTS
DO YOU KNOW THE BASICS?

1. How can you tell what the expected price level is by looking at the *AD/AS* diagram?

2. How can you tell what the expected rate of inflation is by looking at the Phillips Curve?

3. Along a Phillips Curve, how are inflation, unemployment, and output related? What is being held constant?

4. In what sense are workers "fooled" by inflation?

5. How will the economy eventually get to the price level where the *AD* curve intersects the long-run aggregate supply curve?

6. Will a higher rate of inflation always reduce unemployment?

7. What happens to the Phillips Curve when people expect higher rates of inflation?

8. Why must inflation accelerate in order to reduce unemployment below its natural rate?

9. What rate of unemployment and what output level can be sustained in the long run?

10. If wage and price controls worked, how could they help speed the recovery of an economy?

TERMS FOR STUDY

accelerationist theory
cold turkey and gradualism
demand-pull and cost-push inflation
expected rate of inflation

long-run Phillips Curve
natural rate of unemployment
Phillips Curve
tax-based income policy (TIP)

PRACTICAL APPLICATION

1. Use the following Phillips Curve schedule and answer the following questions.

   Inflation Rate: 20 14 10 8 7 6.5
   Unemployment Rate: 3   4   5 6 7 8

   a. If natural rate of unemployment is 6%, what is the expected rate of inflation?

   b. If inflation falls from 8% to 7%, what will happen to unemployment (if expectations about inflation don't change)

2. Construct the aggregate supply curve associated with the above Phillips Curve schedule, assuming (a) the price level in the prior period was 100, (b) full-employment output is 2,000 units, which corresponds with a 6% unemployment rate, and (c) for every 1% change in unemployment, output changes 2% in the opposite direction (this being one version of Okun's Law). To keep the math simple, assume that every 2% change in output equals 40 units of output (2% of 2,000).

3. Workers expect inflation to be 20% and the economy is fully employed. Then the Fed acts to reduce the inflation rate to 10%. What will happen in the short run? In the long run?

4. Describe what is happening in each of the following three graphs. Assume that the initial change (from Point A to Point B) is caused by a shift in the aggregate demand or aggregate supply curve, and then the economy's self-correcting mechanism operates from Point B to Point C. For each panel, identify (a) which curve is shifting (AS or AD), (b) how and why it is shifting, and (c) how the economy gets back to full employment.

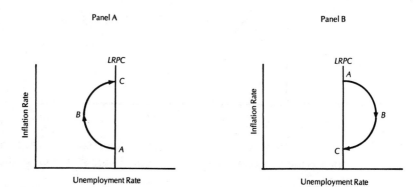

Panel A   Panel B

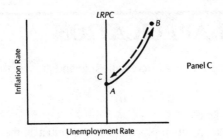

Panel C

5. What phase of the business cycle (the demand-push or the cost-pull phase of an expansion or a recession) is economy in when these statements are made?
   a. "Unions have negotiated for lower wages so as to retain their jobs."
   b. "Unemployment has fallen dramatically as inflation has accelerated."
   c. "Firms have been forced by recent wage hikes to raise their prices and produce less."

6. Wage inflation is related to expected inflation by the following equation:

$$\text{Percent Change in Wages} = \text{Expected Rate of Inflation} + \text{Percent Change in Productivity}$$

   If expected inflation is 10% and productivity increases by 2%, how much will wages change?

7. Use the following graph to answer these questions (assume the economy starts at Point A):

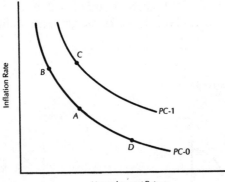

   a. If the Fed increases the growth rate of the money supply, to which point is the economy most likely to move in the short run? In the long run?
   b. If the government decreases government spending, to which point is the economy likely to move in the short run?

    c. Workers come to expect a higher rate of inflation, and they demand higher wages. To which point might the economy move?

8. "Changes in employment and output are caused by how wages and prices change *relative* to each other." Explain.

9. Suppose you own International Widget Works. How could you evade wage and price controls before and after they are enacted?

10. How could wage and price controls appear to be holding down inflation when in fact they are not?

ANSWERS
KNOW THE CONCEPTS

1. The expected price level is where the *AS* curve intersects the long-run aggregate supply curve (i.e., at full employment).

2. The expected inflation rate is where the Phillips Curve intersects the long-run Phillips Curve (at the natural rate of unemployment).

3. More inflation means less unemployment and so more output. The *AS* curve and the expected rate of inflation are held constant along the Phillips Curve.

4. Workers set their wages based upon what they think the price level will be. But if inflation is greater than they expected, they will have been "fooled" into accepting a lower real wage than they wanted.

5. If output differs from the full-employment level of output, workers will adjust their expectations and wages so the *AS* curve shifts the economy along the *AD* curve towards full employment.

6. No. Inflation reduces unemployment only if inflation is higher than expected. If it's lower than expected, unemployment will go up.

7. If people expect higher rates of inflation, they will demand higher wages and raise other factor costs. The Phillips Curve and the *AS* curve will shift up.

8. Because if inflation doesn't accelerate, the expected rate of inflation will catch up with the actual rate, returning unemployment to its natural level.

9. Only the natural rate of unemployment and the full-employment level of output can be sustained in the long run.

10. Wage and price controls could speed the recovery of an economy if they corrected the mistaken judgment of people as to how high prices and inflation will be. This would cause the *AS* curve to shift more quickly towards full employment.

PRACTICAL APPLICATION

1. **a.** 8%
   b. Unemployment will rise to 7%

2. See the figure below.

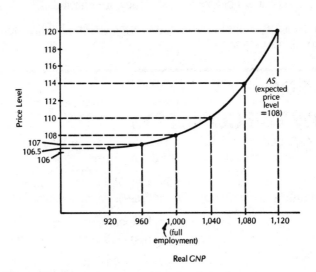

3. Workers will contract for 20% higher wages, but when prices only go up 10%, employers will find they are paying a higher real wage and so will cut back employment. The economy will go into a recession (as *AD* shifts left). In the long run, both unemployment and lower prices will cause workers to adjust their wages down, so the economy will return to full employment (shifting the *AS* curve right).

4. *Panel A:* From Point A to Point B, demand-pull inflation (due to the *AD* curve shifting right). From *B* to *C*, cost-push inflation (due to workers finding out inflation is higher than they had expected and raising their wages), and thus pushing up the *AS* curve.

   Panel B: From Point A to Point B, a demand-pull reduction in inflation (sometimes called "disinflation"). The *AD* curve is shifting left. From *B* to *C*, a cost-push reduction in inflation due to workers finding out inflation is lower than they expected. So they reduce their wages and push down the *AS* curve.

   Panel C: Some event (such as an oil price increase or a worldwide crop failure) has pushed the *AS* curve up and to the left. From Point *A* to Point *B*, the economy experiences a cost-push inflation. From *B* to *C*, there is a cost-push reduction in inflation as workers adjust their wages down so that the *AS* curve shifts right. How far the *AS* curve shifts depends upon whether the long-run *AS* has been reduced.

5. **a.** Cost-push phase of a recession.
   b. Demand-pull phase of an expansion.
   c. Cost-push phase of an expansion.

6. Wages will go up 12%

7. **a.** *Short run:* to *B*. *Long run:* to *C*.
   b. To *D*.
   c. To *C*.

8. When wages *(W)* rise more quickly than prices *(P)*, real wages *(W/P)* are increasing and employment will fall (holding technology and capital constant). When wages rise more slowly than prices, real wages are decreasing, and employment will rise.

9. The trick is to increase your widget price before controls are imposed (since you would not be permitted to increase them after) but also to not lose customers because of your higher price. So you raise your price but offer "special" discounts to your customers (such as coupons, special credit terms, and special volume discounts). Once controls are imposed, you can raise your effective price by cutting back on these discounts. If this is not enough, have your customers pay for some of your costs by picking up the product themselves. Have very strict credit terms or even demand cash in advance for widgets. Have many grades of quality, each with its own price, so you can push up your effective price by reducing the quality in each grade. If your product is in high demand, insist that your customers buy something else from you (at an inflated price) before they can get a widget.

10. If many firms employ the tactics described in Answer 9 above, reported prices will not rise. But the effective price of goods will. So inflation will not be stopped. Note that by evading wage and price controls, firms are actually serving the customers, for otherwise there would be shortages of goods and less output.

15
THE RATIONAL-EXPECTATIONS THEORY

KEY TERMS

nominal shocks shocks that change the price level but leave relative prices unaffected. An unanticipated increase in the money supply, for example, is a nominal shock.

rational expectations expectations that are unbiased and based upon the best available information

real shocks shocks that affect the relative price of goods and inputs. Unanticipated changes in taste, technology, or factor supplies, for example, are real shocks.

shock an unanticipated event.

unbiased forecast a forecast that is neither wrong on average nor systematically wrong.

It seems that once a macroeconomic theory of the economy becomes widely accepted, it no longer works. For example, in the '60s, Keynesianism was at its height, yet in the '70s it seemed to produce more inflation and more unemployment. Then Monetarism was popular, but it too hasn't seemed to work well in recent years.

RATIONAL-EXPECTATIONS THEORY

The **rational-expectations theory** tries to explain why economic theories stop working. The following example illustrates its central ideas. Suppose that the government wants to stimulate the economy and does so by increasing the money supply by 10%. The first time the government does this, it works. But it works by "fooling" workers and other suppliers into accepting lower real wages. Now suppose the government does the same thing again ten times in a row. By the tenth time, people will have caught on and will raise their wages and prices. Then the 10% increase in the money supply will no longer work: It will increase prices—not output. The logic of this example leads rational-expectations theorists to reject any theory that states that people can be systematically fooled time after time. The rational-expectations theory can be explained by a series of assumptions and results:

ASSUMPTIONS

ASSUMPTION 1: PEOPLE WILL TRY TO MAKE GOOD FORECASTS

Businesses need to forecast how well their goods will sell and at what profit. Workers and consumers need to forecast income and price levels. They try to make the *best forecasts*, as follows.

1. *They make unbiased forecasts.* They don't make **systematic errors** (i.e., they don't repeat the same mistake time after time) when estimating inflation, output, and other economic variables.

2. *They use the available information well.* For example, if the government is following a certain policy (such as stimulating the economy before elections), people notice it.

Rational-expectations theorists believe that people will make **random errors** instead of systematic errors. For example, when people's errors in forecasting inflation rates are random, it is impossible for economists to predict whether people will overestimate or underestimate how high inflation will be. (See Practical Application, questions 8 and 9.)

YOU SHOULD REMEMBER

1. An unbiased forecast will be correct on average and not make the same error year after year.

2. According to rational-expectations theory, people will make unbiased forecasts that use information well.

3. The errors people make will thus be random and unpredictable. Any model that assumes people make systematic errors is rejected.

ASSUMPTION 2: PEOPLE TAKE STEPS TO AVOID BEING FOOLED

To keep things simple, consider only workers. In equilibrium, the demand and supply for workers is equal. Now suppose the government increases the money supply unexpectedly. Money wages will rise and workers will initially assume that this represents an increase in their real wages. So they'll work more, and output and employment will go up. But they have been fooled: When prices go up, the workers will find that only their *nominal* wages, not their *real* wages have increased. They have confused a **real shock** (an unanticipated event that changes real wages or real output) with a **nominal shock** (an unanticipated event that changes all prices and costs equally, ultimately leaving real wages and real output unchanged in the long run).

Workers will take steps to avoid this happening again. They will demand cost-of-living adjustments in their wage contracts. They will become more aware of government policy and inflation. The next time the money supply is increased, real output won't be affected.

Some texts say that the rational-expectations theory assumes flexible prices and wages. This is not quite correct. The rational-expectations theory assumes that prices and wages will become more flexible if the government keeps trying to fool suppliers and workers into increasing output and employment. Being fooled is costly. But having flexible wages and prices is also costly. People balance these two costs: When the government tries to fool people more often, people will in turn pay the costs of becoming more flexible.

YOU SHOULD REMEMBER

1. A *shock* is an unexpected event. A *real shock* changes the relative prices of goods and inputs. A *nominal shock* changes all prices and costs equally, leaving relative prices unchanged.

2. Workers (and other input suppliers) will produce more when their wages go up only if they believe that their *real* wages have gone up. Therefore, nominal shocks increase output only when they are mistaken for real shocks (i.e., only if workers are fooled).

3. Workers will avoid being fooled by making their wage payments more flexible (i.e., they will become more responsive to changes in prices and economic conditions).

RESULTS

RESULT 1: ANTICIPATED SHIFTS IN THE AD CURVE HAVE NO REAL EFFECTS

If workers know what the government is going to do, they will set their wage contracts so that they are fully employed. Consider Figure 15-1. The labor market is in equilibrium when output is at full employment *(FE)*. And the *AD* curve is based on what the government is expected to do. What is the expected price level? It is *P*-0, the price level where the *AD* curve *(AD*-0) intersects the long-run aggregate supply curve, *S*-Long Run, at full employment *FE*). People expect the economy to be at full employment and not to systematically be above or below it. So the aggregate supply curve *AS*-A must go through Point *A*.

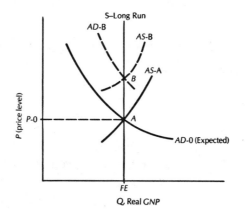

Figure 15-1 Determining that Anticipated Shifts in Supply and Demand Have No Effects on Rational Price Expectations

If *AD* shifts up to *AD*-B and workers have anticipated this, they will raise their wages and the *AS* curve will *also* shift up to Point *B* (to *AS*-B). Anticipated increases in aggregate demand will raise only prices and costs. They have only nominal, not real, effects. (See Practical Application, Question 2.) As an analogy, suppose you are playing poker with someone who always cheats in the last hand of the evening. Once you anticipate this, you can avoid being cheated, by not betting in the last hand.

If the government tries to stimulate the economy (by increasing *AD*) in a way the public anticipates, then it *cannot* increase output. In particular, a policy of always stimulating the economy when there is high unemployment will *not* be effective, since it can be anticipated.

YOU SHOULD REMEMBER

1. In rational-expectations theory, people expect the economy to be at full employment and the price level to be where the *AD* curve intersects the full-employment level of output (on the long-run aggregate supply curve).

2. Anticipated shifts in *AD* will not affect output or relative prices. Only the level of prices and costs will change.

3. The government cannot stimulate output by increasing aggregate demand in any anticipated or predictable manner.

RESULT 2: ONLY UNANTICIPATED SHIFTS IN THE AD CURVE AFFECT REAL OUTPUT

The remarkable conclusion of rational-expectations theory is that shifts in *AD* affect output only when they trick workers and suppliers into increasing output and employment. For example, an unanticipated increase in aggregate demand increases output only because the aggregate supply curve does not shift up with it. (If the poker cheat we described above suddenly starts to cheat in the first hand, the cheat will be able to cheat you until you catch on.)

YOU SHOULD REMEMBER

Unanticipated increases in *AD* increase real output, while unanticipated decreases in *AD* reduce real output.

RESULT 3: FREQUENT AND UNEXPECTED POLICY CHANGES HARM THE ECONOMY

If the government tries to stimulate the economy in any predictable manner (such as when unemployment rises), its policy will become ineffective. On the other hand, if it tries to continually surprise the economy, it may affect output but in negative ways.

For example, every time the government raises the price level to try to fool workers, it is "crying wolf." At first, workers respond (by working more). Eventually, they stop responding. And someday, the wolf does come along, and workers don't respond. For example, new technology may raise real wages, but workers, having been fooled by seemingly good wage increases in the past, don't respond. The result is a sluggish economy and lowered output.

Another example of how frequent policy changes can harm the economy is that workers, to cope with the greater uncertainty produced by the policy changes, will demand higher real wages. Also, savers will demand a higher real interest rate. At a result, employment and investment will contract, reducing output and growth. (Returning to our poker analogy, to play with an unpredictable cheat, you would probably demand higher expected winnings. This in turn would reduce the number of poker games that are played.)

YOU SHOULD REMEMBER

1. It is impossible for the government to systematically fool people into increasing output. Eventually, people catch on.

2. The effects of continued changes in government policy will be to dull the economy's responses to real changes and to increase uncertainty.

MAKING PREDICTIONS WITH THE RATIONAL-EXPECTATIONS MODEL

According to the rational-expectations model, the business cycle stems from (1) people's errors in predicting what the price level will be and (2) real causes. Since the rational-expectations theory holds that people's errors will be random and thus unpredictable, (1) cannot be used to make forecasts with any more accuracy than one can predict when a coin will come up heads.

Rational-expectations economists are thus left with real causes with which to predict future changes in *GNP*. For example, some real causes of recessions could be oil price increases, increases in the marginal tax rate, and a fall in the relative price of a nation's exports. This approach (called the **real business cycle theory**) believes that:

1. Future levels of output depend upon the current state of the economy and how the economy is likely to grow. This depends upon such real factors as changes in technology, tastes, and factor supplies.

2. Depending on the efficiency and type of government spending, economic growth can be hindered or helped by an expansion of government spending.

3. An inefficient tax system (for example, one with high marginal tax rates) can hinder economic activity and reduce output.

4. Finally, the more stable and predictable government fiscal and monetary policy are, the higher the full-employment level of output will be.

In a recession due to real causes, the economy is still fully employed even though unemployment is higher. Recall that at full employment there is always the frictional unemployment from workers and employers adjusting to changing economic conditions and new information. (See Chapter 6.) For example, when OPEC tripled oil prices, many workers in energy-using industries lost their jobs. This increase in unemployment is consistent with full employment, as it takes time for people to adjust to this change and find new jobs.

YOU SHOULD REMEMBER

1. In the rational-expectations model, only real causes can be used to predict future business cycles.

2. The key economic variables our government controls, according to the rational-expectations model, are (1) the efficiency of government spending, (2) the efficiency of the tax system, and (3) the stability and predictability of fiscal and monetary policy. An increase in any of these will make an economy better off.

3. An economy in a recession may still be fully employed when the recession is due to real causes. Adjustment to changes requires unemployment.

CRITICISMS OF THE RATIONAL-EXPECTATIONS MODEL

1. *Expectations may not be rationally formed.* For example, stock market prices (which are in effect forecasts of how firms will do in the future) appear to vary much more than any underlying changes in the economy seem to justify. If so, it may be a reasonable government policy to act to offset unreasonable expectations on the part of the public.

2. *It may take real changes, particularly in unemployment, to force people to change their expectations.* Suppose the best forecasts predict that if workers don't reduce their wages, there will be greater unemployment. Given the inaccuracy of forecasts, it may be rational for workers to wait and see if

unemployment does increase before they agree to reduce their wages. As a consequence, changes in aggregate demand, even if anticipated, may have real effects.

3. *Because of multiyear contracts, workers may not be able to adjust fully during the years the contracts are in effect.* In addition, retailers may be reluctant to change prices too soon in fear of driving away loyal customers. Thus, there may be institutional and economic forces preventing rapid adjustment even if people's expectations are rationally formed.

KNOW THE CONCEPTS

DO YOU KNOW THE BASICS?

1. Suppose you have the price level forecasts that business leaders have made in the past. How can you tell whether their forecasts are unbiased and without systematic error?

2. Why don't rational-expectations economists expect people to make systematic errors in their forecasts?

3. If forecast errors are random, can one predict when a recession is going to occur?

4. Why do workers supply more labor in response to an unanticipated increase in inflation?

5. Why will workers supply no more labor in response to an anticipated increase in inflation?

6. Why can't the government stimulate the economy when it is in a recession?

7. How will an unanticipated expansionary fiscal and monetary policy affect the economy?

8. If firms know the price of their output is going up because people have changed their tastes and increased their demand for the firms' output (this being a real shock), how will firms change their output?

9. If firms know the price increase is due to a nominal shock, how will they change output?

10. How can an active discretionary governmental policy that is designed to increase output actually reduce output in the long run?

TERMS FOR STUDY

random errors	real business cycle theory
rational expectations	systematic errors

PRACTICAL APPLICATION

1. If a baseball player has a .300 batting average, why is it unbiased to predict that for every ten times at bat, he or she should have three hits? Why is predicting four hits (out of ten) a biased prediction?

   Note: A 300 batting average means that the player makes a hit 30% of the time.

2. Use the following table to answer the questions below. This table shows the supply and demand for labor in an economy.

Real Wage	Labor Supply	Labor Demand
4	70	130
5	80	115
6	90	90
7	100	75
8	110	60

   a. What is the real wage *(W/P)* at full employment?
   b. If workers expect a price level of 200 (i.e., $P = 2.00$), what money wage *(W)* will they want?
   c. If workers expect a price level of 200 (and are paid the money wage from (b) above), then what actual price level will cause firms to hire 115 units of labor?

   Note: Assume that firms know what the actual price level is.

   d. If workers come to expect the price level in (c) above, what wage will they demand? What will happen to output?

3. Suppose the Fed announces "We are *not* going to increase the money supply" and then surprises everyone by increasing it by 20%. What will happen? If the Fed does this ten times in a row, what will happen the eleventh time?

4. Continuing Question 3, what will happen the twelfth time the Fed announces "We are *not* going to increase the money supply" if it actually does *not* increase the money supply that time?

5. What is wrong with the following theory: "To get elected, the party in power stimulates the economy just before the election. So we can expect an economic expansion during an election year."

6. When will an unanticipated decrease in the money-supply growth to 2% likely cause a bigger reduction in output:
   a. After a long period of a steady monetary growth of 10%, or

b. After a period when money supply on average grew 10% but grew faster and slower at various times.

7. When can the government reduce inflation without causing a recession?

8. According to "Theory B," the workers' expected price level in Year t (EP_t) equals the prior year's price level (P_{t-1}).
   a. Fill in the EP_t row, the nominal wage (W) row, and the real wage (W/P) row of this table. Assume the full-employment real wage is $12 and that workers at the beginning of each year set their money wage (W) to equal this $12 real wage *based* upon what they expect prices to be (i.e., so that $W/EP_t = \$12$, where $EP_t = P_{t-1}$).

Year (t)	0	1	2	3	4	5	6	7	8	9
Price Level	100	110	120	130	140	150	140	130	120	120
EP_t	—									
W	—									
W/P	—									

   b. In which years will employment (and output) be below its full-employment level? Above? How does the expected price level (EP_t) compare to the actual price level (P_t) when employment and output are below and above their full-employment level?

9. Would "Theory B" in Question 8 be acceptable to an economist who believes in rational expectations?

10. Does everybody have to have "rational expectations" for the rational-expectations model to work?

ANSWERS
KNOW THE CONCEPTS

1. First, find out whether the forecasts were correct on average. Then find out whether the errors were systematic (i.e., whether mistakes were repeated).

2. A person making systematic errors is making the same costly mistake again and again. If people are rational, they will avoid past errors.

3. Only recessions that are due to real causes (such as an OPEC oil price

increase) can be predicted. Those that are due to unanticipated shifts in the *AD* curve cannot, by definition, be anticipated.

4. When firms offer workers higher money wages and ask them to work more, workers accept since they think they are getting higher real wages (but in fact inflation will reduce their real wages).

5. When workers correctly anticipate inflation, they adjust their wages such that they supply the labor they want and no more.

6. According to rational-expectations theory, government cannot systematically trick workers and suppliers into producing more, and in particular, it cannot systematically do this whenever the economy is in a recession (since its actions can then be anticipated).

7. It will increase output in the short run, because aggregate demand will shift right and the aggregate supply curve will not shift.

8. A change in taste that increases the demand for a good means first, that people are willing to pay more in real terms for the good, and second, that the factors that produced the goods now out of favor are now available to be hired. So the firms will produce more, knowing costs won't rise to offset their profits from producing more.

9. If the increase in price is only nominal, there are no new available factors from out-of-favor goods. So costs will rise to offset the output's higher price. Firms will raise their price, not their output.

10. An active discretionary policy adds uncertainty to the economy and reduces the responsiveness of firms to all price changes, whether they are due to real or nominal shocks.

PRACTICAL APPLICATION

1. The forecast of three hits out of ten times at bat is unbiased in the sense that on average it will be right. Sometimes, the baseball player will hit more, sometimes less. Predicting four hits will be right some of the time, but more often it will be too high. So it is biased.

2. **a.** *W/P* at full employment is $6.
   b. $W = $12 ($12/2.00 = $6).
   c. Firms will hire 115 units when the real wage is 5. So to make *W/P* equal to 5, with *W* = $12, we need a price level *(P)* of 240 ($12/2.40 = $5).
   d. Workers will demand a wage of $14.40, since $14.40/2.40 = $6. Output will return to its full-employment level.

3. The first time this occurs, people will not anticipate the increase in the money supply. Output will increase in the short run. But by the eleventh

time, people will anticipate the increase in the money supply, so in the short *and* long run, only prices will increase. Real output will be unaffected.

4. People will expect prices to rise, so the *AS* curve will shift up. But the *AD* curve will be unchanged. So output will fall and prices will rise (there will be a cost-push stagflation). In the long run, output and prices will return to their original levels.

5. Over time, people will come to expect this event, and any attempted expansion before an election will just raise prices.

6. After (a). After (b), prices will be more flexible, so a decrease in price will have less effect. The Great Depression followed a decade of stable prices, which may explain why it took such a long time for the economy to return to full employment.

7. If the public expects inflation to fall, the government can reduce inflation without reducing output (both the *AD* and *AS* curve will shift down the long-run aggregate supply curve together). For example, after World War I, Germany was able to go from a 100% inflation rate per day to stable prices without a recession mainly because the public had confidence in the promises of the German leaders to stop inflation.

8. **a.** The filled-in table follows:

Year:	1	2	3	4	5	6	7	8	9
EP_t	100	110	120	130	140	150	140	130	120
W	12.00	13.20	14.40	15.60	16.80	18.00	16.80	15.60	14.40
W/P	10.91	11.00	11.08	11.14	11.20	12.86	12.92	13.00	12.00

The years when year's employment and output are above full-employment level: 1–5 ($W/P < 12$ and $EP_t < P_t$)
The years when year's employment and output are below full-employment level: 6–8 ($W/P > 12$ and $EP_t > P_t$)
In Year 9, economy at full-employment level: $W/P = 12$ and $EP_t = P_t$.

9. No. In Theory B, the expected price level always lags after the actual price level: This means people are consistently mistaken about inflation in the same way.

10. No. For example, suppose there is an increase in the growth rate of the money supply that good economic models have anticipated. If enough people hiring workers and making investment decisions have this good forecast, their competition will raise wages and nominal interest rates to reflect the higher rate of inflation. So even if workers and savers don't know what is going on, the economy will have the rational-expectations results.

16
ELASTICITY

KEY TERMS

cross elasticity of demand responsiveness of the quantity demanded to a change in the price of *another* good.

elasticity responsiveness of one variable to the change in another, both changes expressed in percentages. The elasticity of Q with respect to P is the percent change in Q for every 1% change in P.

income elasticity of demand responsiveness of quantity demanded to a change in income.

price elasticity of demand responsiveness of quantity demanded to a change in the price.

price elasticity of supply responsiveness of quantity supplied to a change of price.

Note: **Microeconomics** studies the factors that determine the relative prices of goods and inputs. (A review of chapters 3 and 4 is suggested.) This chapter describes how economists measure the response of output to changes in prices and income. Chapter 17 examines the factors affecting demand. Then, chapters 18, 19, and 20 describe what determines supply.

To measure the effects of price and income on demand and supply, economists use "elasticities." **Elasticity** is a measure of responsiveness: It equals the percent change in quantity *divided* by the percent change in the variable that caused quantity to change. That is, it measures cause and effect in percentage terms. The effect is in the numerator; the cause is in the denominator.

THE PRICE ELASTICITY OF DEMAND

The **price elasticity of demand** measures the responsiveness of the *quantity demanded* of a good to a change in its *price*. We will use "$E(Q^d,P)$," which stands for the Elasticity of the Quantity Demanded with respect to Price changes. Formally, we have:

$$E(Q^d,P) = \frac{\text{Percent Change in the Quantity Demanded}}{\text{Percent Change in Price}}$$

where *both* percent changes are expressed as *absolute values.*

When $E(Q^d,P) > 1$, demand is **elastic:** A given percent change in price causes an even greater percent change in the quantity demanded. Just as an elastic rubber ball bounces a lot when one drops it, so it is when demand is elastic: The quantity demanded "bounces" or responds a lot to price changes.

When $E(Q^d,P) < 1$, demand is **inelastic:** A given percent change in price causes a smaller percent change in the quantity demanded. Just as a ball made of an inelastic material like clay doesn't bounce when one drops it, so it is when demand is inelastic: The quantity demanded does not respond much to price changes.

When $E(Q^d,P) = 1$, demand is **unitary elastic:** A given percent change in price causes the same percent change in quantity demanded.

Figure 16-1 shows several demand curves. Panel 1 shows a **perfectly inelastic demand curve** $E(Q^d,P) = 0$): Price has no effect on the quantity demanded. Panel 2 shows a **perfectly elastic demand curve** $E(Q^d,P) = \infty$): an infinitesimally small increase in price above $P0$ reduces demand to 0 and an infinitesimally small decrease in price increases demand to infinity. In Panel 3, at Point F, demand curve C is more elastic than demand curve B, and B is more elastic than A.

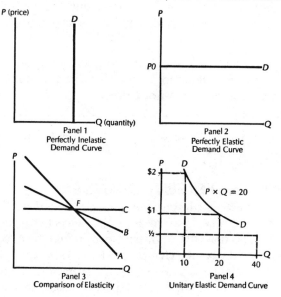

Figure 16-1 The Elasticity of Various Demand Curves

Note: One can compare elasticities by comparing slopes *only* at the point where the curves go through the same point.

Panel 4 shows a **unitary elastic demand curve** ($P \times Q$ is the same at all points on this type of demand curve). Note that Q here represents the quantity of an individual good or service. In the sections on macroeconomics, Q stood for real *GNP*—the national quantity of goods and services.

Economists use the following equation to predict the effects of price on output:

$$\text{Percent Change in Quantity Demanded} = -E(Q^d,P) \times \text{Percent Change in Price}$$

This equation is an approximation that is accurate for small changes in price.

As an example, studies have shown that the price elasticity of demand for candy is 0.5: A 10% increase in the price of candy will reduce the amount bought by 5%. Its demand is inelastic. On the other hand, studies have shown that the demand for electricity in the long run is elastic: $E(Q^d,P) = 2.2$. A 10% increase in the price of electricity will reduce the quantity demanded by 22%.

YOU SHOULD REMEMBER

1. Price elasticity of demand is the percentage change in the quantity demanded for every 1% change in the price.

2. When demand is more elastic, consumers are more sensitive to price changes, increasing or decreasing their purchases more. When demand is inelastic, consumers are more insensitive to price changes.

3. Demand is elastic when output changes by a greater percentage than price does. Demand is inelastic when output changes by a smaller percentage than price does.

MEASURING THE PRICE ELASTICITY OF DEMAND

MEASURING THE PERCENT CHANGE

If the price goes up 10% and the quantity demanded goes down 30%, the elasticity of demand is 3.0. But how do we measure the percent change? For example, if the price was $10 and now it is $7, by what percent did the price fall? To get the percent change, one divides the change in price ($3) by some base price: either the old price ($10), the new price ($7), or an average of the two ($8.50). The percent changes in price, using these respective bases, are 30%, 42.86%, and 35.29%. Like most texts, we will use the *average* price as the base. If P_0 is the original price and P_1, the new price, and Q_0 and Q_1 the similar quantities, we have:

$$\text{Percent Change in Quantity Demanded} = \frac{Q_1 - Q_0}{(Q_1 + Q_0)/2} \times 100$$

$$\text{Percent Change in Price} = \frac{P_1 - P_0}{(P_1 + P_0)/2} \times 100$$

$E(Q^d,P)$ is the ratio of the absolute value of these two terms. This ratio can be simplified to:

$$E(Q^d,P) = \frac{\text{Change in } Q}{\text{Change in } P} \times \frac{\text{Average } P}{\text{Average } Q}$$

where the "Changes" are stated as absolute numbers.

Example: Calculating the Elasticity of Demand.

PROBLEM   At $5, consumers demand 200 records. At $6, consumers demand 160 records. What is the elasticity of demand over this range of prices?

SOLUTION   1.22, or (40/1.00 × $5.50/180). The price increased 18.18% and the quantity demanded fell 22.22%.

MEASURING ELASTICITY ON A STRAIGHT-LINE DEMAND CURVE

A *straight-line demand curve* has several interesting elasticity properties. First, as one moves down the demand curve, the price elasticity of demand becomes smaller (i.e., more inelastic). Starting at *P0*, demand is perfectly elastic [$E(Q^d,P)$ = ∞]; it then falls but remains elastic until halfway down. Halfway down the demand curve (at 1/2 *P0*), $E(Q^d,P)$ equals unity (=1). It then becomes inelastic until at $P = 0$, $E(Q^d,P) = 0$.

On a straight-line demand curve, the elasticity at a given point equals (1) the length of the demand line below the point *divided* by (2) the length of the line segment above it.

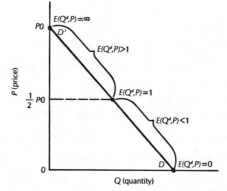

Figure 16-2   The Change in Elasticity Along a Straight-Line Demand Curve

Be sure to notice that all along the straight-line demand curve, the slope is constant but the elasticity changes! So remember that slope and elasticity are not the same thing (and can only be compared where the curves cross, as in Panel 3 of Figure 16-1). Also, because elasticity can change along the same demand curve, when you measure the elasticity of demand, always specify over what range of prices the elasticity was measured.

YOU SHOULD REMEMBER

1. The *percent change in price* is usually calculated by dividing the change in price by the average price (and multiplying by 100).

2. The *elasticity of demand over a segment of the demand curve* is the percent change in quantity demanded divided by the percent change in price (both expressed as absolute values).

3. As one goes down a straight-line demand curve, it becomes more inelastic. It's elastic until halfway down, halfway down it's unitary elastic, and then it's inelastic the rest of the way down.

ELASTICITY AND TOTAL REVENUE

Economists use elasticities to tell what will happen to **total revenue** (price times output) when prices change. Total revenue is the same thing as total sales. In particular, we have:

$$\text{Percent Change in Total Revenue} = (1 - E(Q^d,P)) \times \text{Percent Change in Price}$$

Therefore:

1. If $E(Q^d,P) > 1$, price and total revenue are *negatively related,* or when demand is elastic:
   - An increase in price will reduce total revenue.
   - A decrease in price will increase total revenue.

2. If $E(Q^d,P) < 1$, price and total revenue are *positively related,* or when demand is *in*elastic:
   - An increase in price will increase total revenue.
   - A decrease in price will decrease total revenue.

3. If $E(Q^d,P) = 1$, total revenue is the same whether price goes up or down.

   This result and the following results all assume we are moving along a demand curve and not shifting it! The percent changes in this equation can be positive or negative.

Examples: Effect of Prices on Total Revenue

PROBLEM   The price elasticity of demand for wheat is 0.3. If a bountiful harvest results in 20% lower wheat prices, what will happen to the total revenues of farmers?

SOLUTION   Total revenue will go down by about 14% (.7 × −20%).

PROBLEM   An airline is flying at half capacity. If it lowers its air fares by 10%, will it increase its profits when $E(Q^d,P) = 2.0$? When $E(Q^d,P) = 0.6$? Assume it has the same total cost even though it will have more passengers at the lower price.

SOLUTION   When demand is elastic, the airline will increase its profits by lowering its price (when $E(Q^d,P) = 2.0$, its total revenue will go up 10%, and since its total costs don't change, its profits will go up). But when demand is inelastic, total revenue will fall (by 4% when $E(Q^d,P) = .6$) as will its profits.

Once again, the straight-line demand curve has some special properties: Starting from the price at 0 output and decreasing price to half its level, total revenue increases (this being the elastic portion of the demand curve). Total revenue peaks halfway down, then falls (in the inelastic portion) as the price approaches $0. Figure 16-3 shows an example. Don't make the following common mistake: *Don't confuse total revenue with total profits.* Where total revenue is highest is almost *never* where profits are highest!

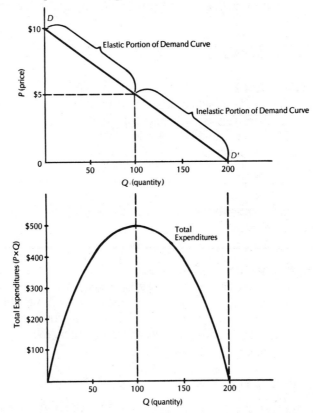

Figure 16-3 Determining Revenue Along the Straight-Line Demand Curve

---

YOU SHOULD REMEMBER

1. *When demand is elastic,* total revenue and price are negatively related: A fall in price increases total revenue and a rise in price decreases total revenue.

2. *When demand is inelastic,* total revenue and price are positively related: A fall in price decreases total revenue and a rise in price increases total revenue.

3. Going down a straight-line demand curve, total revenue increases as the price falls until halfway down, where total revenue is at a maximum, but as the price falls further, total revenue falls.

FACTORS AFFECTING ELASTICITY

PERTAINING TO DEMAND

PRICE ELASTICITY

Most texts list a set of factors that increase the price elasticity of a demand curve. The presence of these factors makes consumers buy even more than otherwise when the price goes down and buy even less than otherwise when the price goes up. But in fact these factors all reflect the effect of one *main factor:*

When *more* **substitutes** for a good become available, demand becomes *more* elastic.

For example, wheat bread is a substitute for white bread. A good that has many close substitutes is like a grocery store in a neighborhood with many other grocery stores: If it charges too much, its customers switch to the other stores. If it lowers its price, it can attract a lot of the other stores' customers. So the demand for its groceries is very elastic. In general then, the more substitutes a good has, the more elastic its demand will be.

Factors Affecting Price Elasticity

1. *The Fraction of Income Spent on the Good:* The more people spend on a good, the more important it is in their budget. So if its price goes up, they are *more* willing to search long and hard for substitutes.

2. *How Narrowly Defined the Good Is:* "Bread" is a more narrowly defined good than is "wheat product"; "white bread" is more narrowly defined than "bread." The narrower the definition, the *more* substitutes the good is likely to have and thus the more elastic its demand will be. For example, the demand for Fords is more elastic than the demand for automobiles; the demand for automobiles is more elastic than the demand for transportation.

3. *How Easy It Is to Find Out About Substitutes:* The easier consumers can find out about the price and availability of substitutes, the more elastic demand will be. Advertising plays a crucial role in increasing the availability of substitutes to consumers.

4. *How Much Time There Is to Adjust to Price Changes:* The more time consumers have to find out about substitutes, the more elastic demand becomes.

Those goods consumers consider to be "necessities" usually have inelastic demands. On the other hand, goods considered to be "luxuries" usually have more elastic demands. But there are exceptions: The demand for ice cream is far more inelastic (0.1) than the demand for food (0.3).

YOU SHOULD REMEMBER

1. The more substitutes a good has, the more elastic its demand is.

2. The larger the good's share of the consumers' budget, the more likely it is that consumers will seek substitutes when its price goes up. The more information available about substitutes, the easier it is for consumers to find substitutes. And the more time consumers have, the easier it is for them to find and adopt the substitutes. The presence of each of these factors increases the elasticity of demand.

3. The more narrowly a good is defined, the more elastic its demand is likely to be.

INCOME ELASTICITY

We denote this as $E(Q^d,I)$:

$$E(Q^d,I) = \frac{\text{Percent Change in Quantity Demanded}}{\text{Percent Change in Income}}$$

As you will recall from Chapter 4, a good is a **normal good** if it goes up in demand when income increases ($E(Q^d,I) > 0$). Most goods are normal. A good is a **superior good** if it goes up in demand when income increases *and* its share in income also goes up ($E(Q^d,I) > 1$). Gourmet food is an example. A good is an **inferior good** if it goes down in demand when income goes up ($E(Q^d,I) < 0$). Examples include cheap red wine and flour for home baking.

If $E(Q^d,I) > 1$, then when income goes up, the good's share of consumer's income goes up. If $E(Q^d,I) < 1$, then when income goes up, its share of consumer's income goes down. In general:

$$\text{Percent Change in Share of Income} = [E(Q^d, I) - 1] \times \text{Percent Change in Income}$$

CROSS ELASTICITY

This measures the responsiveness of the demand for a good to the price of another good. We'll denote it as $E(^d,Pog)$ where *Pog* stands for *Price of the Other Good*. It's equal to:

$$E(Q^d,Pog) = \frac{\text{Percent Change in Quantity Demanded}}{\text{Percent Change in Price of Other Goods}}$$

When consumers buy more of Good A when Good B's price goes up, economists say Good A is a **substitute** for Good B (and Good B is a substitute for Good A): $E(Q^d,Pog) > 0$. For example, when hamburger prices go up, consumers buy more hot dogs.

When consumers buy less of Good A when Good B's price goes up, economists say Good A is a **complement** to Good B: $E(Q^d,Pog) < 0$. Complements often are goods that are used together. Thus, for example, when the price of hot dogs goes up, the demand for hot dog buns goes down.

YOU SHOULD REMEMBER

1. The **income elasticity** of a good is the percent change in the quantity demanded of the good for every 1% increase in income. Normal goods have positive income elasticities: Most goods normally go up in demand when income goes up. Inferior goods go down in demand when income goes up: They have negative income elasticities.

2. A superior good's income elasticity exceeds unity: Its share of income goes up as income goes up.

3. Goods are substitutes when their cross elasticities are positive: The demand for one goes up when the price of the other goes up. Goods are complements when their cross elasticities of demand are negative: The demand for one goes down when the price of the other goes up.

PERTAINING TO SUPPLY

The **price elasticity of the quantity supplied** measures the responsiveness of the quantity supplied to price changes. It will be denoted as $E(Q^s,P)$. It is defined in the same way $E(Q^d,P)$ was:

$$E(Q^s,P) = \frac{\text{Percent Change in Quantity Supplied}}{\text{Percent Change in Price}}$$

Figure 16-4 shows four supply curves: Curve D is more elastic than C, C more than B, B more than A. Curve D is a **perfectly elastic supply curve** [$E(Q^s,P) = \infty$]: A price below $P0$ reduces output to zero; a price above $P0$ increases output to infinity. Curve A is a **perfectly inelastic supply curve** [$E(Q^s,P) = 0$]: A higher price doesn't increase output at all. An example would be the supply of authentic paintings by Vincent Van Gogh.

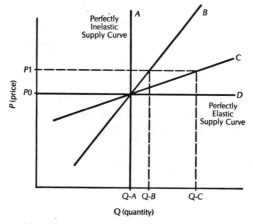

Figure 16-4 'The Elasticity of Various Supply Curves

Factors Affecting Supply Elasticity

1. *How Much Time There Is to Adjust to Price:* It is a basic rule of economic life that the faster one wants something done, the more costly it will be. So when the price of a good goes up, firms at first increase output very little. But then firms adjust by hiring more factors and expanding their plants, and new firms enter the industry. With more time to adjust, the supply response becomes larger. For example, in Figure 16-4, an increase of price from *P0* to *P1* will not immediately affect output *(Q-A)*; the immediate short-run supply curve is *A*. But given some time, *B* becomes the supply curve and *Q-B* the quantity supplied. With even more time, firms enter the industry and existing firms expand, so the supply curve becomes *C* and *Q-C* the quantity supplied.

2. *How Easy It Is to Store Goods:* When the price of a good drops, firms have to choose between selling it now or putting it into their inventory if they believe the drop in price is only temporary. Therefore, the cheaper it is to store goods, the more elastic the supply will be for *temporary changes in the price.* For example, when the demand for steel temporarily falls, steel manufacturers often store their unsold steel rather than reduce their price.

3. *How Cheap It Is to Increase Output:* To increase output is costly. Typically, if an industry tries to buy more inputs, the price of inputs goes up. Similarly, some production processes are quite costly to set up. The less input costs rise and the smaller set-up costs are, the more elastic the supply curve will be.

YOU SHOULD REMEMBER

1. The supply elasticity of a good is the percentage increase in quantity supplied for every 1% increase in price.

2. Supply is more elastic (1) the more time suppliers have to adjust, (2) the less added costs there are to expanding, and (3) in the short run, the cheaper it is to store goods.

KNOW THE CONCEPTS

DO YOU KNOW THE BASICS?

1. When economists say the price elasticity of demand for bananas is 2.0, what do they mean?

2. If consumers of a good are very sensitive to its price, is the good's demand elastic or inelastic?

3. If the output demanded is the same regardless of the price, what is the price elasticity of demand?

4. If one demand curve has a steeper slope than another, is the steeper demand curve more inelastic?

5. What is the main factor that increases the elasticity of demand for a good?

6. When will total revenue go up if the price is reduced?

7. If the income elasticity of demand for a good is greater than 1, what will happen to the demand for the good and to the good's share of people's income when income goes up?

8. How can one tell if two goods are substitutes? Complements?

9. Will firms produce where total revenues are highest?

10. If the demand for a good goes up, what will be the immediate supply response? The longer-term supply response?

TERMS FOR STUDY

price elasticity of demand
elastic, inelastic, unit elastic
total revenue
income elasticity of demand

normal goods, inferior goods
cross elasticity of demand
substitutes, complements
price elasticity of supply

PRACTICAL APPLICATION

1. For the following demand curve, calculate the slope and the price elasticity of demand over each price range ($10 to $8, $8 to $6, etc):

Price	$10	$8	$6	$4	$2	$0
Quantity	0	4	8	12	16	20

Now do the same, but change dollars to cents.

2. **a.** Compare the effect of a $1,000 tax on cars with the effect of a 10% tax on cars. Which tax is likely to have the same impact on the demand for cars (in percentage terms) no matter which year it was imposed?

   Hint: Inflation has increased the price of cars over time, so the $1,000 represents a smaller percentage of car prices in more recent years.

   b. What does your answer imply about the relative advantages of using slopes or elasticities to predict the impact of a price change?

3. **a.** When the wheat harvest falls by 10% due to bad weather, wheat prices go up 40%. What is the price elasticity of demand for wheat?
   b. Using this number, what will happen to the wheat bought by consumers if the government raises the price of wheat by 20%? What happens to the total revenue of wheat farmers?
   c. Still using the elasticity from (a) above, what will happen to the price of wheat if the government destroys 10% of the crop? To the total revenues of wheat farmers?

4. Why will tourists likely have a more inelastic demand curve for restaurant food than will "locals"?

5. Why do merchants often have sales (and cut their prices) on air-conditioners in spring and early summer when demand is highest?

6. Select from each of these groups the good that is likely to have the highest price elasticity of demand:

   Group A: Energy, oil, gasoline, Shell Gasoline, Bill's Shell Station gas.
   Group B: The gasoline bought by truckers, the gasoline bought by weekend drivers.
   Group C: Gas bought from Joe, who has no competitors; gas bought from Bill, who has many competitors.
   Group D: Eyeglasses from Sid's Glass Emporium in a state that does not permit advertising, eyeglasses from the same store in a state that does permit advertising.

7. When Titantown Bus Company raised its bus fare, its total revenues fell. When Petrogard Bus Company raised its bus fare, its total revenues went up. What can we conclude about the elasticity of demand for each company?

8. Which of these groups do you expect to be complements and which do you expect to be substitutes? What is the likely sign of the cross elasticity of demand?

   Group A: Tires and cars.
   Group B: Buses and airplanes.
   Group C: Coal and oil.
   Group D: Hot dogs and hamburgers.

9. You are president of the American Bicycle Federation and you have been asked to predict how the sale of American bicycles will do next year (giving the percent change from this year's sales). Give your answer using the following facts: (1) The price elasticity of demand for American bicycles is 2.5; (2) their income elasticity is 3.0; (3) the cross elasticity of demand with foreign bikes is 4.0; and (4) American bikes will go up 5% in price, foreign bikes will go up 7% in price, and American income will go up 3%. What will happen to the total expenditures of Americans on American bicycles (which equals the total revenues of the American bicycle makers)?

   Hint: Calculate each effect and add the effects together to get the net percent change in quantity demanded. The percent change in total revenue equals the percent change in quantity demand plus the percent change in price.

10. As people earn more income, their food purchases go up but their share of income spent on food goes down. What can we conclude about the income elasticity of food demand?

ANSWERS

KNOW THE CONCEPTS

1. They mean that the quantity demanded will increase 2% for every 1% decrease in price.

2. Elastic.

3. It is perfectly inelastic $[E(Q^d,P) = 0]$.

4. You cannot tell *unless* the two curves cross. At the crossing point, the steeper curve is the more inelastic.

5. The greater availability of substitutes.

6. When the good's demand is elastic.

7. As income goes up, the quantity demanded will go up and the good's share in income will go up.

8. Two goods are substitutes if when the price of one goes up, the demand for the other also goes up. Two goods are complements if when the price of one goes up, the demand for the other goes down.

9. No. Firms will produce where profits are highest.

10. The immediate supply response will be a small increase in supply (or perhaps no increase). But given time, suppliers will increase the quantity supplied.

PRACTICAL APPLICATION

1. The slope is -2 at all points. Between $10 and $8, elasticity is 9, and then 2.33 between $8 and $6, then 1.0, 0.43, and 0.11. Changing from dollars to cents does not affect these elasticities, but it changes the slope from -2 to $-.02$. One of the advantages of elasticities is that their value stays the same when the unit of measuring prices or output changes.

2. **a.** Due to inflation, the $1,000 represents a smaller percentage of car prices over time. When cars were sold for $2,000, the $1,000 in added price meant car prices would go up 50%: we'd expect a huge decrease in demand. When cars sell for $10,000, this is only a 10% increase in price: we expect a smaller decrease in demand. On the other hand, the 10% tax would probably have a similar impact if imposed today or 30 years ago.

   b. Inflation does not harm the usefulness of elasticities; this is one reason why economists use them.

3. **a.** 0.25 (10%/40%).
   b. It will decrease by 5% ($-.25 \times 20\%$). Total revenues will rise 15% $[(1-.25) \times 20\%]$.
   c. Price will go up 40%. (10%/.25); total expenditures on wheat will go up 30%.

4. Tourists have little time to price shop among substitute restaurants, so their demand curve for any one restaurant is likely to be more inelastic. Tourists also lack the substitute of home-cooked meals.

5. In spring and early summer, more people are seeking to buy air-conditioners. This makes the advertising cost *per customer* lower. With more merchants advertising, customers can more easily price shop. So merchants face a more elastic demand curve for their air-conditioners. This leads them to cut prices (to increase their total revenues), causing sales to occur at these times.

6. **a.** Bill's Shell Station gas.
   b. The gasoline bought by truckers (they have more incentive to price-shop).
   c. Bill.
   d. The store in the state that permits advertising.

7. Titantown's demand is elastic; Petrogard's is inelastic.

8. *Group A:* Complements (negative).
   Group B: Substitutes (positive).
   Group C: Substitutes (positive).
   Group D: Substitutes (positive).

9. We sum the effect of price, foreign bike prices, and income: (-2.5×5) $+ (4 \times 7) + (3 \times 3) = 24.9\%$. With 24.9% more bikes sold at a 5% higher price, total expenditures will be up (by approximately the percent change in quantity plus the percent change in price, or 29.9%).

10. The income elasticity is positive (since food purchases went up) but less than unity (since food's share of income went down).

17
THE THEORY OF DEMAND

KEY TERMS

consumer surplus what consumers are willing to pay for a good less what they actually do pay for the good.

income effect effect of a change in real income on the quantity of a good demanded.

marginal utility addition to total utility from consuming one more unit of a good.

substitution effect (of a price change) effect on the quantity demanded of a good when its relative price is changed (and real income is constant): A lower relative price increases consumption.

total utility total satisfaction derived from consuming goods and services.

MARKET AND INDIVIDUAL DEMAND

In this chapter, we analyze how one consumer changes his or her demand for a good when the good's price changes. But is this useful for analyzing a whole market with many consumers? The answer is, yes. The **market demand curve** for a good is the *horizontal sum* of the demand curves of all consumers. Thus, the effect of price on market demand is the sum of its effects on the demand of individual consumers.

In Figure 17–1, we derive the market demand curve for records when there are only two consumers, Abe and Bob. Abe's demand curve is D_{ABE} and Bob's demand curve is D_{BOB}. To get the market demand curve for records, we start with some price (say $5). We find out how much each consumer buys at that price. We then add up these amounts. This gives us the quantity demanded "by the market" at that price. For example, at $5, Abe demands 6 records and Bob demands 4: The market demand at $5 is 10 records. We then do this for all prices.

The result is a market demand curve (D_{A+B}) that is the horizontal sum of D_{ABE} and D_{BOB}.

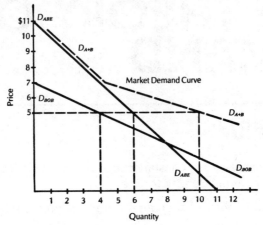

Figure 17-1   How Market Demand Is Affected by Price Changes

YOU SHOULD REMEMBER

1. The market demand curve for a good is the horizontal sum of demand curves for all consumers.

2. Market demand curves sum the effects of price on all consumers.

THE LAW OF DIMINISHING MARGINAL UTILITY

To illustrate the basic theory of demand, assume economists can measure a consumer's satisfaction in "utils." **Total utility** measures a consumer's total satisfaction, or total utils, from a good. When the consumer consumes an additional unit of a good, total utility goes up: Economists call this addition to total utility **marginal utility.**

For example, suppose a consumer eating five units of food has a total utility of 50 utils; adding a sixth unit, total utility increases to 58 utils. The marginal utility of the sixth unit is 8 utils (58 − 50).

The **law of diminishing marginal utility** states that as people consume more of a good in a given period, (1) their total utility goes up, *but* (2) each added unit of the good adds *less* to their total utility. That is, as more of a good is consumed, its marginal utility declines. This law implies that the seventh unit of food in the example above should have a marginal utility that's less than 8 utils of the sixth unit (perhaps 7 or 5 utils).

Note that as more is consumed, total utility is going up. What is "diminishing" is the addition to total utility.

YOU SHOULD REMEMBER

1. Total utility is the total satisfaction or "utils" one gets from consuming some good.

2. Marginal utility is the addition to total utility from consuming one additional unit of the good.

3. The law of diminishing marginal utility states that as people consume more units of a good, the marginal utility of each added unit declines.

THE LAW OF EQUAL MARGINAL UTILITY PER DOLLAR: GETTING THE MOST UTILITY

Consumers want the highest total utility their income allows them to achieve. To show how much of each good they will buy to maximize their utility, let's assume consumers want only two goods: food and clothing.

How much food should the consumer buy? We will use marginal analysis (see Chapter 1) to find out.

How to Achieve Maximum Utility with Marginal Analysis

1. *The consumer wants to maximize total utility. Let the control variable be the units of food the consumer buys.* We assume the consumer spends all his or her income so that buying more food means having less clothing.

2. *The marginal benefit of one more unit of food is how much the one additional unit adds to total utility,* i.e., food's marginal utility:

$$\text{Marginal Benefit} = MU_f.$$

3. *The marginal cost of one more unit of food is the forgone utility from less clothing.* The consumer will forgo P_f/P_c units of clothing when he or she buys one more unit of food, where P_f is the price of food and P_c is the price of clothing. For example, if the price of food is $4 and the price of clothing is $2, then to buy one more unit of food, the consumer must forgo 2 units of clothing. To derive the forgone utility, we multiply the forgone units of clothing by the marginal utility of each unit of clothing:

$$\text{Marginal Cost} = (P_f/P_c) \times MU_c$$

4. *The consumer should demand more units of food as long as marginal benefit* ≥ *marginal cost:*

$$MU_f > (P_f/P_c) \times MU_c.$$

For example, if the consumer gets 8 utils from another unit of food and 3 utils from another unit of clothing and if the price of food is $4 and the price of clothing is $2, the consumer should buy more food and less clothing. The consumer's marginal benefit from another unit of food is 8 utils. The consumer's marginal cost of another unit of food is a loss of 6 utils from 2 less units of clothing (2 units of clothing times 3 utils each). So by consuming one more unit of food, the consumer will on net gain 2 units (8 − 6): the consumer should buy more food.

5. At the highest level of utility, marginal benefit equals marginal cost, or:

$$MU_f = (P_f/P_c) \times MU_c$$

Stated another way, this equality can be stated as:

$$\frac{MU_f}{P_f} = \frac{MU_c}{P_c}$$

The expression on the left is the marginal utility per dollar of food; on the right, the marginal utility per dollar of clothing.

This result reflects the **law of equal marginal utility per dollar**: The highest utility is achieved when the last dollar spent on each good yields the same increase in utility (i.e., when MU/P for each good is equal). To see why this is true, suppose food offered a higher MU per dollar. Consumers could then better their utility by spending one more dollar on food. This means spending one less dollar on clothing, but since this clothing dollar has the lower MU, more is gained than is given up. So if consumers are spending optimally, so that no rearrangement of spending will make them better off, the MU of the last dollar spent on each good should be equal.

When consumers have maximized their utility, economists say they are *in equilibrium* (i.e., they will not change their consumption patterns unless prices or their tastes change).

Examples: Calculating MU

PROBLEM   When $P_f = 4 and $P_c = 2, suppose $MU_f = 8$ utils at the consumer's highest level of utility. What is MU_c? What is MU/P for food and clothing?

SOLUTION $MU_c = 4$ utils. MU/P for both goods is 2 utils.

PROBLEM   The consumer has spent all of his or her income and has MU_f = 6 and $MU_c = 4$ when $P_f = \$4$ and $P_c = \$2$. Is the consumer at the highest level of utility? If not, what should the consumer do?

SOLUTION   No, the consumer is not at the highest level of utility, because $MU_f/P_f = 1.5$, which is smaller than $MU_c/P_c = 2$. The consumer will be better off spending more on clothing (as each dollar spent on clothing has a higher MU) and less on food.

Another way of stating the law of equal marginal utility per dollar is to say the **relative marginal utilities** of goods should *equal* their relative prices $(MU_f/MU_c = P_f/P_c)$. For example, when food costs twice as much as clothing, food should also have twice the marginal utility (*when and only when* the consumer is maximizing his or her utility).

YOU SHOULD REMEMBER

1. The consumer achieves the highest level of utility when the last dollar spent on each good has the same marginal utility.

2. The marginal utility per dollar for a good is derived by dividing its marginal utility by its price.

3. In equilibrium, relative marginal utilities of goods will equal their relative prices: A good that costs twice as much should have twice the marginal utility.

DERIVING THE LAW OF DEMAND FROM THE LAW OF EQUAL MARGINAL UTILITY PER DOLLAR

The **law of demand** states that the quantity of a good demanded will fall when the price of the good rises. This law can be derived from the law of equal marginal utility per dollar.

We begin with consumers at their highest utility (given their income). With food and clothing as the only two goods they consume, we should have:

$$\frac{MU_f}{P_f} = \frac{MU_c}{P_c}$$

Now assume the price of food goes up from P_f to P_f'. Holding the amount of food and clothing consumed constant, neither MU_f nor MU_c changes. But now:

$$\frac{MU_f}{P_f'} < \frac{MU_c}{P_c} \text{ since } P_f' > P_f$$

Because food now has a lower marginal utility per dollar than clothing, food dollars are worth less than clothing dollars: Consumers will buy more clothing and less food. Buying more clothing reduces MU_c and buying less food increases MU_f: This brings the consumer back to equal MU/P. This supports the law of demand (a higher P_f reduces the quantity of food demanded).

A WARNING AND A REMINDER

A Warning

The law of diminishing marginal utility is sometimes incorrectly used to argue that the rich get less utility out of added income than the poor. But utility can't be measured. A greedy rich man, for example, may get more utility from another dollar than a poor ascetic hermit.

A Reminder

The demand curve is the schedule of a good's marginal benefits. Marginal benefits in turn reflect (in dollar terms) the good's relative marginal utility. Thus, the price of a good reflects its marginal value, not its total value. This is why water has a lower price than diamonds. Water has a greater total value but because it is so plentiful, its marginal value is lower.

INCOME EFFECTS AND SUBSTITUTION EFFECTS

When a good's price goes up, two things occur: (1) its relative price goes up *and* (2) consumers' real income goes down (since they can buy less than before). To describe how price changes affect consumers, economists separate the effect of a higher price into these two separate effects:

1. **The Substitution Effect:** The decrease in demand when a good's relative price goes up, holding real income constant. A *higher relative price* for food causes consumers to *buy less* food because the higher price reduces the marginal utility per food dollar, MU_f/P_f. This is true even if the higher price does *not* reduce the real income of consumers. Real income is defined to be "constant" if consumers *can* buy the same amount of food and other goods as before (although in fact they will buy less food).

2. **The Income Effect:** The change in demand when real income changes (holding the *relative* price of the good constant). For a given money income, an *increase* in the actual price of a good will *reduce* real income. This lower real income in itself will *reduce* the quantity demanded of a *normal good*. But it will *increase* the quantity demanded of an *inferior good*.

The total change in the quantity demanded is the sum of these two effects. Table 17-1 summarizes these effects.

Table 17-1 The Effects of a Price Change on Demand

Price Change	Type Of Good	Substitution Effect (1)	Income Effect (2)	Net Effect On Quantity (3) = (1) + (2)
Up	Normal	–	–	–
	Inferior	–	+	?
Down	Normal	+	+	+
	Inferior	+	–	?

Note that it is possible for a higher price to increase demand. This occurs with inferior goods *and* when the income effect is strong. (This case is called the **Giffen Paradox**, which has rarely, if ever, been observed.)

Examples: Using Income and Substitution Effects

PROBLEM   Suppose the government puts a tax on food. To predict the effect of the tax on food consumption, should one use the substitution effect, the income effect, or both combined?

SOLUTION   Use only the substitution effect. Why? Because the nation's income has not changed. The tax merely shifts income from food consumers to those to whom the government gives the tax dollars. (Of course, a poorly designed tax can reduce the real income of a nation, and to the extent it does, economists add in the income effect.)

PROBLEM   When oil prices went up, America was importing one-third of its oil. To predict the effect of higher oil prices on oil consumption in the U.S., economists added the substitution effect to one-third the income effect. Why one-third?

SOLUTION   Because one-third was the fraction of oil the U.S. imported. This represents the lost income from higher oil prices Americans paid to foreign countries. The other two-thirds was only a transfer of income from oil consumers to domestic oil producers and so did not represent a change in national income.

YOU SHOULD REMEMBER

1. The *substitution effect* of a price change is its effect on the quantity of a good demanded due to its effect on the good's relative price, holding real income constant.

2. The *income effect* of a price change is its effect on the quantity of a good demanded due to the effect of the price change on real income.

3. The net effect of a price change is the sum of its substitution and income effects.

4. Taxes and subsidies do not usually change national income significantly, so their main impact is described by the substitution effect.

CONSUMER SURPLUS

Most of us have had the experience of making a good deal when we bought something for far less than what we were willing to pay. Economists refer to this as the good's **consumer surplus**: It is the (1) maximum amount consumers *would* pay for a certain amount of a good *minus* (2) the actual dollars they did pay.

In Figure 17-2, we show the demand curve for a consumer *(DD)*. The consumer pays $3 for each pizza and buys 10 pizzas a month. The distance between the demand curve [which reflects (1)] and the price line *T* [which reflects (2)] is the unit's consumer surplus. For example, the consumer would have paid up to $7 for the fourth pizza but in fact only paid $3: The consumer surplus for the fourth pizza is $4 ($7 − $3). The total consumer surplus from all 10 pizzas equals $35 [= area of triangle *VTU*, which in turn equals the base (*TU* = 10 pizzas) times the height (*VT* = $7) divided by 2].

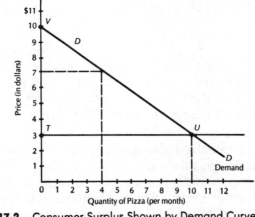

Figure 17-2   Consumer Surplus Shown by Demand Curve

Example: Using Consumer Surplus

PROBLEM In a given month, Sue is willing to pay $10 to see one movie, $8 to see a second movie, and $6 to see a third.

A. If the price of a movie is $7, what is Sue's consumer surplus?

B. If the theater owner offers three tickets for $19, will Sue take the deal? What is the most the theater owner could charge for the three-ticket package deal?

SOLUTION A. $4 ($3 for the first movie plus $1 for the second). Sue will not go to the third movie.

B. Yes. Now her consumer surplus is $5 ($10 + $8 + $6 − $19), which is better than the surplus that results from buying tickets separately. At most, Sue would pay $20, the amount that would leave her with the same consumer surplus ($4) as the option of buying tickets separately ($4 = $24 of value − $20 package-deal cost).

Note: The theater owner makes more money from Sue with the package deal.

YOU SHOULD REMEMBER

1. Consumer surplus measures the difference between what a good is worth to consumers and what they pay.

2. The demand curve reflects the (marginal) value of each unit of the good to consumers.

APPLICATIONS FOR BUSINESS: PRINCIPLE OF EQUAL MARGINAL BENEFIT PER UNIT

We saw that consumers are best off when they get equal marginal utility per dollar. This is a specific case of a more general and powerful tool for decision-making: **the principle of equal marginal benefit per unit**. This principle states that when faced with a limited amount of resources (such as money or time), the decision-maker should allocate the units of the resource to different alternative uses such that *its marginal benefit in each use is equal*. This will achieve the highest net benefit of all possible allocations.

Examples: Equal Marginal Benefit Per Unit

PROBLEM A grocery store has limited shelf space. Every product line generates a yearly profit per square foot of shelf space. As the shelf space devoted to any item is increased, its marginal benefit (i.e., its addition to total yearly profits) goes down. How many square feet should the store owner devote to each item?

SOLUTION   The last square foot devoted to each item should have the same marginal benefit (i.e., should add the same amount to the store's profits). Suppose the last square foot devoted to soup adds $100 to the store's profits while the last square foot devoted to cake mixes adds $80. The store should expand the space devoted to soup and contract the space for cake mixes. For example, one more square foot added to soup that's taken away from cakes will add $20 to the store's profits.

PROBLEM   A business has a policy of never borrowing money but instead generates all of its capital by reinvesting its profits. It thus has a limited amount of capital to invest among many projects. Each added dollar of investment in a project will yield a certain annual return, but usually this rate of return per marginal dollar invested tends to fall as more is invested. How much should the firm invest in each project?

SOLUTION   The last dollar in each project should yield the same marginal benefit. If the last dollar in Project A yields a 10% return while in Project B it yields a 25% return, funds from Project A should be diverted into Project B.

PROBLEM   A business executive has a limited amount of time. Each added hour of time in any task has a certain marginal benefit to the executive. Usually, as more time is devoted to any particular task, its marginal benefit declines. When will the executive be getting the best use of his or her time? Will the most valuable tasks get the most time devoted to them?

SOLUTION   The best use of time will occur when the marginal benefit of the last hour devoted to each task is the same. However, this does not imply that the most time should be devoted to the most valuable task. For example, suppose Task A has a marginal benefit in the first hour of $1,000, in the second hour of $1, and no marginal benefit after that. Task B has a marginal benefit of $3, $2, and $1 for the first, second, and third hour respectively. With five hours, the executive should devote two hours to Task A and three to B. So even though Task A has a higher total benefit ($1,001), less time should be devoted to it.

KNOW THE CONCEPTS
DO YOU KNOW THE BASICS?

1. Why do we add consumers' demand curves together *horizontally* to get the market demand curve?

2. How are total utility and marginal utility related?

3. Does a good with a higher total utility also have a higher marginal utility?

4. What happens to total utility as marginal utility diminishes (as one consumes more of a good)?

5. If the marginal utilities per dollar of two goods are not the same, why will consumers change their consumption pattern?

6. What is the substitution effect of a price increase?

7. What is the income effect of a price increase? How does it differ for normal and inferior goods?

8. Is the marginal utility of a candy bar greater to a poor person or a rich person?

9. Bill has spent $300 for a video recorder. He would have been willing to pay $500. What is his consumer surplus?

10. Even if consumers could still consume the same goods they have been consuming, why will a change in relative prices cause them to change their consumption pattern?

TERMS FOR STUDY

consumer surplus
Giffen Paradox
income effect
law of diminishing marginal utility

law of equal marginal utility
per dollar
marginal utility
substitution effect
total utility

PRACTICAL APPLICATION

1. Suppose a market has only three consumers. Derive the market demand curve from this table.

	Quantity Demanded			
	Price			
Consumer	$4	$3	$2	$1
A	10	14	18	22
B	0	2	4	6
C	5	6	10	16

2. Use the following table to answer these questions. *TU* stands for total utility.

Units	1	2	3	4	5
TU of Good X	6	10	12	13	13
TU of Good Y	7	11	12	12	11

    a. What is the marginal utility *(MU)* of each unit? (Provide your answer in the form of a table.) Is marginal utility increasing or diminishing?

    b. If the consumer has $7 to spend and both goods cost $1, how many of each should the consumer buy?

    c. If the price of good Y goes to $2 while income remains at $7, what will happen to the amounts demanded?

3. For Bill, clothing has a marginal utility of 20 utils and food has a marginal utility of 20 utils. If clothing costs $4 and food $8, is Bill doing the best he can? If not, what can he do to increase his utility?

4. Suppose food costs $12 and clothing costs $2, and at the highest level of utility, clothing has a marginal utility of 6 utils. What is the marginal utility of food?

5. If you are taking a test that has several questions, how should you allocate your time among the questions in order to get the highest score?

6. Mary buys a Cadillac instead of a Chevrolet. The Cadillac costs exactly twice as much as the Chevrolet. What can we conclude about Mary's marginal utility of owning a Cadillac relative to owning a Chevrolet?

7. What is wrong with the following statement: "According to the law of diminishing marginal utility, if you consume less food, the marginal utility you receive from the last unit of food goes up. So you will have greater total utility from consuming less food."

8. Bill is maximizing his utility. He is consuming (among other goods) beer, which costs $1 a can, and pretzels, which cost $.50 a bag. Which good has the higher marginal utility? What is the ratio of his marginal utilities?

9. Suppose the government taxed food and either (1) gave the tax revenues back to Americans in the form of reduced income taxes or (2) gave the tax revenues to a foreign government. In which case (1) or (2) will the demand for food go down more? (Food is a normal good.)

10. Mary has $12 to spend. She buys two beers (which cost $3 each) and three bowls of chili (which cost $2 each). Then the price of beer falls to $2 and chili's price goes up to $3. How will Mary change her consumption of beer and chili? Does this event reflect a substitution effect, an income effect, or both?

ANSWERS

KNOW THE CONCEPTS

1. Because economists want to sum the amounts consumers will buy at each price.

2. Marginal utility is the addition to total utility when one more unit of a good is consumed.

3. The total utility and marginal utility of different goods need not be related. Water, for example, has a high total utility but a small marginal utility.

4. As long as marginal utility is positive, when more of a good is consumed, total utility increases.

5. Because consumers will be better off by consuming more of the good that has the higher marginal utility per dollar. By doing this, they will be gaining more utils per dollar than they are giving up.

6. The substitution effect is the decrease in the quantity demanded of a good that results when the good's relative price goes up (holding the consumer's real income constant).

7. The income effect of a price increase is the change in the quantity demanded due to the decrease in real income caused by the price increase. For a normal good, the quantity demanded falls; for an inferior good, it rises.

8. Since utility between persons cannot be objectively compared, it is impossible to say.

9. $200 ($500 − $300) is Bill's consumer surplus.

10. Those goods whose price fell will now have a higher marginal utility per dollar: Consumers will demand more of these goods.

PRACTICAL APPLICATION

1. The market demand curve will be:

Price	Quantity Demanded
$1	44
2	32
3	22
4	15

2. a.

Units	1	2	3	4	5
MU of X	6	4	2	1	0
MU of Y	7	4	1	0	−1

There is diminishing marginal utility.

b. When each unit costs $1, the above table is also the marginal utility per dollar. To get the answer, buy goods in the order of highest marginal utility per dollar (so you would buy the first Y, then the first X, then the second X and Y, etc.) until all $7 is spent. The answer will be 4 X and 3 Y (both having an equal MU/P of 1).

c. To answer what happens when the price of Good Y goes to $2, we construct the MU/P table:

Units	1	2	3	4	5
MU/P of X	4	3	2	1	0
MU/P of Y	3.5	2	.5	0	−.5

Buying in order of MU/P, the consumer will buy 3 X and 2 Y (with an equal MU/P of 2). Demand for Good Y falls from 3 units to 2. This illustrates the law of demand.

3. MU/P for clothing is 5, for food 2.5. Bill should buy more clothing and less food.

4. From the equality of MU/P, $MU_f/\$12$ = 6 utils/$2. MU_f = 36 utils.

5. You should allocate your time so that the last minute spent on each question adds the same number of points to your total score.

6. For Mary, the marginal utility of owning a Cadillac must be twice as high, or higher, as the marginal utility of owning a Chevrolet.

7. As one less unit of food is consumed, *total* utility decreases by the unit's marginal utility. As less food is consumed, the law of diminishing marginal utility states that this loss in *total* utility becomes bigger.

8. The MU of a can of beer will be twice the MU of a bag of pretzels (the ratio of marginal utilities equaling the ratio of prices).

9. In case (2), because the loss in real U.S. income is greater, so the income effect reduces food demand more.

10. Mary will buy more beer and less chili. Since she could have bought her old quantities at the new prices, her real income has not changed. So this event reflects the substitution effect only.

18
COST AND OUTPUT

SHORT- AND LONG-RUN COSTS

How do costs change with output? The answer, which tells how steep the supply curve will be, is found by looking at two time periods:

1. **The short run,** when the firm can change (either increasing or decreasing) some but *not all* of its inputs in order to produce more or less output. Usually, in the short run, the firm meets a higher demand by hiring more labor and buying more materials, but leaves its plant and equipment unchanged.

2. **The long run,** when the firm can change *all* of its inputs, including its plant size and equipment.

SHORT-RUN COSTS

In using marginal analysis (see Chapter 1), we saw that the *most important cost* for making output decisions is marginal cost. **Marginal cost** (*MC*) is the increase in total cost caused by increasing output by one unit. If six units of output cost $60 and seven units, $77, the marginal cost of the seventh unit is $17 ($77 − $60).

• *MARGINAL COST IN THE SHORT RUN*

Economists generally have found that in the short run marginal costs form a U-shaped pattern with output, first falling as output is increased, but then rising. The section of falling *MC* (from 0 to Point *B* in Figure 18-1) is called the section of *increasing marginal returns*. The section of rising *MC* (from *B* and up) is called the section of *diminishing marginal returns*.

Why does the marginal cost curve have this U-shape? To see why, assume for simplicity that labor *(L)* is the only input the firm can increase in the short run.

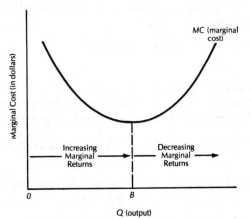

Figure 18-1   The U-Shaped Pattern of Marginal Cost in the Short Run

The **marginal physical product** of labor *(MPP)* is the addition to total output that results when one more unit of labor is added. If ten workers produce twenty shoes and eleven produce twenty-three shoes, the *MPP* of the eleventh worker is three shoes (23 − 20).

MC equals the cost of the added labor needed to produce that unit of output. If an added unit of *L* has an *MPP* of three units, then one added unit of output takes (approximately) one-third of a unit of labor to produce. In general, it takes 1/*MPP* of a unit of *L* to produce one more unit of output. To get the marginal cost of that unit of output, we multiply the wage of labor *(W)* by the labor needed to produce it, 1/*MPP*:

$$MC = W/MPP$$

For example, if *W* = $12 and *MPP* is three shoes, it takes one-third of a unit of *L* to produce a shoe: The shoe's *MC* is $4.

MC changes because MPP changes.

In the section of increasing marginal returns, each added worker provides more than the previous worker to total output: *MPP* is going up. So *MC* (or *W/MPP*) goes down as output is expanded. But the **law of diminishing marginal**

returns states that beyond some level of output, the input's *MPP* declines, such that successive units add less and less to total output. In this section of decreasing marginal returns, *MPP* is going down. So *MC* (or *W/MPP*) goes up once decreasing returns have set in.

To see why *MC* has this U-shape, imagine a large factory fully stocked with equipment and materials. To produce one unit of output will likely take many workers (especially when the factory is based around an assembly line). Thus the first unit of output will have a high marginal cost. But the successive units of output will take fewer units of labor to produce and thus marginal cost will fall. However, at some point, as the plant reaches its capacity in terms of the number of workers it can use, adding more workers no longer adds as much to output as previously (i.e., we have diminishing returns), so each added unit costs more and more to produce. Hence, *MC* will have a U-shape.

Table 18-1 illustrates the relationship between *MC* and *MPP* for a shoe manufacturer when the wage is $12. Up to 3 workers, the firm experiences increasing marginal returns (*MPP* is increasing). The second worker increases output by 4 shoes, so the *MC* of a shoe is $3 ($12/3). But the third worker has a higher *MPP* (5) reducing *MC* to $2.40 ($12/5). Beyond 3 workers, the firm experiences diminishing marginal returns and thus, rising marginal costs.

Table 18-1. The Relationship Between Marginal Cost and Marginal Physical Product

Labor Input	Output	MPP	MC (when W = $12)
0	0	—	—
1	3	3	$4.00
2	7	4	3.00
3	12	5	2.40
4	16	4	3.00
5	19	3	4.00
6	21	2	6.00
7	22	1	12.00

YOU SHOULD REMEMBER

1. Marginal costs are the most important costs in making output decisions. Marginal cost is the increase in total cost needed to produce another unit of output.

2. The short-run marginal cost curve relating marginal cost to output usually has a U-shape. The section of falling marginal costs reflects increasing *MPP*. The section of rising *MC* reflects decreasing *MPP*.

3. The law of diminishing marginal returns states that, beyond some point, as more units of an input are added, its MPP falls. This law applies when the amount of other inputs is not changed.

• *MARGINAL COST AND TOTAL COSTS*

The **total cost** (*TC*) of producing output consists of:

1. **total fixed costs** *(TFC)*: the cost of inputs the firm can't change in the short run (such as plant and equipment), and

2. **total variable costs** *(TVC)*: the total cost of all the inputs (such as workers and materials) the firm *does change* in the short run to produce more. This can be visualized as:

$$TC = TFC + TVC$$

TFC stays the same when output changes. It equals the firm's total cost when output is zero (and thus when $TVC = 0$).

Since *TFC* stays the same as output goes up, both *TVC* and *TC* go up by *MC* when one more unit of output is produced. (Note that this result is true by definition: *MC* is the increase in *TC* due to one more unit of output.)

TVC is the sum of *MCs*. If the marginal cost of the first unit of output is $5, the second unit, $4, and the third, $3, then the *TVC* of one unit is $5, the *TVC* of two units is $9, and of three units, $12.

As *MC* is falling in the section of increasing marginal returns, *TVC* increases, but each increase becomes smaller as *MC* becomes smaller. In Figure 18–2, this occurs as output increases to level *B*. Beyond *B*, *MC* rises, *TVC* increases, and each successive increase becomes bigger. Note that:

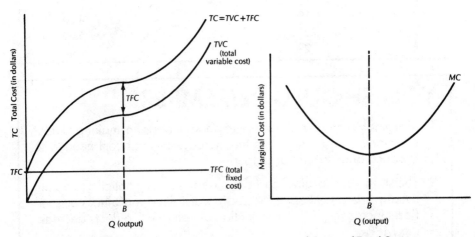

Figure 18-2 The Relationship Between Marginal Cost and Total Cost

1. *MC* is the slope of the *TVC* cost curve.

2. The *TC* curve is the vertical sum of the *TVC* and the *TFC* curves.

3. The *TFC* curve is a horizontal line, since *TFC* is the same when output goes up.

YOU SHOULD REMEMBER

1. *Total fixed cost* is the total cost of all fixed inputs that stay the same when output is changed. *Total variable cost* is the total cost of all variable inputs that increase or decrease with output.

2. *Total cost* is the sum of total fixed cost and total variable cost.

3. Total variable cost at any level of output is the sum of all marginal costs up to that level of output.

4. Total variable cost goes up by marginal cost.

• *MARGINAL COST AND AVERAGE COST*

Average cost is the cost per unit, or, total cost divided by total output. There is an average cost for each type of cost.

Average total cost *(ATC)* equals

$$TC/Q$$

where Q is the number of units of output the firm is producing. We also have:

$$\text{Average Variable Cost } (AVC) = TVC/Q.$$
$$\text{Average Fixed Cost } (AFC) = TFC/Q.$$

Since
$$ATC = TC/Q = (TVC + TFC)/Q,$$

we also have:
$$ATC = TVC/Q + TFC/Q$$

and, finally:
$$ATC = AVC + AFC$$

Since total fixed cost does not change with output, *AFC* is always smaller at higher levels of Q.

To understand how *AVC* and *ATC* change with output, you must first understand how *average* and *marginal* amounts are related.

How Average and Marginal Costs Are Related

1. If we add a number to a sum that is *smaller* than the sum's average, the average will go *down*. For example, if a five-foot man walks into a room of men whose average height is six feet, the average height of the men in the room will go down.

2. If we add a number to the sum *equal* to its average, the average will remain the *same*.

3. If we add a number *larger* than the sum's average, the average will go *up*.

The number being added is the marginal addition. Marginal cost *(MC)* is the number being added to total cost *(TC)*. When the addition (here, *MC*) exceeds the average (here, *ATC*), the average will go up. For example, suppose a firm is producing 50 units and has an *ATC* of $20. If the 51st unit has an *MC* of $25, the *ATC* of 51 units will go up (to $20.10). In general, the change in *ATC* as output increases depends on how it relates to the *MC* of the added output.

(1) If $MC < ATC$, *ATC* goes down.
(2) If $MC = ATC$, *ATC* stays the same.
(3) If $MC > ATC$, *ATC* goes up.

Because *MC* is also the addition to total variable cost as output increases, the resulting change in average variable cost *(AVC)* depends also upon how it compares to *MC*.

(1) If $MC < AVC$, *AVC* goes down.
(2) If $MC = AVC$, *AVC* stays the same.
(3) If $MC > AVC$, *AVC* goes up.

In general, the average cost curve moves toward the marginal cost curve as output increases.

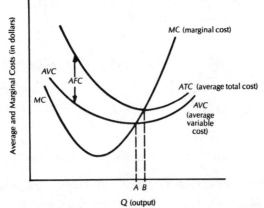

Figure 18-3 The Relationship Between Marginal Cost and Average Cost

Figure 18-3 shows how *MC* and *AVC* are related. *MC* starts out below *AVC*, so *AVC* falls. Then *MC* begins to rise, but as long as *MC* is below *AVC*, *AVC* falls. At *Q* = *A*, *MC* = *AVC*: at this output, *ATC* *is at a minimum!* When *Q* >*A*, *MC* >*ATC* so *AVC* rises as output rises.

The *ATC* curve is the horizontal sum of *AVC* and *AFC*. Since *AFC* is continually falling, the *ATC* curve becomes closer to the *AVC* curve as *Q* increases. At *Q* = *B*, *MC* = *ATC*: at this output, *ATC* *is at a minimum!* (See Practical Application, Question 2, for a numerical example of these relationships.)

YOU SHOULD REMEMBER

1. When output expands, as long as marginal costs is smaller than the average variable cost, AVC falls. MC equals AVC at the minimum AVC. The MC exceeds AVC and AVC rises.

2. Average cost moves towards marginal cost.

3. Average fixed cost becomes smaller as output expands.

4. At the minimum average total cost, MC = ATC. At the minimum average variable cost, MC = AVC.

LONG-RUN COSTS

In the long run, all inputs can be changed. So marginal cost is no longer affected by the law of diminishing marginal product (which assumes some inputs are fixed). When all inputs are increased, economists say the firm has increased its "**scale**". There are three possible cases:

1. *Economies of scale* occur when average total cost falls as output expands. This fall in *ATC* occurs when to produce more output the firm uses fewer added inputs than before. Economies of scale mainly occur because of the economies from specialization and the better utilization rates that result from producing more.

2. *Constant returns to scale* occur when average total cost stays the same as output expands. *ATC* stays the same when the firm can produce more output with the same amount of added inputs as before.

3. *Diseconomies of scale* occur when average total cost goes up as output expands. *ATC* goes up when to produce more output the firm must use more added inputs than previously. Diseconomies of scale often result from the problems and added costs associated with large bureaucracies.

Figure 18-4 shows these three cases.

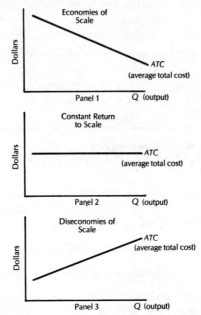

Figure 18-4 The Changing Scales of Cost in the Long Run

Figure 18-5 shows the case for a "typical" firm. Like the short-run *ATC* curve, the long-run *ATC* curve *(LRATC)* is U-shaped. The U-shape reflects the fact that most firms first experience economies, then constant returns, and finally diseconomies as they expand their scale of operations.

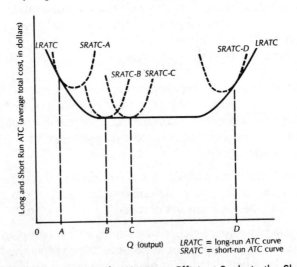

Figure 18-5 Determining the Minimum Efficient Scale in the Short Run and in the Long Run

In the long run, the firm has the freedom to vary all inputs and to choose the most efficient technology and scale. For each level of output, there is one optimal scale with which the firm could choose to produce it. The cost of this optimal scale is shown by the *LRATC* curve: the *LRATC* curve shows the lowest *ATC* at which each level of output can be produced. But in the short run, the firm *cannot* vary all inputs. So it will face a higher cost if it must produce more or less than the level of output for which its current scale is best. For example, in Figure 18-5, the minimum cost of producing output level *A* is shown by the *LRATC*. Suppose the firm has a plant equal to this scale. In the short run, if it wants to produce more or less, its *ATC* will be *higher*: This is shown by the *SRATC-A* curve. For each output, there is a different *SRATC* curve.

In Figure 18-5, output *B*, where *LRATC* just becomes its smallest, is the **minimum efficient scale** for this firm. The larger a firm's minimum efficient scale is relative to the industry's output, the fewer firms there can be in the industry that can compete and produce efficiently.

YOU SHOULD REMEMBER

1. In the long run, all inputs can be increased so that the law of diminishing marginal returns need not apply.

2. The long-run average cost curve shows the lowest *ATC* at which each level of output can be produced.

3. When an increase in all inputs results in a greater than proportionate increase in output, the firm experiences economies of scale. *LRATC* falls.

4. When an increase in inputs increases output proportionately, the firm experiences constant returns to scale. *LRATC* remains the same.

5. When an increase in inputs increases output less than proportionately, the firm experiences decreasing returns to scale. *LRATC* rises.

PROFITS AND COSTS

Each firm has two types of costs:

1. The **explicit costs** it pays for inputs. These are the costs recorded by accountants.

2. The **implicit costs** of its owner's time and investment in the firm. These costs are measured by what the owners could have earned had they worked and invested in their next best alternative (the *opportunity costs of their time and capital*). These costs usually are ignored by accountants.

Since accounting profits ignore implicit costs:

> **Accounting Profits** = Total Revenue − Explicit Costs.

Economic profit is the amount paid in excess of what was necessary to get something done. The amount necessary to get something done is its cost, including *both* explicit and implicit costs. Thus:

> **Economic Profits** = Total Revenue − (Explicit + Implicit Costs)

Considerable confusion is caused by the term "economic profits." It might be better thought of as "excess profits," because it is the excess over what the business owner needs to be paid in order to produce. Thus, while a business needs to make an accounting profit to stay in business, its economic profit can be zero and it will remain in business!

Example: Calculating Economic Profit

PROBLEM   Jerry was a computer programmer who earned $50,000 a year. He decided to go into business for himself, investing $100,000 of his savings (which had been earning 7% in a money market fund). In the first year, his business had $200,000 in revenues and $120,000 in explicit costs. What was his economic profit?

SOLUTION $23,000. Implicit costs equal forgone earnings ($50,000) plus forgone interest ($7,000 = 7% of $100,000). $23,000 = $200,000 − ($120,000 + $57,000).

YOU SHOULD REMEMBER

1. A firm has two costs: the *explicit cost* of the inputs it buys and the *implicit cost* of the time and money invested by its owners.

2. *Economic profit* is the excess of revenue over the firm's costs, when costs include explicit *and* implicit costs.

3. *Accounting profits* ignore implicit costs and so overstate the firm's true economic profit.

KNOW THE CONCEPTS

DO YOU KNOW THE BASICS?

1. Why are average costs lowest in the long run?
2. What is happening to the marginal productivity of workers as marginal costs fall?
3. Why do marginal costs rise?
4. Is the law of diminishing marginal returns true when all inputs are increased together?
5. How is the total variable cost curve derived from the marginal cost curve?
6. How is the total cost curve derived from the total variable cost curve?
7. When $MC < AVC$, how will AVC change when output is increased?
8. How is MC related to AVC and ATC at their respective minimum values?
9. Why does the ATC fall when the firm is experiencing economies of scale?
10. Why would a firm be better off not producing when its economic profits are negative?

TERMS FOR STUDY

accounting profit	law of diminishing marginal returns
average variable, fixed, and total costs	long and short run
constant return to scale	long-run average cost
diseconomies of scale	marginal cost
economic profit	marginal physical product
economies of scale	total cost
explicit costs	total fixed costs
implicit costs	total variable costs

PRACTICAL APPLICATION

1. Assume $Q = 0$ when $L = 0$ and the wage, W (the cost of L) = $60. Fill in the following table to answer the question below:

Labor Input (L)	1	2	3	4	5	6	7	8	9
Output (Q)	2	5	9	14	19	23	26	28	29
MPP									
MC of 1 Q									

At what L do diminishing returns set in?

2. Fill in this table.

Q	MC	TVC	AVC	TFC	AFC	TC	ATC
0	–		–	$112	–		–
1	$16						
2	14						
3	12						
4	6						
5	12						
6	16						
7	22						
8	30						
9	38						
10	44						

    a. Where do diminishing marginal returns set in?
    b. What is the minimum AVC? What is MC at that level of output?
    c. What is the minimum ATC? What is MC at that level of output?

3. Some quick questions:
    a. If ATC = $12 at Q = 5, what is TC?
    b. If AVC = $10 at Q = 10 and AVC = $11 at Q = 11, what is the MC of the eleventh unit?
    c. If ATC = $12 and MC = $15, is ATC rising or falling?
    d. If ATC = $15 and AVC = $10 at Q = 10, what is TFC?
    e. If TC = $150 at Q = 8 and $180 at Q = 9, what is the MC of the ninth unit?

4. If one added worker increases output by ten units, how much labor is embodied in each unit of output? If the added worker costs $12,000, what is the marginal cost of one extra unit of output?

5. Answer true or false:
    a. ATC falls only when MC falls.
    b. At the minimum AVC, AVC = MC.
    c. ATC falls when MC < ATC.
    d. TC increases by MC.

6. Mary Jones can work in a factory and earn $16,000 a year, or alternatively, be a farmer. Assume that except for monetary reward, she doesn't care which she does. To farm, Mary has to invest her savings of $20,000. The annual cost of seed, fertilizer, etc., is $5,000. She could earn 10% annually on her best alternative investment.

a. What is the total cost of farming (including implicit costs)?

b. What is the minimum Mary must make in farming to just make it worthwhile?

c. If her farm revenues are $30,000, what is her economic profit? Her accounting profit? Should she stay in farming?

d. Answer (c) above for revenues of $20,000.

7. Old Fud owns a jewelry store. He didn't raise his prices on the diamonds he bought last year even though diamond prices have since doubled. He says "I'm still making a profit at my old price." Is Old Fud right?

8. Between two towns, one can (a) fly at a cost of $100 taking one hour, or (b) take a bus at $50, which takes five hours. Why are business men and women more likely to choose (a) while relatively more students will choose (b)?

9. Consider the cost curves of a trucking firm.

a. Suppose there is an increase in the price of gasoline. How will each of these cost curves shift up (if they shift at all): MC, ATC, AVC, AFC?

b. Suppose the cost of incorporating and setting up a trucking business goes up. How will each of the above cost curves shift?

10. Suppose a firm's production process can be characterized as having economies of scale. If so, when output doubles, what happens to total cost? To ATC?

ANSWERS

KNOW THE CONCEPTS

1. Because the firm can then select the scale of plant and the amount of equipment that is most efficient for each level of output.

2. MPP is increasing, meaning it takes less labor units to produce each unit of output.

3. Because MPP increases due to the law of diminishing marginal returns, each added unit of output requires more labor units to produce and so, a higher marginal cost.

4. No. It holds true only when some inputs are not increased.

5. TVC is the sum of the MCs.

6. TC is derived by adding fixed costs to TVC.

7. AVC will fall.

8. MC = AVC at AVC's minimum. MC = ATC at ATC's minimum.

9. *ATC* falls since each added unit of output costs less since less added inputs are needed to produce it.

10. Because then it would be better off investing its time and capital elsewhere. Total costs equal the opportunity cost (i.e., the forgone revenues) of the best alternative: If the firm earns less, it's better off with the alternative.

PRACTICAL APPLICATION

1.

Labor Input (L)	1	2	3	4	5	6	7	8	9
Output (Q)	2	5	9	14	19	23	26	28	29
MPP	2	3	4	5	5	4	3	2	1
MC of 1 Q ($)	30	20	15	12	12	15	20	30	60

At $L = 5$, we begin to have diminishing marginal returns (*MPP* falls and *MC* rises).

2.

Q	MC	TVC	AVC	TFC	AFC	TC	ATC
0	—	$ 0	—	$112	—	$112	—
1	$16	16	$16	112	112	128	$128
2	14	30	15	112	56	142	71
3	12	42	14	112	37.33	154	51.33
4	6	48	12	112	28	160	40
5	12	60	12	112	22.40	172	34.40
6	16	76	12.67	112	18.67	188	31.33
7	22	98	14	112	16	210	30
8	30	128	16	112	14	240	30
9	38	166	18.44	112	12.44	278	30.89
10	44	210	21	112	11.20	322	32.20

a. At $Q = 4$.
b. Minimum $AVC = MC = 12$ at $Q = 5$.
c. Minimum $ATC = MC = 30$ at $Q = 8$.

3. a. \$60 ($Q \times ATC = TC$ since $ATC = TC/Q$)
   b. \$21. $Q \times AVC = TVC$ (since $TVC = AVC/Q$). At $Q = 10$, $TC = \$100$ ($10 \times \$10$). At $Q = 11$, $TC = \$121$ ($11 \times \$11$). MC equals in increase in TC: \$21 $= \$121 - \$100$.
   c. Rising (because $MC > ATC$).
   d. \$30. $Q \times ATC = TC$ (since $AFC = TFC/Q$). So $TC = \$150$ ($10 \times \$15$). $TVC = \$100$ ($10 \times \$10$). Since $TC = TFC + TVC$, $TFC = \$50$.
   e. \$30 (\$180 $-$ \$150).

4. One-tenth of a worker is embodied in each unit of output. So each unit costs one-tenth of \$12,000, or \$1,200.

5. a. False.
   b. True.
   c. True.
   d. True.

6. a. \$23,000: Explicit costs are \$5,000. Implicit costs include her forgone earnings of \$16,000 plus the forgone interest of \$2,000 she could have earned had she invested the \$20,000 of savings at 10%.
   b. \$23,000
   c. Economic profit $= \$7,000$. Accounting profit $= \$25,000$. She should farm.
   d. Economic profit $= -\$3,000$ (i.e., a \$3,000 loss). Accounting profit $= \$15,000$. She should not farm.

7. Old Fud is wrong. He is ignoring the higher opportunity costs of diamonds.

8. Businessmen and women usually have a higher opportunity cost of time than students and so are more likely to find flying cheaper. For example, if the opportunity cost of time is \$20 an hour, the plane's cost is \$120 while the bus's cost is \$150.

9. a. MC, AVC, and ATC will shift up. AFC will be unchanged.
   b. AFC and ATC will shift up. MC and AVC will be unchanged.

10. Total costs will less than double, such that ATC falls.

19
COMPETITIVE SUPPLY

KEY TERMS

breakeven price the price at which the firm just covers all its costs.

perfect competition condition that exists when there is enough competition among sellers that no one seller can raise its price without losing all its customers to the other sellers.

shutdown price price below which a firm will shut down.

sunk cost cost that can't be avoided.

RULES OF BASIC DECISION-MAKING

The rules of decision-making are of fundamental importance to both business-people and economists.

CONCERNING COSTS

Four Main Rules in Making a Decision

1. Pay attention only to costs that actually change as a result of the decision. These costs are the marginal costs of the decision. Similarly, in considering benefits, pay attention only to the change in total benefits.

2. Be sure to include implicit costs in total costs.

3. Ignore **sunk costs**. These are the costs that are unaffected by the decision, since they already have been either incurred or committed. Because sunk costs are the same no matter what decision is made, they should play no role in the decision-making process.

4. Make the decision that will secure the largest net benefit.

Example: Application of Decision-Making Rules

PROBLEM   Due to cost overruns, a factory has cost, so far, $4 million to build. It will be useless (not even having a scrap value) unless

256

completed, but this will take another $2 million. If completed, the factory will produce a revenue worth $3 million to the firm. Should the factory be completed?

SOLUTION   Yes. It will produce a revenue worth $3 million, and the marginal cost of completion is $2 million. So the firm will be better off (by $1 million) by completing the factory. The $4 million already spent is sunk cost—not completing the factory won't get rid of the loss, but completing it will make the firm better off by $1 million. If the factory is not completed, the firm will lose $4 million. If it is completed, the firm will lose only $3 million ($3 million in revenue less a total cost of $6 million). So the firm should complete the factory. (This would be true whether the sunk cost were $10 million or $100 million: Sunk costs are ignored in the decision-making process).

PROBLEM   An owner of an apartment complex took out a mortgage to buy the complex. The monthly mortgage payment comes to $300 per apartment. Maintenance and utilities are $250 a month for an occupied apartment and zero for an unoccupied apartment. If the local rents are lower than the owner expected, what is the lowest rent the owner should ever accept?

SOLUTION $250. Any rent above this makes the owner better off by renting (since renting covers at least part of the sunk mortgage costs). But any rent below this does *not* cover the marginal cost of having the apartment occupied (versus having it empty).

CONCERNING OUTPUT

How much should a firm produce? Should it produce at all? The rules for answering these questions are the same for all firms, whether they are monopolists or competitors.

STEP 1: FINDING THE BEST LEVEL OF OUTPUT

Produce Q where MR = MC.

---

where: MC (Marginal Cost) = Addition to Total Costs (due to one more unit of output)

MR (Marginal Revenue) = Addition to Total Revenue (due one more unit of output)

$$Profit = Total\ Revenue\ (TR) - Total\ Cost\ (TC)$$

$$\text{Addition to Profit (due to one more unit of output)} = MR - MC.$$

Using marginal analysis (see Chapter 1), the firm will add to its profits as long as each added unit of output adds more to *TR* than to *TC*. This is the same as saying *MR* > *MC*. The firm will continue to increase *Q* as long as *MR* > *MC*, until *MR* = *MC*, and then it will be at its highest attainable profit.

Note: There may be several *Q*'s where *MR* = *MC*; this rule gives the most profitable level of production if the firm produces at all.

Example: Using Marginal Analysis

PROBLEM Fill in the following table and indicate what is the most profitable level of output.

Output	Total Revenue	Total Cost	MR	MC	Profit	Addition to Profit
0	$ 0	$20	—	—	−$20	—
1	40	25	—	—	—	—
2	70	35	—	—	—	—
3	90	55	—	—	—	—
4	100	95	—	—	—	—

SOLUTION

Output	Total Revenue	Total Cost	MR	MC	Profit	Addition To Profit
0	$ 0	$20	—	—	−$20	—
1	40	25	$40	$ 5	15	$35
2	70	35	30	10	35	20
3	90	55	20	20	35	0
4	100	95	10	30	5	−20

The optimal level of profit is achievable where *MR* = *MC* (at 3, where *MR* = *MC* = $20). Up to this output, *MR* > *MC*, so producing the first and second units of output added to total profits (each unit of output contributed *MR* − *MC* to profits). When *MR* < *MC*, profits fall. (Producing at 3, where *MR* = *MC*, gives the firm the highest attainable profit; other levels may be as profitable, such as 2, but none are better.)

STEP 2: COMPARING TOTAL REVENUE WITH TOTAL AVOIDABLE COSTS

Shut down when total avoidable costs exceed TR.

- *Short-Run Shutdown Rule 1*
  Shutdown if: $TR < TVC$ at Q from Step 1.
  or
  $P < AVC$ at Q from Step 1.

- *Long-Run Shutdown Rule 2*
  Shutdown if: $TR < TC$ at Q from Step 1.
  or
  $P < ATC$ at Q from Step 1.

In terms of the rules for decision-making, only the costs that *change* should be considered in deciding whether to produce or shut down: These are the firm's total avoidable costs. As long as total revenues cover these costs, the firm is better off staying in business. Otherwise, it should shut down.

Fixed costs are costs that do not vary with output and must be incurred for the firm to produce at all. Since producing firms already have incurred their fixed costs, fixed costs are sunk costs in the short run. So firms should ignore fixed costs in the short run. Instead, each firm should compare its total revenues with total variable costs. If $TR > TVC$, then at least it is reducing the burden of fixed costs by producing output. If $TR < TVC$, it is adding to its losses and should shut down.

In the long run, all costs, including fixed costs, are avoidable. For example, factories wear out, and at some point firms have to decide whether to rebuild or shut down. If $TR \geq TC$, the firm is making a profit or breaking even and should stay in business. If $TR < TC$, the firm is incurring a loss, which it could avoid by shutting down.

Why in the short run is the shutdown rule $P < AVC$? Multiply both sides by the Q that the firm would otherwise produce: $P \times Q < AVC \times Q$. We then have $TR < TVC$, or the "Short-Run Shutdown Rule" set forth above. The same logic holds for the long run (if $P < ATC$, the firm should shut down.)

Example: Deciding to Shut Down

PROBLEM   A firm's most profitable level of output is ten machines a year. But it is only the "most profitable" in the sense that when the firm produces ten machines, it is incurring the smallest loss. Its revenues are $100,000, but its fixed costs are $30,000 and its variable costs are $90,000. Should it shut down in the short run? Should it shut down in the long run (when the fixed cost of $30,000 could be avoided)?

SOLUTION   It should not shut down in the short run (since $100,000 > $90,000). If it *did* shut down in the short run, it would be worse off: It would lose $30,000 in fixed costs instead of $20,000 ($100,000 minus a total cost of $120,000). In the long run, the $30,000 of fixed cost no longer is sunk, perhaps because the plant has worn down and is ready to be replaced or because the firm has paid off its debt. So in the long run, the firm must incur a cost of $120,000 to operate. It will choose instead to shut down (since $100,000 in revenues < $120,000 in costs).

HOW COMPETITIVE FIRMS MAKE DECISIONS CONCERNING COSTS AND OUTPUT

We will now describe how competitive firms determine how much output to produce and whether to shut down or not. An industry is **perfectly competitive** when no single firm can raise its price without losing all of its customers. For example, if a farmer tries to sell wheat at $3.51 when the market price is $3.50, no one will buy from that farmer.

Economists describe firms in perfectly competitive industries as being **price takers**. Price takers take the current market price as given, knowing their individual actions have no influence on it.

Conditions Leading to Perfect Competition

1. Many firms are in the industry.

2. Buyers don't care which firm they buy from. They regard all firms as producing similar (homogeneous) products.

3. Buyers are informed enough to know who has the lowest price.

4. Firms can easily enter or exit the industry.

5. Condition 4 (ease of entry) is more important than Condition 1 (many firms). For example, if there are few firms in an industry, but easy and quick entry of new firms, then should any or all of the few firms try charging too much, new firms will enter the industry and push the price back down. Empirical evidence shows that **ease of entry** is more important than the number of firms for creating competition.

While few industries are perfectly competitive, the result from assuming perfect competition applies to all industries to the degree they face competitive pressures over time. Thus, the model of perfect competition is very useful for predicting the effects of demand and cost changes.

Since each price-taking firm has no discernable effect on market prices, the demand curve facing each price taker is *perfectly elastic* (see Chapter 16)—

straight horizontal line at the market price. In Figure 19-1, Panel A shows the demand facing one firm in an industry. Panel B shows the industry's demand curve. The market price is $10 (where supply equals demand). Notice that the single firm's output is very small compared to the industry's output. It is so small that changing the amount it produces doesn't affect price.

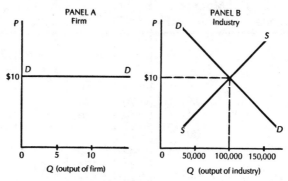

Figure 19-1 Determining the Effect of One Firm on Industry Demand

---

YOU SHOULD REMEMBER

1. In a competitive industry, no single firm has any influence on price.

2. In a competitive industry, each firm is a price taker: We show this by a horizontal demand curve facing each firm.

3. A set of conditions for a competitive industry is many firms, homogeneous product, well-informed buyers, and easy exit and entry. Few firms but easy entry also leads to competition.

RULES OF SUPPLY
• *SHORT RUN*

Short-Run Rule 1: Produce at the Q where P = MC.

The competitive firm can sell all it wants at the market price (*P*). So the marginal revenue from an added unit of output is *P*: *MR* = *P* for price taker. Using marginal analysis, the firm expands output as long as *P* > *MC* and produces at the output (*Q*) where *P* = *MC*.

Now let's apply this rule to Table 19-1. What is the best level of output when $P = \$30$?

Table 19-1. Determining Profits with the Rule of Short Run Supply

Output	Total Revenue	Marginal Revenue (=P)	MC	TVC	AVC	TC	Profit
0	$ 0	—	—	$ 0	—	$ 15	−$15
1	30	$ 30	$40	40	$40	55	− 25
2	60	30	30	70	35	85	− 25
3	90	30	20	90	30	105	− 15
4	120	30	10	100	25	115	5
5	150	30	25	125	25	140	10
6	180	30	30	155	25.83	170	10
7	210	30	41	196	28	211	− 1
8	240	30	60	256	32	271	− 31

Profits are highest ($10) at $Q = 6$ where $P = MC = \$30$.

Short-Run Rule 2: Shut down when P < Minimum AVC.

The firm should shut down if $TR < TVC$ at its best level of Q. If P is less than the firms' *minimum AVC,* then certainly $P < AVC$ at all levels of output. Multiplying each side of $P <$ Minimum AVC by Q, we have $TR < TVC$, which means the firm should shut down. (Note that the minimum AVC is found where the MC curve crosses the AVC curve.)

At what price will the firm in Table 19-1 shut down? The firm's **shutdown price,** the price at which it just covers its variable costs, is $25. At a price any lower, it will shut down.

PLOTTING A FIRM'S SHORT-RUN SUPPLY CURVE

In Table 19-1, what Q should the firm produce if $P = \$41$? Q should be 7 (where $MC = \$41$). At $P = \$60$, $Q = 8$ (where $MC = \$60$). At $P = \$20$, $Q = 0$, since the firm should shut down at any price below $25. In general, the **short-run supply curve** for a competitive firm is identical to the section of its marginal cost curve above its shutdown price (i.e., the section of the MC curve above where it crosses the AVC curve).

The short-run supply curve for a firm (a different firm than shown in Table 19-1) is represented by the darkened line in Figure 19-2.

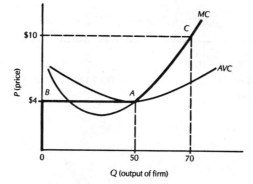

Figure 19-2   The Short Run Supply Curve of a Competitive Firm

Key Procedure for Plotting Firm's Short-Run Supply

1. Start at the top of a graph.

2. Put a straight edge horizontally across the graph. This represents the horizontal demand curve the single competitive firm faces.

3. Go across until you intersect the rising section of the firm's *MC* curve: The firm will supply the amount on the quantity axis at the price on the price axis. (For example, at Point *C* in Figure 19-2, at a price of $10, 70 units of output will be supplied.)

4. Continue down the *MC* curve until you reach the bottom of *AVC* curve—this is the firm's minimum *AVC* (at Point *A*, where the firm will supply 40 units). The firm will shut down below this price ($4). So draw a straight line to the price axis (from Point *A* to *B*), and then draw a line down the axis (from *B* to 0) to show that below $4, no output will be "supplied."

YOU SHOULD REMEMBER

1. Price equals marginal revenue for price takers.

2. In the short run, the firm will shut down if the price of output is below its minimum average variable costs.

3. If the firm produces at all, it will produce where price equals marginal cost.

4. The MC curve above minimum AVC (where AVC = MC) is the firm's short-run supply curve.

• *LONG RUN*

> *Rule:* Produce when $P \geq$ Minimum ATC where $P = MC$.

Our logic is the same as above: The best Q is where $P = MC$. But if P falls below the firm's minimum ATC, then the firm, no matter what Q it produces, cannot cover its costs. It should shut down.

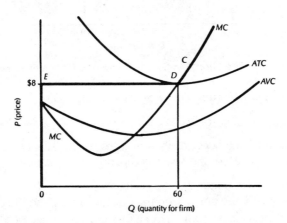

Figure 19-3 The Long Run Supply Curve of a Competitive Firm

Figure 19-3 shows the long-run supply curve for a single firm: its MC curve above its *minimum* average *total* cost. The firm's long-run supply curve goes up from 0 to E (the long-run shutdown price being $8), over to Point D (at $8, the firm supplies 60 units), and then up the MC curve through Point C. Note that in the long run, the firm's **breakeven price** (the price at which its total revenue equals its total cost) is also its shutdown price. (*Proof:* long-run shutdown $P =$ Minimum ATC, and if both sides are multiplied by the Q at the shutdown price, we have $TR = TC$.) Note that the minimum ATC can be found where the MC curve intersects the ATC curve.

YOU SHOULD REMEMBER

1. In the long run, the firm should produce when $P \geq$ Minimum ATC and where $P = MC$.

2. The MC curve above minimum ATC (where $ATC = MC$) is the firm's long-run supply curve.

THE CONSTRUCTION OF THE INDUSTRY'S SHORT RUN SUPPLY CURVE

• *SHORT RUN*

Recall the definition of short run: In the short run, firms have fixed factors that they cannot vary. Let us now add a second condition: Time is too short for new firms to enter or exit the industry. Because there are a fixed number of firms in the short run, any increase in supply can come only from the existing firms. So the industry's supply curve is the horizontal sum of the supply curves of all the firms in the industry. For example, if there are 10,000 firms that are all like the one in Table 19-1, then at a price of $25, 50,000 units will be supplied; at $30, 60,000 units. Note that the supply curve reflects *marginal cost.*

YOU SHOULD REMEMBER

1. In the short run, the industry's supply curve is the horizontal sum of the supply curve of all firms.

2. The supply curve reflects the marginal cost of output.

• *LONG RUN*

In the long run, firms can enter or exit the industry and will do so according to the profits that can be earned. When all firms are alike:

If profit > 0, firms will enter the industry.
If profit < 0, firms will exit the industry.
If profit = 0, the industry will be in long-run equilibrium.

In the long run, *economic profits* equal zero. Recall that economic profits are the excess over what is needed to pay a firm to produce. Thus, when economic profits are positive, new firms are willing to enter the industry. When economic profits are negative, firms will leave. Note that when economic profits are zero, *accounting profits* are positive and equal to the **normal profits** that compensate owners for their implicit costs.

YOU SHOULD REMEMBER

1. The entry and exit of firms cause economic profits to equal zero in the long run.

> **2.** In the long run, accounting profits will be positive and equal to the return to owners for their implicit costs.

• *FROM SHORT RUN TO LONG RUN*

To show how an industry reacts to an increase in demand, we'll examine an industry in which all firms, both entering and existing, have the same cost curves.

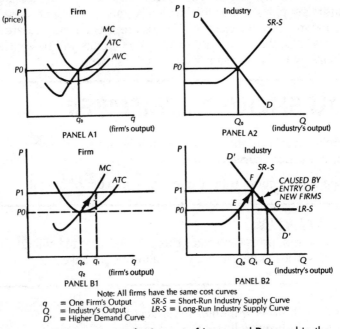

Note: All firms have the same cost curves
q = One Firm's Output $SR\text{-}S$ = Short-Run Industry Supply Curve
Q = Industry's Output $LR\text{-}S$ = Long-Run Industry Supply Curve
D' = Higher Demand Curve

Figure 19-4 Comparing the Impact of Increased Demand in the Short Run and Long Run for One Firm Versus the Industry

In Panels A1 and A2 of Figure 19-4, we show the industry initially in long-run equilibrium. At price $P0$, $P0$ = Minimum ATC = MC. (Note that output is being produced at the *lowest average cost.*) Each firm supplies q_0 and industry supply is Q_0. Assuming we start with 10,000 firms, Q_0 = 10,000 × q_0. $SR\text{-}S$ is the industry's short-run supply curve. It's the horizontal sum of the MC curve (above minimum AVC) of all 10,000 firms.

In Panels B1 and B2, we show the effects of an increase in demand (from DD to $D'D'$). In the short run, the price rises to P_1. Each firm produces q_1 units of output and industry output expands to Q_1 (10,000 × q_1). Each firm is making a profit (since $P > ATC$ at q_1).

In the long run, these profits attract new firms into the industry, increasing the industry's output supplied. New firms enter until the last firm to enter causes all firms to just break even. The long-run supply curve will be $LR\text{-}S$. In the long run, Q_2 will be supplied. Each firm will produce q_0, breaking even in the long run.

Our assumption that all firms have the same costs assures that in the long run, output will be supplied at *PO* since this is the minimum *ATC* of all firms. Any higher price will cause new firms to enter. As we shall see in the next section, an industry's supply need not be horizontal as shown here.

This pattern of response has been observed numerous times. First demand goes up. Price goes up (from Point E to Point F) and this encourages each firm to produce more (increasing Q from Q_0 to Q_1). Initially, the industry is very profitable. Eventually, new firms enter and their competition pushes the initial price increase back down (from F to G) as well as expands total output even more (from Q_1 to Q_2). Profits return to 0. An example of this pattern occurred when hand-held calculators were introduced. At first, they were high priced (over $100). The initial firms making them made large profits. But soon, large numbers of competitors entered the industry, bidding the price down and expanding output.

Alternatively, what if demand goes down? Price goes down (but no further down than the short-run shutdown price). The industry bears large losses and eventually some firms shut down. The exit of firms pushes output down even more, allowing the remaining firms to raise prices. Profits return to zero. Recently, the fall in the price of oil caused many oil-producing firms to suffer large losses. Output only slowly contracted, though, as oil wells were slowly shut down. Eventually, the industry recovered, but at a lower level of production.

Note that output changes much more in the long run (due to the entrance or exit of firms) than in the short run: *Supply is more elastic in the long run than in the short run.*

YOU SHOULD REMEMBER

1. When demand changes, the greatest change in price will occur in the short run. The long-run entry or exit of firms will diminish or eliminate the initial change in prices.

2. In the short run, all firms can suffer losses or enjoy profits. In the long run, profits and losses are eliminated.

3. Supply is more elastic in the long run.

PLOTTING AN INDUSTRY'S LONG-RUN SUPPLY CURVE

In Figure 19-5, Panel A shows the supply curve (*SS*) for a competitive industry when (1) all firms are equally efficient and (2) the industry can buy all the inputs it wants at the same price. The long-run supply curve is perfectly elastic, with firms entering when the price exceeds $8 or exiting when the price falls below $8. This is a **constant-cost industry**. Changes in demand do not affect the long-run supply price (of $8).

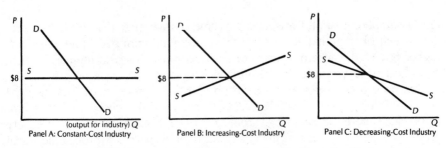

Figure 19-5   Determining the Long Run Supply Curve for Various
Types of Competitive Industries

Panel B shows an increasing-cost industry. If all firms are equally efficient, then the only cause of the rising supply price (as output increases) can be rising prices of some of the inputs the industry employs. For example, construction prices usually go up during economic expansions as building firms bid up the price of building materials. Another reason for increasing costs is that the new firms entering the industry are less efficient than the existing ones.

When all firms are alike, the long-run price will be P = Minimum ATC = MC. (Referring to Figure 19-3, each firm will be at Point D.) When firms differ in efficiency, in the long run, the least efficient firm in the industry will break even (being at Point D) but others will make a profit (Point D being lower on their MC curve). When firm's differ in efficiency, the supply price at each level of output equals the minimum ATC of the *least* efficient firm *in* the industry.

Panel C shows the long-run supply curve of a **decreasing-cost industry.** Minimum ATC falls when the industry expands if the greater output allows more specialization and economies in the supply of inputs: This reduces the price of inputs. For example, expanding sales of video recorders allowed for economies of scale in the production of video recorder components and caused the price of video recorders to fall.

YOU SHOULD REMEMBER

1. When all firms are alike, each firm will produce at its minimum ATC.

2. The minimum ATC of the entering firms determines the long-run supply price as output expands.

3. Increasing costs are caused by rising factor prices or less efficient firms entering the industry.

4. Decreasing costs are caused by economies of scale that reduce the cost of inputs.

EFFECTS OF COSTS ON SUPPLY

Increases in fixed costs (such as the cost of plant and land) and variable costs (such as wages and price of raw materials) affect output and prices as follows:

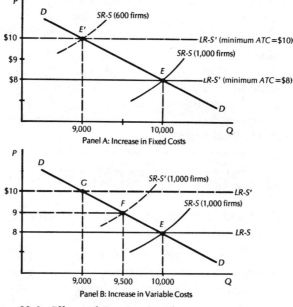

Figure 19-6 Effects of Costs on Supply

Increase in Fixed Costs

Panel A of Figure 19-6 shows a constant-cost industry. Initially, there are 1,000 firms producing 10 units of output each, with a resulting short-run supply curve of *SR-S* (1,000). Since this is also the long run, each firm's minimum *ATC* is $8 and so the long-run supply curve is *LR-S*. Demand equals supply at *P* = $8. Then fixed costs go up (for example, the interest payments on the money firms owe increase). *The MC curve is unaffected by changes in fixed cost.* (Recall that *MC* is the change in *TVC* when output increases by one unit: Changing *TFC* has no effect on *MC*.) So *SR-S* is unchanged: In the short run, neither output nor price are affected (at Point *E*). But firms are losing money. In the long run, some will exit the industry. The industry's long-run supply curve will shift up (to *LR-S'*) to reflect in increase an *ATC* from $8 to $10. Price will go up to $10 and output will fall to 9,000 (at *E'*). But be careful! Each remaining firm still has its old *MC* curve: All that has happened is that the shutdown price has gone up. So each *remaining* firm will produce more, being higher on their *MC* curve. (If, for example, each firm produces 15 units of output, there will be 600 firms left in the industry.)

Increase in Variable Costs

In Panel B of Figure 19-6, start out as before, at *P* = $8 and *Q* = 10,000. Then let variable costs increase (for example, wages go up). An increase in variable costs shifts up each firm's shutdown price *and MC* curve. The industry's supply curve, both short- and long-run, will shift up. This is shown by the shift to *SR-S'* and *LR-S'*.

In the short run (with 1,000 firms), the industry will be where the *SR-S'* curve (the sum of the 1,000 *MC'* curves) equals demand. $P = \$9.00$ and $Q = 9,500$ at Point *F*. In the long run, firms exit the industry and output is where the new *LR-S'* intersects demand at $10 (Point *G*): Output falls to 9,000 units.

Change in Demand

In the short run, an increase in demand always increases price and output (since *MC* is rising). In the long run, an increase in demand will not affect the price in a constant-cost industry; it will raise it in an increasing-cost industry; it will lower it in a decreasing-cost industry. (Check this by drawing a new demand curve to the right of *DD* in Figure 19-4.)

YOU SHOULD REMEMBER

1. Changes in fixed costs have no effect on price or output in the short run in competitive industries.

2. Increases in variable costs increase price and reduce output in the short run. In the long run, price increases even more and output falls even more than they did in the short run as firms exit the industry.

3. In the long run, increases in fixed costs raise prices and lower industry output. But the fewer remaining firms will produce more than before.

KNOW THE CONCEPTS
DO YOU KNOW THE BASICS?

1. Why does a firm increase Q when $MR > MC$?

2. What will a firm lose if it shuts down in the short run? When can it reduce this loss by producing?

3. What will the firm lose if it shuts down in the long run? When will it do better by producing?

4. If a competitive firm can sell 1 widget at $10, at what price will it be able to sell 1,000 widgets? How many widgets can it sell at $10.01?

5. What is the competitive firm's supply curve in the short run? Long run?

6. How do you find the industry's short-run supply curve?

7. How do you describe the long-run supply of the least efficient firm in an industry?

8. Does industrial output increase more in the short run or long run when demand goes up? Why?

9. When do fixed costs affect the industry's supply?

10. What forces determine how prices will change in the long run when demand goes up?

TERMS FOR STUDY

breakeven price
constant-cost industry
decreasing-cost industry
increasing-cost industry
marginal analysis
marginal cost
marginal revenue

perfect competition
price taker
profit
short and long run
short-run and long-run supply
shutdown price
sunk cost

PRACTICAL APPLICATION

1. In Table 19-1, the fixed cost is $15. Redo the table assuming the fixed cost is $35.
   a. Does the change in fixed costs affect marginal cost?
   b. Does it affect the optimal level of output (in the short run)?

2. Some quick questions:
   a. At $Q = 8$, a firm's profit is $40. At $Q = 9$, its MR is $60 and its MC is $55. What is its profit at $Q = 9$?
   b. At $Q = 7$, a firm's profit is $70, and at $Q = 8$, it's $75. The marginal cost of the eighth unit of output is $12. What is its marginal revenue?
   c. At $Q = 9$, a firm's profit is $100; at $Q = 10$, it's $90. What do we know about the tenth unit's marginal revenue and cost?

3. Answer true or false. Assume the firm is a price taker.
   a. The firm should always produce more when $P > ATC$.
   b. The firm should always produce more when $P > AVC$.
   c. The firm should always produce more when $P > MC$ and $P > AVC$.
   d. In the short run, the firm should always shut down when it's incurring a loss.
   e. In the long run, the firm should always shut down when it's incurring a loss.

4. An airline has signed a long-term contract to rent planes at a cost of $200,000 per month. In a given month, suppose each plane can make 100 flights. Each flight costs $5,000 in labor, gas, and other variable costs.

What is the minimum total dollar amount of fares per flight that the airline should accept rather than cancel the flight?

5. Use the following table to answer the questions.

Output	1	2	3	4	5	6	7	8
MC	3	2	1	2	3	4	5	6

    a. What is the minimum AVC? (Recall that TVC is the sum of the MCs and AVC is the average MC.) What is this firm's short-run shutdown price?

    b. What is this firm's short-run supply curve (for prices from $1 to $6)?

    c. If the firm's fixed cost is $9, what is its long-run supply schedule?

6. Suppose there are 100 firms in an industry. Each has the following cost schedules:

Output	1	2	3	4	5	6	7
MC	3	2	1	2	3	4	5
AVC	3	2.50	2.00	2.00	2.20	2.50	2.86
AFC	9	4.50	3.00	2.25	1.80	1.50	1.29

Answer the questions below using the following demand curve for the industry.

Price	$2	3	4	5	6
Q Demanded	940	860	780	700	620

    a. What is the industry's short run supply schedule?

    b. What will price and output be in the short run? How much will each firm produce? What will the profit be?

    c. Allowing for entry and exit, what will the long-run supply curve be?

    d. How much will each firm produce in the long run? How many firms will there be? What will their profit be?

7. We begin this problem by assuming that the industry in Questions 5 and 6 above is in long-run equilibrium. Then demand falls, decreasing by 210 units at each price level. (For example, at $5, demand falls from 700 units to 490 units.)

    a. In the short run, what will happen to price and output? What is the output and profit of each firm?

    b. In the long run, what will happen to price and output? How many firms will be in the industry? What will their profit be?

8. Describe the effects of an output tax of $1 per unit on a constant-cost industry.

9. Why haven't the billions of dollars of government subsidies to farmers improved farm profits?

10. An increase in interest rates increases the mortgage payments of each firm in an industry by $1,000. Describe the short- and long-run effects of this increase in fixed costs on the industry and firm. Assume the industry is a constant-cost industry.

ANSWERS

KNOW THE CONCEPTS

1. Because the firm adds to its profits by producing more when $MR > MC$.

2. If the firm shuts down, its short-run loss will equal TFC. If the firm produces, its short-run loss will equal $TFC - (TR - TVC)$. So if $TR \geq TVC$, the firm will reduce its short-run loss by producing.

3. Long-run shutdown loss equals zero. So the firm should produce only when $TR \geq TC$.

4. $10. At $10.01, it won't be able to sell any.

5. The short-run supply curve is the MC curve above its intersection with the AVC curve (i.e., above the minimum AVC). The long-run supply curve is the MC curve above its intersection with the long-run ATC curve (i.e., above the minimum ATC).

6. Take the horizontal sum of the supply curves of all firms.

7. The least efficient firm will just break even. It will make no profit. It will supply output at its minimum ATC (since for profits to equal zero, $P =$ Minimum ATC).

8. Output increases more in the long run, because new firms enter, increasing total supply.

9. Fixed costs affect the industry's supply curve only in the long run. An increase in fixed costs shifts the long-run supply curve up.

10. The industry's price will go up when demand goes up if new suppliers are less efficient than current suppliers and/or input prices go up when the industry demands more inputs. The price will stay constant if all firms are equally efficient and the industry can get all the inputs its needs at a constant price. The price may go down if input prices go down when more inputs are demanded.

PRACTICAL APPLICATION

1. **Table 19-1. With Fixed Cost of $35**

Output	Total Revenue	Marginal Revenue (= P)	MC	TVC	AVC	TC	Profit
0	$ 0	—	—	$ 0	—	$35	−$35
1	30	$30	$40	40	$40	75	− 45
2	60	30	30	70	35	105	− 45
3	90	30	20	90	30	125	− 35
4	120	30	10	100	25	135	− 15
5	150	30	25	125	25	160	− 10
6	180	30	30	155	25.83	190	− 10
7	210	30	41	196	28	231	− 21
8	240	30	60	256	32	291	− 51

    a. No, MC is not affected. (MC is the change in TC: Each entry in the TC column has gone up 20 but the *change* in TC is still the same.)

    b. No. The optimal level of output is not affected. The firm still produces 6 units of output (the firm loses the least—$10—at Q = 6; note that if the firm shuts down, it loses more—$35).

2. a. $45.

   b. $17.

   c. MC exceeds MR by $10. All answers are from the following equation:

$$\text{Change in profit} = MR - MC.$$

3. a. False.

   b. False.

   c. True.

   d. False.

   e. True.

4. $5,000.

5. a. Minimum AVC = $2 (at Q = 4, also at Q = 3). The shutdown price is $2. The AVC and AFC schedule for this firm is given in the answer to Question 6, below.

   b. The supply curve is obtained by finding the Q at which P = MC. The firm's short-run supply schedule is:

Price	$1	2	3	4	5	6
Firms' Q	0	4	5	6	7	8

c. Its minimum *ATC* is $4 at $Q = 6$. Its long-run supply schedule is:

Price	$1	2	3	4	5	6
Firm's Q	0	0	0	6	7	8

6. a. The industry's short-run supply schedule is:

Price	$1	2	3	4	5	6
Industry Q	0	400	500	600	700	800

     b. Supply equals demand at $P = \$5$ and $Q = 700$. Each firm produces 5 units of Q, making a profit of $6 (*TR* of $30 less $9 of fixed costs and $15 of variable costs; recall that *TVC* is the sum of the *MC*s and *TFC* = $9).

     c. In the long run, P = Minimum *ATC* = $4. So the supply curve will be horizontal at $4 in the long run.

     d. At $4, output demanded will be 780 units. Each firm will produce 6 units. There will be 130 firms (780/6). Profit will equal zero.

7. a. With 130 firms (from Question 6, above), the industry's supply curve in the short run (i.e., 130 × firm's short-run Q) and demand curve will be:

Price	$1	2	3	4	5	6
Industry Q Supplied	0	520	650	780	910	1,040
Q Demanded	—	730	650	570	490	410

     Demand equals supply at $3 (with $Q = 650$). Each firm will produce $5 units at a loss of $5.

     b. Firms will exit the industry until in the long run, $P = \$4 =$ Minimum *ATC*. At $4, 570 units will be demanded. Each firm will produce 6 units, so there will be 95 firms (570/6).

8. First, the short-run effects There are a fixed number of firms in the industry, and each firm will experience a $1 increase in its *MC* at each level of output. The industry supply curve will shift up by $1. Price will rise, but by less than $1 (unless demand is perfectly inelastic). Output will fall as each firm produces less.

Second, the long-run effects: Firms are incurring a loss in the short run due to higher costs. So some firms will exit the industry. As they do, total output will fall and the price will rise. In a constant-cost industry, P will rise by $1.

9. Competition between farmers has bid the price of agricultural output down and the cost of farmland and inputs up so that in the long run, farmers make no *economic* profits.

10. First, the short-run effects: The $1,000 is a fixed cost that is unavoidable in the short run. No firm will shut down and price and output will be unaffected.

Second, the long-run effects: We assume that before the increase in interest costs, all firms were in long-run equilibrium, with $TR = TC$. So the tax will cause a long-run loss. Some firms will leave the industry. Total output will fall and prices will rise (above their short-run level). As the MC curve is unaffected, but the price has increased, each of the remaining firms will produce more.

20
HOW COMPETITION WORKS

KEY TERMS

average-cost pricing pricing of goods at their average cost of production.

free market price price set by forces of supply and demand without government intervention (e.g., no price floors or ceilings).

In this chapter we apply the competitive model to some of our economy's problem areas: agriculture, energy, and natural resources.

AGRICULTURE
THE NEED FOR FEWER FARMERS

The main agricultural problem is that there are too many farmers. If government subsidies were removed, many of our nation's farmers would find themselves looking for work elsewhere.

The farm population has fallen from 35% of the whole population in 1910 to 3% in 1981. Between 1960 and 1981, it fell from 15.6 million to 5.8 million. The following equation shows why:

$$\frac{\text{Number of Farmers}}{\text{Needed}} = \frac{\text{Units of Food}}{\text{Demanded}} \times \frac{\text{Farmers Needed per}}{\text{Unit of Food}}$$

For example, if 500,000 tons of wheat are demanded and one farmer produces two tons of wheat, 250,000 farmers are needed. Now let's consider how economic forces have affected each part of this equation:

1. *Units of Food Demanded*: Food demand has risen very slowly in this century for two reasons:
   a. Food has a very *low income elasticity* (between .2 and 0.08). As a consequence, while real income has risen in this century, food demand has only mildly increased. A further consequence is that food's share in *GNP* has fallen.

277

b. Food has a *low price elasticity* of demand (about .2 to .25 in the aggregate). So despite relatively lower food prices, demand for food per capita has changed little. Population growth has not been sufficiently high to offset this factor.

2. *Farmers Needed Per Unit of Food*: Farm productivity has risen at twice the rate of nonfarm productivity. In 1820, one farmer supported four people, today one farmer produces enough for seventy-eight people. When farm productivity goes up, each farmer is producing more food, and this means *fewer* farmers are needed to produce a given amount of food. This second part of the equation is the main reason the U.S. economy needs less farmers.

COMPETITION AND FARM PROFITS

In a competitive industry, profits are bid to zero in the long run by competitors reducing prices. But the price of many farm goods is held up by the government price floors (which we will discuss below). So instead of prices being bid down, costs have been bid up! In particular, the cost of farmland has risen to reflect the value of the government programs aiding farmers. As a consequence, the benefits of farm programs mainly go to those owning farmland. And this benefit is a one-time affair: Once land prices have gone up, farmers, and in particular, new farmers, will not profit. So any set of farm programs only temporarily helps farmers (and only if they own land). But soon, due to competitive forces, profits are bid away and there is another farm "crisis."

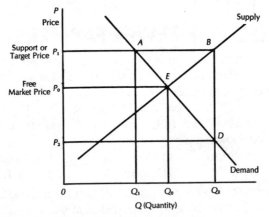

Figure 20-1 The Effect of Farm Price Support Programs

• *FARM SUPPORT PROGRAMS*

Our government uses three types of programs to hold up farm prices.

Support Prices

The government guarantees to buy all crops at a certain support price (this is usually done in the guise of farm loans that can be paid back with the crop being valued at the support price). Usually, the support price is set above the market price. The support price is a price floor. Figure 20-1 illustrates a support price of P_1. Without the price support, the free market price would be P_0, and Q_0 would be sold. But with the support price of P_1, consumers buy Q_1 but farmers produce Q_2. Who buys the excess output $Q_2 - Q_1$? The government (and taxpayers), paying $Q_2 - Q_1 \times P_1$ (which equals the area of the rectangle formed by points Q_1ABQ_2). The surplus food is either stored, given away, or simply destroyed. (For example, perfectly fine oranges are used as pig food.)

The supply of food becomes more elastic in the long run. So as time goes by, farmers produce more and more food at the support price. The program's cost escalates, creating a crisis when Congress no longer wants to pay the many billions of dollars such programs eventually cost.

Target Prices

The government guarantees farmers a certain target price for their crop, lets farmers sell all their crop to the public, and then makes up any difference between the target price and the crop's actual selling price. In Figure 20-1, if P_1 is the target price, farmers produce Q_2. They also sell Q_2 to the public but at Q_2's selling price of P_2 (on the public's demand curve). The government then pays farmers the difference between P_1 and P_2: farmers receive $P_1 - P_2 \times Q_2$ (area P_1BDP_2) from the government. As with support prices, this program also becomes more costly in the long run as supply increases.

Many economists favor target prices over support prices. For the same total cost to the public (taxes *plus* food expenditures: $P_1 \times Q_2$), the public gets more food (Q_2 instead of Q_1). And most economists favor neither, for all food produced beyond Q_1 costs more than it is worth.

> Note: The area *EDB* is considered an **economic waste** since it equals the excess of cost (area Q_0EBQ_2) over benefit (area Q_0EDQ_2) for the output in excess of the free market output Q_0. Recall that in competitive markets, *the demand curve reflects marginal benefits and the supply curve reflects marginal costs.* For example, suppose $Q_0 = 10$ and $P_0 = \$4$. Then the government buys food at \$6 such that 12 units are produced: The marginal cost of the eleventh unit is \$5 and the marginal cost of the twelfth is \$6 (these being points on the supply curve). Suppose the public's marginal benefit from the eleventh unit is \$3 and from the twelfth, \$2 (these being points on the demand curve). The waste is the excess of marginal cost over marginal benefit: \$2 waste for the eleventh unit (\$5 − \$3) and \$4 for the twelfth (\$6 − \$2). The total waste is \$6 (\$2 + \$4).

Acreage Restrictions

The government pays farmers to take farmland out of production. This program illustrates the principle that there is a *substitute* (see Chapter 4) for almost everything. Farmers, with less land, substitute more fertilizer and more labor for land. Recently, 87 million acres of farmland (out of 300 million acres) were idled, yet total farm output was unchanged because farmers farmed the remaining land more intensely.

YOU SHOULD REMEMBER

1. The demand for farmers has fallen mainly because of the growth in farm productivity and the small increase in food demand.

2. The profits from any government program designed to aid farmers are quickly reflected in higher land costs.

3. With support prices, the government buys all the crops farmers can't sell at the support price. With target prices, farmers sell all they produce to consumers and the government pays farmers any difference between the support price and the actual selling price.

4. Because supply is more elastic in the long run, the cost of farm programs escalates over time.

ENERGY
SHORTAGE VERSUS SCARCITY

The energy crisis our nation experienced in the mid-70s illustrates the difference between scarcity and a shortage. Due to OPEC, oil became more scarce worldwide. But only the U.S. experienced shortages, with people waiting in long lines at gas stations and plants closing down because they couldn't get oil. The shortages were caused by a ceiling on gasoline prices that had been imposed by the Nixon Administration. Other nations allowed the price of gas to go up and didn't experience any such shortages.

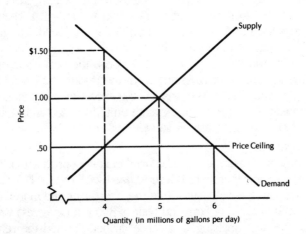

Figure 20-2 The Effect of a Price Ceiling on Gasoline

In Figure 20-2, the free market price of gasoline is $1.00 and output is 5 million gallons (a day). With a ceiling price of $.50, 6 million gallons are demanded but only 4 million are supplied: There is a shortage of 2 million gallons. The excess demand means that there isn't enough gas to go around for everyone who wants it, so everyone scrambles for gas by waiting in long lines. Since consumers are willing to pay $1.50 when supply is 4 million gallons, they will form lines such that the time cost of waiting equals as much as $1 per gallon ($1.50 − $.50). The ceiling price will then raise the effective price of gasoline (including waiting costs) above its market price!

THE EFFECT OF PRICE CEILINGS ON IMPORTS

During the same period, the U.S. had a price ceiling on all domestically produced oil. On the other hand, there was no such ceiling on imported oil. In addition, by law, all oil products had to sell at a price that reflected the *average* price of domestic and foreign oil. So what happened? U.S. oil producers produced less, while U.S. consumers bought more oil than they would have at its higher world price. And the widening difference between domestic demand and supply was imported from OPEC: Oil imports grew despite the higher price! So the U.S. demand for OPEC oil went up. This encouraged OPEC to charge a higher price. The removal of price controls, the more efficient use of energy (caused by higher energy prices), and the competition to supply substitutes for OPEC oil all contributed to the fall in oil prices (from a high of $34 in 1982 to a low of $14 in 1986).

The pricing of oil at its average price is inefficient, since consumers are using oil in uses worth less than the *marginal* cost of the oil. For example, when world oil was priced at $34, the marginal cost of oil to the U.S. was $34 (since all marginal oil was imported). But with an average price of, for example, $16, some of the $34 oil was being used in uses consumers valued at only $16—a waste of $18 ($34 − $16).

YOU SHOULD REMEMBER

1. Price ceilings cause shortages.

2. The price ceiling on domestic oil resulted in a greater dependence on foreign oil.

3. Average-cost pricing is inefficient.

NATURAL RESOURCES
FREE MARKET CONSERVATION

Despite the horror stories about our nation running out of oil and other natural resources, free and competitive markets act to increase the price of goods that are becoming scarcer, and so discourage the exhaustion of natural resources. In turn, higher prices encourage further exploration and better extraction methods.

Example: How the Price of Natural Resources Should Rise in a Free Market

PROBLEM   If you have $900 of oil at current market prices, when will you sell it: now or next year? To answer, compare next year's profit from selling the oil either now or next year. Assume that oil will sell for $1,200 next year, and that the interest rate is 10%.

> **Case (1):** No extraction cost.
> **Result:** *Price of oil should rise at the rate of interest.*

SOLUTION   If you sell now, you can invest the $900 and earn interest. At 10%, your investment will be worth $990 in one year.

Waiting until next year to sell gives you $1,200. You'll choose to wait. The same logic applies to all suppliers. Less oil will be sold today and more will be sold in one year: Current oil prices will rise, and oil prices will fall in the future. For example, the current price could rise to $1,000, and the price in one year could fall to $1,100. The market would then be in equilibrium, with no further price movements, since selling now or in one year would pay the same rate of return: 10%.

Thus, oil prices will rise at the rate of interest.

> **Case (2):** With extraction cost.
> **Result:** *Profit should rise at the rate of interest.*

SOLUTION   With extraction cost, owners of oil wells will compare the profit per unit oil sold today (and invested at 10%) with the profit in one year. In equilibrium, the two should be equal. The profit per unit oil should rise at the rate of interest. So if extracting a unit of oil today has a profit of $1,000, its profit should be $1,100 in one year.

EFFECT OF EVENTS ON PRICE OF OIL (OR NATURAL RESOURCES)

Event 1: Development of substitute (such as solar energy) that is too expensive relative to oil at oil's current prices but eventually will prove economical.

Effect: Pushes down future prices of oil, makes waiting to produce less attractive, and so increases current output and *lowers current price.*

Event 2: New technological advances are expected to lower future (but not current) extraction costs.

Effect: Increases future profits, makes waiting to produce in the future more attractive, and so reduces current production and *raises current price.*

Event 3: Increase in future demand for oil.

Effect: Increases future profits, shifts production to the future, and so *raises current price.*

YOU SHOULD REMEMBER

1. The price of exhaustible resources will tend to rise over time.

2. Resource owners will extract resources so their profits rise at a rate equal to the interest rate.

KNOW THE CONCEPTS
DO YOU KNOW THE BASICS?

1. Why are fewer farmers needed today?

2. Will lower food prices help farmers?

3. Who currently gets the benefits of farm programs started ten years ago?

4. Which program allows consumers to consume more: price support or target price programs?

5. Why is it wrong to say that OPEC caused the gasoline shortages in the U.S.?

6. How is average-cost pricing of oil inefficient?

7. How did the price ceiling on domestic oil production increase our dependence on OPEC?

8. Why don't owners of natural resources sell all they own immediately?

9. Joe owns a natural resource. Under what conditions should he *not* sell any of it today?

10. What happens to keep *future* natural resource prices from rising too fast?

TERMS FOR STUDY

acreage control	price support
average-cost pricing	shortage versus scarcity
exhaustible resource	target price

PRACTICAL APPLICATION

1. During this century, the productivity of workers has risen in almost every industry. Yet, for most of the economy, increases in productivity have meant more jobs, not less as in agriculture. Why has agriculture been different?

2. Suppose farmland sells for ten times a farm's profits *exclusive of land and mortgage costs*. Farmers can borrow at an interest rate of 10% to buy land. Without any government programs, farmland sells for $1,000 an acre; it costs $2,000 in labor, machinery, and material annually to produce a crop; and the crop sells for $2,100. In the long run, the farm's economic profits exclusive of land costs are $100 ($2,100 − $2,000). This just covers the interest payment on the land (10% of $1,000 is $100). Describe the long-run effects of a farm program that raises the value of the crop to $2,500. What will happen to land prices?

3. Use the following table to answer these questions. This table shows the demand and supply for wheat.

Quantity	1,000	2,000	3,000	4,000	5,000
Demand Price	$7	$5	$3	$1	$ .50
Supply Price	$1	$2	$3	$4	$5

   a. What is the free market price of wheat? What is the quantity?
   b. If the government price support for wheat is $5, how much will it buy, and at what cost? How much will consumers buy?
   c. What is the economic waste of this program? (Assume the government destroys the wheat it buys.)

4. Use the table provided in Question (3) above.
   a. If the government sets a target price of $5, how much will it have to pay farmers? How much will consumers buy, and at what cost?
   b. What is the economic waste in this program?

5. Why will acreage restrictions raise the marginal cost (*MC*) of food production over and above its long-run level without restrictions?

6. What type of policy will lead to long lines at gas stations and to plant closings due to a lack of fuel?

7. Suppose domestic oil costs $10 a barrel (because of a price ceiling) and foreign oil costs $30, and the U.S. buys half of each. What is inefficient about requiring oil to sell for its average cost of $20?

Hint: What is the marginal cost of another barrel of oil to the nation?

8. Before OPEC, American and British firms pumped oil in the Mid-East. But these firms were worried (correctly) that they would be nationalized. How would this worry affect their pumping of oil? Once these companies were nationalized, how would we expect oil prices to change (even if OPEC hadn't been formed)?

9. How would the following events affect today's price of zinc, an exhaustible resource?

   Event A: Owners of zinc mines suddenly expect zinc demand to fall next year.

   Event B: Scientists develop zonc, a substitute for zinc, that costs twice as much as zinc but will not go up in price over time.

   Event C: Interest rates fall.

10. You currently own $5,000 worth of gold. The rate of interest is 20%. What is the minimum price of gold you must expect next year for you to hold, not sell, your gold? (Assume you have no other use for the gold other than holding it for its price appreciation.)

ANSWERS
KNOW THE CONCEPTS

1. Because of the dramatic increase in farm productivity and the slow growth in the demand for farm products.

2. No. The demand for farm products is inelastic: A lower price reduces total farm revenues.

3. No one. Owners of farmland got all the benefit ten years ago.

4. Output is the same (for the same support or target price) but consumption is greater under target prices.

5. Because OPEC caused a greater scarcity of oil. Price controls caused the shortages.

6. Average-cost pricing encourages consumers to use the good in uses they value at only the average cost. But if the marginal cost is higher, this means the resources used to produce (or buy) the marginal units of the good would have been more highly valued elsewhere (since cost reflects the value of forgone alternatives). Thus, while consumers gain by buying below cost, they lose *more* elsewhere!

7. The price ceiling on domestic oil reduced domestic production, resulting in the need for more imported oil to make up the difference.

8. Because they expect to do better by conserving their resources and selling the resources when they're worth the most.

9. If the future price of the resource is higher than what Joe can earn by selling today and investing the proceeds, he should not sell today.

10. If future natural resource prices rise too fast, owners will reallocate their resource sales away from the present and toward the future. This shift in quantities will lower future prices and keep them from rising too fast.

PRACTICAL APPLICATION

1. Agriculture has been different because the increase in demand for agricultural products has failed to match the increase in farm productivity. The increase in demand has been greater in other industries because the other industries have higher income and price elasticities of demand.

2. The farm program will raise profits exclusive of land costs to $400. Because farming is competitive, land costs will be bid up to $4,000 an acre (10 × $400). Then the profits including land costs will be 0 ($2,400 less $2,100 in labor and operating costs and $400 in interest cost).

3. a. The free market price is $3, and $Q = 3,000$.
   b. Farmers will produce 5,000 units, and consumers will buy 2,000 units. So the government has to buy the 3,000-unit difference at $5 per unit: Its cost will be $15,000.
   c. The waste is (1) the loss to consumers from consuming less than 3,000 units and (2) the increase in costs from producing more than 3,000 units. (1) is $3,000 (the value of the third 1,000 units not consumed), and (2) is $9,000 (a cost of $4,000 for the fourth 1,000 units and $5,000 for the fifth 1,000 units produced). The total waste is $12,000.

4. a. At $5, farmers will produce 5,000 units. To sell 5,000 units, the market price will be $.50. The government has to pay the difference ($4.50), for a total cost of $22,500 (5,000 × $4.50).
   b. The waste is the excess of marginal cost over value. For the fourth 1,000 units, this is $3,000; for the fifth, it's $4,500. The total waste is $7,500. The waste is less than in Question (3), because with target prices, consumers at least get to consume all that's produced.

5. *MC* is lowest when the firm can vary all factors. But when the use of land is restricted, the law of diminishing marginal returns applies, increasing *MC* over its unrestricted level.

6. A price ceiling that is below the market price will lead to long lines and plant closings.

7. The marginal cost of oil to the nation is $30. The average price encourages consumption worth only $20. This is a waste of $10 ($30 − $20). The price ($20) reflects the marginal benefit of oil, while the cost ($30) reflects its marginal cost. Thus, our nation is giving up $30 worth of resources to buy oil from OPEC that consumers value at only $20—a loss of $10. While it may appear that consumers are getting a good deal, in fact they are giving up $30 of other goods (which the $30 of resources would have produced or bought elsewhere) for oil they value at only $20.

8. With insecure property rights, resource owners will deplete their re-sources too quickly. So the American and British companies probably pumped more oil, and sold it at a lower price. Once these companies were nationalized, the new owners (the government) had a longer time horizon and so would have cut back oil production and raised prices even if OPEC hadn't been formed. Ask yourself: Using the same logic about insecure property rights, why would war between OPEC nations lead to greater oil production and lower prices (assuming the war doesn't destroy oil producing and shipping facilities)?

9. *Event A:* would lower the current price.
   Event B: would lower the current price.
   Event C: would raise the current price. (Since investment of current pro-ceeds would pay less in the future, less would be mined or drilled now.)

10. $6,000 (1.2 × $5,000).

21
MONOPOLIES

KEY TERMS

monopoly the only seller of a good that has no close substitutes.

price searchers buyers or sellers having large enough shares of a market such that when they buy or sell more, they change the market price.

price discrimination the selling of the same good at different prices.

A firm is a **monopoly** (sometimes called a pure monopoly) when (1) it is the only firm selling the good, (2) it has no current or potential rivals, and (3) its good has no close substitutes. Unlike the customers of a perfectly competitive firm, the customers of a monopolistic firm cannot go elsewhere.

A **price searcher** is any buyer or seller who influences price. When a seller is a price searcher, the seller can lower the market price by selling more. In contrast, a perfectly competitive firm is a **price taker** ("taking" the price as given) since the competitive firm can sell all it wants without depressing the market price. Each price taker faces a horizontal demand curve for output; a price searcher faces a downward-sloping demand curve.

A monopoly is one of several types of price searchers that we'll discuss in this chapter and the next.

WHY DO MONOPOLIES EXIST?

Monopolies (and other types of price searchers) exist because of barriers to entry and cost advantages.

BARRIERS TO ENTRY

Barriers to entry keep potential competition away so that a monopoly can make a profit in the long run without worrying about new rivals coming on the scene. The main barriers to entry are:

1. *Legal Restrictions:* The government limits entry into many industries (such as telephone and electricity) and occupations (e.g., by the licensing of doctors and dentists).

2. *Patents:* The government provides barriers to entry to inventors and artists for a certain number of years by granting them patents and copyrights. This prohibits others from copying their ideas.

3. *Control of Strategic Resources:* The ownership of a strategic resource needed to produce a good prevents rivals from entering. For example, most of the world's diamond mines are controlled by DeBeers.

COST ADVANTAGES

A firm may have a monopoly because no one else can produce the good as cheaply. This may be due to:

1. *Economies of Scale:* If economies of scale are so large that a firm can produce all the output of an industry and still have falling average costs, then it will be able to underprice any potential rival, driving the rival out of the business.

2. *Technological Superiority:* By investing in research, a firm may be able to keep ahead of rivals by being able to produce the good at a lower cost than they can.

YOU SHOULD REMEMBER

1. A monopoly is the only seller of a good.

2. A price searcher will reduce the market price for its good when it sells more. A monopoly and other types of price searchers face a downward-sloping demand curve for their output.

3. Monopolies are protected from competition by barriers to entry or by having lower costs.

BASIC ELEMENTS

MARGINAL REVENUE

A monopoly faces a downward-sloping demand curve: To sell more, it must lower its price. Consider Table 21-1.

Table 21-1. The Effect of Price on Marginal Revenue

Demand Curve		Revenue	
Price	Quantity Demanded	Total Revenue (P × Q)	Marginal Revenue
$10	1	$10	$10
9	2	18	8
8	3	24	6
7	4	28	4
6	5	30	2
5	6	30	0
4	7	28	−2
3	8	24	−4
2	9	18	−6
1	10	10	−8

The first two columns show the demand curve facing the monopoly firm. As it sells more, price falls.

$$\text{Total Revenue} = \text{Price} \times \text{Quantity.}$$

Marginal revenue is the change in total revenue due to one more unit of output.

Facts About Marginal Revenue

1. Marginal Revenue = Price − Loss From Price Cut on Prior Output.
   For example, the fourth unit of output in Table 21-1 has a price of $7. So the firm generates $7 in earnings from it. But to sell the fourth unit, the firm had to cut the price by $1, so it lost $3 on the first three units of output. Therefore, it generated $4 in earnings (which equals the MR of the fourth unit).

2. $MR < P$ whenever the firm has to cut its price to sell more. So for all price searchers, $MR < P$! (This is true regardless of the shape of the demand curve, as long as it's downward-sloping.)

3. The firm will *never* produce where MR is negative. This will lower its total revenue and its profits.

4. Total revenue is largest at the level of output at which $MR = 0$. Up to this point, each added unit of output increases the firm's total revenue (since $MR > 0$). But don't confuse total revenue with total profit: The firm will *not* produce where total revenue is highest but rather where total profit is highest.

5. When demand is elastic, more output increases total revenue, and so $MR > 0$. In general, we have:

Table 21-2. How Elasticity of Demand Affects Marginal Revenue

ELASTICITY OF DEMAND	MARGINAL REVENUE
Elastic (>1)	Positive
Unitary Elastic (=1)	Zero
Inelastic (<1)	Negative

6. Because of 3 and 5 above, a firm will never produce where the firm's demand is inelastic. Remember that we are talking about the demand curve *facing the firm*! For example, farmers produce where the market demand for wheat is inelastic. But this does not contradict what we just said, because the demand curve facing *each* farmer is *perfectly* elastic.

7. If the demand schedule is a downward-sloping straight line, then (a) the marginal revenue curve is twice as steep as the demand curve (for example, in Table 21-1, for every $1 fall in price, *MR* falls $2) and (b) the *MR* curve intersects the bottom axis at half the output the demand curve does. In Figure 21-1, the demand curve intersects the horizontal axis at $Q = 10$, while the *MR* curve hits it as $Q = 5$. Remember that this is true only of *straight-line demand curves*!

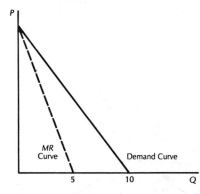

Figure 21-1 The Effect of Demand on Marginal Revenue

8. The total revenue curve shows the total revenue at each level of output. *MR* is the slope of the total revenue curve: it's the "rise" in *TR* over the "run" of one more *unit*.

YOU SHOULD REMEMBER

1. Marginal revenue is the increase in total revenue from selling another unit of output.

2. MR = P − Loss from Price Cut on Prior Output.

3. Price > Marginal Revenue (for all but the first unit of output).

4. Monopolies will produce only where MR ≥ 0 and the firm's demand curve is elastic.

THE OUTPUT DECISION

Short-Run Rule: Produce where $MR = MC$ if $P \geq AVC$.

Long-Run Rule: Produce where $MR = MC$ if $P \geq ATC$.

By following these rules, the firm will maximize its profits (at $MR = MC$) and shut down only when it can't cover its avoidable costs. Note that P, AVC, and ATC are all evaluated *at the output* the firm would produce (the Q where $MR = MC$) if it produces at all.

Figure 21-2 shows the demand and costs curves facing a monopoly. The monopoly will maximize its profits at $Q0$ (the Q where $MR = MC$). $P0 > AVC$ at $Q0$ ($AVC = I$ at $Q0$) so it will produce in the short run. $P0 > ATC$ at $Q0$ ($ATC = G$ at $Q0$), so it produces in the long run. Its profits will be the average profit per unit ($P − ATC$) times output: $P0 − G \times Q0$ (or area *GFEP0*).

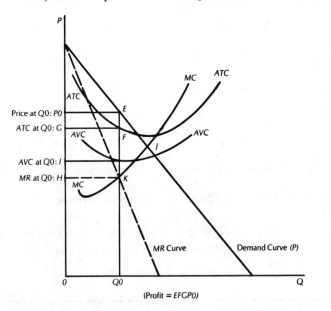

Figure 21-2   The Demand and Cost Curves of a Monopoly

If its fixed costs were higher such that the *ATC* at $Q0 > P0$, it would shut down in the long run but produce in the short run. In the short run, a monopoly *can* make a loss. In Figure 21-3, the optimal output level (if output is to be produced) is at $Q = 3$ ($MR = MC = \$4$). In the short run, the firm will not shut down because $P = \$7$ exceeds its AVC of $6. It is making a loss of $15 (TR = 3 × $7 = $21 less TC = 3 × $12 = $36 equals a loss of $15). But in the long run, it will shut down since $P = \$7$ does not cover its ATC of $12.

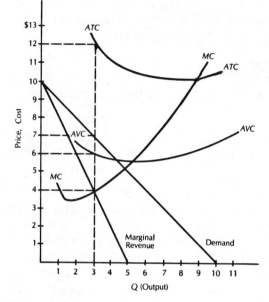

Figure 21-3 Visualizing a Monopoly's Shut-Down in the Long Run

FALLACIES AND FACTS

• *FALLACIES*

"Monopolies charge the highest price they can get."

The highest price comes from producing just one unit of output. As long as $MR > MC$, a monopoly will profit by selling more—which requires it to lower its price.

"Monopolies always make a profit."

In the short run, monopolies can incur losses, like other firms.

"Monopolies produce where they make the highest average profit per unit."

A firm making the highest profit per unit is *not* making the highest profit. It should produce more. For example, suppose the first unit of output adds $3 to profits; the next, $2; the third, $1; and the fourth, subtracts $1 from profits. The highest average profit ($3) is from producing one unit. But the *highest profit* ($6) is from producing three units (its average profit per unit of output is then only $2). A firm should always produce more when the additional output adds to profits, even if it adds less to profits than the average profit and thus lowers average profits.

• *FACTS*

Monopolies don't necessarily produce at the lowest average cost.

With perfect competition, in the long run, firms must produce at their lowest average cost (or be driven out of the business by those who do). Monopolies have no such competition. They may produce where *ATC* is falling, is at its minimum, or is rising (depending upon where $MR = MC$).

Monopolies produce only where demand is elastic.

Only over the range of output where demand is elastic is $MR > 0$. Since $MC > 0$, it can only be over this range that the profit-maximizing condition can hold: $MR = MC$.

Price exceeds marginal cost.

$P > MR$. Since $MR = MC$ at the monopolist's profit-maximizing level of output, it follows that $P > MC$.

A monopoly does not have a supply curve.

A supply curve tells how much firms will produce at each price. But the monopoly is not a price taker: The monopoly sets it's own price. A supply curve showing the quantity a monopoly will produce at a given price is *impossible to construct* because the same price on different demand curves will elicit different quantities from a monopoly. For example, while a monopoly will usually supply more when the price goes up, the opposite can happen. (See Practical Application, Question 5.)

Monopolies produce less than competitive firms.

If an industry has the same costs regardless of whether it has many firms or just one firm, then total industrial output will be greater when the industry is competitive (with many firms) than when it is monopolized by one firm. When there is only one firm, the one firm, operating as a monopoly, will see industry's demand curve as its own, such that its $MR < P$. When there are many firms, each firm's share of total output will be so small that each firm's $MR = P$. Thus, competitive firms will produce until $P = MC$, while a monopoly will stop short at a smaller output, where $P > MR = MC$. For example, if both marginal cost and average cost are \$2, in Table 21-1, the monopoly would produce 5 units of output (where $MR = MC = \$2$). If the same monopoly is replaced by many competitive firms with the same \$2 average and marginal cost, they will produce 9 units of output (where $P = MC = \$2$). Be careful! Both monopolies and competitive firms produce where $MR = MC$. The *difference* is that when the monopoly produces more, its price falls: its $MR < P$.

YOU SHOULD REMEMBER

1. To get the highest profits, a monopoly will produce where $MR = MC$ and will shut down if it can't cover its avoidable cost. In the

> short run, it will shut down if *at* its best output, $P < AVC$; in the long run, if $P < ATC$.
>
> **2.** For a monopoly, price exceeds marginal cost.

PRICE DISCRIMINATION

So far, we've assumed the monopoly sells all its output for the same price. But the monopoly may be able to charge a different price for different units. This is called **price discrimination** if the differences in price do *not* reflect cost differences (such as transportation costs). Recall that:

$$MR = P - \text{Loss on Prior Units From Price Cuts.}$$

By charging different prices, the monopoly does not have to cut its price on its prior output. As a result, its *MR* will be greater.

But to charge different prices, it is *essential* that buyers cannot *resell* their purchases. Otherwise, the buyers who can buy at the lower price will resell to all other buyers, thereby destroying the ability of the monopoly to charge less to some but not all buyers.

Price discrimination results in:

1. More profits (because of the higher *MR*).

2. More output (because of the higher *MR*).

Perfect price discrimination occurs when the monopoly gets the demand price for *each* unit. In Table 21-1, the perfect price discriminator would sell the fourth unit for $7, the fifth for $6, the sixth for $5, and so forth. Thus, the monopoly does not lose from cutting its price on its prior output! Its $P = MR$. It produces the same output that a competitive industry would with its costs. For example, if its average and marginal cost is $2 at all levels of output, the monopoly would produce 9 units (as would a competitive industry).

TWO MAIN METHODS OF PRICE DISCRIMINATION
Method One: Volume Discounts

With **volume discounts**, customers pay less per unit when they buy more. If these discounts do not reflect a cost saving to the seller, then they are a form of price discrimination.

Example: More Profits from Volume Discounts

PROBLEM   A firm has a monopoly on a special spring water, which it produces at an average cost and marginal cost of $0 (i.e., it has no costs). Each customer's demand price for one quart of spring water is $4; for the second quart, $3; third, $2; fourth, $1; fifth, $-1. How much should the firm charge if it charges the same price for all units? How can it enhance its profits by using volume discounts?

SOLUTION If it charges the same price for all units, its best profit per customer is $6 (at $P = \$2$ for three quarts). But if it uses volume discounts, charging the demand price for each unit ($4 for the first quart, $3 for the second, and so on), it will sell 4 quarts to each customer and will have a $10 profit per customer.

Some examples of volume discounts include the "frequent flier" bonuses offered by airlines, the "builders' discount" offered by building supply companies, and "buy two, get one free" offers.

Method Two: Segregated Markets

The monopoly may be able to segregate and separate markets and charge a different price in each. This will increase profits if the different markets have different elasticities of demand. Without segregating its markets, at its optimal output, the monopolist's demand curve has an elasticity that equals a certain average of the elasticities in each separate market. But by separating its markets, it will pay the monopoly to (1) raise prices in those markets that have the more inelastic demands and (2) lower prices in those markets with the more elastic demands.

The basic rule of making the most profits from separate markets is to (1) sell to each until the last unit sold in each has the *same* marginal revenue and (2) have $MR = MC$.

Example: Benefits of Price Discrimination

PROBLEM Without separating two markets, a firm's $MR = \$15$, an average of Market A's MR of $25 and Market B's MR of $5. How can the firm gain by separating the two markets?

SOLUTION By separating the two markets, the firm can withdraw one unit of output out of Market B (losing $5) and sell it to Market A (gaining $25), and so on net increase its total revenues by $20. The firm should continue doing this until both markets have the same MR (*and* a MR equal to its MC).

Examples of ways businesses segregate markets (and offer those with more elastic demand curves lower prices) include senior citizen discounts on drugs and travel, cents-off coupons (so that only those with coupons get a lower price), special subscription rates for college students, and lower rentals by apartment owners only to new tenants.

YOU SHOULD REMEMBER

1. Price discrimination is the selling of the same good at different prices. Price differences reflecting only cost differences do not represent price discrimination.

2. Perfect price discrimination is when the seller prices each unit of output at its demand price.

3. For price discrimination to work, it must be difficult for buyers to resell to one another.

4. If a firm can sell its output at different prices in separate markets, it should allocate its output so that the last unit sold in each has the same marginal revenue *and* $MR = MC$. By doing this, the firm will charge more to those with inelastic demands and less to those with elastic demands.

5. All forms of price discrimination raise total output and increase total profits.

TAXES AND MONOPOLIES

LUMP-SUM TAX

A **lump-sum tax** is a tax that is the same no matter what the monopoly produces. Just as a change in fixed costs has no effect on MC, a lump-sum tax has no effect on MC and so has no effect on the monopoly's optimal output (where $MR = MC$) or price.

In contrast, a lump-sum tax will raise prices and reduce output in the long run in a competitive industry.

The lump-sum tax will force a monopoly to shut down in the short-run if it exceeds $TR - TVC$, and in the long run if it exceeds $TR - TC$.

UNIT TAX

A **unit tax** is a tax per unit of output (for example, a $1-per-unit-output tax). It increases MC. So it has the same effect as an increase in wages or other variable costs. A unit tax *reduces output and raises prices* in both the long and short run.

The increase in price will be *less* than the increase in the unit tax for a straight-line demand curve.

Example: Effect of Unit Tax on Monopoly

PROBLEM   A monopoly has the demand schedule shown in Table 21-1. Both its average cost and marginal cost are $4 for all units of output. The government then imposes a $2 unit tax on the monopoly's output. How much will its price go up?

SOLUTION   By $1. Before the tax, the monopoly had the highest profit by producing 4 units of output (whose $MR = MC = \$4$) and then selling them at a price of $7. The tax increases the firm's effective MC to $6, so the firm will produce 3 units of output (whose $MR = \$6$) and will sell them at a price of $8.

YOU SHOULD REMEMBER

1. An increase in fixed costs or a lump-sum tax will not affect a monopoly's output or price. The only exception is if the increase is so large that it forces the monopoly to shut down.

2. An increase in variable costs or a unit tax will decrease a monopoly's output and raise its price.

KNOW THE CONCEPTS
DO YOU KNOW THE BASICS?

1. What causes price to exceed marginal revenue for a monopoly?

2. Why does $P = MR$ for a competitive firm?

3. If a monopoly finds itself in the inelastic portion of a demand curve, how will it change its output?

4. Can monopolies make losses?

5. Does a monopoly produce where it makes the highest profit per unit of output?

6. Why doesn't a monopoly produce where $P = MC$?

7. How does price discrimination increase MR?

8. If a firm sells in different markets, in which ones should it charge a higher price?

9. How will a lump-sum tax affect a monopoly's output?

10. When will a monopoly's behavior differ from that of a competitive industry when a lump-sum tax is imposed?

TERMS FOR STUDY

marginal revenue
monopoly
perfect price discrimination

price searcher
price discrimination

PRACTICAL APPLICATION

1. A monopoly is currently producing 10 units of output. At $Q = 10$, $P = \$14$ and $MC = \$12$. At $Q = 9$, $P = \$15$. Should it have produced the tenth unit of output?

2. A monopoly that has both a constant average cost and marginal cost of $5 faces the following demand curve:

Quantity	1	2	3	4	5	6	7	8
Demand Price	$9	$8	$7	$6	$5	$4	$3	$2
Marginal Revenue								

   a. Fill in the marginal revenue of each unit.
   b. How many units will the monopoly produce?
   c. What is its profit?

3. If the monopoly in Question 2 above is a perfect price discriminator, then:
   a. What is the marginal revenue of each unit?
   b. How many units will the monopoly produce?
   c. What is its profit?

4. a. What lump-sum tax would shut down the monopolist in Question 2 (assuming it does not price discriminate as in Question 3)?
   b. What would be the effect of a smaller lump-sum tax?
   c. What would the effect of a $2 unit tax be on price and output?

5. While an increase in demand will usually cause a monopoly to produce more, this need not always be true, as this question shows.
   a. Suppose a monopoly can sell one widget at $4, two at $3, and three at $2, and that its marginal cost for each unit is $1. How many widgets will it produce?
   b. Now suppose the demand curve shifts up so the monopoly can sell one unit at $10, two at $5, and three at $3. How many widgets will it produce now?

6. The following are examples of price discrimination. Indicate which group has the higher elasticity of demand.
   a. Theaters often charge children half the adult rate.
   b. Airlines give frequent fliers free airline tickets.

c. A German automobile manufacturer may charge $10,000 more in America than it does in Germany.

7. Suppose a rental agency has the exclusive right to rent cottages on Air Head Island. These cottages are owned by private individuals. Assume the rental agency has no costs whatsoever (so its $MC = 0$) but it earns 30% of the total rentals. Owners have an upkeep cost of $100 for each weekly rental. The rental agency sets the weekly rental rate.
   a. If the rental agency wants the highest profits, what will MR be when profits are highest?

Hint: See Figure 16–3.

   b. From the owners' point of view, will the rental rate the agency sets be too low or too high?

Hint: What will the MR be when the rental agency maximizes its earning? Compare this to the owners' MC of $100.

8. What is wrong with the following statements?
   a. "If a monopoly is making a loss where $MR = MC$, then it can raise its price to get rid of its loss."
   b. "Monopolies tend to be in markets where demand is inelastic."
   c. "Monopolies react to an increase in demand by raising price, not output."

9. In Market A, one unit sells for $10 and the quantity demanded goes up one unit for every $2 price decrease. In Market B, the demand price for one unit is $6 and the quantity demanded goes up one unit for every $1 price decrease. If you were a price discriminator with a constant marginal cost of $2, what price would you charge in each market?

10. Mary would pay $5 for one widget, $3 for a second, and $1 for a third. The widget store advertises "Buy two widgets for $4 each, get one free." How is the widget store price discriminating? Why is it price discriminating?

ANSWERS

KNOW THE CONCEPTS

1. Because the demand curve facing a monopoly is downward-sloping, to sell another unit of output, a monopoly has to reduce P for all its output. $MR = P -$ Loss due to price cut on prior output. So $MR < P$.

2. The competitive firm can sell all it wants without reducing its price. So $MR = P$ since it has no loss due to price cutting.

3. In the inelastic portion of the demand curve, the monopoly can cut output and increase total revenue. Since less output also lowers total cost, profits will go up. So the monopoly decreases output until demand is no longer inelastic.

4. Yes, in the short run.

5. No. As long as added output adds *anything* to profit, even when it adds less than the average profit, it should be produced.

6. A monopoly has to lower its price to sell more, and this causes a loss on its prior output. Its $MR < P$, and so it will stop production before $P = MC$ since then $MR < MC$.

7. Because the firm does not cut the price on prior output when it practices price discrimination (or does not cut it as much as when it sells all output at the same price), the MR of added output is higher.

8. In the markets with more inelastic demands (and lower marginal revenues).

9. If it does not cause the monopoly to shut down, it won't affect its output (or price) at all.

10. A lump-sum tax (or change in fixed cost) has no effect on monopoly output. In a competitive industry, it will reduce output in the long run.

PRACTICAL APPLICATION

1. No. $MR = \$5$ ($\$14 \times 10 - \$15 \times 9$). Since $MR < MC$, the firm should not produce the tenth unit of output.

2. **a.** Since MR is the increase in TR, we have:

Quantity	1	2	3	4	5	6	7	8
Demand Price	$9	$8	$7	$6	$5	$4	$3	$2
Marginal Revenue	$9	7	5	3	1	−1	−3	−5

    b. $Q = 3$ (where $MR = MC = \$5$; $Q = 2$ also gives the same profit.
    c. Profit $= \$6$ ($\$21 - \$15$).

3. **a.** Same as the demand price: 1, $9; 2, $8; 3, $7; etc.
    b. $Q = 5$.
    c. Profit $= \$10$ ($TR = \$9 + 8 + 7 + 6 + 5 = \$35$ and $TC = 5 \times \$5 = \$25$).

4. **a.** Any lump-sum tax exceeding its profits of $6.
   b. No effect on *MR* or *MC* and so none on *P* or *Q*.
   c. *Q* would be reduced to 2 units (where *MR* = new *MC* of $7); the price would be increased by $1 to $8.

5. **a.** It will produce two widgets (*MR* > *MC* for the first ($4 > $1) and second unit ($2 > $1) but *MR* < *MC* for the third ($0 < $1).)
   b. One widget. When demand goes up, in this case, supply goes down!

6. Price discriminators charge lower prices to those with more elastic demand curves. In these cases, children, frequent fliers, and automobile buyers in Germany have more elastic demand curves. Recall that price discrimination depends upon buyers not being able to resell their goods easily. But in the back of *The Wall Street Journal*, you will find ads for frequent flier coupons and for "grey market" automobiles shipped from Germany.

7. **a.** The rental agency will maximize its profits by maximizing total rentals (i.e., where *MR* = 0) since it earns 30% of total rentals.
   b. Owners on the other hand want a positive *MR* of $100 (to cover their *MC* of $100). So owners would want a higher rental rate (and fewer rentals) than the rental agency.

8. **a.** If *MR* = *MC*, the monopoly is making its best profit. A higher (or lower) price will only make it worse off.
   b. Monopolies will always be in the elastic region of the demand curve (where *MR* > 0).
   c. An increase in demand changes *MR*. It usually—but not always—increases it. If it does increase *MR*, the monopoly will increase output.

Output	1	2	3	4	5	6
MR-Market A	$10	6	2	−2	−6	−10
MR-Market B	$ 6	4	2	0	−2	−4

9. You would change the price at the *Q* where *MR* = $2. This price is $6 in Market A and $4 in Market B.

10. The price for the third unit is 0 so the widget store is charging a different price for different units. If it charged $4 a unit, its total revenue from Mary would be $4. But with this deal, it makes $8. In fact, this is the most it can get from Mary for three units.

22

BETWEEN MONOPOLY AND COMPETITION

KEY TERMS

cartel an arrangement among sellers in a market to jointly set prices and output.

monopolistic competition market like that of perfect competition (many sellers, easy entry and exit, and perfect information), except that each seller sells a closely related but not identical product.

oligopoly Market with few sellers and medium to high barriers to entry.

perfectly contestable markets markets with unimpeded and costless entry and exit of firms.

We have described markets that are perfectly competitive (in Chapters 19 and 20) and, at the other extreme, markets controlled by monopoly (in Chapter 21). We will now describe some of the in-between cases. We begin with the most competitive case and progress to increasingly monopolistic cases.

There are two forces pulling at any market. One force in the pull of the monopoly profits that could be earned if all firms *colluded* by agreeing to charge a high price. The other force is the pull of the profits that one firm could make if it *competed* with other firms by cutting its price to get more business. *The force of collusion leads the market to monopoly; the force of competition leads it toward perfect competition.*

Example: When Is Competition Likely to Occur?

PROBLEM   Suppose a professor puts a dollar down on a table once every minute until one student in the class raises his or her hand: That student gets all the money on the table. How will the class get the greatest amount of money?

SOLUTION   The class will get the most by colluding and agreeing to wait until the professor runs out of money (and then dividing the money). But each student has an incentive to cheat by raising his or her hand and taking it all (this being a form of competition). What is more, each student knows that if he or she doesn't raise his or her hand, someone else will. As can be predicted, the competitive result (a hand being raised early) becomes more likely (1) the more students there are, (2) the less students know each other, and (3) the less likely the losing students will or can retaliate against the student getting the money.

As we shall see, the same forces are at work in the marketplace to make the competitive results come about.

YOU SHOULD REMEMBER

The two main forces affecting firms are (1) the pull of collusion, which increases industrial profits if all firms act collusively like a monopoly and (2) the pull of competition, which rewards an individual firm with more profits when it cuts its price.

PERFECTLY CONTESTABLE MARKETS

NATURE
The central feature of this type of market is that any firm can enter or exit costlessly. There are no legal barriers, nor are there any start-up costs. There can be one firm, a few firms, or many firms.

RESULT
Output and prices will be at the competitive level. Economic profit $= 0$; $P = MC$ in the short run and $P = MC =$ Minimum ATC in the long run.

EXPLANATION
If any firm makes an economic profit, another entering firm can undercut its price and take away its business. Either this will occur or the firm, knowing this, will set its price as low as it can. The minimum price is the minimum of the firm's long-run ATC curve.

EXAMPLE
An airline has all the flights between two major cities. At first glance, it would seem this airline would act as a monopoly. But it may be quite easy for another airline to enter this market should the first airline charge any price exceeding its cost. If so, the first airline will charge the competitive price.

YOU SHOULD REMEMBER

1. No matter what the market structure, the cheaper entry is the more competitive prices and output will be.

2. In perfectly contestable markets (those with costless entry and exit), prices and output will be the same as set by perfect competition. In the long run, P = MC = Minimum ATC.

MONOPOLISTIC COMPETITION

NATURE

The nature of monopolistic competition is the same as the nature of perfect competition (many firms, easy entry and exit, and perfect information) *except* that firms sell similar but not identical products. (For example, restaurants compete with one another, but don't serve the same fare.)

Each seller practices **product differentiation**, trying to differentiate its product from those of its competitors by advertising, service, quality, and/or location.

Each seller has a range of customers, some very loyal to its product and others, not. As a consequence, dut to product differentiation, each seller faces a downward-slopping demand curve.

Examples include most retail establishments (including dress shops, restaurants, and grocery stores) in large cities.

RESULTS

Each firm is like a small monopoly: it faces a downward-sloping demand curve and produces where $MR = MC$ but $P > MC$. In the short run, the firm can make a profit or loss.

In the long run, any economic profits are bid away by new firms entering. So in the long run, we still have $MR = MC$. We also have $P = ATC$ (Economic profits $= 0$ when $P = ATC$). But $P >$ Minimum ATC due to product differentiation (and the resulting downward-sloping demand curve).

Since the firm does not produce at minimum ATC, it has **excess capacity** (more could be produced at a lower cost).

EXPLANATION

Figure 22-1, Panel A, shows the short-run results (before any new firms can enter this market). The firm faces a downward-sloping demand curve, its more loyal customers willing to pay the higher prices. Like a monopoly, it chooses to produce where $MR = MC$ but $P > MC$. Here, the firm produces 100 units, $MR = MC = $10, and the price is $15. Its ATC is $11, so it makes a $400 economic profit ($P = $15 less $ATC = $11 equals $4 profit per unit $\times$ $100).

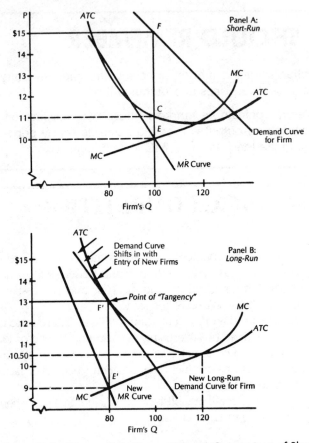

Figure 22-1 Monopolistic Competition: A Comparison of Short-Run and Long-Run Results

Because of free entry, new firms will enter, offering similar (but not identical) products. This reduces the demand for the firm's output. Entry continues. The firm's demand curve keeps shifting left, until the firm makes no economic profit: Panel B shows the long-run results. The long-run (and lower) demand curve just touches the ATC curve at Point F'. This **tangency** (the demand curve just touching the ATC curve) is what differentiates monopoly from monopolistic competition.

P = ATC = \$13 and the firm makes no economic profits. The firm produces 80 units of output, MR = MC = \$9. The firm's excess capacity is 40 units (since it could produce 120 units at its minimum ATC of \$10.50).

EXAMPLE

Two gas stations are located on the opposite ends of a small town. If both charge the same price, customers will go to the station closest to their homes. But if one station charges more than the other, its share of the town's business falls until only those living next to the station use it. In the short run, the two stations are likely to set the same price, each getting about half the business and making a good profit. But this will attract new gas stations. Each new gas station splits the market further. Entry continues until profits go to 0. These will have excess capacity in that the original two stations could have served the whole town.

The two gas stations could have lowered their prices to prevent the entry of new competitors (this is called **limit pricing**). If entry were quick and easy, they would have done so (giving the result of perfectly contestable markets). But if entry is slow and costly, they may be better off with higher prices and more profits now even if it means more competition and less profits in the future.

YOU SHOULD REMEMBER

1. Monopolistic competition is like perfect competition except for product differentiation.

2. Each firm faces a downward-sloping demand curve. If the industry is profitable, entry will shift each firm's demand curve to the left until it just touches and is tangent to its ATC curve.

3. The long-run result will be no profits, $P > MC$ and $P = ATC >$ Minimum ATC (i.e., excess capacity).

4. Limit pricing is the practice of lowering one's price, making less profits now, but also discouraging the entry of new competitors.

OLIGOPOLY

NATURE

In an oligopoly, there are few firms, and new firms face high (or medium) barriers to entry (often because existing firms have large economies of scale and can, if need be, drive new firms out of business with a costly price war).

There is **mutual interdependence** because the actions of one seller significantly affect the others. This is in contrast to competition, where the actions of any one firm have no affect on the market price or the sales of other firms. With mutual interdependence, one firm cutting its price can take away a large part of another firm's business. The goods can be identical or differentiated.

Examples of oligopolies include the automobile, the cigarette, the main-frame computer, and the breakfast cereal industry.

RESULTS AND EXPLANATION

The results are indeterminate because they depend upon how each firm acts. Figure 22-2 shows one of, say, four firms in an oligopoly. If all firms charge the

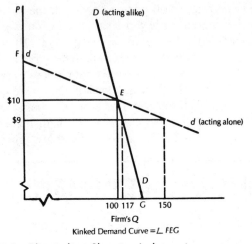

Figure 22-2 Oligopolies: Showing Indeterminacy

same price, we'll assume that each gets one quarter of the quantity demanded. This is shown on the *DD* ("All Act Alike") demand curve for one of these firms. If all firms charge $10, each will sell 100 units (and total industry-wide demand will be 400 units). If all firms charge $9, each will sell 117 units (total industry-wide demand being 458). But if the other three firms charge $10, then the demand curve facing this one firm is *dd* ("Acting Alone"). At $10, it sells 100 units (as above). But when it charges $9 (and the others still charge $10), it gets some of the other firms' customers, selling 150 units.

So if the firm does charge $9, it will sell 117 units if others also cut their price to $9. It will sell 150 units if they don't. Or, it will sell somewhere between 117 and 150 units when the others cut their price (but not all the way down to $9). So the results are *indeterminate* because of mutual interdependence.

This indeterminacy makes it very difficult to model or predict how oligopolies will act. For example, suppose two contractors are bidding to build a bridge for a city. Each can build it at a cost of $5 million and each knows the city will pay up to $12 million to have it built. Each has to submit a sealed bid (i.e., a bid that the other one can't see) at the same time; the lowest bid gets the contract. What will the winning bid be? If they collude, it will be $12 million. If they compete, it will be $5 million. If they partially collude, the bid may be between $5 million and 12 million. The results are indeterminate because what one contractor does affects the other.

An oligopolic firm faces a **kinked demand curve** when (1) other firms maintain their price when it raises its price but (2) other firms match its price cuts. In Figure 22-2, the kinked demand curve would be *FEG*.

The same demand curve is shown in Figure 22-3. Beneath it is the marginal revenue curve *FEHIJ*. From 0 to 100 units of output, the *MR* curve from demand curve *dd* applies (this being the *FH* segment of the *MR* curve). From 100 on, the *MR* curve from the demand curve *DD* applies (this is *IJ*). Since this curve is

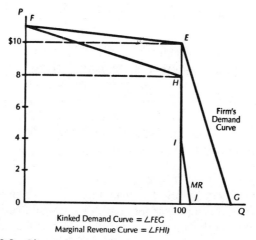

Figure 22-3 Oligopolies: Comparing the Kinked Demand Curve with the Marginal Revenue Curve

lower, there is vertical segment at 100 units between *I* and *H* (between $4 and $8).

If marginal cost at *Q* = 100 falls between $4 and $8, the firm will produce 100 units and charge $10. This makes the output and price of the oligopolistic firm facing a kinked demand curve inflexible with respect to changes in cost. Falling marginal costs will not reduce prices until costs fall below $4; rising marginal costs will not increase the price until it goes above $8.

In the long run, economic profits can be made since entry is costly. Depending upon the degree of collusion or competition, the results can be monopolistic or competitive. The main forces affecting this outcome are discussed later in this chapter in the section on "cartel cheating."

YOU SHOULD REMEMBER

1. In oligopolies, what one firm does has a large impact on the sales of the other firms. This mutual interdependence makes the price and output outcome difficult to predict.

2. A kinked demand curve for each firm results when it raises its prices alone but other firms retaliate by cutting their prices when it lowers its price. This can result in the same price and output over a wide range of costs.

SPECIAL MODELS OF OLIGOPOLIES

To get specific results, we need to specify how oligopolistic firms will react to one another. These are some of the models.

• *DOMINANT-FIRM OLIGOPOLY*

NATURE
In this industry, one firm dominates the market and many other small firms compete for the remaining fraction of the market. There is limited entry, so the dominant firm does not worry about the smaller firms taking away most of its business.

An example was OPEC when Saudi Arabia dominated the oil industry and was willing to cut back on its oil production to drive up oil prices. (Due to changing times, this seems no longer to be the case.)

RESULTS
The dominant firm sets its price to maximize profits, taking into account the effect of its price on the supply of the many other small firms. Like a monopoly, it can make a profit in the long run, with $P > MC$ and $P >$ Minimum ATC. But unlike a monopoly, it controls only a fraction of the market and so sets its price lower than a monopoly would.

EXPLANATION
Since there are many small firms which act competitively, the dominant firm has to take into account what the small firms will supply at each price. The dominant firm then figures out how much it can sell by subtracting the small firms' supply from market demand. With this information, the dominant firm sets its price where $MR = MC$. Consider Table 22-1.

Table 22-1. Dominant-Firm Oligopoly: Determining Dominant Firm's Residual Demand Schedule

Price	$9	$8	$7	$6	$5
Market Q	700	750	800	850	900
Supply of Other Firms	300	250	200	150	100
Q of Dominant Firm	400	500	600	700	800
Dominant Firm's TR	$3,600	$4,000	$4,200	$4,200	$4,000
MR (per 100)	$600	$400	$200	$ 0	−$200
MC (per 100)	$200	$200	$200	$200	$200

The first row shows the quantity demanded *(Q)* in the market at each price. The second row shows how many units the small firms (i.e., the "other firms" in the industry) will supply at each price. The third row shows the difference: This is the dominant firm's **residual demand curve**, showing how much the dominant firm can sell at each price. The last row shows that it will produce 600 units, since here $MR = MC$. It will sell its output at a price of $7, at a marginal cost (per 100 units) of $200, or an MC of $2 per unit. Other firms will produce 200 units.

Some conclusions about dominant-firm oligopoly are:

1. *The more elastic the supply of other firms, the more elastic the demand facing the oligopolistic firm.* This will reduce the price it sets. For example, suppose the quantity supplied by the small firms at each price in Table 22-1 increased by 50% (so for example, at $7, they supplied 300 and at $6, 225 units). The market price would fall to $6 and the firm would then produce 625 units. (Work this out! Note that lowering the price from $7 to $6 increases the firm's TR by $250. This raises its output by 125 units, so its MR per unit becomes $2, which equals its per-unit MC.)

2. *The smaller the total industrial output the dominant firm has (at any given price), the more elastic the residual demand curve will be.* The result will be a lower price.

YOU SHOULD REMEMBER

1. A dominant-firm oligopoly is one where one firm dominates the industry. It acts monopolistically but the many others act competitively. The dominant firm sets its price so $P > MC$.

2. The dominant firm faces a residual demand curve: At each price, it can sell the market output less what the other firms sell.

3. The more elastic the supply of other firms and the smaller the dominant firm's share of total output, the lower the market price.

• *PRICE LEADERSHIP OLIGOPOLY*

NATURE

One firm dominates the industry. There are few firms, and the other firms have found it to their advantage to set their prices equal to that of the dominant firm (which is thus the **price leader**).

The price leader often gets its position by being able and willing to punish firms that undercut its price. This it does with a **price war**. The price war inflicts losses on all, but the lesson learned (not the cut prices) pays off in the long run. The willingness to suffer losses (which in the short run may seem irrational) is a **credible threat** when it results in greater long-run profits.

RESULTS

Like the dominant firm, the price leader faces a residual demand curve. Its MR = its MC and $P > MC$ and $P >$ Minimum ATC. But if the price leader charges too much, the other firms may *not* follow its lead and may instead charge a lower price. The price leader, knowing this, will take this into account by setting a lower price. Note that in the dominant-firm model, the other firms are already charging their lowest price, so the dominant firm doesn't worry about the price being undercut.

YOU SHOULD REMEMBER

1. Price leadership occurs when one firm sets the price and all other firms follow.

2. The price leader will set the price to maximize its profits, taking into account the fact that a lower price increases the odds that other firms will follow its lead and not undercut its price.

3. The price leader often holds its position by making the credible threat of a price war if the other firms try to undercut its price.

• CARTEL

NATURE

A **cartel** has an explicit and sometimes even a formal (and legal) agreement to centrally set prices and output. Cartels are illegal in the U.S., but several illegal cartels have existed (with short life spans). In Europe, cartels are legal. A cartel is like an oligopoly: a few firms in an industry with high barriers to entry. OPEC is, of course, the most famous example of a cartel.

RESULTS

The cartel acts to maximize the profits for the whole industry. It therefore acts like a monopoly: $P > MC$. Output need not be at the minimum ATC.

Cartels and oligopolies both suffer from **the cartel cheating problem**: the tendency for each member to try to cut its price. As a consequence, an important part of the cartel's function is to police its members and make sure they charge the cartel price and not less.

EXPLANATION

The cartel will make the largest profit by treating the industry's demand curve as its demand curve, and then allocating output to the firms with the lowest cost. It sets $MR = MC$ at the same output and price a monopoly would.

One way a firm can cheat on a cartel is by secretly giving its customers a lower price. For example, using the illustration at the beginning of the oligopoly section, suppose the cartel sells 400 units at $10. Assume the average and marginal cost of output is $6. There are four firms and each gets to sell 100 units. Their joint profit is $1,600. If they all cut their price to say, $9, their joint profit falls (to

$1,404; TR = \$9 × 468 less TC = \$6 × 468). At P = \$10, each firm gets \$400 in profits. All firms are worse off if all cut their price to \$9 (and each earns a smaller profit of only \$351, the joint profit divided among the four firms).

But suppose only one firm cuts its price for all its customers to \$9: Its sales will increase to 150 units and its profits will go up from \$400 to \$450 (\$3 profit per unit × 150). So, it pays firms to cheat if they can get away with it.

Because $P > MC$, it pays each firm to seek new customers by offering them lower prices (while maintaining the same price for old customers). But customers become adept at playing one firm off another, with the result that when many firms practice price cutting, the cartel will break apart (as most have eventually done). An example of this cheating process occurred when OPEC collapsed as each oil-exporting nation cut its price in order to earn more profits, with the result that oil prices collapsed.

Another form of cheating is **non-price competition**, where firms compete by offering better quality and service and by advertising more. The results of this type of cheating, if left unchecked, will be that the added costs of the extra service and quality will eventually rise until they wipe out much if not all the cartel's profits.

YOU SHOULD REMEMBER

1. Cartels are oligopolies with explicit agreements to set prices and outputs centrally. They will act like a monopoly, with the same price and output.

2. Cartels and all other types of oligopolies suffer from cheating. Each firm can profit from cutting its price (but only if the others don't).

3. Another form of cheating is non-price competition, which increases the cost of all its members. Forms of non-price competition include advertising, better service, and better quality.

FORCES THAT PROMOTE COMPETITION

Cheating is a form of competition: It destroys collusion. Forces that promote cheating promote the competitive results.

In the hand-raising example at the beginning of this chapter, we saw that (1) the greater the number of firms, (2) the less that firms know about what the other firms are doing, and (3) the less likely that firms can retaliate (for example, with a price war), the *more likely cheating will occur* and the more likely prices and output will be at the competitive level.

Competition will also be greater when it is difficult to detect whether firms are cutting their prices. Detection will be more difficult and competition more likely: (1) when prices are not public knowledge but instead are privately set between buyers and sellers, (2) the more output demand varies from year to year (so when sales go down, other firms don't know if a price cutter is the cause), (3) when there are many types of products (varying in quality and service), and (4) when there is frequent innovation with new products and improvements.

Cheating is also more likely when it pays more: when price greatly exceeds marginal cost. Then another sale will bring more profits. Often, this occurs when an industry has high fixed costs, low variable costs, and excess capacity due to a fall in demand. At such times, cartels (such as OPEC) tend to break apart as each firm finds the temptation to go its own way too great to resist.

Cheating is also more profitable the *more elastic the industry's demand curve is*. A more elastic demand increases the gain in sales from price cutting.

YOU SHOULD REMEMBER

1. Price cutting (or cartel cheating) is a force for competition. It benefits society and consumers.

2. Price cutting is more likely: (1) the harder it is to detect, (2) the less it's punished, (3) the more it pays, and (4) the more elastic demand is.

3. Collusion is less likely in industries with varying demand, heterogeneous products, frequent innovations, and excess capacity.

KNOW THE CONCEPTS

DO YOU KNOW THE BASICS?

1. What force pushes an industry towards monopoly?

2. What force pushes an industry towards lower prices?

3. With free and costless entry into an market with only one firm, at what level will the price be set?

4. Why does a monopolistic competitor face a downward-sloping demand curve?

5. How is monopolistic competition like perfect competition?

6. What is the source of indeterminacy for whether an oligopoly will act competitively or monopolistically?

7. Why do farmers help each other out, while in other industries businesses are glad to see their rivals go out of business?

8. When and why does it pay a firm to undercut the industry's price?

9. How do price wars serve to discipline an industry?

10. Why is the competitive result more likely when it's easy for firms to undercut a collusively set price level?

TERMS FOR STUDY

cartel
cartel cheating problem
collusion
credible threat
dominant firm oligopoly
monopolistic competition
mutual interdependence

limit pricing
oligopoly
perfectly contestable markets
price leadership
price war
product differentiation

PRACTICAL APPLICATION

1. Identify which type of market (perfect competition, perfectly contestable markets, monopolistic competition, and oligopoly and its various types) these conditions most likely describe?
   a. Few firms and high barriers to entry.
   b. A Dairy Board that tells dairies how much milk to produce and requires all milk be sold to it.
   c. Many restaurants in a town, each serving a slightly different menu. It is easy to enter the restaurant business.
   d. One major firm dominates the computer industry but many small firms actively compete.

2. Use the following table (which shows the demand curve for a given market) to answer the questions below:

Quantity Demanded	1	2	3	4	5	6	7
Demand Price	$10	9	8	7	6	5	4

   a. What price and output would a monopoly have if it has a constant average and marginal cost of $4 per unit?

    b. If there are two firms (with $AC = MC = \$4$), what price and output will they set if they collude successfully?

    c. Given that the price in (b) has been set, how will it pay one of the firms to cut its price?

    d. If both firms continue to cut prices, what price will emerge?

3. In the table in Question 2, suppose one firm has a marginal cost of $2. It is the sole firm in the industry. New firms can enter, but their marginal and average costs equal $5.

    a. Without the threat of entry (if new firms cannot enter), what price would the firm set?

    b. With the threat of entry, what price will it set? (This is called limit pricing.)

4. Suppose a firm faced a kinked demand curve that is described by this table. Answer the questions below.

Quantity	1	2	3	4	5	6	7	8	9	10
Price	$20	19	18	17	16	15	12	9	6	3

    a. Where is the "kink" in this demand curve? What are other firms doing above the kink? Below it?

    b. If this firm has a constant $MC = AC$ of $3, what output and price will it choose?

    c. How far can its MC go up before it raises its price?

    d. How much can its MC fall before it lowers its price?

5. If you ran a cartel, why might you limit the amount of advertising each member can do?

6. Suppose all students who get within ten points of the highest grade on a test will get an A. All others will get an F. The test is to be multiple choice. Before the test, all the students meet and agree to answer all questions with "B." Identify if the following promotes collusion (all students answering "B") or competition (some students putting down the correct answers):

    a. The teacher publicly announces each student's score.

    b. Students live with each other in the same dorm.

    c. The brightest students are also the most athletic, and thus able to protect themselves against reprisals if they get caught putting down the right answers.

    d. A few students are "loners" and "unsocial."

    e. The class is very large.

7. A leading industrialist complains "These young upstart firms in our industry are cutting prices. They have no community spirit or integrity. They just cause trouble and losses." As a consumer, would you agree?

8. On a street corner, enough newspapers are sold to yield a profit of $100 a day. One newspaper vendor could handle these sales. If other jobs pay a daily wage of $20, how many newspaper vendors will locate on this street corner? (Assume sales are evenly divided between vendors.) How is this excess capacity?

9. In an industry with high fixed costs and low variable costs, why will a fall in demand increase price cutting pressures?

10. How does the football rivalry between two schools differ from the rivalry between two businesses?

ANSWERS

KNOW THE CONCEPTS

1. The promise of monopoly profits.

2. Competition and the profits to be made from undercutting the industry's price whenever $P > MC$.

3. The perfectly competitive price level of $P = $ Minimum ATC.

4. Product differentiation results in its customers differing in their loyalty to (or liking for) its product. A higher price drives away those less loyal and a lower price attracts new customers.

5. As in a perfectly competitive market, profits encourage entry, and the competition from the new entrants drives economic profits to zero in the long run.

6. The source of indeterminacy is that each firm does not know how its rivals will react when it changes its price.

7. Because there are so many farmers, there is no mutual interdependence. So by helping another farmer stay in business, each farmer is not hurting himself or herself. But when there are few rivals, one going out of business helps the others: There is mutual interdependence in this case.

8. Whenever $P > MC$, it pays to get some extra sales (by offering new customers a lower price).

9. A price war can serve to punish firms that undercut the industry's collusively set price. Of course, a price war can also signal the movement towards greater competition.

10. More firms will undercut the price, and the rewards from acting collusively will be smaller and more short-term. This makes the competitive outcome more likely.

PRACTICAL APPLICATION

1. **a.** Oligopoly.
   b. Cartel.
   c. Monopolistic competition (and perhaps perfectly contestable markets).
   d. dominant firm oligopoly.

2. **a.** $MR = MC = 4$ at $Q = 4$ and $P = \$7$.
   b. Same as a. Output has to be distributed between them. Most likely, each will get 2 units of Q.
   c. Each firm initially produces 2 Q. If it gets a new customer (not already in the market), it could sell another unit at $6 and add $3 to its profit (increasing its profits from $6 to $9). If it could attract a current customer of the other firm, it could charge, say, $6.95 and add $3.95 to its profit.
   d. The competitive price of $4 will emerge.

3. **a.** $MR = MC = \$2$ at $Q = 5$ and $P = \$6$.
   b. Its limit price will be $5, and Q will equal 6.

4. **a.** Between 6 and 7 Q. Above $15, only this firm is raising its price: below $15, other firms are matching its price cuts.
   b. For $Q = 6, MR = 10$. For $Q = 7, MR = -6$. So $Q = 6$ and $P = \$15$.
   c. To increase $P, MC > \$10$.
   d. Even if $MC = 0$, this firm will not cut its price.

5. Advertising is a form of non-price competition. Like price cutting, each firm on its own will advertise too much in the sense that total industrial profits will be reduced. Advertising for the industry becomes unprofitable when each firm is mainly trying to offset each other firm's advertising rather than to attract new customers into the industry.

6. **a.** Collusion.
   b. Collusion.
   c. Competition.
   d. Competition.
   e. Competition.

7. The upstarts are promoting competition, which is good from the consumer's point of view.

8. Five vendors will locate on the corner. This is an excess capacity of four, since one could do the job alone.

9. Given high fixed costs, the industry will likely have a high price (at least in the long run). Given low variable costs, it will have a low MC. A fall in demand usually results in excess capacity. And with excess capacity, each firm will be looking for ways to use it. One way is to seek new customers by cutting price.

10. In football, there is only one winner. In competition, there can be many winners, with each firm taking a certain fraction of the market.

23
EFFICIENCY AND REGULATION

KEY TERMS

allocative efficiency (also pareto efficiency) when no possible trade or reallocation of goods and inputs will make some people better off without making others worse off.

THE COMPETITIVE PROCESS

Society has to answer three questions about how it's going to use and allocate its scarce resources:

1. *What goods are going to be produced?*

2. *How are these goods to be produced?*

3. *Who should get these goods?*

The unique point about the competitive economy is that it tends to reward (with profits) firms that answer questions 1 and 2 correctly. Firms that market and produce the right goods efficiently are profitable. Those that don't, make losses and go out of business.

The main way to make economic profits in a competitive economy is to *innovate:* to find a better way to do something. Innovations include finding cheaper* ways to produce a good or finding more valued goods to produce. Profits lead others to copy the innovator and ultimately bring the innovation's full benefit to consumers in the form of cheaper prices for the same goods or better goods for the same price. In the long run, the pursuit of profits will cause economic profits to be bid back to zero.

---

*Note: The fact that a good has become cheaper to produce means it takes fewer resources to produce, not that the good itself has been cheapened in quality.

YOU SHOULD REMEMBER

1. Economic profits in a free and competitive economy come from innovation.

2. Economic profits reward firms for finding new and better ways to make and market their goods.

3. Competition bids economic profits back to zero, passing the benefits of innovations on to consumers.

THE EFFICIENCY OF COMPETITIVE MARKETS

Efficiency is one of the main concerns of economists. But why should anyone care about efficiency? Because when an economy is efficient, it is getting the best value for the least cost. A loss in efficiency is the equivalent of the destruction that results from war. But some people say that an equitable distribution of income is more important than efficiency as an economic goal and are willing to sacrifice some efficiency to get greater equality. But even here, it is better for everyone concerned, poor and rich alike, that greater equality be achieved at the lowest possible loss in efficiency. So even those concerned about equality should be concerned about efficiency.

Suppose an economy has the marginal benefits (*MB*) and marginal costs (*MC*) shown in Table 23-1. The good involved is lunch boxes. How many lunch boxes should the economy produce to maximize its net benefits?

Table 23-1. Determining the Optimal Production Rate

Quantity	1	2	3	4	5	6
MB	$6	$5	$4	$3	$2	$1
MC	$1	$2	$2.50	$3	$4	$5

Using marginal analysis, the first lunch box should be produced, because it adds $6 to total benefits and only $1 to total cost. Similarly, the second and third lunch boxes add more to benefits than to costs (*MB* > *MC*) and so increase net benefits. On the fourth lunch box, *MB* = *MC*: This is the optimal number of lunch boxes, the number that maximizes society's net benefits.

If the lunch box industry is competitive, *the socially optimal quantity* of lunch boxes will be produced. To see why, recall that the demand curve is the marginal benefit curve: The demand price (P^d) equals the value that consumers place on the marginal lunch box, so $MB = P^d$. For example, consumers will pay $4 for the third lunch box, because that is the marginal value it adds to their utility. Also, the supply curve is the marginal cost curve: The supply price (P^s) equals the cost of the marginal lunch box, so $MC = P^s$. Since demand equals supply in competitive markets, it follows that $P^d = P^s$ and $MB = MC$: The optimal number of lunch boxes will be produced.

Economists measure the gain in net benefits by the **total surplus** from producing a good. Each unit of the good contributes to net benefits the difference between MB and MC. For example, the first lunch box added $5 to net benefits ($6 − $1) and the second, $3 ($5 − $2). The total surplus when $Q = 4$ is $9.50 ($5 + 3 + 1.50 + 0).

The surplus going to consumers is the **consumer surplus**: the amount consumers would pay for the good less what they actually did pay for the good. For $Q = 4$, the consumer surplus is $6 (the total value of $6 + 5 + 4 + 3 less the payment of $12 for all 4 units).

The surplus going to producers is the **producer surplus**: what producers are paid less their marginal costs. For $Q = 4$, this equals $3.50 (the price of $3 × 4 minus the sum of MCs of $1 + $2 + $2.50 + $3, or $12 − $8.50).

The total surplus is largest when $MB = MC$ and demand equals supply. In Figure 23-1, at the competitive level of output ($Q0$), (1) the consumer surplus is the area below the demand curve but above the price ($P0$): Area *GFI*, (2) the producer surplus is the area below the price ($P0$) and above the supply curve: Area *HFG*, and finally, (3) the total surplus is the sum of (1) and (2): Area *HFI*.

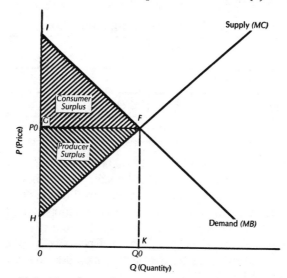

Figure 23-1   Visualizing Consumer and Producer Surplus

An economy is **allocatively efficient** when all possible reallocations of goods (and inputs) will make someone worse off. Alternatively stated, an economy is allocatively efficient when no additional mutually beneficial trades can be made between any two persons (or groups). This occurs when marginal benefit equals marginal cost: at the competitive industry's price and output.

YOU SHOULD REMEMBER

1. A free and competitive economy maximizes net benefits.

2. Consumer surplus measures the excess of a good's total value over what was paid for the good.

3. Producer surplus measures the excess of producers' total revenue over their marginal costs.

4. Allocative efficiency exists when there are no more mutually beneficial trades to be made between people. A competitive economy is allocatively efficient when $P = MC = MB$.

THE SOCIAL LOSS FROM MONOPOLY

Because $P > MC$ for a monopoly, this means that the last unit of output is worth more than it costs. Thus, the economy would be better off if monopolies produced *more*. Consider Table 23-2.

Table 23-2. Determining Social Loss

Quantity	4	5	6	7	8	9	10
Demand Price	$16	$15	$14	$13	$12	$11	$10
Marginal Revenue	—	$11	$ 9	$ 7	$ 5	$ 3	$ 1
Marginal Cost	$9.50	$ 9	$ 9	$ 9.50	$10	$11	$13

The monopolist will produce 6 units of output (since $MR = MC = \$9$ at $Q = 6$). But to secure the largest net social benefit, 9 units should be produced. At $Q = 9$, marginal benefit *to consumers,* as reflected by the demand price (P^d), equals marginal cost ($11). The social loss from monopoly is the loss in net benefits because *monopolies produce too little.* If 9 and not 4 units of output were produced, this would add $5.50 to society's net benefits (the sum of $P^d - MC$ or $3.50 for the seventh, $2 for the eighth, and $0 for the ninth). Thus, the social loss from monopoly is $5.50.

In Figure 23-2, the monopolist produces 4 units of output where $MC = MR = \$4$. $P = \$8$. As long as the value consumers place on output (shown by the demand curve) exceeds marginal cost, society would be better off with more produced. The net benefit to society is greatest when $Q = 7$ where $P = MC =$

$5. The social loss from monopoly is the sum of the differences between *P* and *MC* between 4 and 7 units: Area *EFJ*. (Using the formula for finding the area of a triangle, we have 1/2 × base (3 = 7−4) × height ($4 = $8 − $4), or a loss of $6 (1/2 × 3 × $4).

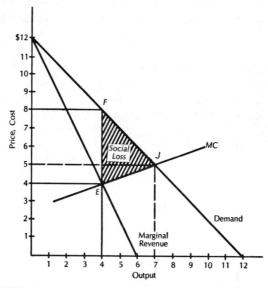

Figure 23-2 Determining Social Loss from Monopoly

It is important to remember that a monopoly causes a social loss because it produces too little, not because it's making a large profit. In fact, if the monopoly is a perfect price discriminator (see Chapter 21), it will produce as much as competitive firms and thus cause no social loss. Yet it will be making its largest possible profit!

YOU SHOULD REMEMBER

Because *P* > MC for the last unit of output, monopolies could increase the net benefit to society by producing more (until *P* = MC). The social loss from monopoly is the total net gain from the added output that should have been produced as measured by this added output's excess of *P*ᵈ over MC.

REGULATING MONOPOLY

• *PRICE CEILINGS*

A price ceiling on a monopoly can, if correctly placed, increase its output. For the range of output where the price ceiling is below the price on the demand curve (P^d), the monopoly will regard the ceiling price as its marginal revenue: MR = ceiling price. Why? Because like the perfectly competitive firm, if the monopoly produces more in this range of output, its price—the ceiling price—does not fall. In Table 23-2, a price ceiling of $11 would cause the monopoly to produce 9 units. This particular price ceiling (P^c) is socially optimal since P^c equals the MC at the intersection of the MC curve and the demand curves (so P^c = P^d = MC). A lower or higher ceiling will cause less than 9 units to be produced. For example, if P^c = $13, Q = 7; if P^c = $9.50, Q = 7. If the ceiling is *too* low, the monopoly will shut down (e.g., if P^c is below $9).

A monopoly facing the demand and cost curves in Figure 23-3 would produce 3 units of output (where MR = MC = $4) at a price of $7. A price ceiling of $5 would give the monopoly an effective demand curve that is horizontal between *A* and *B* and then from *B* to *D*. Along the *horizontal segment,* the monopoly's new *MR equals P*! The monopoly will produce 5 units of output.

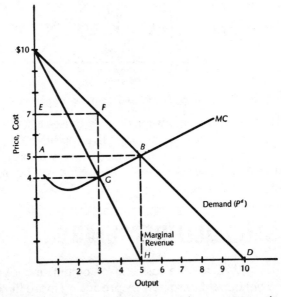

Figure 23-3 The Effect of Price Ceiling on Monopoly

Key Procedures for Drawing *MR* Curves With Price Ceiling

1. At the ceiling price (P^c), draw a horizontal line to the demand curve. Along this line, MR = P^c.

2. For output whose P^d < P^c, the old *MR* curve is still valid.

3. At the output where P^d = P^c, the *MR* curve is a vertical line connecting P^c with the old *MR* (below it).

For example, with a price ceiling of $7, the *MR* curve runs horizontally from *E* to *F*, then down from *E* to *G*, then along the old *MR* curve from *G* to *H*. The firm would produce 3 units of output (since *MR* = *MC* at *Q* = 3). A price ceiling of $4 will also elicit a monopoly output of 3 units (the *MR* curve would be *LGH*). Any price ceiling above $7 would not affect output (since it's above the price the monopoly would freely choose to charge). A price below $4 would reduce the monopoly output below its freely chosen level of 3 units. This would make society worse off (since less would be produced).

• *DO REGULATIONS WORK?*

The above analysis of price ceilings provides the central rationale for the public regulation of monopolies. Certain industries are regarded as having such large economies of scale that one firm can meet all the demand and still not achieve its most efficient scale. These industries will tend to be **natural monopolies** since the first firm in the industry can expand and eliminate any potential competition and yet still make monopoly profits (assuming, of course, entry is costly so that the industry is not a perfectly contestable market). In these industries, economies of scale produce falling *MC*. Some economists consider railroads and such public utilities as electricity and water natural monopolies (but this is disputed by others).

Figure 23-4 shows the cost curve of a natural monopoly. Its efficient scale of output (where the *ATC* curve bottoms out) is larger than the market, allowing it to drive out any competitors. Its price will be P_m. But from a social point of view, its output should be Q_0, where $MC = P^d = P_0$. But if this ceiling price is imposed, the price will not cover the monopoly's cost ($ATC_0 > P_0$). The monopoly will go out of business. The alternative is to subsidize the monopoly or allow it to charge a price equal to its average total cost (P_1).

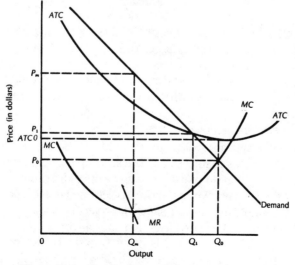

Figure 23-4 The Cost Curve of a Natural Monopoly

The Limits of Price-Ceiling-Type Regulations

1. Usually, the government guarantees regulated industries such as public utilities a certain return on their costs. Thus, regulated firms have less incentive to hold down costs. In fact, often the more costs they have, the higher the price and profit they are allowed.

   For example, regulatory agencies have allowed many electrical companies to make consumers pay for their huge losses from nuclear power plants. Other studies suggest that regulated utilities pay their workers about 30% too much and spend too much on plant and equipment.

2. The **capture hypothesis** postulates that regulatory agencies tend to be "captured" by the industry they regulate and act in the industry's behalf rather than the consumers'. Regulators are often drawn from the industry, later returning as consultants or employees. So they may be inclined to favor the industry. Also, the industry itself has a much more focused interest than the general public does in seeking favorable regulations.

   Often, when a regulatory agency is "captured," a price ceiling becomes a price floor forced upon consumers (such as utility rates).

   For example, regulation of the trucking industry limited entry and raised fares. Between 1940 and 1970, the number of licensed carriers declined; in addition, trucks were prohibited by government regulations from carrying freight on return trips. When the industry was deregulated in the late 70s, truck fares declined significantly. Similarly, when the airline industry was deregulated, air fares fell about 30%.

• *ANTITRUST*

If a monopoly does not have economies of scale, then an alternative to regulation is to break the monopoly up into smaller firms. The Sherman Antitrust Act (1890) outlawed any contracts or conspiracies leading to monopoly. The Clayton Act (1914) reenforced the Sherman Act by outlawing specific practices, such as price discrimination (in particular, larger firms getting a lower price from suppliers than smaller firms), tying contracts (contracts that force buyers buying one item to buy another item from the firm), and interlocking directorates (where the same persons serve on the board of directors of several firms in the same industry). In addition, the Celler-Kefauver Act (1950) prohibited mergers that would lead to greater monopolizing of an industry.

The drawbacks of antitrust policy are that (1) a firm may be dominant in an industry because it is more efficient, and breaking up the firm reduces efficiency and (2) some of the outlawed practices (such as price discrimination and "predatory" price cutting) may at times make society better off. For example, the Robinson-Patman Act (1936), in the name of protecting society from monopoly, outlawed discounts for large purchases and special concessions to any favored set of buyers. The real purpose of this law was to discourage grocery and department store chains from competing with local stores. Thus, the law promoted the monopoly of less efficient local merchants.

IS MONOPOLY BAD?

Monopoly, oligopoly, and monopolistic competition often exist because (1) as with all innovations, someone has to be first and thus, by definition, a "monopoly," (2) they have economies of scale that allow them to produce at a lower cost than if the industry were made up of many firms and (3) because customers prefer buying brand names and having a smaller range of choice. Perfect competition in these cases may be too costly and not desirable. For "perfect" competition to exist in the restaurant business, all restaurants in a town would have to serve the same food. Most consumers would reject perfect competition and instead favor variety, even if it meant higher restaurant prices. A good brand name is something a seller wants to protect with quality controls—and something consumers also value because they then can be more certain of what they are buying. The fact that many consumers choose brand names over generic brands shows that they do not want perfect competition in all products. In addition, competition can wipe out an innovator's profit too quickly and discourage further research and inventiveness (this is recognized in our patent and copyright laws).

Nevertheless, when a monopoly makes its profits from withholding output, it causes social harm. Interestingly, some economists contend that our government is the main source of monopoly in our economy. It supports cartels for various agriculture products (including milk and peanuts), it prevents foreign competition with tariffs and quotas, and supports unions that hold a monopoly on the supply of labor inputs to certain industries.

WHEN WON'T A COMPETITIVE ECONOMY BE EFFICIENT?

Even without monopoly, competitive firms will not produce the socially optimal level of output when the price does not reflect all the marginal benefits of the good or when marginal costs do not reflect the full cost of producing the good. This occurs when some of the benefit or cost of the good is borne by someone *other* than those buying and selling it. An example is when a firm does not have to pay for the damage its pollution causes. Another example is when viewers receive a television's station signals but don't pay for the benefit. We will cover this issue in detail in Chapter 27.

YOU SHOULD REMEMBER

1. A price ceiling imposed upon the price of a good produced by a monopoly can, if it's not placed too low, cause the monopoly to produce more of the good. The price ceiling eliciting the greatest output is equal to the price where the demand curve and the marginal cost curve intersect.

2. Natural monopolies occur when the efficient scale of production is large relative to the market size of the industry. As a result, only one (or a few) firms will dominant the industry and will tend to act monopolistically.

3. Government regulations, such as those on electrical utilities, seek to effectively put a price ceiling on monopoly goods. The capture hypothesis suggests that regulations will tend over time to favor the industry over the consumers as the regulatory agencies are "captured" by the industries they control.

4. Antitrust seeks to break up firms and to discourage practices believed by lawmakers to encourage monopoly.

KNOW THE CONCEPTS

DO YOU KNOW THE BASICS?

1. How can a firm profit by finding a more valuable good to produce?

2. Who ultimately gets the economic profits in a competitive economy?

3. What is the contribution to net benefits of the last unit of a good produced in a competitive economy?

4. In Figure 23-1, what area represents the total value of QO units of output?

5. In Figure 23-1, what area represents the total cost of producing QO units of output?

6. What is Area *IFH* in Figure 23-1?

7. Why is a minimum wage law not allocatively efficient when it prevents workers from getting a job?

8. How does a monopoly create social losses?

9. Will a price ceiling always cause a monopoly to produce more?

10. When might a competitive economy produce too much of a good (from a social point of view)?

TERMS FOR STUDY

allocative efficiency   producer surplus
capture hypothesis   total surplus
consumer surplus

PRACTICAL APPLICATION

1. Identify whether the profits from these innovations came from (1) finding a cheaper method of production or (2) finding a more valued good to produce.
   a. The decision to market light beer to beer drinkers who drink a lot of beer (as as less fattening way to drink a lot).
   b. The repackaging of U.S. bonds making annual payments into bonds that make just one large payment after a certain number of years (called zero coupon bonds).
   c. The use of genetic engineering to produce insulin at a lower cost.

2. Suppose consumers suddenly want fewer action movies and more romances than are now being produced. Describe how profits will play a role in getting movie producers to switch.

3. Use this table to answer these questions.

Quantity	1	2	3	4	5	6
Demand Price	$14	$12	$10	$8	$6	$ 4
Supply Price	$ 4	$ 6	$ 7	$8	$9	$10

   a. What level of output will yield the largest net benefit?
   b. In a competitive economy, what level of output would be produced and sold?
   c. What is the consumer surplus? The producer surplus? Their sum? And what is the net benefit?

4. Suppose a price ceiling of $4 is placed on the good in Question 3.
   a. What will be the net benefit? The consumer and producer surplus?
   b. Show that the price ceiling on the price in a competitive industry is inefficient, using (1) marginal analysis, (2) consumer and producer surplus, and (3) allocative efficiency.

5. Using the table from Question 3, assume the firms in the industry establish a monopoly.
   a. What output will they produce?
   b. What will the social loss be (as compared to when the firms acted competitively)?

6. A price ceiling on the price in an industry monopolized by one firm can be efficient. In question 5, what price ceiling will maximize social output?

7. What is wrong with this statement: "When business firms make large profits, it is healthy for the economy. So the government should encourage firms to get together and set a common price, and the government should punish firms that undercut this agreed-upon price."

8. Why is it inefficient for Customer B to be paying $2 for a hamburger that costs Customer A $1?

Hint: Find what mutually beneficial trades could take place.

9. If in the table in Question 3, firms by mistake produce 6 units of output and sell them for $4 each, why is society worse off than if firms had not made this mistake?

10. Suppose the government restricts all families to owning only one car. Why would this be allocatively inefficient?

Hint: Assume one person values one car at $12,000 and would value a second at $7,000. A second person values one car at $5,000. What trade would make both of these persons better off when people are allowed to own more than one car?

ANSWERS

KNOW THE CONCEPTS

1. In the long run, a set of inputs costing $10 will produce $10 of output. A firm that finds a good to produce that consumers value at $12 can make a $2 profit. In the long run though, the price will return to $10, so consumers get the "profit" in the form of a $12 good costing them only $10.

2. Consumers, in the form of lower prices.

3. The last unit just covers its cost: It adds nothing to net benefits. But up to the last unit, each additional unit increases net benefits.

4. The area under the demand curve: *OIFK*.

5. The area under the supply curve: *OHFK*.

6. *IFH* is the difference between the area under the demand curve and the area under the supply curve. It's the net benefit of *QO* units of output or the total surplus.

7. If employers would have to hire workers whom the minimum wage prevents from working, then the minimum wage has prevented a mutually beneficial trade from taking place. So it's not allocatively efficient.

8. A monopoly could produce more output whose value (i.e., price) exceeds its cost, but it doesn't because its *MR* < *P.* The social loss comes from the fact that it could produce more (*not* from the fact it makes a large profit).

9. No. A low enough price ceiling can cause a monopoly to produce less or even shut down.

10. When the producers of the good don't bear all of the cost of producing the good.

PRACTICAL APPLICATION

1. **a.** (2).
   b. (2).
   c. (1).

2. Initially, action movies will make losses and romances will make profits. The producers that switch first will make profits. The profits reward those producers that produce the goods consumers want. The losses penalize those who don't. Of course, when public tastes change again, movie producers again will switch to making the movies the public demands.

3. **a.** 4
   b. 4
   c. Consumer surplus: $12. Producer surplus: $7. Their sum: $19. Net benefit of 4 units: $19 (the same as the sum of consumer and producer surpluses).

4. **a.** Only 1 unit will be produced. The net benefit from 1 unit will be $10. Consumer surplus: $10. Producer surplus: $0.
   b. (1) Marginal analysis: The second, third, and fourth units have $MB \geq MC$ and should be produced.
   (2) The consumer plus producer surplus is bigger at $Q = 4$ ($19 versus only $10).
   (3) There are consumers who are willing to pay producers at least their cost or more for the second, third, and fourth unit of output. The price ceiling prevents these mutually beneficial trades so it is not allocatively efficient.

5. Use the following table:

Quantity	1	2	3	4	5	6
Demand Price	$14	$12	$10	$8	$6	$ 4
Supply Price	$ 4	$ 6	$ 7	$8	$9	$10
Marginal Revenue	14	10	6	2	−2	−6

   a. The monopoly will produce 2 units of output (recall that the supply price equals the MC: for the first 2 units of output, $MR > MC$).
   b. The social loss is $3 ($3 loss from not producing the third unit plus $0 for the fourth).

6. The price ceiling should be set, where $P^d = MC$, $P^c = \$8$.

7. Profits that result from monopoly are detrimental to the economy. Allowing firms to set a common price (i.e., establish a cartel) harms the economy because the firms will produce less than the competitive level of output.

8. Customer B would be willing to buy a hamburger from Customer A at a price above Customer A's MB (of $1). Both could benefit (e.g., if Customer B paid $1.50). (A different price for the same good is not allocatively efficient.)

9. Because of the mistake, society is worse off by $3 for the fifth unit (since it cost $3 more than it's worth) and by $6 for the sixth unit. The net benefit of 6 units is $10 (down from $19 at $Q = 4$). The loss in net benefits and surplus is $9.

10. Suppose it's Owner A who values his car at $5,000. Owner B values her car at $12,000 and would pay $7,000 for a second car. These two owners could be better off if Owner A could sell Owner B his car (say at $7,000). So restricting the number of cars a person can own is not allocatively efficient.

24

FACTOR DEMAND AND PRODUCTIVITY

Note: "Inputs" and "factors" are the labor, capital, materials, and land that a firm employs to produce output.

Why is Barbara Walters worth $1 million to ABC? Because she attracts viewers and without her, ABC would be worse off by at least a million dollars. And why would it lose this amount? Because its customers who buy advertising time would pay it at least a million fewer dollars. So Barbara Walters's salary is *derived* from what her employer can earn from its customers.

So it is with all inputs, whether they are labor, land, or capital. This chapter describes the forces that determine the *derived* demand for all inputs. Chapter 25 will show how the analysis of derived demand applies to labor markets, and Chapter 26 will cover the markets for land, capital, and entrepreneurship.

HOW TO MEASURE PRODUCTIVITY AND PROFITS

A firm wants to know how many units of an input it should hire. Let's suppose the firm wants to know how much labor it should hire. The firm will use marginal analysis.

Using Marginal Analysis to Determine Input

1. The firm wants to maximize its profits:

$$\text{Profits} = \text{Total Revenue} - \text{Total Cost}$$

The firm breaks the hiring decision into steps of hiring one more unit of labor at a time. The "unit" of labor could be an additional hour of work or an additional work year, depending upon what is convenient for the firm to add.

2. The *marginal benefit* of one more unit of labor is the amount it adds (by increasing output) to total revenue:

Marginal Revenue Product = *Increase in Total Revenue*
    (MRP)   *Due to One More Unit of Input*
                (here, due to one
                more worker being hired).

3. The *marginal cost* of one more unit of labor is the amount it adds to total cost:

Marginal Factor Cost = *Increase in Total Cost*
    (MFC)   *Due to One More Unit of Input*
                (here, the added
                cost of employing another
                worker—including wage and
                fringe benefit costs).

4. As long as each additional worker adds more to revenue than to cost, profits go up. So the firm will continue to hire as long as:

$$MRP \geq MFC.$$

5. It will maximize its profits and hire enough workers so that:

$$MRP = MFC.$$

Firms can be price takers (perfectly competitive) or price searchers (such as monopolies) in the markets in which they sell their output: This affects how they value the output a worker produced (the *MRP*). They also can be price takers or price searchers in the market in which they buy inputs: This affects how they value the cost of an added worker (the *MFC*). We will now study the four possible cases.

YOU SHOULD REMEMBER

1. Marginal revenue product (MRP) is the addition to total revenue due to employing an additional unit of an input.

2. Marginal factor cost (MFC) is the addition to total cost due to employing an additional unit of an input.

3. The firm will maximize profits by hiring until MRP = MFC.

DETERMINING MARGINAL BENEFIT BY MARGINAL REVENUE PRODUCT

CASE ONE: PRICE TAKER IN AN OUTPUT MARKET

A perfectly competitive firm (i.e., a price taker) can increase output and still sell it at the same price. So if $P = \$10$ and a worker adds four units to total output, the worker adds $40 to the firm's total revenue—this is the worker's *MRP.* For a price taker,

$$MRP = \text{Price} \times MPP.$$

MPP is the **marginal physical product** of the input: how much the added input increases total *physical* output.

Table 24-1 shows the *MRP* for a price-taking firm whose price is $4. The *MPP* schedule shows diminishing marginal returns (or diminishing *MPP*) throughout.

Table 24-1. The Marginal Revenue Product for a Price-Taking Firm

Units of Input	1	2	3	4	5	6	7
Output	8	15	21	26	30	33	35
MPP	8	7	6	5	4	3	2
MRP = P × MPP	$32	$28	$24	$20	$16	$12	$ 8

The third input, for example, adds 6 units to total output $(21 - 15)$. Each unit sells for $4, so the third unit adds $24 to total revenue (check this out by directly calculating the change in total revenues).

Using marginal analysis, if marginal factor cost is $20, the firm will hire 4 units of input. If *MFC* then falls to $16, the firm will hire 5 units. As a consequence, we have this result: *The* MRP *schedule is the derived demand curve for the input.*

Figure 24-1 shows the derived demand for labor by this firm when $P = \$4$.

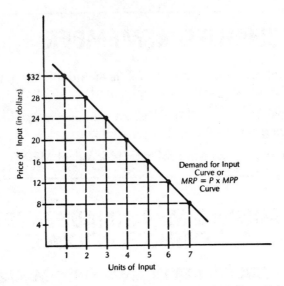

Figure 24-1 Derived Demand Curve for Input for a Price-Taking Firm

The derived demand curve is negatively sloped because of the law of diminishing marginal returns. (See Chapter 18.) Thus, the other inputs are being held constant when the firm calculates the marginal worth of an added worker.

CASE TWO: PRICE SEARCHER IN AN OUTPUT MARKET

As a price searcher (such as a monopoly) sells more, the market price of its good goes down. So $MR < P.$

Suppose another worker adds four units to output, and these four units sell for a total of $40 (or at an average price of $10 each). But to sell these four units, the price searcher had to cut its price. Assuming this price cut reduced its revenues on its prior output by $28, these four units added $12 to total revenue ($40 − $28) and had an average marginal revenue of $3 each. So we have MRP of a price searcher:

$$MRP = MR \times MPP.$$

Here, MR = $3 and MPP = 4, so MRP = $12.

Note that the formula $MRP = MR \times MPP$ also applies to price takers, since $MR = P$ for price taker. But because $MR < P$ for a price searcher, a price searcher will place a *lower* value on inputs and hire fewer of them (other things being equal).

The price searcher's derived demand curve for an input (its MRP curve) slopes downward because of (1) diminishing MPP and (2) falling MR.

YOU SHOULD REMEMBER

1. For a price taker, $MFC = P \times MPP$.

2. For a price searcher, $MFC = MR \times MPP$.

3. For a price taker, MRP declines as the firm hires more because of diminishing MPP. For a price searcher, MRP declines even more because besides falling MPP, its MR also falls as it hires more.

4. For both price takers and price searchers, the marginal revenue product schedule is the demand schedule for the input.

• *FACTORS SHIFTING THE DERIVED DEMAND FOR AN INPUT*

Table 24-2. shows how various factors change the demand for an input.

Table 24-2. Factors Shifting the Derived Demand for Inputs

Factor	Shift in Factor	Shift in Derived Demand
1. Demand For Output (Change in P and MR)	Increase Decrease	Increase (to right) Decrease (to left)
2. Change In Productivity	MPP Up MPP Down Industry-wide Increase	Increase Decrease Up if Demand Elastic; Down if Inelastic
3. Price of Substitute Input	Price Up Price Down	Uncertain Uncertain
4. Price of Complementary Input	Price Up Price Down	Decrease Increase

An increase in output demand *that raises price and marginal revenue* increases the amount of input firms want to hire. An increase in *MPP* increases what firms are willing to pay for each input.

An industry-wide increase in productivity (and not just at the firm level) has an uncertain effect on labor demand. When all firms become more productive, the same set of inputs produces a higher output. *If demand is elastic,* this higher output will increase the industry's total revenues and thus what firms pay for inputs. But *if demand is inelastic,* this higher output will reduce total revenues and input demand.

How does an increase in the price of another input, such as an increase in the cost of machinery, change labor demand? First, the machine's higher price raises the cost and price of output, which in turn reduces output demand (this is the **output effect**). Second, when labor and machinery are substitutes (such that one input can to some degree replace the other), then the firm, to *produce a given amount of output,* will use more labor and less machinery (this is the **substitution effect**). So the output effect of a higher machine price reduces labor demand, while the substitution effect increases it. The net effect is uncertain.

Complements are inputs used closely together. When the price of one goes up, less of both will be used. So the output effect and this effect reenforce each other. For example, most highly skilled workers have jobs that use much energy. When energy prices went up, the demand for highly skilled workers went down, even in those industries where output didn't fall.

• *FACTORS AFFECTING THE ELASTICITY OF DERIVED DEMAND*

By what percentage will labor demand go down when wages go up by 1%? To find out, economists use the elasticity of labor demand.

$$\text{Elasticity of Input Demand} = \frac{\% \text{ Change in Quantity of Input Demanded}}{\% \text{ Change in Input's Price}}$$

Note that both percent changes are stated as absolute values. For example, the elasticity of labor demand in many industries is 0.5: A 10% wage increase reduces the quantity of labor demanded by 5%.

Labor demand is more elastic when the quantity of labor demanded goes down *more* when wages go up. Input demand will be *more elastic:*

1. *When MPP Falls Less:* When *MPP* falls less as more of the input is employed, the input demand schedule is thus flatter and more elastic. When *MPP* falls quickly, it is more inelastic. For example, if a bakery needs only one truck driver to make deliveries, the *MPP* of added truck drivers falls quickly. So its demand for truck drivers is inelastic: A lower wage for truck drivers will not increase the number of truck drivers it hires.

2. *When the Demand for Output Is More Elastic*: When an input's cost goes up, so does the price of output. So the more elastic output demand is, the more output and thus input employed will fall when the price of output (and wages) go(es) up. For example, the growing competition from foreign car makers has made the demand for U.S. cars, and thus the demand for U.S. auto workers, more elastic.

3. *When It Is Easier to Substitute Other Inputs:* The more close substitutes there are for an input in the production process, and the more readily available these substitutes are, the more firms will replace the input when the input's price goes up. For example, a greater ability for firms to easily hire nonunion workers makes the demand for unionized labor more elastic.

4. *When the Input's Initial Share of Total Cost Is Larger:* The larger its share, the more a given increase in the input's price increases the price of output in percentage terms. And the more price goes up (in percentage terms), the more output and thus inputs employed will fall. As an *approximation,* we have:

% Change in Price = Input's Share × % Change in Input's Price

For example, labor costs represent about 25% of a car's total cost. So a 10% wage increase will increase car prices about 2.5%. But if labor's share were 90%, the price would go up 9%—and labor demand would fall more. An exception to (4) (and this approximation) occurs when inputs have close substitutes, but this is rare for such major inputs as capital and labor.

YOU SHOULD REMEMBER

1. The demand curve for an input is shifted by changes in the demand for output, by changes in the price of other inputs, and by changes in productivity.

2. When input demand goes down more when its price rises, its demand is more elastic. When the quantity of an input demanded is insensitive to price changes, its demand is inelastic.

3. The demand for an input will be more elastic when (1) its *MPP* curve is flatter, (2) the demand for output is more elastic, (3) it has close substitutes, and (4) its share of total cost is larger.

DETERMINING MARGINAL COST BY MARGINAL FACTOR COST

CASE THREE: PRICE TAKER IN AN INPUT (FACTOR) MARKET

Most firms, even large firms, employ only a small fraction of the total work force. So almost all firms are price takers in the markets in which they buy inputs: They can hire what they want at a constant price. Even firms that are monopolies in the markets in which they sell are usually price takers in hiring.

MFC for Price Takers = Price of the Factor

Labor's MFC is its wage (including fringe benefits and training costs).

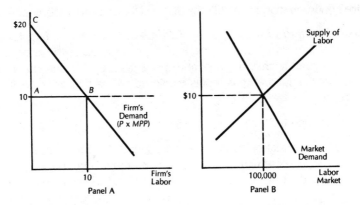

Figure 24-2 Demand and Supply of Labor from the Point of View of a Price Taker in an Input Market

Figure 24-2 shows the demand and supply for labor from the firm's (Panel A) and input market's (Panel B) point of view. At a wage of $10 an hour, the firm in Panel A hires 10 workers and the market in Panel B hires 100,000 workers. The market demand curve reflects the sum of firms' demands (but takes into account that as all firms hire and produce more, the price of output falls). The supply curve of labor shows that at higher wages, more persons want to work.

CASE FOUR: PRICE SEARCHER IN AN INPUT (FACTOR) MARKET: MONOPSONY

The vast majority of factor markets are competitive. But in some cases, there is a **monopsony**, a firm so dominant in a factor market that its hiring decisions affect the input's market price. A monopsony in the labor market, for example, has to pay a higher wage if it wants to employ more workers. The cost of an added worker is the worker's wage *plus* the cost of paying a higher wage to all its previously higher workers. Or in general:

MFC for Price Searcher = Price of the Factor *plus* Added Cost of Paying Higher
Price to Already Hired Inputs

Example: MFC *for a Monopsony*

PROBLEM   A firm has hired nine workers at $400 a week. To hire a tenth worker, it must pay $410 a week. Suppose the tenth worker's MRP is $450. Should the firm hire the tenth worker?

SOLUTION   No. The worker would cost $410 *plus* the added pay of $10 each for the other 9 workers: The worker's *MFC* is $500 ($410 + 9 × $10). Since *MFC* > *MRP*, the worker should not be hired.

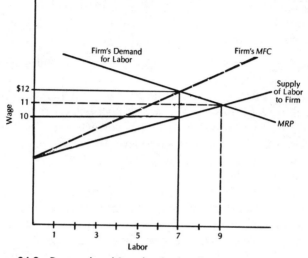

Figure 24-3   Demand and Supply of Labor from the Point of View of a Monopsonist

Figure 24-3 shows the demand and supply for workers of a monopsony. *SS* is the supply curve facing this firm: It's upward-sloping (instead of flat like that of the price taker). *MFC* exceeds the wage. When the supply curve is a straight and upward-sloping line, *MFC* rises twice as fast as the supply curve. The *MRP* curve is the firm's demand curve for labor. This firm will hire until *MRP* = *MFC* at $12.00, paying a wage of $10 to 7 workers. If this firm were forced to act competitively, it would hire more workers (9) at *W* = *MRP* = $11.

YOU SHOULD REMEMBER

1. A price searcher in its output market can be a price taker in its input market.

2. For price takers in the input market, MFC = Price of Input.

3. For a price searcher in the input market, MFC = Price of Input *Plus* Added Cost of Paying Higher Wages to Already Hired Inputs.

4. For the price searcher, MFC > Price of Input.

EFFICIENCY

We will now examine why input markets are efficient when firms are price takers in both their output *and* input markets. Our example will involve workers, but it also applies to land and capital.

Each price taker will hire labor until:

$$\text{Wage} = \text{Price} \times \text{Marginal Physical Product } (W = P \times MPP).$$

Suppose that for all firms, $W = \$10$ and $P = \$2$ with $MPP = 5$. To show that this is optimal, we have to show that total output will be reduced when firms hire a different number of workers than they currently are hiring. Suppose one worker is taken from Firm A and given to Firm B. In Firm B, the worker's MPP < 5 (due to diminishing MPP); in Firm A, an MPP of 5 will be lost. So total output will fall. Obviously, this is inefficient.

Workers want to be with the firm paying them the highest wage (other things being equal). The desire for high wages causes workers to allocate themselves to firms efficiently (since they will go where they are most valued). In the above case, the worker would not want to work for Firm B, since Firm B would pay less than $10 while Firm A pays $10. So the worker will stay with Firm A, as is efficient.

When all factors are paid this way, we will have, for any two inputs, for example, capital (K) and labor (L):

$$\text{Wage} = P \times MPP \text{ of } L$$
$$\text{Capital Rental} = P \times MPP \text{ of } K$$

Or (solving out P)

$$\frac{MPP \text{ of } L}{\text{Wage}} = \frac{MPP \text{ of } K}{\text{Capital Rental}}$$

Capital's cost is calculated as an hourly "rental" so that it is expressed in hourly terms, as worker's wages are expressed.

This is the criterion for maximizing profits. Recall the principle of *equal marginal benefit per unit.* (See Chapter 17.) The firm can hire several inputs. It should hire each until the last dollar spent on each yields the same marginal benefit. The marginal benefit per dollar of any input is $MR \times MPP$/Input Cost. When this is equal for all inputs, the firm is getting the most output for its money. This above expression meets this criterion (after canceling out the MR terms).

Example: Making Hiring Decisions

PROBLEM   An added worker costs $10,000 a year. An added machine costs $20,000 a year. The marginal worker adds 50,000 units to total output. The marginal machine adds 80,000 units. How can the firm produce more at its current total cost?

SOLUTION   It can produce more by hiring more workers and fewer machines. The worker adds 5 units per dollar (50,000/$10,000), the machine, 4 (80,000/$20,000). So, for example, getting rid of one machine and using the $20,000 savings to buy two workers will on net increase output by 20,000 units (− 80,000 from one less machine but + 100,000 from two workers). So at the same total cost, the firm can produce 20,000 more units of output. The firm will continue to hire more units of labor (lowering labor's *MPP*) and fewer units of capital (increasing capital's *MPP*) until both yield the same marginal addition to output *per dollar cost.*

YOU SHOULD REMEMBER

1. When firms are price takers in both the markets they sell in and the markets they buy factors in, inputs will be allocated to their most valued use.

2. Firms will hire inputs until the marginal physical product of each per dollar cost is the same. This will give it the most output for a given cost (and equivalently, the least cost for a given output).

INCOME ALLOCATION

When a firm is a price taker and pays all inputs according to Input Price = Output Price × *MPP* of Input, the total revenue of the firm will be fully (not more nor less) spent in the long run on the factors it employs. The proof of this assertion is beyond the scope of this book, but its implications are important and so are discussed here.

Consider again Table 24-1. Suppose the wage is $16. The firm will hire 5 workers. But the firm's total revenue will be the sum of the revenues added by each worker (*TR* = Sum of *MRP*s): $32 + $28 + $24 + $20 + $16 = $110. But the firm spends only $80 on workers (5 × $16). So it has a $30 "surplus." But this surplus is what will be paid for capital inputs and land inputs when they are paid their marginal revenue product. So the firm itself makes no economic profit or loss in the long run. In terms of Figure 24-2, Panel A, labor is paid $100 and other inputs receive the area equal to triangle *ABC* (or ½ of base times height: $50). *TR* is $150.

YOU SHOULD REMEMBER

1. When all factors are paid their marginal value (P × MPP), total revenue will equal total costs in the long run.

2. The surplus of each factor will be the income of other factors, and vice versa.

KNOW THE CONCEPTS

DO YOU KNOW THE BASICS?

1. When American textile workers lose their jobs, why are consumers and not their employers responsible?

2. What is the benefit of hiring one more worker? The cost?

3. When will the firm stop hiring more workers?

4. When will a firm that is a price taker in both its output and input market stop hiring?

5. Is the following true: "Monopolies are also price searchers (monopsonies) in their input markets."

6. Why don't monopolies hire enough workers from a social point of view?

7. Why does labor cost more than its wage to a monopsony?

8. What rule should firms follow to allocate workers to their most valued use?

9. "If there were no workers, no output could be produced. So workers deserve more than their marginal worth." Comment.

10. How does marginal physical product differ from marginal revenue product?

TERMS FOR STUDY

complements and substitutes in
   the production process
elasticity of input demand
marginal factor cost (*MFC*)
marginal revenue product (*MRP*)
monopsony

output effect
price taker and price searcher
   in input market
price taker and price searcher
   in output market

PRACTICAL APPLICATION

1. The federal government owns 95% of the land in Alaska. If it cut back its holding to 90%, this would double the land available for private development. It has been argued that this would lower Alaskan land prices (which is true) and that "the lower price of land would make Alaskans poorer." Why is the assertion in quotes wrong?

2. If a firm can hire 100 workers at $100 per worker per week and 101 workers at $101, what is the cost of worker number 101?

3. Use the following table to answer these questions. Assume the firm is a price taker in all markets.

Labor Units	1	2	3	4	5	6	7	8
MPP	20	18	16	14	12	10	8	6

   a. If the firm hires 4 workers, how much is it producing (assuming Q = 0 when it hires no workers).
   b. If the wage is $12 and the price of output is $1, how many workers should the firm hire?
   c. Answer the same question for W = $24 and P = $2; W = $36 and P = $3; W = $48 and P = $4 (You will find that only the *ratio of wages to prices* (W/P) matters for employment decisions.)
   d. If W = $35 and P = $2, how many workers should the firm hire (if it can hire only whole labor units.

4. Indicate whether the following events will increase, decrease, or have an uncertain effect on the quantity of labor demanded by U.S. automobile manufacturers.
   Event A: Demand for U.S. cars falls.
   Event B: Wages of auto workers go up.
   Event C: Price of machinery goes up. (Machinery and auto workers are complements.)
   Event D: Price of machinery goes up. (Machinery and auto workers are substitutes.)
   Event E: Total productivity goes up in U.S. auto making. Demand for U.S. cars is elastic.

5. A firm can sell fifty widgets for $5 each and fifty-two for $4.90 each. When it hires another worker, its output goes up from fifty to fifty-two units. The firm can hire all the workers it wants at $8.
   a. Should it hire this worker?
   b. If instead fifty firms were producing one widget each, would one of them hire this worker?

6. This problem illustrates the substitution effect. The widget industry can produce one widget with one of two technologies. Technology A uses two units of labor and three units of capital, while Technology B uses three units of labor and two units of capital.
   a. If wages are $2 and capital cost $1.50 a unit, which technology will the widget industry use?

   Hint: Which costs less per widget?

   How many workers per unit of output will the industry employ?
   b. If wages are still $2 but capital costs $2.50, which technology will the widget industry use? How many workers per unit of output will it employ?
   c. What was the substitution effect?

7. Continuing with Question 6 above, we will now show the output effect. The demand curve for widgets is:

Demand Price	$8	$8.50	$9	$10	$11	$12
Output Demand	400	375	350	300	250	200

   a. When wages are $2 and capital cost is $1.50, what is the cost per widget? Assuming the cost per widget equals the price per widget (as it does in the long run in a competitive industry), how many widgets will be demanded?
   b. When wages are $2 but capital costs $2.50, what is the cost per widget? Output demand?
   c. What is the output effect?
   d. How many units of labor were demanded in (a)? in (b)?

   Remember: Labor Demand = Output Demand × Labor per unit of output.

8. One hour of labor cost $10 and an hour of machine time costs $30. The MPP of an hour of labor is 30 added widgets. The MPP of an hour of machine time is 120 widgets. How can the firm produce more at the same cost?

9. Each unit of capital costs twelve times the cost of a unit of labor. If labor costs $100 and its MPP is ten units of output, what does one unit of capital produce (if the firm is efficient and a price taker in its input market)?

10. In both Industry A and Industry B, the first worker adds five units to total output: the second, four units; the third, three units; the fourth, two; and

the fifth, one. Both industries are price takers. There are six workers in the labor market.

    a. If the price of output in industry A is $2 and the price of output in industry B is $1, how many workers will work in each industry? At what wage?

    b. If the price of A then falls to $1.50 and the price of B rises to $1.50, how many workers will work in each industry? At what wage?

    c. How does the labor market respond to the change in consumer demand that is reflected in the change from A to B?

ANSWERS

KNOW THE CONCEPTS

1. While the news media often blames employers for plant closings and firings, the employers are only reflecting the desires of consumers: Here, consumers no longer want to buy American-made textiles. The demand for labor is a *derived demand!*

2. The benefit is the addition to total revenue (the marginal revenue product, or *MRP*). The cost is the addition to total cost (the marginal factor cost, or *MFC*).

3. When workers no longer add more to total revenue than to total cost: when *MRP* = *MFC*.

4. When Price of Output × Marginal Physical Product = Price of Input (from *MRP* = *MFC*).

5. No. Almost every firm, monopoly or competitor, is a price taker in the markets in which it buys factors.

6. For the last worker hired by a monopoly, we have *MR* × *MPP* = Wage. But the value of the worker's output to consumers is Price of Output × *MPP*. Since *P* > *MR* for a monopoly, society would gain (as its marginal benefit exceeds the marginal cost) from more employment.

7. A monopsony has to raise its wage to all its workers to hire one more worker. So its cost of another worker is:

    Wage + Added Cost of Higher Wage for Workers Already Hired

    So, its *MFC* > Wage.

8. Workers should be allocated to the job where they have the *highest* marginal worth: where Wage = Price of Output × *MPP* is highest. This is exactly what competitive markets do.

9. The same is true for capital, for land, and for materials. But if they all get more than their marginal worth, total costs will exceed total revenues by several times. So the position taken in the quote is an economic impossibility. At the level of the whole economy, it says that all imputs should get more than they produce.

10. *MPP* is the addition to total output due to an added input. *MRP* is the addition to total revenue due to an added input. The first is a physical measure, the second, a monetary measure.

PRACTICAL APPLICATION

1. The fact that private land is so costly in Alaska tells us it has a high marginal physical product. So more land would raise total Alaskan output a great deal. Alaskans as a whole would be better off. Sometimes it is easy to forget the simple fact that more inputs mean more output.

2. $201

3. **a.** 68. Total Output = Sum of *MPP*s.
   b. 5 workers.
   c. As long as $W/P = 12$, the firm will hire 5 workers.
   d. 2 workers. The first worker adds $40 to total revenue and the second worker adds $36 to total revenue. Both cost less, $35, so the firm hires both. But the third worker would add $32 to *TR* but would cost $35, so the third worker should not be hired.

4. *Event A:* Decrease (shift demand for labor curve to left).
   Event B: Decrease (move along demand for labor curve).
   Event C: Decrease (shift to left).
   Event D: Uncertain effect. Data suggest that it would decrease labor demand.
   Event E: Increase (shift to right).

5. **a.** No. The worker adds $4.80 to total revenue ($52 \times \$4.90 - 50 \times \$5$) and $8 to total cost.
   b. Yes. The worker adds $9.60 ($2 \times \$4.90$) less 10¢ lost on the first unit of output, or $9.50 to total revenue.

6. **a.** Technology A (because it costs less). The industry will use two units of labor per unit of output. (Technology A costs $8.50, while B costs $9.)
   b. Technology B. The industry will use three units of labor per unit of output. (A costs $11.50 and B costs $11.)
   c. The substitution effect was the one-unit increase in labor per unit of output due to the higher price of capital.

7. **a.** $8.50. $Q = 375$.
   b. $11.00. $Q = 250$.
   c. The output effect is the reduction in demand by 125 units (from 375 to 250) caused by the higher price of capital.
   d. 750 (375 × 2) and 750 (250 × 3) respectively.
   Note that the higher price of capital has two effects on labor demand: Its output effect is negative (as Q falls from 375 to 250) but its substitution effect is positive (as labor per unit of output increases from 2 to 3). In this case, these effects exactly offset one another.

8. The marginal product per dollar for labor is 3 (30 /$10) and for capital, 4 (120/$30). The firm is getting more value per dollar spent on capital, so it should use more capital and less labor. For example, if it got rid of 3 worker hours (losing 90 units of output) and used the $30 to buy one machine hour (gaining 120 units of output), it could increase output by 30 units (120 − 90) with no change in cost.

9. *MPP* of Capital = 120.

10. **a.** Four workers to Industry A; two workers to Industry B. (We assign workers to A and B in order of highest *MRP*.) The marginal worker in each adds $4 to total revenue, so the wage = $4.
    b. Three workers to each: wage = $4.50.
    c. The fall in A's price reduces its wage: for four workers, it will pay a wage of only $3. B will pay an added third worker $4.50. So one worker from A will leave and go to B to get the higher wage. Now with three workers, A too pays $4.50. Now all workers are content to stay where they are. The change in wages, reflecting the consumers' change in the value of output, pulls workers to their most valued use.

25
WAGES, LABOR MARKETS, AND UNIONS

WORKERS AND JOBS

Why do workers of the same ability earn different wages? Why do doctors earn more than school teachers? How do unions affect wages? To answer these questions, this chapter presents two labor market models and their modifications.

MODEL 1: WORKERS ALIKE, JOBS ALIKE

ASSUMPTIONS

1. All workers are equally skilled.

2. All jobs are exactly alike in terms of amenities, fringe benefits, and so forth.

3. Competition exists among employers (there are no monopsonies) and workers (there are no unions).

4. Workers are well-informed about what jobs pay.

5. Workers can change jobs easily and employers can change workers easily.

These assumptions will be modified as we move towards more realistic cases.

RESULTS

1. The wage level will be set so the labor market clears.

2. All firms pay the same wage.

EXPLANATION

Figure 25-1 shows the demand and supply for workers in a given labor market. The equilibrium wage is $8, where the demand for workers (70 jobs) equals the supply (70 workers).

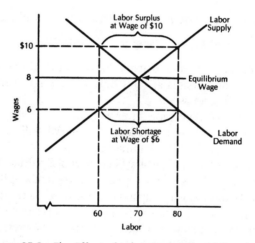

Figure 25-1   The Effect of Labor Demand and Supply

If wages are too high, there will be a surplus of workers. At a wage of $10, for example, there is a surplus of 20 workers. The surplus workers will bid wages down.

If wages are too low, there will be a shortage of workers. At a wage of $6, there is a shortage of 20 workers. Employers who cannot get enough workers will bid wages up.

If one firm pays a wage below the market, all its workers will quit and no others will apply. The firm must raise its wage or go out of business. If it pays a wage above the market, it will have a surplus of applicants. This surplus will alert the employer to the fact that it is paying too much. It will lower its wage or be underpriced in the output market and driven out of existence by competing firms.

Note how each assumption listed earlier is necessary for this result. All workers are equally skilled, so employers value all workers equally and can pay each the same wage. All jobs are alike in nonmonetary (or nonpecuniary) aspects, so workers compare wages alone and go to the job paying the highest wage. Workers are informed and can easily change jobs. Employers are not restrained by unions from lowering wages and can replace their workers easily if workers demand wages that exceed the market level.

IMPLICATIONS

1. A firm can determine how its wages compare to what other firms are paying by looking at its resignation rate and its application rate. When resignations are high and applications few, it's paying too little.

2. Competition among workers forces wages down. Competition among employers forces wages up. (This is an example of the "invisible hand" moving people by self-interest to outcomes that are actually in the economy's interest.)

3. Any factor that *increases the demand* for workers will increase wages.

$$\text{Wage} = \text{Price of Output} \times \text{Marginal Physical Product}$$

Any factor that increases demand for output (and thus its price) or *MPP* will increase labor demand (and thus wages). For a nation as a whole, wages will be higher when:
   a. The nation has more capital per worker.
   b. The nation has better technology, managerial skills, and know-how.
   c. The nation has abundant natural resources.

When workers in one industry become more productive (because of an innovation or perhaps more capital), the benefits spill over into other industries. As the industry expands, drawing workers from other areas of the economy, wages elsewhere will rise. This phenomenon is sometimes referred to as "a rising tide lifting all ships": Workers benefit from the higher productivity and wages of others.

4. Any factor that *decreases the supply* of workers will increase wages.

In the thirteenth century, the black plague wiped out one third of Europe's population, but left the capital, land, and technical know-how intact. Real wages doubled in many areas. Besides plague, war, and pestilence, some of the factors affecting the supply of labor include:
   a. Population.
   b. Labor-force participation rate. (This is the fraction of the population that wants to work and is working or seeking a job.)
   c. Hours of work per worker.

To get total work hours supplied, we multiply $(a) \times (b) \times (c)$. In the next section, we'll discuss the factors affecting (c).

YOU SHOULD REMEMBER

1. When workers are alike in skills and jobs are alike in amenities, all jobs will pay the same wage.
2. At equilibrium wage, the quantity of workers demanded equals the quantity supplied.
3. Factors increasing worker productivity increase wages: More capital, more natural resources, and better technology all increase a nation's wage level.
4. Factors decreasing the supply of workers increase wages; a smaller population, a smaller fraction of persons who work, and fewer hours of work per worker all increase a nation's wage level.

• *HOURS OF WORK FOR AN INDIVIDUAL*

In this century, real wages have risen. As a result, males have worked fewer hours (in 1900, the average work week was 55 hours; today it's 37 hours) while females have worked more (their labor-force participation rate has increased from 21% in 1900 to over 54% today). To understand these divergent results, the main thing to remember is that a person's decision to supply *more* hours of work is also a decision to demand *less* leisure time.

An *increase* in the real wage has two effects:

1. *The Substitution Effect:* Economists divide the time of workers between work and leisure. Work is any activity for which the worker gets paid. Leisure time includes the remaining hours for which the worker doesn't get paid. Thus, leisure may involve a great deal of effort and energy (for example, cleaning a home or taking care of children) and yet is not "work" by this definition.

    A higher real wage increases the reward for working and thereby increases the opportunity cost of leisure time. This higher relative cost of work time, by itself, will cause workers to *substitute* (i.e., give up) some leisure time in order to work longer hours so as to get the greater amount of goods the higher wage now buys.

2. *The Income Effect:* Leisure is a normal good (see Chapter 17). So when income goes up, people usually want to "buy" more leisure and work less.

The net effect of higher wages depends upon whether the substitution effect or the income effect is stronger. Figure 25-2 shows a typical **backward-bending supply curve of labor** for a worker. In Figure 25-2, the worker works only if wages exceed $4. From $4 to $8, the substitution effect dominates the income effect as higher wages elicit more hours of work. For $8 to $10, the two effects precisely offset each other: In this wage range, the supply of hours for this worker is perfectly inelastic. From $10 up, the income effect dominates the substitution effect as higher wages result in fewer work hours.

For males, the income effect has dominated the substitution effect: Higher real wages have reduced their hours of work. For females, the opposite has been true.

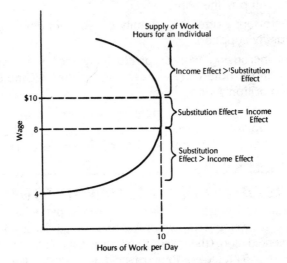

Figure 25-2 The Backward Bending Supply Curve of Labor

YOU SHOULD REMEMBER

1. One more hour of work means one less hour of leisure time. Therefore, the supply of work hours is the mirror image of the demand for leisure hours.

2. A higher wage has two effects. The substitution effect increases work hours because the higher wage makes leisure time more expensive. The income effect reduces work hours because higher income increases the demand for leisure time.

3. The net effect of a wage increase depends upon which effect is stronger. When the income effect dominates, a higher wage means workers want to work fewer hours and a lower wage means workers want to work more hours. When the substitution effect dominates, a higher wage means workers want to work more hours and a lower wage means less hours.

MODEL 2: WORKERS ALIKE BUT JOBS DIFFER

ASSUMPTIONS

Assumptions 1, 3, and 4 of Model 1, *plus*:

2'. Jobs differ in their working conditions. Some are pleasant, some dangerous, and so forth.

5. Workers place the same value on amenities and disagreeable working conditions.

Assumption 2' means workers now will compare not only wages but working conditions as well. Assumption 5 assures that all workers place the same value on any particular job's working conditions and so are willing to accept the same money wage for that particular job.

RESULTS

The **full wage** of all jobs will be equal. Money wages will vary to compensate workers for the nonmonetary differences between jobs.

EXPLANATION

Full wages are the full monetary value workers place on working in a given job. Full wages serve the same role as money wages did in Model 1: Any job whose full wage is too high will have a surplus of applicants, and any job whose full wage is too low will have a shortage of workers. Only when all jobs pay the same full wage will the labor market be in equilibrium: No workers will want to change jobs.

Those jobs with disagreeable aspects will have to pay a higher money wage; those jobs with positive nonmonetary aspects will be able to pay a lower money wage. These **compensating wage differentials** compensate workers for differences in working conditions. For example, garbage collectors are paid reasonably well because their job is unpleasant.

IMPLICATION

Employers with better working conditions can pay lower money wages. This gives an incentive to employers to provide pleasant working conditions. Employers will improve working conditions as long as the dollar savings from lower wages covers the employers' cost of providing better working conditions.

EXTENSION

We can modify Assumption 5 by assuming (more realistically) that workers differ in the value they place upon many amenities. For example, the extra pay differential workers would demand to work on a high-rise construction project most likely will vary widely from worker to worker. If so, workers in any given job will have the same or *higher* full wage than they can get elsewhere. Those workers getting higher full wages in their current job than they can earn elsewhere are earning economic rents. An **economic rent** is any payment in excess of opportunity cost (here, it's the excess in full wages over what the worker can get elsewhere). In Models 1 and 2, all jobs paid the same full wage in equilibrium so that no workers received any economic rents.

YOU SHOULD REMEMBER

1. When workers are alike in skill and taste but jobs differ, then all jobs will pay the same full wage.

2. Differences in money wages will compensate for differences in nonmonetary aspects of work. These wage differentials are called compensating wage differentials.

OTHER MODELS OF DIFFERENCES IN WAGES

In the above models, workers were equally skilled and were considered interchangeable by employers. Now let's modify this assumption.

• HUMAN CAPITAL

Human capital is the set of skills that a worker acquires through schooling and experience that improves the worker's productivity and income. The cost of schooling includes its direct costs (such as tuition and books) plus its forgone cost (mainly what could have been earned had one not been in school). The benefit of extra schooling is the value of the increase in future earnings that occurs as a result of the extra schooling.

How do we know that more schooling will lead to higher wages? In the short run, we do not know for certain. For example, a particular skill may suddenly no longer be in demand. But in the long run, people will not bear the cost of learning a skill unless it pays to do so. Thus, higher wages in the long run compensate workers for the costs of schooling and training.

• NONCOMPETING GROUPS

Certain skills and attributes, either natural or acquired, may be in high demand. The workers who have these skills will earn more than those who don't. Those who don't have the skills may not be able to get them (at least not quickly). So an economy can have **noncompeting groups**—whole groups of workers who have special skills and earn economic rents. For example, when oil prices went up, the salaries of experienced oil geologists quadrupled. They earned much more than they could get in any alternative career.

• *SPECIAL SKILLS*

Entertainers, professional athletes, and top managers often have unique skills that make them special. They earn salaries far greater than what they could earn elsewhere. Their high salaries are mostly economic rents and not a compensating differential nor a reflection of opportunity costs. For example, a movie star making $400,000 a year who otherwise would have made $40,000 as a salesperson is earning an economic rent of $360,000.

YOU SHOULD REMEMBER

1. The fact that education is costly means that in the long run educated workers must be paid more (or they won't become educated).

2. Whole groups of workers can earn economic rents if there are no other competing groups of workers to bid down their wage.

3. A single worker can earn an economic rent as a result of having a skill or other attribute that is unique.

DISCRIMINATION

Discrimination occurs when workers with the same ability as other workers are denied well-paying jobs or receive less pay because of their race, sex, or other characteristics not related to productivity.

Suppose brown-eyed workers get lower pay than blue-eyed workers. Why would employers ever hire blue-eyed workers when they cost more? Why then don't all workers get the same full wage, as in Model 1 or 2? Some possible explanations of this are:

1. Customers refuse to deal with brown-eyed workers.

2. Co-workers may refuse (or demand a wage premium) for working with brown-eyed workers. If employers can't keep brown-eyed workers separate from other workers, employers will hire them only when they work for less.

3. Employers may themselves dislike brown-eyed workers. If there are enough unprejudiced co-workers and employers and thus enough jobs for brown-eyed workers from nondiscriminatory employers, then brown-eyed workers will get the same pay. This suggests that a group will be *more* discriminated against the larger the group and the smaller the fraction of unprejudiced employers.

4. Employers may find it too costly to discover a worker's true ability. Employers may find, for example, that height is a good "cheap screening device" for selecting managers. They may believe that tall people make "natural leaders." So tall children, knowing this, become leaders early, acquiring skills that later will reinforce the employers' belief that they deserve high-paying leadership jobs.

Some economists believe that the forces of competition and profit-seeking will, with time, wear down the barriers caused by discrimination. Laws against discrimination may speed this process. But these laws may fail if employers avoid hiring minorities because they fear the lawsuits that may result if they dismiss a minority worker.

YOU SHOULD REMEMBER

1. The key to understanding discrimination is understanding why employers would ever hire workers of the same ability at higher wages than those discriminated against.

2. The lower wages caused by discrimination may reflect the employers' distaste (or prejudice), the customers' distaste, or the distaste of other workers.

3. Discrimination may reflect its use as a cheap screening device by employers; widespread discrimination may result in a self-fulfilling prophesy.

UNIONS

UNIONS IN PRICE-TAKING FIRMS

A union has a monopoly on the supply of labor to the firms it has organized. Figure 25-3 shows the industry's demand for labor (*DD*) and the workers' supply of labor (*SS*). If the union wants the most members, it will set the wage at $6. If it wants the biggest total wage payments (Wages × Manhours), it will set the wage at $7, employment being at 70 workers where the union's marginal revenue curve intersects the axis. If it wants the most profits (the total difference between wages and supply costs), it will set the wage at $10 (for a profit of $160): This is at the point the marginal revenue curve intersects the supply curve.

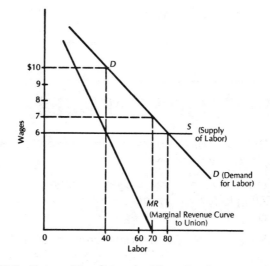

Figure 25-3 Unions: Visualizing the Wage/Employment Trade-Off

Whatever the union's goals (and they can certainly be other than those above), if the union wants higher wages, it must accept the fact that it will then have fewer members. Unions in the 1970s, for example, pushed their wages up from 12% to 25% higher than nonunion wages. Union employment and membership fell as a result.

Unions achieve a higher wage by (1) prohibiting employers from paying a lower wage (say, by setting wages at $10 in Figure 25-3) and (2) limiting the supply of workers in the industry (say to 40 in Figure 25-3). Craft unions, which represent workers with a certain type of skill, typically try to restrain entry into the profession. For example, the American Medical Association helped close down many medical schools at the beginning of this century. Industrial unions, which represent all types of workers in the same industries, more often set wages (although a few seek to limit entry and training also).

Some unions try to raise wages by limiting how much each worker produces. Although the same goal could be achieved by reducing the number of workers, a union in a declining industry may feel pressured to keep its current members employed. Limiting productivity will prove useful in increasing labor demand only when the price elasticity of output demand is inelastic (see Chapter 24).

Unions have two effects on nonunion wages:

1. **The *Spill-Over Effect:*** In Figure 25-3, if the union increases the wage from $6 to $10, 40 workers will be out of work. They will spill over into the nonunion sector and lower wages there.

2. The *Wage Threat Effect:* Nonunion firms, to avoid being unionized, may raise their wages. Note that when this effect predominates, both union and nonunion workers will lose jobs.

YOU SHOULD REMEMBER

1. Unions face a trade-off between employment and wages when they organize a competitive industry.

2. Unions may achieve higher wages by setting a minimum wage; by restricting labor supply; and, when output demand is inelastic, by reducing productivity.

3. Unions have two effects on nonunion wages. First, those losing jobs in the union sector will spill over into the nonunion sector, lowering nonunion wages. Second, nonunion employers, to avoid the threat of being unionized, may pay a higher wage.

UNIONS AND MONOPSONISTIC EMPLOYERS

Unions may face employers who act as a monopsony. In this case, over some range of wages, it is possible for unions to get both higher wages *and* more employment.

Whenever a monopoly (here, the union) faces a monopsony (the employers), we have a **bilateral monopoly.**

Figure 25-4 shows the marginal revenue product (*MRP*) of labor to the monopsony, the supply curve (*SS*), and its marginal factor cost (*MFC*) to the monopsony. If employers were competitive and workers were not in a union, the wage would be $8 and employment 100. If workers are not in a union but the employers are monopsonistic, the monopsony will pay a wage of $7 and hire 60 workers (where *MFC* = *MRP* = $10).

But when the workers are represented by a union, the union can present a wage the monopsony must pay.

Key Procedure for Finding Employment for a Bilateral Monopoly

1. Start at the monopsony wage and employment where *MFC* equals *MRP* ($7 and 60 workers).

2. Draw a horizontal line across the graph at whatever union wage you want (as long as it is above 1's level).

3. Employment will be where this line intersects the labor supply curve (*SS*) or the marginal revenue product curve (*MRP*), *whichever comes first.*

4. The highest employment will be at the point the supply curve intersects the *MFC* curve.

Starting at $7, as the wage goes up to $8, employment moves from 60 to 100 along the *SS* curve. At $8, the industry has the highest employment. Then going up from $8, employment falls as we move up and inward on the *MFC* curve. At $10, for example, 60 workers will be employed.

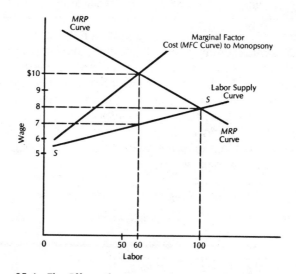

Figure 25-4   The Effect of a Union on Monopsony Employers

What wage the union will choose depends upon its bargaining power and its goals. It is possible for the union to get higher wages and more employment, but in actuality, the union could choose a wage that reduces employment.

YOU SHOULD REMEMBER

1. Unions, facing a monopsonist (a monopoly buyer of labor) can increase employment *and* wages (this does not mean they will).

2. The highest level of employment is at the wage where the supply of labor intersects the *MRP* curve.

THE MINIMUM WAGE

In Chapter 3, we saw that the effect of a minimum wage, like that of any other price floor, is to create a surplus of workers Studies have shown that for every 10% increase in the real minimum wage, teenage employment falls between 1% and 3%. In addition, we saw above that employers offer better working conditions when they can offer and attract workers at a sufficiently lower money wage. But the minimum wage (because it prevents lower wages) discourages firms from offering better working conditions. Some studies suggest that the minimum wage causes firms to cut back on working conditions (including on-the-job training) to such a degree that the minimum wage reduces full wages.

Theoretically, a minimum wage could have the same effect of increasing employment as a union could, *when* employers are monopsonistic. But almost all low-skilled workers can work in a wide range of jobs, so their employers are not monopsonists. So while the monopsonist argument is often used to justify the minimum wage, it has little basis in fact—especially since a minimum wage reduces, not increases, employment.

Another justification given for a minimum wage is that it helps the poor. But studies show that most workers whose income falls below the poverty level earn substantially more than the minimum wage. (Most minimum wage workers are middle-class teenagers.) Thus, a higher minimum wage can't substantially help the poor.

KNOW THE CONCEPTS

DO YOU KNOW THE BASICS?

1. How can an employer tell if it is paying its workers too little (compared to other firms)?

2. If a firm lowers its wages, what will happen to the firm's application and resignation rates?

3. Are workers worse off when they work in dangerous jobs with disagreeable working conditions?

4. Why do employers give their workers fringe benefits?

5. What is the main cost of a college education?

6. Will a higher wage always make workers work more?

7. When can unions raise both wages and employment?

8. Why is it costly for employers to not hire workers that are discriminated against?

9. What keeps a union from raising wages too much?

10. If nonunion firms are not worried about being unionized, how will a higher union wage affect nonunion wages?

TERMS FOR STUDY

backward-bending supply
   curve of labor
bilateral monopoly
compensating wage differential
economic rent

full wages
human capital
income and substitution effects
   on work hours
noncompeting groups

PRACTICAL APPLICATION

1. Using Model 2, suppose (a) Job A has dangerous working conditions, which workers would be willing to pay a minimum of $2 an hour to remove and (b) Job B has a better fringe benefit program, which workers would pay up to $1 an hour to get. How will the hour money wages compare between these two jobs? Which job will workers prefer to take?

2. Why do barbers in India earn less than U.S. barbers, even when both have the same equipment and know-how?

3. Why does attendance in MBA programs go up during recessions?

4. How will the following events affect a worker's hours of work?
   Event A: The worker inherits $500,000.
   Event B: A male worker's wage goes up. (Assume that his income effect is stronger than his substitution effect.)
   Event C: A female worker's wage goes up. (Assume that her substitution effect is stronger than her income effect.)

5. If the government stopped subsidizing the cost of college and fewer people went to college as a result, what would be the short-run and long-run impact on the earnings of college graduates?

6. Unions tend to demand higher wages the more *inelastic* the demand for labor is (because then the trade-off between wages and employment is lessened). How will the following factors affect union wage demands (other things being equal)?
   a. The demand for output is highly elastic.
   b. Labor represents a small fraction of total cost.
   c. It is easy to substitute capital for labor.
   d. The union controls only a small fraction of the industry.

7. Which of the following best explains why American workers are paid more than workers in Mexico:
   a. American unions.
   b. The minimum wage.
   c. American workers are more productive.

8. Use the following table to answer these questions. The table shows weekly wages and the supply of labor at that wage.

Workers	1	2	3	4	5	6	7	8
Wages	$100	125	150	175	200	225	250	275
MRP	$400	375	350	325	300	275	250	225

   a. If firms in this industry are price takers in this factor market, how many workers will they hire? At what wage?
   b. If this industry is a monopsony (having only one employer or a cartel of a few employers), then how many workers will the monopsony hire?

   Hint: Calculate the monopsony's MFC.

9. The United Mine Workers have favored government-imposed standards of safety for all coal mines, whether unionized or not. How would these standards, imposed by the government, help increase the wages of union coal miners?

10. Professional accountants are pushing for higher requirements for entry into their profession, including more years of education. How would this impact the wages and number of accountants? How would it benefit new accountants? Old accountants?

ANSWERS

KNOW THE CONCEPTS

1. When its resignation rate is too high and its application rate is too low.

2. Its application rate should fall and its resignation rate should rise.

3. No. Workers in dangerous jobs are getting the same or higher full wage than they could get elsewhere. Their higher money wage compensates for the poor nonmonetary aspects of the job.

4. With higher fringe benefits, employers can attract workers while paying lower wages. If the reduction in wages covers the fringe benefits' cost, employers will offer them.

5. Forgone earnings, i.e., the amount that could have been earned if instead of going to school the person had worked.

6. No. If the income effect (higher wages making leisure more desirable) dominates the substitution effect (higher wages making leisure more expensive), workers will work less.

7. When the union faces a monopsony.

8. Because those discriminated against are cheaper to employ. By hiring these workers, the firm can make more profits and become more competitive.

9. With higher wages, there will be less employment.

10. It will lower nonunion wages as unemployed union workers spill over into the nonunion sector looking for jobs.

PRACTICAL APPLICATION

1. Job A must pay $3 more than Job B. This compensates the workers for having the $2 dangerous working conditions and for not having the $1 better fringe benefits. Workers will then have the same full wage in both jobs: They'll take either one. Note that *only* in equilibrium are workers indifferent between jobs.

2. The opportunity cost of being a barber is higher in the U.S. Thus, all jobs benefit from the fact that in the U.S., there is more capital, know-how, and resource per worker.

3. A major cost of schooling is forgone earnings. In a recession, this cost is reduced. So more people continue their schooling (unless they believe the earnings of MBA holders is also going to be depressed in the future).

4. *Event A:* Hours of work will decrease.
   Event B: Hours of work will decrease.
   Event C: Hours of work will increase.

5. In the short run, an increase in the cost of college would reduce the number of people getting a college education. Wages of college graduates would fall until their numbers dwindled (which could take years). In the long run, the stock of college graduates would fall, increasing the wages of college graduates as their fewer number increased their marginal product. Ultimately, the cost of going to college would once again pay for itself,

but (a) college graduates would earn more to justify the higher cost of college and (b) there would be fewer college graduates, so they will have a higher marginal product to cover their higher cost.

6. **a.** Reduce wage demands.
   b. Increase wage demands.
   c. Reduce wage demands.
   d. Reduce wage demands (the smaller the fraction of the industry a union controls, the more elastic the demand for union output will be because of the competition from the nonunion firms).

7. Answer (c). Americans earn more because they produce more.

8. **a.** The industry will hire 7 workers at a wage of $250.
   b. The following table shows the monopsony's *MFC*.

Workers	1	2	3	4	5	6	7	8
Wages	$100	125	150	175	200	225	250	275
MRP	$400	375	350	325	300	275	250	225
MFC	$100	150	200	250	300	350	400	450

The *MFC* is the increase in total cost. For example, for a monopsony hiring all workers, 3 workers cost $450 (3 × $150) and 4 cost $700 (4 × $175): hiring the fourth worker increases total cost by $250. The monopsony will hire until *MRP* equals *MFC* or 5 workers at a wage of $200.

9. Higher coal safety standards would raise the nonlabor costs of all mines, particularly for the smaller nonunion mines. Since union mines already meet these standards, the effect would be to push up the costs of nonunion mines and put many of them out of business. This would allow the union to demand higher wages without the fear of competition from nonunion workers.

10. The impact would be to reduce the number of accountants over time and thus raise the wages of those who are accountants. Old accountants would benefit. New accountants would get higher wages, but only to offset their higher costs of becoming accountants, so they would not benefit (or would benefit by less than those who are already accountants).

26

RENT, INTEREST, AND PROFITS

Economic rent is a payment to any factor in perfectly inelastic supply. In other words, economic rent has *no* impact on supply. As noted in Chapter 25, economic rent is also any payment in excess of a factor's opportunity cost. This is an equivalent definition. Why? Because once a factor receives its opportunity cost, any added payment leaves its supply unchanged.

Economic profit is the excess of total revenues over costs (including the opportunity costs of the owner's time and investment). Economic profit is like a rent, except competition eliminates economic profits in the long run. (Note, however, that a monopoly doesn't face competition and thus can earn long-run economic profits.)

Interest is a payment for the use of funds over a period of time. These funds may finance the production of **capital**, a durable manmade resource of production that yields a return over several years. The income from capital is called its **yield** or **return**, and is stated as a percent of the original investment. So if a $2,000 machine yields $200 a year, its **rate of yield** or its **rate of return** is 10% ($200/ $2000 × 100).

At one time, "rent" was defined as the return on land and "interest" as the return on capital. But today, economists recognize that all factors can earn rents, interests, *and* profits. For example, suppose an actor invests $100,000 in acting lessons. The alternative interest he could have earned on the $100,000 is 10%.

Without acting lessons, he would have earned $20,000 a year in some other profession. With lessons, skill, and luck, he earns $70,000 a year as an actor. Of the $70,000, $20,000 compensated him for the opportunity cost of his time and is the "wage" portion of his compensation. His interest income on his investment in acting lessons is $10,000 (10% of $100,000). And $40,000 is an economic rent (the payment in excess of his opportunity cost of $30,000).

ECONOMIC RENT

Economic rent is any payment that doesn't affect the supply of the input. As a consequence, economic rent is a *purely demand-determined payment.* For ex-ample, suppose a farm grows a given amount of cotton and nothing else. And suppose cotton costs (in fertilizer, labor, and other nonland costs) $5,000 to grow. Any payment for this farm's annual crop in excess of $5,000 is an economic rent (because above $5,000, cotton will be grown regardless of how high the price is). If the crop is worth $12,000, for example, the economic rent is $7,000 ($12,000 − cost of $5,000). When cotton demand falls and the crop's price falls to $7,000, economic rent falls by an equal amount, to $2,000. When demand goes up and crop's price goes up to $20,000, economic rent rises to $15,000.

Some factors earn economic rents because they are more efficient. Figure 26-1 shows the supply cost (or the nonland cost) of growing cotton on different land. We assume each acre of land grows the same amount of cotton but at different costs. As we move from left to right on the supply-of-land curve, we move from the most efficient land to the least efficient land. The first acre put into production

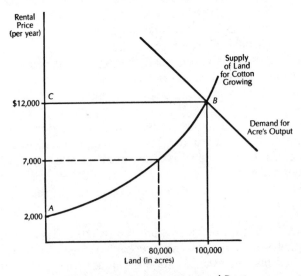

Figure 26-1   Determining Land Rent

grows the crop at a cost of $2,000. The 80,000th acre's cost of growing the crop is $7,000. Demand equals supply at Point B: 100,000 acres will be cultivated, each acre producing $12,000 worth of cotton. The best land has a growing cost of $2,000 and so earns an economic rent of $10,000. The 80,000th acre earns an economic rent of $5,000 ($12,000 − $7,000). And the 100,000th acre put into production has a growing cost of $12,000: It earns no economic rent. The 100,000th acre of land represents **marginal land.** Marginal land's nonland cost is just covered by what it produces. If land sells for ten times its economic rent, then the first acre would sell for $100,000, the 80,000th acre for $50,000, and the 100,000th acre, the marginal land, for zero dollars.

Total economic rent received from all land is the sum of all rents, or Area *ABC.* This area is the producer's surplus (see Chapter 23) for cotton farmers.

Now let's consider several propositions about taxes and rents:

1. A *tax only on economic rent* will not affect the supply or allocation of the factor. The most profitable use for the factor before the tax is still its most profitable use after the tax. So the tax does not harm efficiency: Resources are still allocated to their best use.

2. A *price ceiling on economic rent* will not affect supply but will affect the allocation of the factor. Suppose three people want an apartment: A will pay $800 for it, B will pay $600, and C will pay $400. Without a price ceiling, A will get the apartment. But with a price ceiling of, say, $300, A or B or C may get it. There is no assurance that the apartment will go to the person who most values it (A). From an economic point of view, price ceilings on economic rent are allocatively inefficient.

3. A *tax on the actual rent* from land that exceeds its *economic* rent will reduce the supply of productive land. For example, in Figure 26-1, a tax of $5,000 an acre will reduce the after-tax return on land to $7,000 and acreage to 80,000 acres.

YOU SHOULD REMEMBER

1. Economic rent is a payment to a factor whose supply is fixed. Economic rent is purely demand-determined: It goes up or down by the change in what consumers pay for the factor's output.

2. A tax on economic rent affects neither the supply of resources nor how they are used.

3. Rent provides an incentive to allocate resources to their most efficient and productive use. Price ceilings on rent remove this incentive.

INTEREST

Most business firms borrow to finance their investments. **Investment** is the *addition* firms make to their current capital stock. Their current capital includes their plants, equipment, special know-how (technology), and any other durable manmade inputs. Capital has a productive life beyond a year, while "materials" are used up within the year.

Interest is the price the firm pays to borrow funds. If it pays $1,000 a year to borrow $5,000, its interest *rate* is 20%. On the other hand, the investment's yield (or return) is its payoff. If a $5,000 investment pays back $1,500 a year, its rate of return (rate of yield) is 30%. To maximize profits and wealth, a firm should borrow when the rate of return on its investment exceeds the interest rate.

Example: How to Maximize Profits and Wealth

PROBLEM　An investment cost $6,000 and pays back $1,500 a year forever. The interest rate is 10% (for simplicity, we assume the firm can both borrow and lend at this rate). Should the firm make the investment?

SOLUTION　Yes. The project yields a rate of return of 25% ($1,500/$6,000 × 100), which exceeds the interest rate of 10%. By borrowing $6,000 and then paying back $600 (10% of $6,000) a year in interest, the firm will increase its profits by $900 a year ($1,500 return − $600 in interest payments).

PROBLEM　If the above project returns $500 a year (instead of $1,500), should the firm make the investment?

SOLUTION　No. The interest rate (10%) exceeds the project's yield (8.33%). The firm would be better off lending the $6,000 at 10% and earning $600 a year (instead of this project's return of only $500).

Figure 26-2 shows the demand and supply for loanable funds. The *supply* of loanable funds (*SS*) comes from savers (including households, pension funds, and foreign investors). At higher interest rates, more funds are supplied (or lent) to business firms. The *demand* for loanable funds (*DD*) comes from borrowers (mainly business firms) and shows the rates of return their investments pay: As more is invested, the yield on each added investment falls.

Demand equals supply at Point *E*; $200 billion will be lent by savers and borrowed by businesses. The interest rate will be 12%.

Note: Some of the demand for loanable funds is by households for durable household goods such as homes and cars and for financing current consumption such as trips.

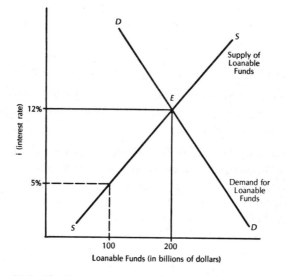

Figure 26-2   The Demand and Supply of Loanable Funds

Banks do *not*, in the *ultimate* sense, "lend money." *Savers* lend money. Instead, banks and many other financial institutions are "middlemen" or financial intermediaries, collecting money from savers and lending it out for the savers. For this service, banks earn the difference between their lending rate and the rate they pay to savers.

One role of interest rates is to assure that only the most productive projects are financed. A **usury law** sets a price ceiling on the interest rate charged on loans. A **usury ceiling** prevents the efficient allocation of capital.

Suppose the usury ceiling is 5%. In Figure 26-2, $100 billion will be saved. However, that is only one-half of what would have been invested and saved at the market rate of 12% if not for the usury ceiling. Thus, usury laws *reduce total savings and total investment*! Furthermore, projects paying less than 12% may be financed. For example, if a project paying 12% is pushed aside for one paying 7%, the economy will lose the 5% difference. As a result, usury ceilings can reduce economic growth, reduce total investment, and misallocate capital.

What factors determine the market rate of interest? Recall that when savers buy a bond, they are lending money to the firm that issued the bond. The interest rate on any particular bond (or other loan) is determined by the following factors.

Factors That Determine the Market Rate of Interest

1. *Real Rate of Interest:* Most people prefer a dollar's worth of consumption today over the same amount of consumption in a year. So it is necessary

to pay them *more* in a year to get them to give up a dollar's worth of consumption today. The real rate of interest reflects this extra payment. If in order to save $1,000 in real goods today, savers must be paid $1,100 in real goods in a year, then the real rate of interest is 10%. This "pure" rate of interest reflects people's time preference for the present over the future.

2. *Premium for Default Risk:* The issuer of the bond may not pay back the loan or bond (i.e., may **default**). If savers anticipate a high risk of default, a high interest rate will be offered.

3. *Risk Premium for Interest Rate Changes:* Most bonds pay a fixed rate of interest. When interest rates go up, the value of these bonds falls. To compensate savers for this risk, bonds may carry an added risk premium. Since longer-term bonds and loans are more exposed to this risk, they typically pay a higher interest rate. The **normal yield curve** for bonds is for bonds with greater maturity (i.e., longer terms) to pay higher interest rates.

A recent trend has been for bonds and loans to pay a variable interest rate (usually based upon the three-month U.S. treasury bill rate). These bonds have little interest rate risk and so usually pay less interest.

4. *Inflationary Premium:* Savers want more dollars back in interest when they expect inflation: They then can get the *real* interest rate they want. For example, the savers in (1) above want to be paid $1,100 in real goods in a year. If they expect prices to go up 10%, they'll want 10% more dollars, or $1,210, so they can still buy $1,100 worth of real goods. If r is the real interest rate and p is the expected rate of inflation, then i, the nominal interest rate quoted on the bond market, will equal:

$$i = r + p + (r \times p).$$

Here, $i = 21\%$ [$.21 = .10 + .10 + (.10 \times .10)$]. Usually the $r \times p$ term is so small that it is ignored. In this case, we write $i = r + p$.

5. *Premium for Administration Costs:* Interest also has to cover the cost of administering the loan. For small loans (such as those on credit cards), this cost can be significant.

YOU SHOULD REMEMBER

1. Interest is a payment to savers for giving up current consumption and lending the resulting savings.

2. A firm borrows as long as its investment projects have a higher (or the same) rate of return as the market rate of interest.

3. The supply of loanable funds reflects how much people want to save. The demand reflects the expected rates of return on investment projects.

4. Investments represent *additions* to the current capital stock.

5. The interest rate is the real rate of interest, *plus* a premium for default risk, *plus* a risk premium for possible changes in the value of the loan (or bond), *plus* an inflationary premium, *plus* a premium to cover administrative costs.

MAKING INVESTMENT DECISIONS

Firms making an investment decision have to compare current costs with future returns. The main method of doing this is using present value.

The Steps in Making an Investment Decision

Step 1: Calculate the present value of returns.

The present value (*PV*) of a return of *R* dollars in *N* years is:

$$R/(1 + i)^n,$$

where *i* is the market interest rate stated as a decimal number (see Chapter 12). **Present value** is the *discounted* value of the *R* dollars: It's the amount one would borrow today at *i*% to pay back *R* dollars in *N* years.

Take the returns for each future year, calculate their present values, and then add them together. The resulting number—the present value of the returns—is the amount that can be borrowed today and paid back with the returns.

Step 2: Calculate the cost.

If the firm is buying capital now, there is no need to discount. But if costs are incurred over several years, these costs will have to be discounted just as returns are.

Step 3: Invest if present value of returns ≥ cost.

If a project costs $500 and has returns whose present value is $700, the firm can borrow $700, invest $500 to pay off the $700 loan, and have $200 left over as a profit. (Recall that the $700 present value is the amount the returns can be used to borrow against.)

Example: Using Present Value to Make an Investment Decision

PROBLEM   A machine costs $2,000. It lasts two years and has no scrap value. In the first year, it produces $990. In the second year, it produces $1,210. Should the firm invest in the machine if the interest rate is 10%?

SOLUTION No. *Step 1: PV* = $990/1.10 + $1,210/1.21 = $1,900. *Step 2:* Cost = $2,000. *Step 3: PV* < Cost.

PROBLEM You can buy or lease a car for one year. If you buy the car, you pay $10,000 now and can sell it for $8,640 in one year. You can lease it for one year for $2,600 (which has to be paid now). In both cases, you have the same maintenance and gas costs. When the interest rate is 20%, should you buy or lease?

SOLUTION Lease. Find out the *PV* of buying the car for one year. It's $10,000 less the *PV* of getting back $8,680 in one year: $10,000 − $8640/ 1.20, or $2,800. Here, leasing is cheaper since it costs only $2,600.

VALUE OF AN ASSET

The value of a piece of land is the present value of all its future rentals. Similarly, capital's value is the present value of all its future rentals. If an asset's yearly "rental" is R per year and if the asset lasts forever, then its present value—when the interest rate is i%—is shown by the following formula:

$$PV = R/i,$$

where i is stated as a decimal. So an asset paying $200 a year forever is worth $2,000 when the interest rate is 10%. (One could borrow $2,000 at 10% and pay back $200 a year forever.) But if the interest rate fell to 5%, the asset would be worth $4,000 ($200/0.05).

ECONOMIC PROFITS

Economic profits are residual payments. They are the excess of total revenues over total costs (including the costs of the owner's time and capital). Unlike economic rents, economic profits disappear in the long run when subjected to competitive pressures. Economic profits are "quasi-rents," because they are like economic rents except that they disappear with competition.

Note: We are talking about *economic profits*. Recall that accounting profits ignore the opportunity cost of an owner's time and investment and do not disappear in the long run.

Economic profits arise from several sources:

1. *Innovation:* An entrepreneur discovers a cheaper way to produce an existing good or finds a more valued use for existing resources (e.g., by discovering a new and more valuable good to produce with these resources). Either way, entrepreneurs earn on economic profits until competitors copy their methods and bid their profits away.

2. *Monopoly:* By reducing output produced from its competitive level of production, a monopoly can earn economic profits.

3. *Risk-Bearing:* In many industries, only a fraction of those entering will ever succeed (e.g., the restaurant industry). It seems reasonable then that the few winners must earn more than their costs. Otherwise, no one would be willing to bet their resources in these risky enterprises.

A central role of economic profits is to tell producers what goods consumers want them to produce. Economic profits signal what goods consumers want more of, while losses signal what goods consumers want less of.

YOU SHOULD REMEMBER

Economic profits are rents that can be bid away by competition. They arise from innovation, risk-bearing, and the reduction of output due to monopoly.

KNOW THE CONCEPTS

DO YOU KNOW THE BASICS?

1. Economists sometimes refer to economic rent as a payment to a factor that no one can produce more of. How does this match our definition?

2. Is the "rent" paid on an apartment purely an economic rent?

3. If a factor's payment is totally an economic rent and its demand curve shifts down 50%, what will happen to the factor's payments? To its supply?

4. Why do interest rates reflect "the public's impatience and capital's productivity."

5. Who are the lenders and borrowers of a bond?

6. Why do bonds with longer maturities normally pay more?

7. Why does a price ceiling on rents or interest lead to allocative inefficiencies and lower output?

8. How can a college student earn an economic profit by his or her choice of study?

9. How does risk lead to profits for some?

10. What two roles do all factor payments play?

TERMS FOR STUDY

economic profit
economic rent
inflationary premium
interest
marginal land

rate of return
real (or pure) rate of interest
risk premium
usury ceiling

PRACTICAL APPLICATION

1. There are five plots in a town that are suitable for locating gas stations. The nonland cost (in annual terms) of developing and operating the first plot is $10,000. For the second plot, the cost is $20,000, for the third plot, $30,000, and so forth.
   a. If each location generates $100,000 in annual revenues, what is each plot's economic rent? Is any plot marginal?
   b. If each location generates $40,000 in annual revenues, what is each plot's economic rent? Is any plot marginal?

2. Identify the source of economic profits in these cases:
   a. A cigarette company finds that it can make a profit by marketing a special cigarette "for the sporting woman."
   b. U.S. car manufacturers enjoyed higher profits due to the import quotas imposed on foreign cars.
   c. An owner of a gold mine made a huge profit when gold's price went up thirty times.

3. A firm has four possible projects in which it can invest. Their rates of return are 15%, 12%, 10%, and 7%. What will determine how many of these projects it finances? Does it matter whether the firm has to borrow to finance the projects, or whether the firm has to finance the projects from its own funds?

4. A college town has two types of renters: town people and students. There are 200 student renters who are willing to pay $500 a month for an apartment. Of the renters who are town people, 100 are willing to pay $600 for an apartment and another 150 town people are willing to pay $400. There are 240 identical apartments in the town.
   a. What is the free market rent?
   b. What would the rent be if there were no students?
   c. Who causes high rents: apartment owners or renters?
   d. A rent control law imposes a rent ceiling of $300. Suppose that at this low rent, no apartment owner will bother renting to students unless there is no one else to whom he/she can rent. Who gains from the rent ceiling? Who loses?

5. A researcher concludes, "High rents are caused by high land prices." Is this conclusion correct?

6 Which of the following is the best example of someone collecting an economic rent:
   a. A landlord who rents an apartment at an amount just covering her cost.
   b. A student who buys a ticket for $10 but would have paid $15.
   c. An auto dealer who sells a car for $12,000 and would have taken $10,000.

7. A firm has a project returning $1,000 a year in perpetuity (i.e., forever). Assume the market rate of interest is 5%.
   a. What is the present value (*PV*) of the returns from this project?
   b. What is the maximum cost the firm will bear to build this project?
   c. If the project cost $5,000, what will happen to the firm's value?

8. Why is a tax on economic rent more efficient than a tax on interest or wages?

9. Suppose all farmland is good only for farming. Will a fall in the price of farmland reduce agricultural output?

10. How will the following events affect the interest rate that a bond pays and the price of the bond?
    Event A: An increase in the expected rate of inflation.
    Event B: A growing confidence that the firm issuing the bond will survive and prove creditworthy.
    Event C: A growing concern that future bond prices will prove more variable.

ANSWERS

KNOW THE CONCEPTS

1. The quantity of a "nonreproducible" factor cannot be increased. So its supply is inelastic and it thus earns a rent.

2. No. Some, if not most, of an apartment's rent is a return on improving the property (by building the apartments) and a compensation for maintenance.

3. The factor's payment will fall 50% and its supply will be unchanged.

4. The supply of loanable funds reflects the impatience of savers: The more impatient they are, the less they supply. The demand for loanable funds reflects the productivity of capital. The more productive capital is, the more firms demand. Thus, the equilibrium interest rate is influenced by both these factors.

5. Firms borrow money by issuing bonds. The savers who purchase the bond are lending their money to firms.

6. Because they are exposed for a longer period of time to the risk of their value falling (due to interest rates rising, greater inflation, or default).

7. With a price ceiling, owners no longer have an incentive to allocate their resources to their most valued use. So a price ceiling results in the misallocation of resources.

8. If a student can anticipate before others do which fields of study will pay better, then by choosing to major in a well-paying field he or she can make a profit. But in the long run, other students will perceive the field's value and compete its profits away.

9. Without profits for some, none would be willing to risk money. Profits for some make up for the losses of others.

10. Factor payments give an incentive to people (1) to supply the factor (*except* for economic rent) and (2) to allocate the factor to its most valuable use.

PRACTICAL APPLICATION

1. a. Plot 1: $90,000. Plot 2: $80,000. Plot 3: $70,000. Plot 4: $60,000. Plot 5: $50,000. No plot is marginal.
   b. Plot 1: $30,000. Plot 2: $20,000. Plot 3: $10,000. Plot 4: $0. Plot 5: Will not have gas station (unless it's already built and it's cost a sunk cost). Plot 4 is marginal.

2. a. Innovation.
  b. Monopoly (restricted entry of competitors).
  c. Risk-bearing.

3. The market interest rate determines how many projects it will build. If the rate is 11%, the firm will undertake only the first two projects (paying 15% and 12%). Even if the firm can finance all four projects with its own funds, it would never invest in the projects paying 10% and 7%. When the interest rate is 11%, it would be better off to lend the funds out and earn 11%.

4. a. $500.
  b. $400.
  c. Renters.
  d. Those who gain are the 240 town people who pay less rent than they would have paid otherwise. Those who lose are the apartment owners and students who can't find an apartment.

5. No. Land prices reflect the present value of future rents. So rents affect land values, not the other way around.

6. c. The dealer earns a $2,000 rent.

7. a. $20,000.
  b. $20,000.
  c. It will go up to $15,000. (For example, the firm could borrow $20,000 today and pay its loan from the project's returns. After deducting the $5,000 cost, it will have added $15,000 to its current value.)

8. A tax on an economic rent changes neither its supply nor how the factor is allocated. A tax on interest and wages will reduce supply and may affect allocation.

9. No. The land has no alternative use and so will be used in farming as long as farm prices cover the nonland costs of farmers.

10. The interest rate and the price of a bond are *inversely* related.
  Event A: Increase interest rate; reduce bond price.
  Event B: Reduce interest rate; increase bond price.
  Event C: Increase interest rate; reduce bond price.

27
PUBLIC CHOICE AND EXTERNALITIES

SOCIAL OPTIMALITY AND FREE MARKETS

Without fraud, misinformation, *and* externalities, people, left alone, will select the best goods to consume and produce them in the most efficient manner. This follows from the fact that free trade allows people to reallocate goods and inputs to their most valued use.

But in the presence of externalities, the free market may *not* produce the socially optimal quantities of goods. Externalities lead to **market failure**—from a social point of view, the market produces either too much or too little of a good.

There are two types of externalities. **Negative externalities** result when activities impose uncompensated costs on people. This means that a good's **social cost** (the cost borne by everyone to produce the good) exceeds its **private cost** (the cost borne by those producing the good). For example, a steel firm dumping its waste in a stream may harm the health of those downstream. Here, steel's social cost exceeds its private cost because the firm doesn't pay for the harm its dumping does to others. When a good has *negative externalities,* producers pay only a fraction of the good's total cost. Therefore, they will produce *too much* of the good from a social point of view.

Positive externalities result when an activity benefits people who don't pay for those benefits. This means that a good's **social benefit** (the benefit to everyone) exceeds its **private benefit** (the benefit received by the good's producers). For example, a farmer's apple trees may allow local honey producers to raise more bees. Here, an apple tree's social benefit exceeds its private benefit because bee producers do not pay for the benefits they get from the tree. When a good has *positive externalities,* producers only get a fraction of its total social benefits and so will produce *too little* from a social point of view.

YOU SHOULD REMEMBER

1. Externalities occur when an activity's social costs and benefits are not borne privately by those producing the good.

2. In free markets, too much of a good with negative externalities is produced. Too little of a good with positive externalities is produced.

SOLUTIONS TO MARKET FAILURES CAUSED BY EXTERNALITIES

ASSIGN PROPERTY RIGHTS

Assigning property rights to all of a good's benefits gives owners the right to the property's benefits; the owners then have the incentive to use the property wisely. A major property right is the right of people to sue for the damage done to them by others. For example, polluters will bear the cost of their pollution when citizens can sue for the damages done to them.

The absence of clear ownership rights results in the **problem of the commons.** In England, commons were unowned areas where any farmer could graze field animals. No farmer expected to benefit from saving grazing land for future use, because other farmers coming along would get the benefit instead. As a result, farmers overgrazed and destroyed the commons. On the other hand, an owner would have had an incentive to maintain that land and prevent overgrazing. Just as the unowned commons were abused in the past, currently oceans are over-fished and public timberlands are overcut since without property rights, no one has an incentive to maintain the future value of these unowned resources.

ENCOURAGE LOWER TRANSACTION COSTS

According to the **Coase Theorem**, people can get rid of any market failure by bargaining among themselves if *transaction costs are low*. What's more, the distribution of property rights does not affect this outcome. Consider the following example.

A factory dumps its waste into a nearby stream. This costs the people downstream $20,000 in damages each year. To clean up its waste, the factory would have to spend $12,000 annually. From a social point of view, society would be better off cleaning up the waste since the benefits exceed the costs.

What would happen if the factory has the right to dump unclean waste water into the stream? Without transaction costs, the downstream citizens could (and would) get together and pay the factory $12,000 not to pollute.

Now suppose the factory does not have the right to dump without the downstream citizens' permission. In this case, it will also not pollute because its dumping costs would be $20,000 (to compensate the downstream citizens for damages) while clean up costs are only $12,000.

Thus, in both cases, the outcome—no pollution—is the same regardless of who has the property rights to the stream.

The presence of high transaction costs can cause this socially optimal result not to occur. For example, when the factory has the right to dump, it may be too costly for downstream citizens to get together and pay the factory not to pollute. One way to lower transaction costs would be to allow for class-action suits against polluters, rather than requiring each person to go to court individually.

GOVERNMENT TAXES AND SUBSIDIES

Taxes on negative externalities and subsidies for positive externalities can correct market failures.

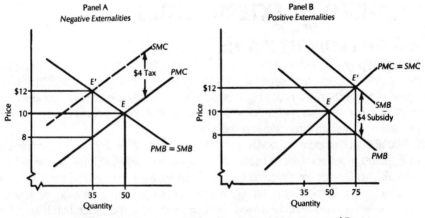

Figure 27-1 How Taxes and Subsidies Correct Negative and Positive Externalities

Panel A of Figure 27-1 shows the case when producing widgets results in negative externalities. Due to pollution, the social marginal cost (*SMC*) is $4 per unit above the private marginal cost (*PMC*). In a free market, firms produce 50 widgets and sell them at $10. The marginal social *and* private benefit is $10 *but* the widget's social cost is $14: Too much is being produced. Ideally, the government could impose a $4 tax per widget: This would raise widget's private cost to its true social cost. Firms would then produce 35 widgets and sell them at a price of $12. At this output, social marginal benefit equals social marginal cost.

Panel B shows the case when there is a positive externality in the consumption of widgets (but no negative externalities). Due to the uplifting effect of widget consumption, its consumers benefit others by $4 for each unit they consume. In a free market, 50 widgets are consumed at a price of $10. But the fiftieth unit's social marginal benefit ($14) exceeds its social *and* private marginal cost of $10. More should be produced. With a subsidy of $4 per unit, suppliers will treat the social marginal benefit curve (*SMB*) as their new demand curve. They will produce 75 units at a price of $12.

GOVERNMENT REGULATION

Government regulation tells firms what they can and cannot do. For example, all firms may have to install a certain type of pollution control.

The limits of regulation are that:

1. Because most regulations apply equally to all firms regardless of their individual costs and benefits, regulations can be inefficient. For example, all cars in the U.S. have about $1,000 worth of pollution-control equipment, whether they are used in Los Angeles or in Utah. Yet in Utah, pollution is so low that the marginal benefit of less car pollution is negligible.

2. Standardization in regulations does not allow for individual tastes. For example, in certain communities, citizens would prefer to breathe polluted air rather than suffer the loss of jobs caused by the imposition of pollution standards.

YOU SHOULD REMEMBER

1. When no one owns a resource, no one has an incentive to maintain its value, since anyone can get the benefits of the upkeep. The lack of property rights leads to market failure.

2. The Coase Theorem states that without transaction costs, the socially optimal amount of each good will be produced.

3. Cures for market failures include (a) assigning property rights, (b) lowering transaction costs, (c) imposing government taxes (for negative externalities) and subsidies (for positive externalities), and (d) imposing government regulations.

4. Government regulations, when made standard for all, result in added costs.

PUBLIC GOODS

A pure **public good** is a good that people can consume without reducing what others consume. Examples include (up to a point) the services of a lighthouse, a musical concert, and national defense. Basically, a public good is a special case of a positive externality.

Two central aspects of public goods are:

1. The marginal benefit of a public good is the *sum* of its benefits to everyone. Figure 27-2 shows A's demand curve for the public good and B's demand curve. For the fourth unit, A will pay $5 and B, $7. So the social demand for the fourth unit is $12. The **social demand curve** is the *vertical* sum of the individual demand curves.

2. Public goods will *not* be optimally supplied by the free market when *the cost of exclusion* is high. **Exclusion cost** is the cost of excluding a potential consumer of a good (especially a public good) or from enjoying the benefits of the good.

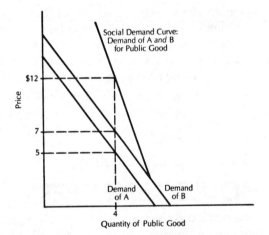

Figure 27-2 Comparing Social Demand and Marginal Benefit of a Public Good

When exclusion costs are high, there is a **free-rider problem**. A free rider enjoys the benefits of the public good without paying for it. When enough people are free riders, the public good is not supplied. Therefore, everyone, including the free riders, is then worse off.

For example, suppose roads are paid for with voluntary contributions. While any one driver might like well-maintained roads, his or her contribution will have little effect. So why should the driver contribute? There's little added benefit for the cost. But if most drivers thought like this, there would be few roads. However, if noncontributors can be excluded from using the roads (for example, by collecting tolls), the free-rider problem is eliminated.

An example of a public good whose exclusion cost is low is a concert: Free riders are easily excluded by allowing only those who buy tickets to hear the concert. On the other hand, it is impossible to exclude any citizens from the benefits of national defense. Thus, all nations pay for national defense with taxes.

YOU SHOULD REMEMBER

1. One person's consumption of a pure public good does not decrease anyone else's consumption of that good.

2. The marginal benefit of a public good is the sum of its benefits to all persons. Its social demand curve is the vertical sum of all individual demand curves.

3. When exclusion costs are high, the free-rider problem results. Free riders get a public good's benefit without paying any of its cost. When there are too many free riders, too little of the public good is produced.

AN APPLICATION: POLLUTION CONTROL

Pollution is costly (in terms of health, aesthetics, and so forth). Getting rid of it is also costly. Socially, society wants to minimize this sum:

Total Cost = Pollution Cost + Pollution-Abatement Costs.

The socially optimal level of pollution is the level that minimizes this total cost. Note that the optimal level of pollution is *not* zero when the cost of achieving zero pollution exceeds its benefits.

Getting rid of pollution is a public good—this suggests that government action is needed to reduce pollution to its optimal level. Marginal analysis is used to derive the optimal level of pollution. The control variable will be tons of pollution per year. The *marginal benefit* of more pollution is the *marginal reduction in pollution-abatement costs.* Figure 27-3 shows the marginal benefit (*MB*) schedule of more pollution. To see why the *MB* curve for pollution has a negative slope, start at 90 tons. The ninetieth ton of pollution costs nothing to get rid of (so this will be the level of pollution without government intervention). If the government acts to reduce pollution, we move left. Moving left, the *MB* curve measures the marginal cost of getting rid of each additional unit. For example, it costs only $10 to get rid of the seventieth ton, while it costs $40 to get rid of the thirtieth ton. Since the marginal cost of getting rid of pollution goes up as more is eliminated, the *MB* curve (which shows the marginal cost saved) rises as we move left and falls as we move right.

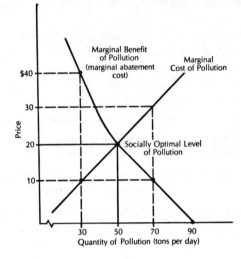

Figure 27-3   Determining the Socially Optimal Level of Pollution by Comparing Marginal Benefit and Marginal Cost

The marginal cost (*MC*) schedule shows the marginal cost of pollution. This is the damage an additional unit of pollution does to people's health and property. The thirtieth ton, for example, harms society by $10, and the seventieth ton, by $30.

In a sense, the *MC* curve is society's supply curve for pollution while the *MB* curve is society's demand curve. But the *MB* curve is not a demand "for pollution." Rather, it is a demand to keep the cost of reducing pollution down.

The socially optimal level of pollution occurs where marginal benefit equals marginal cost: at 50 tons. Too *little* pollution, say 30 tons, costs more to get rid of than it's worth (e.g., getting rid of the thirtieth unit costs $40 but is only worth $10). On the other hand, too *much* pollution is also harmful. For example, getting rid of the seventieth unit costs $10 but saves society $30 in health costs. *Not* getting rid of the seventieth unit makes society worse off.

The government can get firms to produce the optimal amount of pollution by (1) imposing a tax equal to the public's marginal cost of pollution or (2) restricting pollution to 50 units through regulations.

Regulations are not generally favored by economists, because changing technology and tastes can make the regulated level either too low or too high from a social point of view. But given that the government is going to regulate the amount of pollution allowable, the most efficient method to achieve this aim is to allow producers to buy and sell the rights to pollute. In this way, those producers with the lowest cost of pollution abatement will be the ones to reduce pollution. (See Practical Application, Question 7.)

YOU SHOULD REMEMBER

1. Pollution is socially costly, but so is getting rid of pollution.

2. The marginal benefit of a unit of pollution is the pollution abatement cost saved by not reducing pollution by one unit. The marginal cost of pollution is its social cost. More pollution should be allowed as long as marginal benefit exceeds marginal cost.

3. One method of reducing pollution is to impose a tax on polluters equal to the marginal social cost of pollution.

4. Another method of reducing pollution is to regulate how much each firm can pollute. This is most efficiently done if firms are allowed to trade their rights to pollute.

PUBLIC CHOICE

A central criticism of the free economy is that businesspeople are "greedy." The implicit assumption is that government officials are motivated by the unselfish desire to serve the public and are better regulators of our lives. Although only the most naive believe that government bureaucrats and politicians are not also selfish and greedy, many economists have assumed that government always acts unselfishly in the public interest. Recently though, economists have tried to understand how those in government act. The **theory of public choice** analyzes how governments operate.

To understand public choice in a democracy, we begin by comparing voting with buying goods. When consumers buy a particular brand of bread, they are in effect "voting" for how the economy should be organized. The same is true with voting at election time. While with private "voting," people choose often and between many goods, with public voting, people choose only once every several years between "package deals." Since public voting is less frequent and there are fewer choices, economists generally believe that it transmits less information about people's desires than does the marketplace.

Because voters face package deals set before them by politicians, a central issue of public choice is whether the votes on these "deals" reflect the true preferences of consumers. The **voting paradox** states that *how* a majority will vote on a set of issues can depend on the order in which the issues are presented. They may vote for A over B. And for B over C. And yet, they may vote for C over A! (See Practical Application, Question 5, for an example.) Since how a majority will vote can depend on the *order* of the issues, who controls the public agenda matters a great deal. In particular, economists expect government agencies to set the public agenda to favor their interests. As one example, budget-cutting in most government agencies usually results in the most popular and necessary programs being cut first. In this way, public officials try to create a crisis in which their funding will be restored.

The **median voter model**, another model of public choice, predicts that when two people are running for office, they will position themselves near the opinions of the median voter. The **median voter** is the voter at the fiftieth percentile. If one candidate gets too far from the median, the other candidate will win the election. Suppose we have 100 voters. The first feels that government spending should be $1, the second voter wants $2 spent, and so forth. The median voter wants $50 to be spent. Suppose one candidate for office favors $60. The other candidate merely has to promise to spend $59 and will win with 59% of the vote. So both candidates, if they want to win, will promise to spend $50, giving each an equal chance at winning. Any other position will lose.

DEALING WITH SPECIAL INTERESTS

Unfortunately, the median voter model does not explain why so many laws favor only a small minority of the population. To explain this, public choice theorists point out that one way to achieve a majority is to combine many special interest groups by promising each something they feel strongly about. This is called **logrolling**—the trading of votes to get legislation favoring only a minority passed. For example, farmers in the farm states may want a price-support program. The textile mill owners in southern states want a tariff on foreign textiles. To get their bills passed, the farm state representatives and the southern state representatives agree to vote for each other's bills. With this type of trading, the "log" of bills gets pushed through Congress.

Such special interest legislation benefits only a small fraction of the population but costs everyone (in higher taxes and prices). This is socially harmful when it costs the nation more than it benefits the special interests. For example, consumers paid $150,000 per year for every job saved by the auto import quota imposed by our government. Yet, the jobs saved only paid $30,000. (And what is worse, the $150,000 would have created three or more jobs elsewhere.)

To see why such **pork-barrel legislation** gets passed (along with the dynamics of logrolling), suppose we hypothetically offered each congressional representative a special program that is worth $10,000 to his or her district but that costs taxpayers *nationally* $30,000. The conditions are that they must vote for a whole log of programs, such that only representatives who vote for the log of programs get a special program. The nation would be better off without any of these programs. But all representatives may vote for the log of programs. By joining the logroll, their district gets $10,000. By refusing, the log of programs may still pass. If it passes, the district does not benefit but still pays higher taxes. But by joining, the *addition* to taxes for the district from having its program included is very small. (For example, with 500 districts, the $30,000 total cost of adding its program to the log is only $600 ($30,000/500).) So each representative will vote for the whole log of programs.

If special interest legislation is so prevalent, why don't voters oppose it? The model of **rational voter ignorance** states that voters rationally do not have any incentive to make fully informed votes. This follows because one person's vote has little effect on an election's outcome. Since it is very costly to become informed about public issues, rational voters, balancing a large cost against a small likely benefit, will be ignorant voters.

On the other hand, special interest groups benefit from legislation that focuses benefits upon them. They can concentrate their efforts on key legislators. Because the legislation's costs are diffuse (perhaps only a few dollars per voter), few in the public have an incentive to oppose it.

Legislation can result in rents (and profits) to special interest groups. But **rent-seeking** by seeking favorable legislation can be costly (e.g., in contributions to campaigns). In the extreme, rent-seeking behavior will use up all the benefits of the legislation. From a social point of view, rent-seeking produces a net social loss, in that it increases costs without any corresponding benefit to society.

One solution to exploitative special interest group legislation is to require more than a majority vote, and in the extreme, **unanimity**. But as the consent of more is needed, society runs into the **hold-out problem**. For example, suppose a program is worth, after deducting its costs, $100 million to the nation. If unanimity (the consent of everyone) was needed, then one representative could hold out by demanding, say, $50 million for his or her district in exchange for his or her consent. And since each representative has an equal incentive to be a hold-out, any legislation, productive or not, would be difficult to pass. Thus, as a greater proportion of votes is needed for passage, society gains by having less special interest legislation but loses by having less legislation in the public good.

Another solution is for legislation to be considered *only* at the governmental level (local, state, or national) at which its benefits are felt. In this way, those benefiting will also have to pay its costs. In addition, the smaller the area legislation covers, the greater the freedom citizens have of moving away. To see why the ability to move is important, suppose citizens can move at will between cities at no cost. Then each city would have to provide the optimal amount of social services (parks, sewers, etc.) at the lowest price (i.e., taxes) per unit of service, or be bid out of existence as its citizens move to cities offering the optimal package of services and taxes. Therefore, smaller governments and greater mobility of citizens and firms between cities, states, and nations produces better government. (This result is called the **Tiebout Hypothesis**.)

YOU SHOULD REMEMBER

1. The voting paradox is that different results can be voted for, depending upon the order in which issues are presented to voters.

2. In two-person races, both candidates will try to take positions close to the median voter's positions.

3. During logrolling, representatives vote for each other's special interest legislation.

4. The optimal level of government services and taxes occurs when (a) governments compete with each other and (b) citizens can freely and at low cost move from one governing unit (such as city or state) to another.

KNOW THE CONCEPTS

DO YOU KNOW THE BASICS?

1. Does the existence of an externality imply a market failure?

2. How does voting differ from using market prices as a means of allocating resources in the economy?

3. Why does the absence of private property rights lead to the overuse and poor maintenance of the property?

4. Why would there never be a market failure if all transactions were costless?

5. When will society be better off with more pollution?

6. Why don't private goods suffer from the free-rider problem?

7. Why is the average voter under-informed?

8. What determines whether a public good will be underproduced without government intervention?

9. How can special interest groups gain benefits at a greater expense of the whole economy?

10. How does the international mobility of citizens and multinational firms improve government?

TERMS FOR STUDY

Coase Theorem
exclusion cost
hold-out problem
logrolling
median voter
negative externality
paradox of voting

positive externality
private good
problem of the commons
public good
rational ignorance of voters
unanimity

PRACTICAL APPLICATION

1. Use the following to answer the questions below:

Quantity	1	2	3	4	5	6	7
MSB	$10	$8	$6	$4	$3	$2	$ 1
MSC	$ 1	$2	$3	$4	$6	$8	$10

MSB is the marginal social benefit of the good; MSC, the marginal social cost.

a. If there are no externalities, how many units of this good should be produced? How many will be produced?

b. If there are positive externalities so that each buyer gets one-half of the social benefit of the good, how many units should be produced? Will be produced? What would the government have to do to get the optimal amount produced?

c. If there are negative externalities so that each seller pays half the social cost of the good, how many units should be produced (assume there are no positive externalities)? Will be produced? What should the government do to get the optimal amount produced?

2. To illustrate why oceans will be overfished, suppose a professor puts twenty beads on her desk and promises the class that she will double the number of the beads on the desk every five minutes. Any student can come up any time and take any number of beads. At the end of the class, she will pay 10¢ a bead.

a. What policy is best for the class as a whole?

b. What policy is best for each student?

c. How would property rights help?

3. There are fifty farmers in a valley. Each year the valley floods, destroying all crops. A dam can be built at $2,000 for each foot in height (this cost is an annualized cost). The first foot saves *each* farmer $100 per year in damages, the second foot saves each farmer an additional $90 in damages, the third, $80; and so on.

a. Suppose the dam is three feet high. What is the social benefit of one more foot?

b. What is the socially optimal height of the dam?

c. Suppose forty of the farmers get together and agree to share costs: How high will their dam be? Why are the remaining ten farmers "free riders"?

4. Mr. Jones lives next to Mrs. Smith in an apartment building with thin walls. Mrs. Smith sings opera, which she values at $20 a day. Mr. Jones hates

Mrs. Smith's singing and would pay up to $30 a day for her to stop singing.
   a. What type of externality is this?
   b. What will happen if the apartment contract states that anyone can sing if they want?
   Hint: Use the Coase Theorem and assume no transaction costs.

   c. What will happen if the apartment contract states that to sing, one must get permission from his or her neighbors?

5. Smith, Jones, and Parker each have a vote on the city council. They are to vote on which of three projects are to be built. Their ranking of these projects (with 1 being the one they want most and 3 the least) is as follows.

	Project A	Project B	Project C
Smith	1	2	3
Jones	3	1	2
Parker	2	3	1

The projects are brought up in pairs.
   a. Between Projects A and B, which will win?
   b. Between Projects B and C, which will win?
   c. Between Projects C and A, which will win?
   d. How does this illustrate the voting paradox?

6. Why might smaller school districts produce better schools?

7. In Smogville, the government will allow only 6 units of pollution. There are two firms, Widget International and Smokestack, Inc. The government can either (1) have the same standards for both, allowing each 3 units of pollution or (2) give each firm the right to pollute 3 units and allow the right to be sold to the other company. Without pollution controls, each would put 6 units of pollution into the air. The marginal abatement costs (*MAC*, the cost of reducing pollution by one unit) are:

Units of Pollution	1	2	3	4	5	6
MAC of Widget	$100	$ 90	$ 80	$ 70	$ 60	$50
MAC of Smokestack	$500	$400	$300	$200	$100	$80

   a. What will the total abatement cost of option (1) be?
   b. In option (2), how many units of pollution will Smokestack, Inc. buy from Widget International? What is the total abatement cost in this case?
   c. Why is option (2) more efficient?

8. Why do Democrats running in primaries usually sound more liberal than they do in the main election? (Assume that Democratic voters are more liberal on average than the general population.)

9. A polluting firm argues "If I have to pay for the damage my pollution causes, this will raise my costs and the social cost of my products." Is the firm correct?

10. Mary and Jane each value listening to an hour of classical music on the radio at $5. They each value a small pizza at $5. What is the social benefit of the music? Of the pizza?

11. In a large apartment house, all tenants had to pay for their own utilities. The rent was $500. Each tenant used $200 of water and electricity a month, yielding a total cost of $700. Then, the apartment owner decided to pay for all utilities and adjusted the rents to reflect the *average* cost for all apartments. Each apartment owner can now use as much water and electricity as he or she wants. How does the new rent compare with $700?

ANSWERS
KNOW THE CONCEPTS

1. No. Market failures occur only in the absence of clear property rights and when there are high transaction costs.

2. Because consumers make choices among many goods and because they directly benefit from their market choices, consumers send a more frequent and informed "signal" to producers than they do when voting.

3. Without property rights, those who maintain the property won't necessarily benefit. So they have no incentive to keep the property up or prevent its overuse.

4. Because those harmed by a negative externality could get together and pay those responsible for it to stop. Similarly, those helped by a positive externality could get together and pay those responsible to produce more

5. When the marginal cost of getting rid of it is greater than the margina' benefit from getting rid of it.

6. Because when one person consumes a private good, others are by definition excluded from enjoying it.

7. Because the likelihood of affecting the outcome is small. So the benefit of voting correctly is small.

8. Too little of the good will be produced without government intervention if the cost of excluding free riders is high. When exclusion costs are low, free riders can be forced to pay: The optimal amount will be produced.

9. Because the per-taxpayer cost of special interest legislation is so low that it doesn't pay anyone to oppose it.

10. Mobility forces nations to compete for citizens and businesses. This pushes them towards offering the optimal mix of public goods and taxes.

PRACTICAL APPLICATION

1. a. Four units should be and will be produced.
   b. Four units should be produced. Three units will be produced. The government would have to establish a subsidy of $2 per unit.
   c. Four units should be produced. Five units will be produced. The government should impose a tax of $3 per unit.

2. a. The class should wait until the end of the period to "harvest" the beads.
   b. Each student should rush up and grab all twenty beads immediately. If he or she doesn't someone else will.
   c. If one of the students owned the beads, he or she would allow their value to grow to its highest level because he or she would be assured through property rights of getting this value.

3. a. The marginal social benefit of the fourth foot is $3,500 (50 farmers × $70 marginal benefit to each).
   b. Seven feet high [the seventh foot's marginal social benefit is $2,000 (50 × $40)]. Its marginal cost is $2,000.
   c. Six feet high (the sixth foot is worth $2,000 to the forty farmers). The remaining ten farmers are free riders since each is getting $450 in benefits ($100 + $90 + ... + $50) at no cost. On the other hand, the forty farmers had to pay $300 each for the same benefit.

4. a. A negative externality.
   b. Mr. Jones will pay Mrs. Smith $20 at a minimum and up to $30 for her to stop singing. She will agree not to sing.
   c. Mrs. Smith will offer Mr. Jones $20 to give his permission to sing, but Mr. Jones will refuse.

5. a. Project A.
   b. Project B.
   c. Project C.
   d. If Project A is compared to Project B, and then the winner (A) with Project C, C will win. But if B is compared to C, and then the winner (B) compared to A, A will win. So a different agenda produces a different outcome. (How would you pair the choices so B would win?)

6. Parents have greater mobility between smaller school districts. This forces school districts to compete for students and thus do a better job. In the last twenty years, school districts have been merged and enlarged. According to some economists, the resulting loss in competition is partly to

blame for the higher administrative costs per pupil and the lower student performance observed over the same period. (Of course, these results also have many other causes.)

7. a. Each firm will get rid of its fourth through sixth unit of pollution. The total abatement cost will be $560.

b. Smokestack will buy two of Widget's rights to pollute. The first saves it $200 and cost Widget only $80. A price between $200 and $80 will benefit both. The second saves Smokestack $100 and cost Widget $90. Once again, at some price between these numbers, both benefit by the trade. The third is not worth it: it saves $80 but cost Widget $90. The total abatement cost (with Widget getting rid of 5 units of pollution and Smokestack just 1) will be $430.

c. Because the trading of rights induces those with the lowest cost of abating pollution to cut back on pollution.

8. Using the median voter model, the median voter in the Democratic primary will be more liberal than in the general election. So Democratic candidates will be more liberal in the primary than in the general election (just as Republican candidates are usually more conservative-sounding in the primaries).

9. No. Its pollution is a cost to society, whether it pays it or someone else does. Forcing it to pay this cost doesn't change the total social cost. Furthermore, as it cuts back its production, the marginal social cost of the good it produces will *fall* (see Panel A of Figure 27-1).

10. The social benefit of one hour of music is $10, and of one pizza, $5.

11. Because the social cost of utilities is now higher than its private cost (since one renter's added utility cost is spread over all renters), renters now use more water and electricity. Rents now exceed $700. Note that renters are worse off. This suggests that unless monitoring and charging renters for the utilities they use is more costly, renters will prefer apartments where they pay for utilities.

28
GOVERNMENT SPENDING AND TAXATION

KEY TERMS

average tax rate percentage of income paid in taxes.

deadweight loss (or excess burden) of a tax social loss from taxes that exceeds the tax revenues collected.

marginal tax rate percentage of *added* income paid in taxes.

progressive tax system tax system under which those with higher incomes are subject to higher marginal and average tax rates.

In 1985, the federal government spent $3,500 per person, and state and local governments spent an additional $1,870 per person. This represented 40% of *GNP*. This government spending went for (1) goods and services (such as defense, highways, education, and police services) and (2) transfer payments. **Transfer payments** are payments made to individuals without any service or goods being required in exchange. Examples are welfare payments, Social Security payments, and unemployment compensation.

Social Security (and such related programs as Medicare and federal pensions), national defense, and interest payments on the public debt represent 75% of federal spending (the percents in 1985 were 35%, 28%, and 12% respectively).

COST-BENEFIT ANALYSIS OF GOVERNMENT SPENDING

From the standpoint of efficiency, government spending on goods and services should be undertaken only when benefits exceed costs. One method to achieve this goal is to require governments to analyze the costs and benefits of each program. Unfortunately, the ability of government officials to do this accurately may be limited. For example, one study showed that the actual costs of government projects were on average two to three times higher than the government's projected cost. Also, benefits are often difficult to measure.

The common emphasis on employment rather than efficiency in government spending is detrimental to the economy. Suppose there are two projects using only labor. Both yield $100,000 in benefits but one takes two workers and the other ten. Which is better? The one with two workers, because its opportunity cost is lower. To see why, recall that the only way to increase income per person is to increase output per person (see Chapter 25). That is, when *fewer* persons— and *less employment*—are needed to produce a given amount of output, per capital income goes *up*!

YOU SHOULD REMEMBER

1. When the costs of government projects exceed their benefits, our economy becomes less efficient.

2. Efficiency, not employment, is the means by which the highest output and income per person is achieved.

THE ECONOMICS OF TRANSFER PAYMENTS

Transfer payments can be either (1) cash or (2) payments-in-kind (that is, in the form of specific goods and services). Examples of payments-in-kind include free schooling, free medical care, and free food.

If the government gives someone $10,000 in free education, what is the impact of this spending? First, it replaces what the person would have spent anyway on education (say this is $8,000). Second, the difference between what the person would have spent and what the government supplied increases the amount spent on education. In this example, the difference is $2,000. So the $10,000 in free education increases the amount spent on education not by $10,000 but by $2,000. *An in-kind payment increases total spending on the in-kind good by less than the in-kind payment.*

What is the $10,000 in free education worth to the person getting it? If the person had been given $10,000 in cash (instead of $10,000 in education) and spent it all on education, then the person valued the free education at least as much as $10,000, since he or she was willing to pay that amount for education. But if the person would have spent only part of it on education (say, only $8,000), then the person values the education by less than $10,000. Why? Because the $2,000 in extra education was not worth $2,000 to the person (or it would have been spent on education and not on something else). To the recipients, *in-kind payments are worth less than (or at best the same as) the same amount paid in cash.*

If the government's goal is to increase the utility of recipients, then all transfer payments should be in cash and not in-kind.

YOU SHOULD REMEMBER

1. The total quantity of a good demanded will increase by less than any in-kind payment made in the form of that good.

2. In-kind payments are worth less than their cash equivalent.

TAXATION

Most people, when asked how much they pay in taxes, will tell you what they pay in *income* taxes. Yet the income tax represents only 44% of federal taxes and about one-third of all taxes (including state and local taxes). The rest of federal taxes is made up of payroll (or Social Security) taxes (36%), the corporate tax (10%), and many other smaller taxes. Local and state taxes are evenly divided between property tax, income tax, sales (or excise) tax, and other taxes. Most taxes are **direct taxes** on persons or legal entities such as corporations (such as personal and corporate income taxes) but some are **indirect taxes** on goods and services (such as sales or excise taxes, and tariff duties on imports).

A central concept for understanding the impact of taxes is the **marginal tax rate**. This is the percentage of added income paid in taxes. For example, if Joe is in the 45% tax bracket and his earnings rise from $50,000 to $52,000, his taxes will go up $900 (45% of the $2,000 increase in income). *The marginal tax rate— not the average tax rate—affects incentives* to work and invest since it determines the *marginal* benefits of working and investing.

A **progressive tax system** is one under which, as a person earns more, his or her marginal tax rate rises. A **proportional tax system** has the same marginal tax rate at all levels of income. A **regressive tax system** is one under which, as a person earns more, his or her marginal tax rate falls.

The **average tax rate** is the percentage of total income paid in taxes. In a progressive tax system, the average tax rate rises with income, but is less than the marginal tax rate. In a proportional tax system, the average tax rate stays the same at all levels of income, and it equals the marginal tax rate. In a regressive tax system, the average tax rate falls as income goes up, and it is greater than the marginal tax rate. See Practical Application, Question 2, for an example. (Be careful! It is not necessarily true that the rich pay less taxes in a regressive tax system. They may pay more taxes even though they pay a smaller percentage of income in taxes.)

YOU SHOULD REMEMBER

1. The marginal tax rate (the tax rate on one's added income) affects incentives.

> **2.** When average and marginal taxes go up with income, the tax system is progressive. When they are equal and constant, the tax system is proportional. When they fall with income, the tax system is regressive.

EQUITY IN TAXES

Since most people would like to pay less taxes, their basic notion of what is fair and equitable often coincides with what produces less taxes. Other less biased principles of **equity** include:

1. **Horizontal Equity**: Equals should pay equal taxes. If two persons are exactly alike, consistency requires that both should pay the same tax. For example, consider the double-taxation of corporate income. It is commonly argued that it is "fair" to tax corporations at the same rate as individuals. But the income from corporations that is paid out in dividends is first taxed at the corporate level and then taxed at the personal level. Thus, dividend income is taxed at a higher rate rather than at the same rate as other income. The principle of horizontal equity holds that dividend income should be taxed only once (say, by allowing corporations to deduct their dividends as expenses).

2. **Vertical Equity**: Unequals should pay different taxes. If Smith and Jones earn different incomes, then it seems right they should also pay different taxes.

3. **Benefits Principle**: People should pay taxes in proportion to the benefits they receive from the government. For example, taxes on gasoline are paid for by drivers, who benefit from good roads; these taxes support road construction and maintenance. The rationale for this principle is that, except for helping the poor, it isn't right to benefit one group of people at the expense of others—those who get the benefit from a government program should pay for it. The same principle is used to condemn stealing and slavery.

4. **Ability to Pay Principle**: People who are able to pay more taxes should pay more. This implies that people who earn more should pay more. However, this result is consistent even with some regressive tax systems, depending on what the vague term "ability to pay" means, so it is not a useful criterion. Note that this principle is inconsistent with the benefits principle.

TAXES AND EFFICIENCY

Taxes distort economic decisions. One criterion of selecting taxes is to choose those that distort decisions the least. To measure the distortions caused by taxes, economists measure their **deadweight loss** (also called **the excess burden of taxation**). Taxes impose a burden upon the private sector (the buyers and sellers of goods) exceeding the tax revenue collected. The deadweight loss is the excess of private sector's burden over the tax revenues collected. The excess burden of the tax on a good (or its deadweight loss) is the excess of its cost to buyers and sellers over the tax revenues collected.

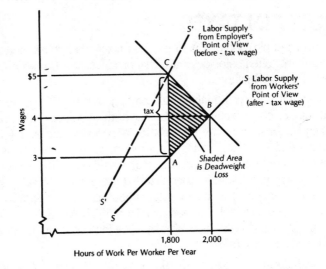

Figure 28-1 Tax on Wages Compared with Deadweight Loss

In Figure 28-1, we show the demand and supply for labor in an economy with 100 million workers. Without any tax, each worker will work 2,000 hours at a wage of $4. With a 40% tax rate, workers must be paid more in before-tax wages to get the same after-tax wages. The after-tax wage labor supply schedule is SS (the same one as when there are no taxes). The before-tax wage schedule is S'S'.

Key Procedure for Showing Effects of Taxes

1. The impact of a tax can be represented by shifting the demand curve down or supply curve up. It doesn't matter which is used. We'll shift the supply curve up.

2. The original supply curve (which reflects what suppliers must be paid) is also the after-tax curve. In Figure 28-1, SS shows the wages workers get after taxes.

3. Next, we construct the supply curve showing the supply price *including taxes*. We *add* the tax vertically to the original supply curve to get the new supply curve including taxes. For example, if the supplier's price is $10 and the tax is $2, the supply price including taxes is $12. Thus, the supply curve including taxes is $2 above the original supply curve. In Figure 28-1, the vertical distance between S'S' and SS equals the taxes workers pay.

In Figure 28-1, labor supply drops to 1,800 hours per worker, the before-tax wage is $5, the after-tax wage is $3 (60% of $5), and taxes are $2 (40% of $5). Total tax revenues are $3,600 per worker ($2 × 1,800 hours). The cost of the tax to workers and producers is $3,600 in the taxes they paid plus the lost surplus measured by the area of triangle *ABC*. *The deadweight loss is Area ABC.* It is equal to $200 per worker. (The area of a triangle is ½ of base × height or ½ × $2 × 200 hours.) The deadweight loss for every dollar of taxes collected is 5.5 cents ($.055 = $200/$3,600). One study suggests that the actual deadweight loss is 30 cents per tax dollar collected. Other studies show varying deadweight losses.

The $200 deadweight loss represents the loss in social net benefits that no one gets. It occurs here because people are working less than is socially optimal.

The more inelastic demand and supply are, the smaller the deadweight loss from a given tax. Note that when demand and supply are more inelastic, output will fall less when a given tax is imposed. So the less a tax changes output, the smaller the deadweight loss is likely to be. For example, a tax on a good whose supply is perfectly inelastic will not affect its output at all so there is no distortion or deadweight loss.

YOU SHOULD REMEMBER

1. The deadweight loss (or excess burden) of a tax is the private sector's loss less the taxes collected.

2. The deadweight loss is less the more inelastic demand and supply are.

MAJOR DISTORTIONS IN OUR CURRENT TAX CODES

By taxing some activities and not others, our tax codes redirect resources away from their most efficient use. Some of the major distortions in our current codes are caused by:

1. *The Use of Historical Costs for Depreciation:* Businesses can deduct depreciation expenses only on the basis of the historical cost of assets. But inflation increases the replacement cost of assets. As a result, using historical costs *understates* costs, *overstates* profits, and thus *increases* the effective tax rate on true profits.

2. *Allowing Homeowners to Deduct Mortgage Interest Payments:* Since homeowners can deduct these payments without having to also record the implicit rental of their homes and the change in their homes' value as a source of income, homes, in effect, become businesses that can deduct expenses

and yet do *not* have to report income—a very good deal! Tax laws thus favor homeownership over business investment. See Practical Application, Question 6.

3. *Allowing Tax-Free Bonds:* While the federal government taxes most interest income, it does not tax the interest income from state and municipal bonds. As a result, capital is diverted from private investment into state and municipal projects.

Because of their competitive advantage, tax-free bonds pay a lower interest rate. When should someone buy a tax-free bond? If the person's marginal tax rate is t and a municipal tax-free bond pays i% and a corporate bond pays r%, then the municipal bond should be bought when:

$$i\% > (1 - t) \times r\%.$$

Example: Comparing Tax-Free Bonds With Other Bonds

PROBLEM　If a municipal bond pays 9% and the corporate bond pays 10% and a person is in the 40% tax bracket, should the person buy the municipal bond?

SOLUTION　Yes. The after-tax return on the corporate bond is 6% (10% − 4% taken away in taxes), so the municipal bond pays more (9%) in after-tax dollars. The corporate bond would have to pay 15% before it would pay the same in after-tax income as the municipal bond (15% = $i\%/(1 - t)$ or 9%/.6).

4. *Taxing Inflation-Caused Capital Gains:* Current tax laws tax all the price appreciation of certain assets (such as stock and land) as capital gains. But part of an asset's price increase just reflects inflation. This part of its price rise is *not* real income (since it merely maintains the real value of the asset), yet it is taxed. Suppose Mr. Jones buys a stock at $100 and a year later sells it for $110. In the same year, prices go up 6%. However, $6 of the price increase was not real income: Only the $4 is a true capital gain. If Mr. Jones pays a 20% tax on capital gains, he'll pay a tax of $2 on the price increase of $10. But this is an effective tax rate of 50% on the true capital gain (.50 = $2/$4).

All these distortions add to the deadweight losses of taxes. It is probably impossible to have a tax that doesn't distort the economy in some way. Nevertheless, the deadweight loss can usually be reduced when (1) all types of income are treated equally and (2) taxes are imposed only upon true real income, removing the distortions caused by inflation on replacement value and the price of assets.

YOU SHOULD REMEMBER

1. Whenever the government taxes one type of income and not another, a distortion results. People will invest less in earning the taxed income and more in earning the untaxed income. Too little will be invested in earning the taxed income.

2. When inflation is not properly accounted for, a distortion results. Inflation increases the effective tax rate of corporate profits because business firms can write off only historical costs. Inflation reduces the effective tax rate on homes because it increases the interest rate and thus the tax write-off on new fixed-rate mortgages and on all variable-rate mortgages.

SOME SPECIAL TAXES

Some economists have proposed the following taxes as being better than our current taxes.

THE VALUE-ADDED TAX (VAT)

The **value-added tax** is a tax on a company's "value added" (the difference between its sales and what it buys from other firms). Each firm reports what it sells and also what it has bought and pays a certain percentage of the difference in taxes. By reporting on what it has bought and *from whom*, the tax authorities can see if other firms are correctly reporting their sales. So while VAT is like a sales tax, tax cheats are more easily caught with a VAT.

THE FLAT TAX

The **flat tax** is a proportional tax. In 1985, a flat tax of 20% would have collected the same revenues the income tax collected. The flat tax has the advantage of reducing the marginal tax rate and increasing economic activity. A deduction is usually proposed so it doesn't affect the poor too severely.

The **Laffer Curve** suggests that as the marginal tax rate increases, total tax revenues first increase and then fall when the marginal rate becomes excessive (see Chapter 10). The flat tax (or a less progressive tax) is one way to take advantage of this result: By getting rid of excessively high marginal tax rates, more tax revenues might be collected.

THE CONSUMPTION TAX

Unlike the income tax, a **consumption tax** taxes people only on their consumption spending. As with the income tax, people would report their income. But they would *also* report their savings, i.e., what they have *added* to their assets and savings accounts. Then they would deduct their savings from their income and pay taxes only on their consumption. This has the advantage of rewarding savings, which in turn will be used to finance more investment and thus increase economic growth. Individual Retirement Accounts (IRAs) are a step in the direction of a consumption tax.

TAX INCIDENCE AND TAX SHIFTING

The persons paying a tax are not necessarily those who bear the tax. For example, the corporate income tax may reduce wages (so that workers bear the tax) or raise prices (so that consumers bear the tax). This is the problem of **tax incidence**: Who bears the tax? Because of **tax shifting** (through higher prices or lower costs), the burden of the tax need not be borne by those who pay it.

For example, suppose the international supply of capital is perfectly elastic to the United States at a 10% interest rate and that our nation borrows extensively from other countries. Who then bears the incidence of a corporate income tax (assuming there are only two factors, labor and capital)? The answer is that labor will bear the corporate income tax. Any reduction in capital's return below 10% (due to the corporate income tax) will cause an exit of capital from the U.S. until capital's *after-tax* rate of return rises back to 10%. Capital will not suffer. But the reduction in capital will reduce wages until workers fully bear the tax.

As a general rule of thumb, those whose supply or demand is most inelastic bear more of the burden of a tax while those with more elastic supplies and demands bear less.

YOU SHOULD REMEMBER

1. A value-added tax is like a sales tax, but it is easier to catch tax evaders with a VAT tax.

2. A consumption tax encourages savings since it does not tax income that is saved. Only once the income is spent is it taxed.

3. Who pays a tax and who bears the tax can be entirely different because of tax shifting.

4. Those with more inelastic supplies and demands will bear more of a tax.

KNOW THE CONCEPTS

DO YOU KNOW THE BASICS?

1. If you give a poor family 100 pounds of cheese, will the family's consumption of cheese go up by 100 pounds?

2. Would senior citizens prefer free food or the equivalent amount in cash?

3. In a progressive tax system, Mr. Smith pays 20% of his income in taxes. Is his marginal tax rate greater than, equal to, or less than 20%?

4. Is it always true that in all regressive tax systems the rich pay less taxes than the poor?

5. How does the deadweight weight loss reflect lost net benefits?

6. "The less a tax affects people's behavior, the more efficient it is." Is this true? If so, why?

7. How does inflation affect the allocation of capital between building homes and building plants and equipment?

8. Why do municipal and state bonds pay a lower interest rate than do corporate bonds?

9. Why will a VAT tax of 8% have the same effect as a sales tax of 8%?

10. "We would be better off if the government required employers to double the number of workers needed to do each job." Is this true?

TERMS FOR STUDY

ability-to-pay principle	marginal tax rate
average tax rate	payments-in-kind
benefits principle	progressive, proportional, and
deadweight loss (or excess	regressive tax systems
burden) of tax	tax shifting and tax incidence
direct and indirect taxes	transfer payments
horizontal equity	vertical equity

PRACTICAL APPLICATION

1. In Freedonia, Mrs. Clark earns $50,000 and pays $20,000 in taxes Mrs. Smith, her neighbor, earns $100,000 and pays $30,000 in taxes. Is Freedonia's tax system progressive, regressive, or proportional?

2. Three countries have the following marginal tax rates:

Marginal Tax Rate	Countries		
Income Levels	Country A	Country B	Country C
0–$10,000	10%	20%	30%
$10,000–$20,000	20%	20%	20%
$20,000–$30,000	30%	20%	10%

a. What type of tax system does each country have?
b. What taxes will a person earning $15,000 pay in each country? What is the person's average tax rate? Marginal tax rate?
c. What taxes will a person earning $25,000 pay in each country? What is the person's average tax rate? Marginal tax rate?

3. What principle of equity applies to these situations:
a. A property tax that pays for city improvements.
b. The equal taxation of income from wages and the interest earned on a corporate bond.
c. The bank robber, who when asked why he always robbed banks, answered "Because that's where the money is."

4. Mrs. Fearn is a school teacher. Her average tax rate is 20% and her marginal tax rate is 50%. She has to decide whether to teach summer school. She would earn $2,000, but she would have to give up summertime activities that she values at $1,200. Should she teach summer school?

5. Suppose a poor family spends 10% of its income on cheese. The family's income is $6,000. The government gives the family $2,000 in free cheese.
a. How will this affect the family's total cheese consumption?
b. Is the family better off by $2,000 or by less than $2,000?
Assume the family cannot resell the cheese.

6. Mr. Jones borrows $100,000 to buy a $100,000 home. When inflation is 0%, he pays $10,000 a year in interest. When inflation is 15%, he pays $25,000 a year in interest (since he has a variable interest rate mortgage that goes up with the rate of inflation). His house also increases in value by the rate of inflation. In both cases, he can deduct his interest payment from his income of $50,000. He plans to sell his home when he retires and won't pay any tax on any gains in his home value. Both his average and marginal income tax rates are 50%.
a. What taxes does Mr. Jones pay when inflation is 0%?
b. What taxes does he pay when inflation is 15%?
c. How does inflation affect the value of buying a home?

7. Suppose a municipal bond pays 8% and a corporate bond of the same maturity and degree of risk pays 12%.
   a. What tax bracket do you have to be in to be just willing to buy the municipal bond?
   b. Who would buy municipal bonds in a regressive tax system: the rich or the poor?

8. Steve values a painting at $15,000 and the painting costs $12,000. But the government imposes a $4,000 tax on the painting. What is the deadweight loss of this tax?

9. Use the following table to answer the questions below:

Quantity	1	2	3	4	5	6
Demand Price	$11	$8	$6	$4	$2	$1
Supply Price	$1	$2	$3	$4	$5	$6

   a. What will the price and quantity bought and sold be?
   b. The government imposes a $10 tax. Derive the supply curve including the tax. What will the price and quantity bought and sold be?

10. Which of the following are transfer payments?
   a. Unemployment compensation paid to a laid-off worker.
   b. Money the government pays to buy buses.
   c. Salary received by postal workers.
   d. Money given by parents to their child as a present.

ANSWERS

KNOW THE CONCEPTS

1. No. It will go up only by the difference between 100 pounds and how much cheese the family had been buying before.

2. The cash.

3. Greater than 20%.

4. No. In a regressive tax system, the rich can pay more taxes but less in percentage terms.

5. The lost consumer and producer surplus is the loss in net benefits to society.

6. Yes. The more inelastic demand and supply are, the less people will change and the smaller the deadweight loss.

7. Inflation raises the tax on the profits from plants and equipment and lowers it on homes. Thus, it pushes the allocation of capital towards homes.

8. Because corporate bonds, to compete, have to pay more in before-tax interest to give savers the same after-tax interest that tax-free municipal and state bonds pay.

9. A good's final price is the sum of the value added by those making and selling the good. So an 8% tax on one is the same as an 8% tax on the other.

10. No. Output per worker would be cut in half, as would income per person.

PRACTICAL APPLICATION

1. Mrs. Clark's average tax rate is 40%. Mrs. Smith, who earns more, has an average tax rate of 30%. Freedonia's tax system is regressive.

2. **a.** Country A has as progressive tax system; B has a proportional tax system; C has a regressive tax system.
   b. In Country A: $2,000 in taxes, an average tax rate of 13.3%, and a marginal tax rate of 20%.
   In Country B: $3,000 in taxes, an average tax rate of 20%, and a marginal tax rate of 20%.
   In Country C; $4,000 in taxes, an average tax rate of 26.7%, and a marginal tax rate of 20%.
   c. In Country A: $4,500 in taxes, an average tax rate of 40%, and a marginal tax rate of 30%.
   In Country B: $5,000 in taxes, an average tax rate of 20%, and a marginal tax rate of 20%.
   In Country C: $5,500 in taxes, an average tax rate of 22%, and a marginal tax rate of 10%.

3. **a.** The benefits principle.
   b. Horizontal equity.
   c. The ability to pay principle.

4. It is the *marginal* tax rate that affects Mrs. Fearn's choice. The $2,000 more in income will be taxed at a 50% rate, leaving her with $1,000 after taxes. This will not cover her $1,200 opportunity cost of teaching, so she should not teach.

5. **a.** Cheese consumption will go up by $1,400.
   b. The family is better off by less than $2,000. If given $2,000 in cash, the family would have bought $800 in cheese (10% of $8,000) and preferred other goods to cheese for the remaining $1,200. So the remaining $1,200 in cheese the family would not have bought, if given the choice, is worth less than $1,200 to the family. The family is better off, but by less than $2,000.

6. a. $20,000 (50% on a taxable income of $40,000).

 b. $12,500 (50% on a taxable income of $25,000).

 c. Inflation increases the after-tax income of homeowners (notice that any loss in having to pay a higher interest rate is compensated by increases in the home's value). Therefore, inflation makes homes more valuable.

7. a. The "breakeven" tax bracket is the one with the tax rate t where $(1 - t) \times 12\% = 8\%$. So $t = 33.3\%$. If one is in this tax bracket or higher, the municipal bond should be bought.

 b. In a regressive tax system, the poor will have the higher marginal tax rates and so will buy municipal bonds.

8. $3,000. Steve will not buy the painting, since with the tax added on, it costs $16,000 and Steve values it at only $15,000. So the government collects no tax revenue. But Steve is worse off by the lost consumer surplus of $3,000 ($15,000 value − cost of $12,000). The deadweight loss is $3,000.

9. a. 4 units at $4.

 b.

Quantity	1	2	3	4	5	6
Demand Price	$11	$8	$6	$4	$2	$1
Original Supply Price	$1	$2	$3	$4	$5	$6
Supply Price— Including Taxes	$11	$12	$13	$14	$15	$16

Suppliers will produce and sell one unit at a before-tax price of $11 (the price paid by demanders) and an after-tax price of $1 (the amount received by suppliers).

10. (a) and (d) are transfer payments.

29
INTERNATIONAL TRADE

We are all traders. For example, as workers, we trade our time and effort for the goods and services our wages buy. In studying international trade, remember that *what's true about trade is true about international trade*. These truths are:

> *Trade is mutually beneficial.* Two people don't exchange goods and services unless *both* expect to benefit. Just because one person "profits" from trade, it doesn't mean the other "loses": Both sides profit or they wouldn't trade.

> *Exports are what you sell and imports are what you buy.* Workers export time and effort and import purchased goods and services. Nations **export** goods in order to buy **imports**. Sometimes you hear the claim that "Exports are good and imports are bad." In other words, this claim says it's better for a nation to give away (i.e., sell) more than it takes back (i.e., buys)! Instead, a smart nation tries to get the *most* back for what it sells.

> *The cheaper imports are, the better off a nation is.* The more a person gets back for what he or she gives away, the better off the person is. It's the same for nations. When a nation's imports cost less, a given amount of its exports then buys more imports.

Inflows of monies tend to equal outflows. Have you ever worried about whether California sells more to the rest of the U.S. than it buys back? Or about your town's trade imbalance? No one worries about these issues, because people don't sell goods except to buy back other goods. The same is true for world trade. Nations *sell* to the U.S. to get the dollars to *buy* from the U.S. The U.S. export industry would be devastated if U.S. citizens stopped buying imports.

In recent years, the U.S. has had a serious trade imbalance. It is importing more goods than it exports. But nations also trade assets (such as stocks and bonds). When one adds in these other items, it turns out that what the U.S. spends on other nations' goods *and* assets just about equals what they spend on our goods and assets! For example, in 1984, the U.S. imported $114 billion more goods than it exported. But the U.S. spent only $3 billion more on foreign goods *and* assets than foreigners bought from the U.S. (the change in U.S. official reserve assets most closely measures this difference). So the flows of monies in and out of the U.S. are about equal.

YOU SHOULD REMEMBER

1. People don't trade unless both sides expect to benefit.

2. Imports are what a nation gets back in exchange for giving away exports.

3. The cheaper imports are, the more a nation gets back in trade.

WHEN WILL A NATION BENEFIT FROM TRADE?

Recall that the relative price of Good A is the amount of Good B that has to be given up to get one more unit of Good A. When Good A costs $12 and Good B costs $6, the relative price of Good A is 2 (since two units of B have to be given up to buy one unit of A). So:

$$\text{Relative Price of A} = P_a/P_b,$$

where P_a is the price of Good A and P_b, the price of Good B.

Two nations should trade whenever the relative prices of goods (before trade) are different. To show this, assume there are only two goods: food and clothing. Assume food sells for $20 a unit and clothing for $10 a unit (so the relative price of food is 2). Then Martians land and quote the following prices: Food is 6 Blops a unit and clothing is 2 Blops per unit. Their relative price for food is 3.

Should we humans trade with the Martians? The answer is, yes: The Martians have a different relative price (3 instead of our 2). They value food more highly than we do. So we can benefit by specializing in food production and buying clothing from them. For each two units of clothing we stop producing (which cost $10 each to produce), we can produce one unit of food (at a cost of $20), sell it to the Martians (for 6 Blops), and buy back three units of clothing (worth $30)! By giving up producing two units of clothing (and producing food instead), we get three units of clothing back!

But if the Martian prices were 4 Blops for food and 2 Blops for clothing, both humans and Martians have the same relative prices and there would be no gains from trade.

On the other hand, if Martian prices were 2 Blops for food and 2 Blops for clothing, their relative price for food would be 1. This is lower than our relative price for food. So we humans would gain by specializing in producing clothing and buying food from the Martians. By producing one less unit of food, we could produce two more units of clothing and trade them for two units of food.

It doesn't matter which way relative prices differ—what matters is that they differ! Remember, we are talking about relative price differences *before* trade takes place. After trade, relative prices tend to become the same.

Why do relative prices (before trade) differ between nations? The main reasons are (1) differences in relative costs of producing goods, due to differences in labor, capital, and technology, (2) differences in taste, and (3) differences in natural resources and climate.

WHAT GOODS SHOULD A NATION TRADE?

A nation should sell those goods that other nations value at a higher relative price than it does. A nation should buy those goods that other nations are willing to sell at a lower relative price than it has. Buy low, sell high!

In the example above, our relative price for food was 2. When the Martians' relative price was 3, we sold (exported) food. When it was 1, we bought (imported) food.

YOU SHOULD REMEMBER

1. Differences in before-trade relative prices make trade beneficial.

2. When relative prices differ, a nation can always get more of one good without giving up the consumption of the other.

3. Relative price (as compared with the other nations' relative prices) determines which goods to produce and export and which goods to import.

> **4.** A nation should produce more of the good that it has a lower relative price of producing and should export that good.
>
> **5.** A nation should produce less of the good that it has a higher relative price of producing and should import that good.

THE LAW OF COMPARATIVE ADVANTAGE

The **law of comparative advantage** summarizes the main points of the two preceding sections. It states that a nation should compare its relative prices before trade. The nation should then *export* those goods that it can produce at a *lower* relative price than other nations and *import* those goods that it otherwise would have to produce at *higher* relative price. The nation can have *more of all goods* by doing this. (And so will the other nations trading with it!) How is this possible? Because when each good is produced by those nations with the lowest relative price of producing it, more of all goods can be produced.

To show this, suppose there are "units of resource" (part labor, part capital, and part land) that nations use to produce food and clothing. The following table shows what this unit can produce in the U.S. and France:

Table 29-1. Illustrating the Law of Comparative Advantage

Country	Output of 1 Unit of Resource			Relative Price of Food
	Food		Clothing	
U.S.	5	or	10	2
France	2	or	8	4

For example, 1 unit of resource can produce 5 units of food *or* 10 units of clothing in the U.S. Here, the price of food in the U.S. is one-fifth of a unit of resource; the price of clothing is one-tenth of a unit of resource. So the relative price is 1/5 divided by 1/10, or 2. For every unit of food produced, the U.S. must give up 2 units of clothing.

In this example, the U.S. has an **absolute advantage** in producing food *and* clothing: It can produce more food or more clothing with a unit of resource than France can. But even though the U.S. is more efficient in each, it still gains by trading with France! Why?

The U.S. has a **comparative advantage** in producing food: It has a lower relative price of producing food (2 versus France's 4). Just invert the relative price of food to get the relative price of clothing: It is one-half a unit of food for the U.S. and one-fourth a unit of food for France: France has the comparative advantage in producing clothing. According to the law of comparative advantage, the U.S. should produce and export food; France should produce and export clothing.

To show how this will increase world output, let's start with no trade. Then the U.S. moves 1 unit of resource from producing clothing and reallocates it to producing food. France moves 2 units out of food production into clothing. The net result is shown in Table 29-2.

Table 29-2. Impact of Transfer of Resources

Transfer	Impact on Food	Impact on Clothing
In US		
1 unit		
from Clothing		−10
to Food... +5		
In France		
2 units		
to Clothing..		+16
from Food..................................... −4		
Net Impact on World Output:	+1	+6

With more of both goods, there will be some mutually acceptable trading terms that will make both nations better off.

The **terms of trade**—the relative price that goods trade at—will fall between the before-trade relative prices. So food's relative price after trade will fall between 2 and 4. Supply and demand will determine its final relative price.

YOU SHOULD REMEMBER

1. Each country should produce more of the good that it has a lower relative price of producing.

2. World output will be increased when all nations produce those goods that they have a comparative advantage in producing.

3. By trading, two countries can both end up with more than they had before trade.

4. The terms of trade for a good will fall between the before-trade relative prices of both countries.

GRAPHICAL ANALYSIS OF COMPARATIVE ADVANTAGE

Note: This section is for those who have been required to graph the effects on international trade. Other readers may not benefit from this section (as it repeats the prior material in this chapter).

To show the benefits of trade, we begin with the production possibility curves for U.S. and France, based upon Table 29-1. We'll assume the U.S. has 100 units of resources and France has 150. Figure 29-1 shows the before-trade production possibility curves: This also shows the consumption possibilities when there is no trade. For example, the U.S. can have 1,000 units of clothing and no food (when all 100 units of resources produce clothing) or 500 units of food and no clothing, or some combination of each shown by Line *AA*. The absolute value of the slope equals the relative price of food (for the U.S., 2; for France, 4). Let's assume for the sake of illustration that each country consumes at Point *C* (e.g., the U.S. consumes 500 units of clothing and 250 units of food).

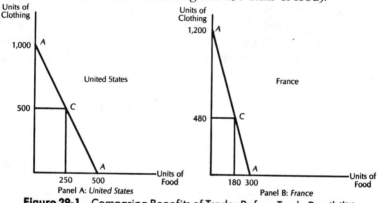

Figure 29-1 Comparing Benefits of Trade: Before Trade Possibilities

Now we introduce trade. Let the world terms of trade be 3. The U.S. will produce all food and no clothing: It will be at Point *D* in Figure 29-2. Then it starts to sell each unit of food for 3 units of clothing. As it does so, it moves up and to the left on Line *DE*. It can stop at any point and consume food and clothing at any point on this line. Because of trade, the U.S. consumption possibility curve (*DE*) is above its production possibility curve (*AA*). It can get more of *both* goods.

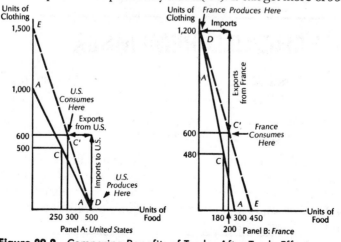

Figure 29-2 Comparing Benefits of Trade: After Trade Effects

If its new consumption is at Point C', it has 600 units of clothing (instead of 500) and 300 units of food (instead of 250). How does it do this? It produces 500 units of food and sells (exports) 200 units to buy (import) 600 units of clothing.

France will specialize in producing clothing (at Point D in Panel B of Figure 29-2). It can then sell each unit of clothing for one-third a unit of food: It can consume on Line DE. If it chooses Point C', it will export 600 units of clothing in exchange for 200 units of food. It too will have more food and clothing with trade than it did without trade.

Key Procedure for Graphing Effects of Trade*

1. For each country, calculate how much of the good on the vertical axis it could produce if it devoted all of its resources to producing that good and none of the other. Do the same for the good on the horizontal axis. Plot these points on the respective axes and connect them: the connecting line is the *production possibility curve.*

2. Each country produces only the good it has a lower relative cost of producing. Plot this point. Then assume the country sells all it produces and buys the other good at the world's terms of trade: Plot this point. Then connect these two points. This is the country's *consumption possibility curve.* If plotted correctly, it will be above and to the right of the production possibility curve (plotted in step 1).

3. Each country will select some combination of the two goods to consume: this combination will be shown by a point on its consumption possibility curve.

4. A nation's imports will be equal to its consumption of the good it does *not* produce (as plotted in step 3).

5. A nation's exports equals the difference between the total output of the good it produces and the amount it consumes.

YOU SHOULD REMEMBER

1. Without trade, a nation can consume only along its production possibility curve.

2. With trade, a nation will specialize in producing one good. It will export that good, and import the other.

3. The absolute value of the slope of the production possibility curve equals the before-trade relative price of the good on the bottom axis. The absolute value of the slope of the consumption possibility curve equals the terms-of-trade relative price for the good on the bottom axis.

---

*Note: This procedure applies only to straight-line production curves.

> **4.** By producing the good whose before-trade relative price is less than the terms-of-trade price, a nation can consume more of both goods.

THE EFFECT OF TARIFFS AND QUOTAS

Tariffs are a tax on imports. One study estimated that tariffs (and other trade restrictions) cost every American $500 annually in the form of higher prices.

Figure 29-3 shows the effect of trade. *DD* and *SS* are the *domestic* demand and the *domestic* supply for clothing in the U.S. (that is, the demand and supply of the nation's citizens). Without trade, the price of clothing is $10. Let's assume the world price of clothing is $6. The world's supply curve is *W-S*. At $6, consumers will buy 700 units of clothing, domestic producers will produce 300 units, and the U.S. will import the remaining 400 units.

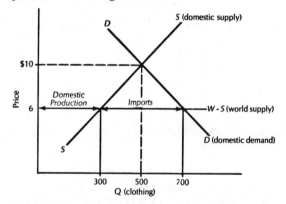

Figure 29-3 Effects of World Trade in a No-Tariff Situation

Figure 29-4 shows the effect of a $2 tariff on clothing imports. The domestic price of clothing will rise to $8. Consumers will buy 600 units (down from 700), domestic producers will produce 400 units (up from 300), and imports will be 200 units (down from 400). *The effect of a tariff on a good is to reduce the good's consumption, increase its domestic production, and reduce imports.*

From a social point of view, what has happened?

1. Area *A* is the *cost of inefficient production.* This is how much over and above the $6 world price the U.S. is paying in added production costs for the added domestic output of 100 units (from 300 to 400). Area *A* = $100 (remember, the area of a triangle equals 1/2 base × height).

2. Area *B* is the *tariff revenues* collected. Area *B* = $400.

3. Area *C* is the *lost consumer surplus* caused by the fall in consumption from 700 to 600 units. Area *C* = $100.

4. Area *E* is the *added profits* to producers because of clothing's higher price. Area *E* = $700.

5. Areas *A* + *B* + *C* + *E* = the *total loss to consumers* because of the higher price. This Area = $1,300.

The *social* loss is Area *A* plus Area *C*. Consumers lose Areas *A* + *B* + *C* + *E*. But the government gets Area *B* in taxes and producers get Area *E* in profits. On net, Areas *A* and *C* are *a deadweight loss:* No one benefits from this loss. Consumers lose *more* than others gain. Consumers lose $1,300, and the government and producers gain $1,100, so the deadweight loss is $200.

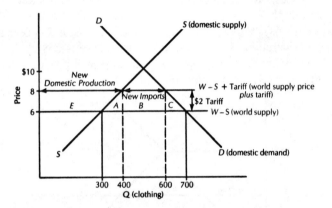

Figure 29-4   Effects of World Trade in a $2-Tariff Situation

A **quota** is a limit on the amount of imports. If set correctly, it has the same effect on output and consumption as a tariff. In Figure 29-4, a quota limiting imports to 200 units of food will push food prices up to $8.

All areas will be the same except for Area *B*: The government will not collect any tariff revenues. Where does this $400 of lost tariff revenues go? Usually, the government gives importers a certain quota so the importers get the $400 (since they can buy 200 units at $6 and sell them for $8). With the U.S. "voluntary export quotas" on Japanese automobiles, the Japanese auto firms get the implicit tariff revenues (which is one reason they are happy to "volunteer" to limit exports)!

YOU SHOULD REMEMBER

1. A tariff raises domestic prices, reduces consumption, increases domestic production, and reduces imports.

2. Consumers lose more than others gain: The difference is the deadweight loss of the tariff.

> **3.** A quota can have the same effect as a tariff, except that the government does not collect any tax revenues.

TRADE AND UNEMPLOYMENT

In the examples above, trade caused the U.S. to shift production away from clothing and into food. In this shift, workers became temporarily unemployed in the clothing industry until they could find jobs in the food industry. But then all workers earned a higher real wage. So while unemployment is costly, it results in everyone being better off.

This is *not* the case if some workers *specialize* in the clothing industry and are thus unable to transfer their skills to food production. Those workers will *lose* by having to produce clothing at lower wages or by becoming unemployed. The same will be true of other workers specializing in clothing production. Nevertheless, since the nation as a whole benefits from free trade, it is possible to compensate "losers" for their losses and for everyone to be better off.

Several economic studies have shown that the total cost borne by workers who are thrown out of work because of foreign trade is on average $4,000 per worker. Yet the cost to consumers of protecting one job with a tariff is at a minimum $30,000. Tariffs seem a very expensive method of "job protection." While economists differ on the exact numbers, most economists condemn tariffs as highly inefficient.

ARGUMENTS FOR TARIFFS

Protection From Cheap Foreign Labor: This is a fallacious argument. A country benefits from trade whenever it has a *comparative* advantage in some goods, even when it does not have an absolute advantage in any good (see the example of France above).

The U.S. is quite capable of competing with low-wage countries because it has more capital and skilled labor. In a sense, it has *cheap* skilled labor compared with "low-wage" nations. The worry over competition from cheap foreign labor is misplaced. The U.S. faces its greatest competition from the more advanced countries, such as Japan and Germany.

Protection of American Way of Life, Self-Sufficiency, and Military Preparedness· Any of these goals, if desirable, are far cheaper to achieve by subsidies

Protection of Infant Industries: Some argue that tariffs should be used to protect beginning (or "infant") industries from competition until they can grow and become profitable. However, this makes sense only if the present value of future profits makes up for the current losses to consumers due to the higher prices caused by the tariff. Thus, those infant industries which want tariff protection should be required to pay back later in higher taxes the current cost to consumers of the tariff protection. In this way, only those industries which truly believe that they have a valid case for a tariff will seek tariff protection. Most likely, the number of valid cases would prove to be small.

Bettering the Terms-of-Trade: This is one of the few possibly valid arguments for tariffs. If the U.S. has monopsony power so that when it buys less, the world price of an imported good falls, then some tariff can make the U.S. better off. But this assumes that other nations won't retaliate with higher tariffs. If they do, all nations will likely be worse off.

YOU SHOULD REMEMBER

1. Tariffs are a very expensive form of job protection. There are far cheaper ways to help workers in their transition between jobs.

2. The only two possibly valid reasons tariffs are to protect infant industries and to better the world terms of trade. But both reasons apply only in limited circumstances.

KNOW THE CONCEPTS
DO YOU KNOW THE BASICS?

1. Mary buys a car from Joe's Car Sales. Joe is the only dealer in the area and makes a big profit from the sale. Does Mary benefit or lose from her purchase?

2. If Japan sold imports to the U.S. but did not buy any exports from the U.S., would the U.S. be worse off?

3. When will two nations not benefit from trade?

4. "Cheap imports are hurting the U.S. economy." Is this true?

5. How are farmers (who export a large volume of their output) hurt by tariffs on imports?

6. Which goods should a nation specialize in producing when it trades with other nations?

7. According to the law of comparative advantage, how can the world produce the greatest output?

8. Who benefits from tariffs? Who loses? How do the total losses compare with total benefits?

9. Why would foreign producers prefer a quota over a tariff that had the same impact?

10. "Everyone should do what he or she is best at." Is this true?

TERMS FOR STUDY

absolute advantage	law of comparative advantage
comparative advantage	relative price
exports	tariffs
imports	terms of trade
infant industries	quotas

PRACTICAL APPLICATION

1. Peru can produce 16 units of corn or 8 units of wheat with a unit of resource. Mexico can produce 12 units of corn or 4 units of wheat.
   a. Which country has the absolute advantage in producing each good?
   b. What is the relative price of wheat in each country? Of corn?
   c. If these are the only countries in the world, which should produce wheat? Corn?
   d. In what range will the terms of trade for wheat fall?

2. Suppose Santa Claus was real and gave gifts to children at Christmas.
   a. Who would benefit?
   b. Who would be hurt?
   c. Would our nation on net be better or worse off?
   d. From a social point of view, does the dumping of goods by foreign nations harm our nation?

   Note: "Dumping" is the selling of imports below cost. Santa Claus is guilty of dumping.

3. The U.S. annually spends billions of dollars subsidizing the export of goods from the U.S. Does this help or hurt the U.S.?

4. In science fiction literature, robots are often banned from Earth because they "can do everything better, leaving nothing for humans to do."
   a. Would robots cause humans to have nothing to do?
   b. Which tasks would humans perform?
   c. Would humans be better or worse off?

5. Countries Y and Z have the following production possibility schedules for food and clothing:

Country Y	Food	0	4	8	12
	Clothing	12	8	4	0

Country Z	Food	0	4	8	12
	Clothing	36	24	12	0

    a. Before trade, what is the relative cost of food in each country?
    b. With trade, which country will produce food? Clothing?
    c. Show the consumption possibility schedule for both countries when the terms of trade for food is 2.

6. At a gas station, Bill can change the oil on 5 cars in an hour or pump the gas on 20 cars in an hour. Susan can change the oil on 10 cars in an hour or pump gas on 60 cars in an hour. Who should do what?

7. Assume that the world price of oil is $15 per barrel. At that price, the U.S. imports 400 million barrels a day and consumes 600 million barrels a day. The government then imposes a $5-per-barrel tax on oil imports. For every $1 increase in oil prices, domestic consumption goes down 20 million barrels a day while domestic production goes up 40 million barrels a day.
    a. What will the new oil price be (assume the world supply is perfectly elastic at $15).
    b. What will the new consumption, domestic production, and import levels be? How much will the government collect in taxes?
    c. What will be the cost of inefficient production, the loss in consumer surplus, and deadweight loss? (Use the triangle formula of 1/2 × change in price × change in quantity for both the loss in efficiency and the loss in consumer surplus.)
    d. Why, from an efficiency point of view, would a $5 tax on *all* oil be better than the $5 tax on oil imports?

8. Suppose trade follows this pattern: The U.S. buys cars from Japan, Japan buys oil from the Middle East, and the Middle East buys machinery for the U.S. What then is wrong with reciprocity legislation requiring *each* country to buy from the U.S. exactly the amount it sells to us? (This type of trading pattern is called *multilateral trade,* as opposed to *bilateral trade* between two nations.)

9. Use the following table:

Price of Clothing	$8	$7	$6	$5	$4	$3	$2
Domestic Demand	100	200	300	400	500	600	700
Domestic Supply	900	800	700	600	500	400	300

    a. Without trade, what will the price of clothing be?

b. If the world price of clothing is $6, what will happen? If it's $2?

c. Construct a table of this country's demand for clothing imports (which is its *excess demand for clothing at each price*) and its supply of clothing exports (which is its *excess supply of clothing at each price*).

10. Use this table:

Price of Clothing	$5	$4	$3	$2	$1
Other Nations' Demand	1300	1400	1500	1600	1700
Other Nations' Supply	2600	2400	2200	2000	1800

a. What is the excess supply curve of other nations for clothing? (Give your answer in the form of a table.)

b. Using the table in Question 9 above, what will the world price of clothing be? How much will the U.S. import from other nations?

ANSWERS

KNOW THE CONCEPTS

1. Mary benefits, or she would not have bought the car.

2. The U.S. would be better off: It would have the imports without having to pay for them.

3. When their relative prices are the same.

4. No. Cheap imports mean the U.S. is getting back more for the exports it sells.

5. Tariffs reduce foreign sales to the U.S. This means foreigners have fewer dollars with which to buy U.S. goods. In turn, this reduces foreign demand for U.S. agricultural products.

6. The goods that have relative prices that are lower than their world terms-of-trade relative prices.

7. When each country produces the goods it has the lowest relative price of producing, world output will be maximized.

8. The gainers are (a) producers and factors of production that are specialized in producing the good the tariff is imposed upon and (b) the government. The losers are consumers (including the nonspecialized factors producing the good). Total losses exceed total benefits.

9. Because a quota allows the producers, rather than the government, to benefit from the higher price.

10. No. Everyone should do what he or she has a *comparative* advantage in doing, not what he or she has an absolute advantage in doing. What is true for nations is also true for people.

PRACTICAL APPLICATION

1. **a.** Peru has the absolute advantage in both goods.
   b. For wheat: Peru, 2; Mexico, 3.
   For corn: Peru, 1/2; Mexico, 1/3.
   c. Peru should produce wheat. Mexico should produce corn.
   d. Between 2 and 3.

2. **a.** Consumers of toys.
   b. Factors specialized in toy production.
   c. Better off: The factors released from toy production could produce other goods. So, the nation could have more toys *and* more other goods.
   d. No. Dumping makes the U.S. better off.

3. It hurts the U.S. It's the equivalent of giving away goods without getting anything back.

4. **a.** No. Unless the robots have the same relative price of doing things as humans do, they (or their owners) would want to trade with humans.
   b. Humans would perform those tasks that they have a lower relative price performing than robots have.
   c. Humans would be better off.

5. **a.** Y: 1. Z: 3.
   b. Y will produce food. Z will produce clothing.

c.	Country Y	Food	0	4	8	12
		Clothing	24	16	8	0
	Country Z	Food	0	6	12	18
		Clothing	36	24	12	0

6. Bill's relative price of doing an oil change is 4 gas pumpings. Sue's relative price is 6. So Bill should change oil, and Sue should pump gas.

7. **a.** $20 (World price of $15 + $5 tariff).
   b. *Consumption:* 500 million barrels a day ($5 price rise reduces consumption by 5 × 20 million from 600 million).
   Domestic Production: 400 million barrels a day. (Domestic production was 200 million; it goes up by 5 × 40 million to 400 million.)

Imports: 100 million barrels a day (consumption of 500 million less domestic output of 400 million).

Taxes: $500 million a day ($5 × 100 million barrels imported).

c. *Cost of Inefficient Production:* $500 million a day (1/2 × price change of $5 × change in domestic oil production of 200 million).

Consumer Surplus Loss: $250 million a day (1/2 × price change of $5 × change in consumption of 100 million).

Deadweight Loss: $750 million a day (sum of the above).

d. A tax on all oil has no cost of inefficient production (since domestic supply will remain at 200 million barrels). There is only the consumer surplus loss of $250 million a day. Also, more tax revenue will be collected, because all oil is taxed: tax revenues will be $2,500 million a day ($5 × 500 million barrels a day consumed). So the tax on all oil has a lower deadweight loss per tax dollar. For the import tax, the deadweight loss was $1.50 per tax dollar collected. For the all-inclusive tax, it is 10 cents per tax dollar collected.

8. With more countries specializing in the goods they have a comparative advantage in supplying, world output and the welfare of the U.S. will be greater. But multilateral trade means the U.S. will have trade surpluses with some (here, the Middle East) and trade deficits with others (here, Japan). Forcing reciprocity will reduce the gains from comparative advantage and make the U.S. worse off.

9. a. $4   b. At $6, the U.S. will export 400 units of clothing. At $2, the U.S. will import 400 units of clothing.

c.

Price	Exports	Imports
$8	800	—
7	600	—
6	400	—
5	200	—
4	0	0
3	—	200
2	—	400

10. a.

Price	Excess Supply to U.S.
$5	1,300
4	1,000
3	700
2	400
1	100

b. The world price will be $2. Other nations will have an excess supply of 400 units of clothing at $2. This matches the U.S.'s excess demand of 400 units of $2. The U.S. will import 400 units.

30
EXCHANGE RATES AND THE INTERNATIONAL MONETARY SYSTEM

EXCHANGE RATES

In this chapter, to keep things simple, we will talk exclusively about what determines the value of the dollar. The "value of the dollar" refers to the **exchange rate** for the dollar: how many units of foreign currency foreigners are willing to pay for a dollar. For example, if the dollar's exchange rate against the Swiss franc is 2.5, 2.5 francs buy one dollar. (The symbol for the Swiss franc is SwF, so this is quoted as 2.5 SwF/$.)

1. *How to Convert Foreign Prices Into Dollars:*

$$\text{Dollar Price} = \text{Foreign Price/Exchange Rate}$$

If a Swiss watch costs 100,000 francs and the exchange rate is 2.5 SwF/$, then the U.S. price will be $40,000.

2. *How to Convert Dollar Prices Into Foreign Prices:*

Foreign Price = Dollar Price × Exchange Rate.

If a Chevrolet costs $12,000 and the exchange rate is 2.5 SwF/$, then the Chevrolet will cost 30,000 francs.

3. *How to Convert Exchange Rate for Dollars Into Exchange Rate for Foreign Currency:*

Foreign Exchange Rate = 1/Dollar Exchange Rate.

If 2.5 francs buy a dollar, it will take $.40 to buy a franc.

Hint: Recall the old trick from chemistry class of labeling all numbers and then canceling the labels to see what you've got. For example, in (1) above, we have $ = SwF/(SwF/$). Canceling labels on the right-hand side gives $.

WHAT DETERMINES THE EXCHANGE RATE?

The U.S. has **flexible exchange rates**. With some exceptions, the government lets the dollar's exchange rate be set by the free market forces of demand and supply.

This section focuses on what determines the Swiss franc price of the dollar. The demand and supply of the dollar as a function of its franc price is shown in Figure 30-1.

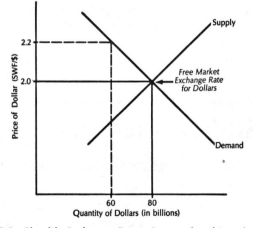

Figure 30-1   Flexible Exchange Rates: Demand and Supply of the Dollar

The main things to note are:

1. *The demand curve is the demand by foreigners for U.S. dollars.* Foreigners (here, Swiss citizens) demand dollars to buy (1) U.S. goods and services, (2) U.S. physical assets (by, for example, building a factory in the U.S.), and (3) U.S. financial assets (such as stocks, bonds, and treasury bills).

2. *The demand curve has a negative slope: As the dollar becomes cheaper, Swiss citizens demand more dollars.* When the price of the dollar falls (when it takes fewer francs to buy a dollar), the dollar has **depreciated**. As a result, the franc price of U.S. goods, services, and assets becomes cheaper. For example, at 2.2 SwF/$, a $12,000 Chevrolet costs 26,400 francs; at 2.0 SwF/$, only 24,000 francs. So demand for Chevrolets exported to Switzerland goes up as the dollar depreciates. As the dollar depreciates, the demand for all U.S. exports goes up, as does the demand for U.S. dollars with which to buy them. In Figure 30-1, the quantity of dollars the Swiss want goes from 60 to 80 billion (per year) as the dollar depreciates from 2.2 to 2.0 SwF/$.

3. *The supply curve is the supply by U.S. citizens of dollars in exchange for Swiss francs.* Why would U.S. citizens be willing to give up dollars in order to get Swiss francs? So they can buy Swiss goods, services, and assets. It takes Swiss francs to buy Swiss goods, so U.S. citizens must give up (i.e., supply) dollars to get Swiss francs.

4. *The supply curve has a positive slope.* When the value of the dollar goes up (so one dollar trades for more francs), the dollar has **appreciated**. The positive slope means that as the value of the dollar rises, U.S. citizens want more francs and so are willing to supply more dollars. Why? Because the U.S. price of Swiss goods is then lower. For example, a watch costing 100,000 francs costs $50,000 when the exchange rate is 2 but only cost $45,455 when it's 2.2 SwF/$.

5. *In equilibrium, the demand and supply of dollars are equal.* This occurs in Figure 30-1 at 2.0 SwF/$. At this price, the Swiss want $80 billion (per year) with which to buy U.S. goods, services, and assets. And U.S. citizens are willing to supply $80 billion (per year) to buy $80 billion worth of Swiss goods, services, and assets. The **equilibrium exchange rate** has been reached.

YOU SHOULD REMEMBER

1. The exchange rate is the price of one country's currency stated in terms of another's.

2. When the dollar appreciates, its exchange rate has gone up (SwF/$ goes up). When the dollar depreciates, its exchange rate falls (SwF/$ goes down).

---

3. When the dollar appreciates, import prices fall and the price of U.S. exports to other nations rises.

4. When the dollar depreciates, import prices rise and export prices fall.

5. The demand for the dollar by foreigners reflects their demand for U.S. goods, services, and assets. The supply of dollars to foreigners by U.S. citizens reflects the citizens' demand for foreign goods, services, and assets.

6. At the equilibrium exchange rate, the dollars demanded equal those sold: The dollar value of the goods, services, and assets bought by foreigners and sold by U.S. citizens will be equal.

FACTORS AFFECTING THE EXCHANGE RATE

The factors affecting the value of the dollar are shown in Table 30-1.

As an example, if U.S. citizens suddenly want more Swiss watches and cheese and start traveling more to Switzerland, the supply curve in Figure 30-1 will shift to the right and the dollar will decrease in value.

The *combined factors* are:

1. *Relative U.S. Price Level:* According to the doctrine of **purchasing power parity**:

$$\frac{\text{U.S. Exchange Rate}}{(\text{SwF/\$})} = \frac{\text{Swiss Price Level}}{\text{U.S. Price Level}}$$

To illustrate the forces behind purchasing power parity, suppose the only good traded is steel and that the U.S. steel price is $100 per ton and the Swiss steel price is 200 francs per ton. Further, for simplicity, assume that transportation costs are zero. Then the exchange rate will be 2. At 2, the price of steel, whether imported or produced domestically, will be the same ($100) and thus competitive. If the exchange rate is higher, Swiss steel will be cheaper. For example, if it's 4, Swiss steel will cost only $50. This will increase the demand for Swiss steel by U.S. citizens until the exchange rate returns to 2. If it's lower, U.S. steel will be cheaper (e.g., if it's 1, U.S. steel will cost 100 francs). Swiss demand will go up for U.S. steel until the exchange rate returns to 2. The doctrine of purchasing power parity asserts that exchange rates will change so that all traded goods will have the same price (whether imported or produced domestically). For this reason this doctrine is also known as the *law of one price*.

Table 30-1. Factors Affecting Value of Dollar

Factor	Change in Factor	Effect on Dollar
Single Factor		
Affecting Demand		
• Foreign demand for U.S. Goods and Services (i.e., Demand for U.S. Exports)	Increase	Appreciation
	Decrease	Depreciation
• Foreign demand for U.S. Physical Assets (such as plants in U.S.) and Financial Assets (such as bonds and stocks)	Increase	Appreciation
	Decrease	Depreciation
Affecting Supply		
U.S. demand for Foreign Goods and Services (i.e., Demand for Imports)	Increase	Depreciation
	Decrease	Appreciation
• U.S. demand for Foreign Physical Assets and Financial Assets	Increase	Depreciation
	Decrease	Appreciation
Combined Factors		
• US Price Level *Relative To* Foreign Price Level	Increase	Depreciation
	Decrease	Appreciation
• US Interest Rates *Relative To* Foreign Interest Rates	Increase	Appreciation
	Decrease	Depreciation
• US Growth Rate *Relative To* Foreign Growth Rate	Increase	Depreciation
	Decrease	Appreciation

This doctrine works best in the long run and when countries have large differences in their inflation rates. *It predicts:*

a. The U.S. dollar will *appreciate* when the U.S. inflation rate is *below* foreign inflation rates (so that foreign price levels rise relative to the U.S. price level).

b. The U.S. dollar will *depreciate* when the U.S. inflation rate is *above* the foreign inflation rates.

2. *Relative Interest Rates:* According to the doctrine of **interest rate parity,** capital flows towards those nations paying the highest interest rates until, in equilibrium, all nations pay the same interest rates *adjusting for the risk of default and the risk that the nation's currency will depreciate. This doctrine predicts:*

a. When U.S. interest rates go *up* (or other nations' interest rates go down), international capital flows into the U.S. This increases the demand for U.S. assets and causes the dollar to *appreciate.*

b. When U.S. interest rates go *down* (or other nations' interest rates go up), capital flows out of the U.S., increasing the supply of dollars: The dollar will *depreciate.*

3. *Relative Growth Rates:* If the U.S. grows *faster* than other nations, our demand for imports will expand faster than their demand for imports (which, of course, are our exports): The dollar will *depreciate.* When the U.S. grows *slower* (or other nations grow faster), the dollar will *appreciate.*

YOU SHOULD REMEMBER

1. Any event that increases the demand for U.S. dollars by foreigners will cause the dollar to appreciate. Such events include: an increase in the demand for U.S. goods and assets, a U.S. inflation rate that is lower than foreign inflation rates, a U.S. interest rate that is higher than foreign interest rates, and higher foreign growth rates.

2. Any event that increases the supply of U.S. dollars to foreigners by U.S. citizens will cause the dollar to depreciate. Such events include: an increase in demand by Americans for foreign goods, services, and assets; a U.S. inflation rate that is higher than foreign inflation rates; a U.S. interest rate that is lower than foreign interest rates; and a higher U.S. growth rate.

3 According to the doctrine of purchasing power parity, the relative price levels of nations determine exchange rates. The exchange rate changes until all traded goods, whether produced domestically or imported, sell at one price. This result is called **the law of one price.**

4. Capital flows to those nations offering the highest interest rates.

FIXED EXCHANGE RATES

At one time, most nations had **fixed exchange rates**. Under fixed exchange rates, a government buys and sells its currency at a certain exchange rate against all other currencies. To do this, governments need to accumulate large holdings of other nations' currencies in order to sell them to maintain the value of its own currency. As a result, the demand and supply of the currency *no longer have to be equal* since the government makes up any differences from its reserves of currencies.

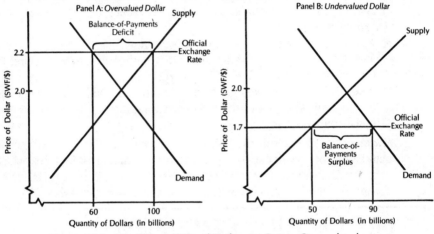

Figure 30-2   The Effect of Fixed Exchange Rates: Overvalued, Undervalued

In Figure 30-2, Panel A, we show the effects of an **overvalued currency**: The government tries to set the exchange rate *above* its free market level. Here, the U.S. government holds the exchange rate of the dollar at 2.2 SwF/$ while its free market level is 2.0. Supply exceeds demand: Foreigners wan 40 billion fewer dollars than U.S. citizens want to supply. In this case, the U.S. has a **balance-of-payment deficit**. The U.S. government has to buy the 40 billion excess supply of dollars with its Swiss franc reserves. This balance-of-payments deficit reduces the U.S. government's reserves of francs. Eventually, if these deficits continue, the government will have to **devalue** the currency by lowering the official exchange rate. Governments are often forced to do this suddenly, as currency speculators, sensing a coming devaluation, stage a **run on the currency**, demanding that the government exchange its Swiss francs for the speculators' dollars.

In Figure 30-2, Panel B, the U.S. government has **undervalued** the dollar by setting the exchange rate **below** its free market value (at 1.7 instead of 2.0). Now there is an excess demand of $40 billion—the U.S. has a **balance-of-payments surplus**. Demand exceeds supply: Foreigners want more dollars than U.S. citizens want to supply. To satisfy the excess demand, the U.S. government will hand out dollars for francs, increasing its reserves of francs.

At some point in time, the U.S. might want to stop accumulating francs. If so, it will **revalue** the dollar by raising its official exchange rate. Note that when a currency is overvalued, dwindling reserves force the government to devalue; no such pressure forces countries to revalue an undervalued currency since the government can go on accumulating reserves without limit if it wishes.

> Hint: To remember these results, remember that *an excess demand for dollars equals the excess supply of foreign currency.* So an overvalued dollar (relative to Swiss francs) means an excess supply of dollars, an excess demand for francs, and, as a result, decreasing U.S. government reserves of francs. An undervalued dollar means an excess demand for dollars, an excess supply of francs, and a resulting increase in the U.S. government reserves of francs.

YOU SHOULD REMEMBER

1. Under fixed exchange rates, the government buys and sells its currency at a fixed rate.

2. An overvalued currency is one whose fixed exchange rate is above its free market value.

3. When a government overvalues its currency, it will have a balance-of-payments deficit. It will have to run down its reserves of foreign currency. Eventually, its reserves will run out, forcing it to devalue its currency by lowering its official exchange rate.

4. An undervalued currency is one whose fixed exchange rate is below its free market value.

5. When a government undervalues its currency, it will have a balance-of-payments surplus. It will accumulate foreign currency reserves. To avoid accumulating too much, it may revalue its currency by increasing its exchange rate.

ADJUSTMENTS UNDER FIXED EXCHANGE RATES

A country running a balance-of-payments deficit finds its reserves of foreign currency falling. Temporarily, it can borrow these reserves from other nations, but this only puts the problem off until later. If the country doesn't want to change its fixed exchange rate, it then has two options. It can either (1) impose **exchange controls** prohibiting its citizens from trying to exchange the nation's currency for foreign currency or (2) decrease the excess supply of its currency.

With option (1), the government hopes to reduce the outflow of its foreign currency reserves. But exchange controls harm a nation by reducing its international trade.

With option (2), the government can reduce the supply of its currency by decreasing real income (by restrictive fiscal policy) or by decreasing its money supply. Restrictive fiscal policy, by decreasing national income, reduces the demand for imports. Restrictive monetary policy reduces the general price level. Both restrictive fiscal and monetary policies shift the free market exchange rate up towards the official rate and thus get rid of the deficit.

YOU SHOULD REMEMBER

1. To get rid of a balance-of-payments deficit, a nation can (1) impose exchange controls, (2) use a restrictive fiscal and/or monetary policy to reduce import demand, or (3) allow exchange rates to change.

2. If a nation rejects (2) and (3), then it can no longer have an independent monetary and fiscal policy. Its monetary and fiscal policy will be determined solely by the need to keep a sufficient level of foreign currency reserves.

THE CURRENT AND CAPITAL BALANCE

Under flexible exchange rates, there are no balance-of-payment deficits or surpluses since exchange rates move to eliminate them. Total dollars going into our economy thus equal the dollars going out. To keep track of these flows, the government keeps a **balance-of-payments account**.

The balance-of-payments account has two parts: (1) The **current account**, which keeps track of *goods and services* flowing on net *out of* the U.S., and (2) the **capital account**, which keeps track of *physical and financial assets* flowing on net *into* the U.S.

Think of the current account as the nation's checking account. When U.S. citizens buy (import) more than they earn (by exporting), the U.S. *checking account is negative,* showing a deficit. To pay for the excess imports, the U.S. has to borrow from foreigners or sell some of its assets to them. The capital account shows the changes in what the U.S. owes the world. So when the U.S. borrows, *the capital account is positive* and equal in value to its checking account deficit: It shows the U.S. owes other nations more. But when the U.S. receives more than it spends (when exports exceed imports), its *checking account is positive,* showing a surplus. This surplus is lent to foreigners or used to buy their assets: The *capital account will be negative* and equal in value to the U.S. surplus. It shows that the U.S. owes other nations less.

With flexible exchange rates, the balance of payments sums to zero. Therefore, we have:

Balance on Current Account + Balance on Capital Account = 0.

Table 30-2 shows a sample balance-of-payment account. **Credits** in this account are items that bring foreign currency into the U.S. **Debits** are items that take dollars out of the U.S. Credit items represent forces that increase the demand for dollars; debits, items that increase the supply.

Table 30-2. Balance-of-Payment Account (in billions of dollars)

Account	Credit	Debit	Sum
Current Account			
1. Merchandise Exports	200		
2. Merchandise Imports		250	
1 + 2: Balance of Trade			−50
3. Net Military Transactions		4	
4. Net Investment Income (and other services)	40		
5. Net Travel and Transportation Receipts		3	
1 through 5: Balance on Goods and Services			−17
6. Unilateral Transfers		6	
1 through 6: Balance on Current Account.....			−23
Capital Account			
7. Change in U. S. Assets Abroad		80	
8. Change in Foreign Assets in U.S.	100		
7 + 8: Net Private Capital Flows			20
9. Change in U.S. Reserve Assets		6	
10. Change in Foreign Official Assets in U.S.	9		
9 + 10: Net Government Capital Flows			3
7 through 10: Balance on Capital Account.....			23

Notice that there are changes in net government capital flows. Under pure flexible exchange rates, governments would not be buying and selling currency, and these numbers would be zero. Often, governments intervene to influence exchanges rates. This is called a **dirty float** or a **managed float**.

In 1984, the balance of trade was −$114 billion, the balance on the current account was −$107 billion, and net private capital flows were $82 billion.

YOU SHOULD REMEMBER

1. Under flexible or floating exchange rates, the balance of payments will always be zero.

2. The balance on the current account reflects mainly the net export of goods and services from this nation.

3. The balance on the capital account reflects mainly changes in what the U.S. owes other nations. This is equivalent to the net inflow of capital into the U.S.

4. The balance on the current account plus the balance on the capital account sum to zero: When one is negative, the other is positive by the same amount.

5. When the U.S. buys more than it sells, the balance on the current account (and net exports) is negative. To pay the difference, the U.S. must increase what it owes other nations and capital must flow into the U.S.: The capital account will be positive.

6. When the U.S. sells more than it buys, the balance on the current account (and net exports) is positive. The world must borrow from the U.S. to pay the difference. What the world owes the U.S. thus increases and capital flows out of the U.S.: The capital account will be negative.

THE MACROECONOMICS OF AN OPEN ECONOMY: THE KEYNESIAN VIEW

By definition, aggregate demand (*AD*) equals:

$$AD = C + G + I + \text{Net Exports}$$

where *C* is consumption spending, *G* is government spending, *I* is investment spending, and Net Exports = Exports − Imports. In the simple Keynesian Model:

1. An increase in exports increases aggregate demand through the multiplier process.

2. An increase in imports decreases aggregate demand (by taking dollars out of the economy) through the multiplier process.

A trade deficit is thus thought to be undesirable. But saying trade deficits are always undesirable ignores the forces that created the deficit. Suppose Britain buys and sells $100 million of goods to the U.S. In this case, there is no deficit. But suppose Britain sells $100 million of goods to the U.S. and uses it to build factories in the U.S. Now, there is a $100 million deficit (since British investments in the U.S. don't count as exports). Yet, aggregate demand is the same in both cases! (The British investment shows up in *I*, investment). The same is true when the British buy U.S. government bonds (allowing a higher *G*) or stocks and bonds from U.S. citizens (increasing *C*). All these occur with the U.S. having a trade deficit and yet do not affect aggregate spending. Thus, the trade deficit need not be undesirable.

Monetarists view trade deficits as decreasing aggregate demand *only* to the degree that they represent an increase in the demand for U.S. dollars by foreigners. Suppose Britain sells $100 million of goods to the U.S. and puts the dollars into a vault. This results in a trade deficit. But in addition, it represents an increase in money demand, and any increase in money demand reduces aggregate demand. But this can be quickly remedied by the Fed printing more dollar bills. By doing so, our nation will be better off since it will get $100 million worth of goods in exchange for 100 million pieces of paper.

YOU SHOULD REMEMBER

1. According to the simple Keynesian Model, imports depress aggregate demand while exports stimulate it.

2. According to Monetarists, a trade deficit reduces aggregate demand only to the degree that it reflects an increase in dollar demand by other nations.

WHAT CAUSES TRADE DEFICITS?

Consider the following equation:

Spending − Domestic Output = Imports − Exports (= trade deficit)

= Borrowing from Other Nations.

When the U.S. spends more than it produces, it buys more from other nations than it sells (imports exceed exports), creating a trade deficit. So the U.S. has to borrow from foreigners to support its excess spending.

Is this borrowing bad? No, not if it finances profitable investments, since the profits on these investments will pay for the borrowing. Yes, if the borrowed funds are used unwisely. Then Americans in the future will have to cut back consumption to pay back the foreign loans.

Many economists believe that the government's deficit causes the U.S.'s trade deficit. As the U.S. government borrows more, this runs up interest rates, attracting foreign capital. This increases the demand for the dollar, raising its value and putting the U.S. export manufacturers at a disadvantage (since the higher exchange rate increases the world price of U.S. exports): Thus the U.S. trade deficit. The solution is to raise taxes or reduce government spending.

Other economists point out that empirically, government deficits "do not matter" (they affect neither interest rates nor net exports). These economists believe that the U.S. economy's recovery and President Reagan's tax cuts increased the rate of return on investments in the U.S., attracting foreign capital. Foreigners, in order to get the dollars to invest in the U.S., are willing to sell the U.S. more than they buy back: thus the trade deficits. In this context, the trade deficit is good, because it reflects a needed infusion of capital into the U.S. To raise taxes would be harmful.

YOU SHOULD REMEMBER

1. When a nation spends more than it produces, its imports exceed its exports and it must borrow from other nations.

2. Borrowing from other nations and trade deficits go together. The capital account measures borrowing from other nations; the current account reflects the trade deficit.

3. Borrowing will be beneficial when it is productively invested. Otherwise, future consumption will have to be reduced to pay back the debt.

KNOW THE CONCEPTS

DO YOU KNOW THE BASICS?

1. Who demands dollars? Why? Who supplies dollars? Why?

2. Can all currencies appreciate at the same time?

3. Can all countries export more than they import?

4. Why is the doctrine of purchasing power parity called the "law of one price"?

5. What does the balance on the capital account reflect?

6. When the dollar appreciates, what happens to the prices of imports? To the foreign price of U.S. exports?

7. Under fixed exchange rates, what happens when a nation overvalues its currency? Who might benefit from an overvalued currency?

8. Can a nation have a fixed exchange rate, no exchange controls, and an independent monetary and fiscal policy?

9. How can a nation spend more than it produces? How is this reflected in the current and capital accounts?

10. If the U.S. spends $200 billion more than it produces, what does the trade deficit (imports − exports) equal?

TERMS FOR STUDY

appreciation and depreciation
   of a currency
balance-of-payment account
capital and current accounts
devaluation and revaluation
   of a fixed exchange rate

fixed exchange rate
foreign exchange rate
flexible (or floating) exchange
   rates
interest rate parity
purchasing power parity

PRACTICAL APPLICATION

1. For each of the following events, determine whether it is *supply* or *demand* for the dollar that is affected, whether the curve shifts to the *left* or to the *right,* and whether an *increase* or a *decrease* in the value of the dollar results.
   Event A: Rambo Part IV sells big in Europe.
   Event B: Americans flock to Britain.
   Event C: American stocks and bonds sell well in Europe.
   Event D: Japan builds a factory in Iowa.
   Event E: American interest rates move above those of other nations.
   Event F: American monetary policy becomes more expansionary, increasing the U.S. price level.
   Event G: Americans buy more French wine.

2. The exchange rate for the dollar is 0.90 British pounds per dollar and 260 yen per dollar.
   a. How many dollars will it take to buy 1 pound? 1 yen?
   b. What will a $12,000 Chevrolet cost in Britain? In Japan?
   c. What will a suit costing 200 pounds cost in the U.S.? A 20,000-yen suit?

3. If the exchange rate for the dollar changes from Question 2's values to 0.80 pounds and 300 yen, then answer questions (a) through (c) above, plus:
   d. How has the dollar appreciated or depreciated against the pound and the yen?

4. How would you treat the following transactions in the balance-of-payments accounts? Are they credits or debits? Are they in the current or capital accounts?
   a. A Californian wine maker sells wine to France.
   b. A Californian buys a Toyota car made in Japan.
   c. Foreigners earn interest on the U.S. treasury bills they hold.
   d. Arabs buy farmland in Kansas.
   e. An American company builds a factory in Hong Kong.

5. Two countries, A and B, produce and sell only wheat. In Country A, a ton of wheat sells for 20 Ables. In Country B, it sells for 5 Babels.
   a. If there are no trade barriers or transportation costs, what must the exchange rate be for Ables?
   b. What if the exchange rate is higher?
   c. Lower? (Hint: Use the doctrine of purchasing power parity.)

6. Some economists view trade flows as reflecting capital flows. If so, how will the following events affect the net exports of these countries?
   Event A: New investment opportunities develop in Canada.
   Event B: Sweden imposes higher taxes on its businesses.
   Event C: Poland suffers a crop failure viewed as being a temporary setback.

7. Suppose a British bond pays 15%: it costs 1,000 pounds and will pay back 1,150 pounds in one year. The current U.S. exchange rate is 2.0 £/$ and is expected to increase 5% by next year to 2.10 £/$.
   a. What is the expected rate of return on this bond *in dollars?*
   b. How much would an equivalent U.S. bond have to pay to beat this rate?

8. A nation having a fixed exchange rate has been running a deficit in its balance of payments. It is running short of foreign currency reserves. It wants to get out of this problem.
   a. Has it overvalued or undervalued its currency?
   b. If it changes its exchange rate, will it devalue or revalue its currency?
   c. If, instead, it changes its monetary policy to get rid of this deficit, will it increase or decrease its money supply?
   d. Alternatively, if it changes its fiscal policy, will it raise or lower taxes?

9. Japan has one of the highest saving rates in the world (it saves about 30% of its income, compared with the U.S.'s 6%). How will this likely affect its

net exports? Its balance on its current account? The United States has condemned Japan for saving so much. If Japan saved less, would the U.S. be worse or better off?

10. Assume that because of the U.S.'s low rate of inflation, foreigners want to hold more dollars (since dollars hold their value better than the foreigners' own currency).
   a. What will happen to the U.S. trade deficits? Exchange rates?
   b. If the U.S. money supply remains unchanged, what will happen to aggregate demand (using the Monetarist Model)?

ANSWERS

KNOW THE CONCEPTS

1. Foreigners demand U.S. dollars to buy U.S. goods, services, and assets. U.S. citizens supply U.S. dollars (exchanging them for foreign currency) to buy foreign goods, services, and assets.

2. No. If one currency appreciates against the other, the other has depreciated.

3. One nation's exports are another nation's imports. So summing over all nations, exports equal imports.

4. Because in the simple purchasing power parity model, the exchange rate changes to assure that domestic goods and imported goods sell at the same price (there thus being *one price* for the same goods).

5. It reflects how much what the U.S. owes the rest of the world has changed in a year. When the U.S. owes more, the balance is positive. It reflects whether capital is flowing into the U.S. (then it's positive) or out (then it's negative).

6. Imports become cheaper and exports cost more abroad.

7. An overvalued currency results in balance-of-payments deficits. A higher exchange rate makes imports cheaper and benefits consumers who buy imports.

8. No. It can have only two of the three.

9. A nation can spend more than it produces only by importing more than it exports. Its net exports are thus negative: Its current account will be negative. In terms of capital flows, it has to borrow to pay for its excess spending: Its capital account will be positive.

10. $200 billion.

PRACTICAL APPLICATION

1. *Event A:* Demand, Right, Increase.
   Event B: Supply, Right, Decrease.
   Event C: Demand, Right, Increase.
   Event D: Demand, Right, Increase.
   Event E: Demand, Right, Increase.
   Event F: Demand, Left, Decrease; Supply, Right, Decrease.
   Event G: Supply, Right, Decrease.

2. **a.** 1.11 $/£. and .00384 $/yen.
   b. 10,800 pounds and 3,120,000 yen.
   c. British suit: $222.22. Japanese suit: $79.92.

3. **a.** 1.25 $/£ and .00333 $/yen.
   b. 9,600 pounds (it's cheaper than in Question 2).
   3,600,000 yen (it's more expensive than in Question 2).
   c. British suit: $250 (it's more expensive than in Question 2).
   Japanese suit: $66.67 (it's cheaper than in Question 2).
   d. Against the pound, the dollar has depreciated. Against the yen, the dollar has appreciated. Note the effect on import and export prices!

4. **a.** Credit. Current account.
   b. Debit. Current account.
   c. Debit. Current account.
   d. Credit. Capital account.
   e. Debit. Capital account.

5. **a.** 0.25 Babels per Able. This assures that Country B's wheat sells for 20 Ables in Country A and that A's wheat sells for 5 Babels in B.
   b. If Ables are overvalued (say at .5 Babels per Able), B's wheat will be cheaper (only 10 Ables). A's citizens will want to import wheat from B and will try to exchange their Ables for Babels. The increase in demand for Babels will increase the value of the Babel and reduce the value of the Able back to 0.25.
   c. If Ables are undervalued (say at 0.1), A's wheat will be cheaper (only 2 Babels). B's citizens will demand A's wheat and thus demand more Ables to buy it with: Ables will appreciate back to 0.25.

6. *Event A:* Canada's net exports will be negative. To get the Canadian dollars to invest in Canada, other nations must sell more to Canada than they buy.
   Event B: Sweden's net exports will be positive as capital leaves.
   Event C: Poland's net exports will be negative as Poland borrows to tide itself over this crisis.

7. **a.** In dollars: you invest $500 today to get $547.62 in one year: a 9.5% return. As an approximation, the net U.S. interest rate on foreign bonds equals:

Net U.S. Interest = Foreign Interest Rate − Expected % Appreciation of
   Rate on Foreign   Dollar (against Foreign
   Bonds   Currency).

   b. You would invest in the U.S. bond when it pays 9.5% or better.

8. a. Overvalued.
   b. Devalue.
   c. Decrease.
   d. Raise.

9. When Japan's savings exceed domestic investment opportunities, as is the case, Japan will have a positive net export balance (as it invests its excess savings in the rest of the world). Its current account will be positive. Japan invests much of its savings in the U.S. This helps increase the U.S.'s capital stock, productivity, and future growth rates. Japan also buys government bonds, which allows the U.S. government to spend more and delay tax payments until later. This is also positive, unless our government unwisely spends what it borrows (but this is hardly Japan's fault, nor would Japan's saving less correct this problem).

10. a. Foreigners will sell more good to the U.S. than they buy back, creating a larger U.S. trade deficit. The increase in demand for dollars will cause the dollar to appreciate.
    b. Any increase in money demand reduces aggregate demand.

APPENDIX

GLOSSARY

absolute advantage ability to produce a good with fewer inputs

accelerationist theory theory that unemployment cannot be permanently reduced through inflation

accounting profits profits ignoring implicit costs. Equals total revenue less explicit costs.

actual or realized investment total investment spending, including unsold output put into inventory

added buyer effect a lower price for a good attracts new buyers into a market, increasing its quantity demanded.

aggregate demand total real quantity of goods and services demanded in an economy

aggregate demand curve curve showing how aggregate demand increases when the price level of all goods and services falls

aggregate supply total real quantity of goods and services produced in an economy

aggregate supply curve (long run) a vertical curve showing in the long run (when costs have adjusted to price changes) that aggregate supply equals the full-employment level of output, no matter what the price level is

aggregate supply curve (short run) curve showing how aggregate supply increases in the short run when prices go up but factor costs don't change

allocative efficiency (also termed "pareto efficiency") when no possible trade or reallocation of goods and inputs will make some better off without making others worse off

appreciation when it takes more of another nation's currency to purchase a nation's currency

assets what people own or what other people owe them

average tax rate percent of income paid in taxes

backward-bending supply curve of labor a curve showing that as real hourly wages go up, workers first supply more and then fewer hours of work.

balanced-budget multiplier number that a change in government spending must be multiplied by to get resulting change in *GNP when* taxes increase the same amount as government spending

balance-of-payment account account made up of two accounts that keep track of goods, services, and assets flowing in and out of a nation. See also **capital account** and **current account.**

barter trade without money

bilateral monopoly market where a monopsony and monopoly deal with each other

bond IOU issued by a borrower promising to pay a fixed amount of dollars on specified dates to the holder of the bond

breakeven price price at which the firm just covers its costs

built-in stabilizers government spending that automatically increases and taxes that automatically decrease when *GNP* falls

businesses producers of goods and services

capital stock of plants, equipment, inventory, and other resources of production useful for more than one year

capital account account keeping track of physical and financial assets flowing on net into a country

capture hypothesis hypothesis that regulatory agencies tend to be "captured" by the industry they regulate and act on the industry's behalf rather than the consumers'

cartel an arrangement among sellers in a market to jointly set price and output

cartel cheating problem all collusive agreements suffer from the tendency of each member to cut its price and take a bigger share of the market.

coase theorem theory that people can get rid of any market failure by bargaining among themselves when transaction costs are low

collusion attempt, either explicit or implicit, to not compete

commodity money a widely traded good valued both for its use as a medium of exchange and for itself. The main example is gold.

comparative advantage ability to produce a good at a lower relative cost

compensating wage differentials differences in money wages compensating for differences in nonmonetary aspects of work (such as differences in working conditions and fringe benefits)

complementary inputs inputs used closely together. When the price of one goes up, less of both will be used even if output is unchanged.

complements two goods that go together (such as peanut butter and jelly). When the price of one goes up, the quantity demanded of the other goes down.

constant-cost industry industry with perfectly elastic long-run supply curve

constant returns to scale when long-run average total cost stays the same as output expands. Results when a given increase in all inputs increases output in the same proportion.

consumer surplus what consumers are willing to pay for a good minus what they do pay

consumption household spending on consumption goods and services

consumption function function showing consumption at different levels of disposable income

consumption goods goods and services that are consumed or used up within the year, such as food and electricity. (Although in practice, many goods counted as consumption goods last longer, such as dresses, cars, and toasters.)

contradictory gap see *GNP* gap.

control variable variable that decision-maker can increase or decrease to get the best net benefit or profit. For example, a control variable for a firm is the output that it produces.

cost-push inflation inflation caused by upward shift in the aggregate supply curve. Usually a reaction to demand-pull inflation.

credible threat threat that in the short run seems irrational (as it harms the person making it) but is credible because it results in long-run profits. An example is a dominant firm's threat to cut its price and drive out of business any competitor charging less than it does.

cross elasticity of demand responsiveness of the quantity demanded to a change in the price of *another* good. Percent change in quantity demanded of a good due to a 1% increase in the price of another good.

crowding out decreases in private investment spending (which is mainly financed by borrowing) due to increases in government borrowing (that push up interest rates)

current account account keeping track of goods and services flowing on net out of a country.

cyclical unemployment unemployment due to downturns in the economy

deadweight loss loss to society without any offsetting gains

deadweight loss of a tax total loss to producers and consumers from a tax minus tax revenues collected. Also termed "excess burden of a tax."

decreasing-cost industry an industry with a long-run supply curve that is downward sloping

"deficits do not matter" theory that equilibrium income will be the same if government spending is paid for with taxes or borrowings

deflation decrease in price level

deflationary gap see *GNP* gap.

demand curve any downward sloping curve that shows a greater quantity of a good demanded at a lower price, provided that other determinants of demand (such as income and prices of other goods) are held constant

demand-pull inflation inflation caused by rightward shift in aggregate demand curve

depreciation decline in the value of an asset over a given time, usually a year. (For calculating national income, depreciation is called the "capital consumption allowance.")

depreciation (of a currency) when the value of a currency goes down (i.e., it takes less of another nation's currency to purchase it)

desired or planned investment total investment spending that businesses *want* to make. It does *not* include unwanted inventory accumulation.

discount rate interest rate the Federal Reserve system charges banks that borrow funds from it

discretionary economic policy changing economic policy to actively affect the economy

discrimination workers not getting the same well-paying jobs or getting less pay than others with the same ability because of their race, sex, or other characteristic not related to productivity

diseconomies of scale when long-run average total cost goes up as output expands. Results when a given increase in all input results in a smaller than proportional increase in output.

disinflation decrease in rate of inflation

disposable income after-tax income available for consumption spending and saving by households

economic profit payment in excess of what is necessary to get something done. Economic Profits = Total Revenue − (Explicit + Implicit Costs).

economic rent any payment to a factor in excess of its opportunity cost. Also, payment to factor in perfectly inelastic supply.

economics study of how people choose among alternative uses of their scarce resources

economies of scale when long-run average total cost falls as output expands. Results when a given increase in all inputs results in a more than proportional increase in output.

effectiveness lag time it takes for government action to affect economy

efficiency when people produce all that can be, given their resources. To produce more of one good, an efficient economy must produce less of other goods and is on its production possibility curve.

elastic demand when a given percent increase in price causes a greater percent decrease in the quantity demanded, decreasing total revenue

elasticity responsiveness of one variable to the change in another, both changes expressed as percents. The elasticity of Q with respect to P is the percent change in Q for every 1% change in P.

equation of exchange $MV = PQ$, or money times velocity equals price times output

equilibrium in aggregate demand when spending equals income

equilibrium price price at which the quantity demanded equals the quantity sold. Also termed the "market clearing price."

expansionary gap see *GNP* **gap.**

explicit costs dollar costs actually paid out

exports goods and services sold by domestic citizens to other nations

factor of production any input used to produce output (the main factors being land, labor, and capital)

fiat money a money not backed by gold or any other valuable good. For example, the dollar.

final good good produced for final use and not for resale within the year.

fiscal policy policy involving government spending and taxation

fixed costs costs that neither increase nor decrease as output changes

fixed exchange rate exchange rate set and supported by a nation's government, which buys and sells its currency at that rate.

flexible exchange rate an exchange rate that is set by free market forces without government intervention. Also called "floating exchange rate."

foreign exchange rate the price of one nation's currency in terms of another nation's currency

45° line a valuable reference line since all points on this line have the same value on the vertical and horizontal axes

fractional reserve banking banking system where banks lend money out they owe their depositors.

free good good that is not scarce; good whose supply exceeds demand at a zero price

free-rider problem while everyone benefits from a public good, each tries to be a free rider by not paying for it. As a result, the good may not be supplied in a free market.

frictional unemployment unemployment due to the normal workings of an economy

full-employment deficit what the deficit *would be* if the economy were at full employment (also called the "active" or "structural" deficit).

full-employment level of output output where the demand and supply for labor (and other factors) are equal, there being neither a shortage nor a surplus of workers. Also termed "potential output."

full wage total monetary value of a job (per period); the sum of money wages plus the monetary value of all the nonmonetary aspects of work.

Giffen good good whose demand decreases when price goes down. The good must be an inferior good for this to occur.

GNP gap gap between actual and full-employment output. When output is above its full-employment level, there is an "inflationary" or "expansionary" gap; when it's below, a "deflationary" or "contractionary" gap.

government debt total accumulated borrowings of the government

government deficit excess of government spending over taxes collected (for a year)

government surplus excess of taxes over government spending (for a year).

graph visual presentation of how two variables are related to each other

gross national product (*GNP*) total money value of all final goods and services produced by an economy within a given period, usually a year

hold-out program whenever the consent of a higher percent of people is needed, each person has a greater incentive to hold out his or her consent, with the result that less is achieved.

households owners of all factors in the economy. Households provide the services of labor, land, capital, and ownership to businesses.

human capital skills and ability acquired through investment in schooling and on-the-job training

implementation lag time it takes for the government to implement its policy and take action

implicit costs costs incurred because of alternative opportunities given up. For a firm, these include the costs of its owners' time and investment.

imports goods and services that are bought by domestic citizens and are produced by other nations

income highest level of sustainable consumption. Income minus consumption equals addition to wealth.

income effect effect on the quantity demanded of a good when real income changes

income effect of a price change a lower price for a good is like giving consumers more income. Some of this "income" may go for buying more units of the good, increasing its quantity demanded.

income elasticity of demand percent change in quantity demanded for every 1% change in income

income velocity see **velocity**.

increasing-cost industry industry with rising long-run supply curve

inelastic demand when a given percent increase in the price causes a smaller percent decrease in the quantity demanded, increasing total revenue

inferior good a good that people demand less of when their income goes up

inflation rise in general level of prices. Usually refers to persistent rise in prices over time.

inflation rate percent increase in price level over a year

inflationary gap see *GNP* **gap**.

inflationary premium addition to real interest rate to compensate savers for expected loss in purchasing power from inflation

inflationary premium effect of money supply growth higher and expected growth rates in the money supply increase interest rates.

injections any form of spending other than consumption. Includes investment and government spending.

innovation finding a better way to do something, including a cheaper way to produce a good or a more valued good to produce

input see **factor of production**.

interest payment for use of funds over a certain period of time

interest rate parity when capital flows between nations until all nations pay the same interest rates, adjusting for the risk of default and the risk that the nation's currency will depreciate

inverse relationship see **negative relationship.**

joint products two goods produced together because it is difficult to produce them separately (e.g., leather and beef)

kinked demand curve hypothetical demand curve that an oligopolic firm faces when other firms maintain their price when it raises its price but match its price when it lowers its price

labor force all persons employed or unemployed

Laffer curve curve showing that as the marginal tax rate increases, total tax revenues first increase and then fall as the marginal rate becomes excessive

law of comparative advantage nations are better off when they produce goods they have a comparative advantage in supplying

law of demand quantity demanded and price are inversely related—more is demanded at a lower price, less at a higher price (other things being equal)

law of diminishing marginal returns after some point, as a firm adds more and more units of an input, the input's marginal physical product diminishes (i.e., it adds less to total output than before)

law of diminishing marginal utility as people consume more of a good in a given period, its marginal utility declines

law of equal marginal utility per dollar the highest utility is achieved when the last dollar spent on each good has the same marginal utility

law of increasing relative cost as more of a good is produced, its opportunity cost rises

law of one price see **purchasing power parity.**

law of supply quantity supplied and price usually are directly related—more is supplied at a higher price, less at a lower price (other things being equal)

leakage any allocation of income that is not directly spent on goods and services. Includes taxes and savings.

liabilities what people owe others

lifecycle model of consumption consumption spending is a function of people's expected future income and spending, including the effects of age and retirement

liquidity ease with which an asset (such as a stock or bond) can be converted into cash

liquidity effect of money supply growth when people do not expect higher inflation, an increase in the money supply reduces interest rates and increases investment spending

logrolling the trading of votes to get positions favorable only to minority interest groups voted in

long run period when firm can change all inputs, including its plant size and equipment. Also, period when firms can enter or exit an industry.

long-run neutrality of money see **neutrality of money.**

M1 measure of the money supply counting only cash held by the public plus checking accounts

macroeconomics study of the economy as a whole, including the causes of the business cycle, unemployment, and inflation

marginal analysis solving economic problems by using small steps and evaluating the costs and benefits of each marginal step

marginal benefit increase in total benefit due to one more unit of output, labor, or other control variable being increased

marginal cost addition to total cost due to increasing output by one unit

marginal factor cost *(MFC)* addition to total cost when one additional unit of an input is employed

marginal physical product *(MPP)* addition to total physical output due to an added unit of an input

marginal propensity to consume *(MPC)* added consumption spending due to $1 more of disposable income

marginal propensity to save *(MPS)* added savings due to $1 more of disposable income

marginal revenue increase in total revenue due to additional unit of output

marginal revenue product *(MRP)* addition to total revenue when one additional unit of an input (such as labor or capital) is employed

marginal tax rate percent of additional income paid in taxes

marginal utility addition to total utility from consuming one more unit of a good

marginal value value of least importance that a unit of a good (or resource) is currently being put to; the loss suffered due to one less unit of the good.

median voter model when two people are running for office, they will position themselves near the opinions of the median voter

microeconomics study of factors determining the relative prices of goods and inputs

minimum efficient scale level of output where long-run average total cost achieves its minimum

monetary base essentially all the cash in the economy. The sum of bank reserves and currency held by the public. Also termed "high-powered money."

monetary policy policy determining level and growth rate of the money supply

money the medium of exchange; what people use to pay for goods and services

monopolistic competition market like that of perfect competition except sellers sell a closely related but not identical product

monopoly only seller of a good with no close substitutes

monopsony a firm so dominant in a factor market that its hiring decisions affect the input's market price. Faces higher input price as it employs more.

mutual interdependence when one firm's actions affect another firm's in the same industry significantly, and vice-versa

natural monopoly industry having such large economies of scale that one firm can meet all the demand and still not achieve its most efficient scale

natural rate of unemployment level of unemployment when people's expectations about prices match the actual level of prices. (Occurs at full employment when government and union interventions are absent.)

negative externalities activities imposing uncompensated costs upon others. Also termed "external diseconomies."

negative relationship X and Y are negatively related if when X goes up, Y goes down and vice versa. (Also called an "inverse relationship.")

net investment addition to the capital stock of the nation. Equals gross investment minus depreciation.

neutrality of money in the long run, a larger money supply has no effect on output or on relative prices

Nominal *GNP* *GNP* valued at prices belonging to the same period goods were produced in (referred to also as "*GNP* in current dollars")

nominal interest rate actual rate of interest; the extra *money* borrowers have to pay back to lenders, in excess of the loan amount expressed as percent per year of the loan.

nominal shock shock changing the price level but leaving relative prices unaffected. (An example is an unanticipated increase in the money supply.)

nominal value value of goods in terms of their prices at the time they were produced and sold. Also called "value in terms of current dollars"

nominal wage hourly money earnings

non-price competition competition between goods on aspects other than price (such as quality and service)

non-price rationing any method of equating supply and demand other than price. Its two main forms are waiting lines and discrimination.

normal good a good that people demand more of when their income goes up

normal profits long-run accounting profits in an industry, just covering the owner's implicit costs

Okun's law for every 2% real *GNP* is below its potential full-employment level over a year's time, the unemployment rate will increase by 1%.

oligopoly market with few sellers and medium to high barriers of entry

open market operation main method government changes money supply. The buying and selling of government securities by the Federal Open Market Committee (FOMC).

opportunity cost value of best alternative that had to be given up in order to undertake a given course of action

overvalued currency currency whose exchange rate is above its free market equilibrium rate

payment-in-kind payment in goods or services rather than in money

perfect competition whenever there is enough competition that no one seller can raise its price without losing all its customers to other sellers

perfectly contestable markets markets with unimpeded and costless entry and exit of firms

perfect price discrimination when seller charges a different price for each unit of the good that's equal to the unit's demand price

permanent income expected average value of future earnings

permanent-income hypothesis consumption spending is a constant fraction of peoples' permanent income

Phillips curve curve showing trade-off between inflation and unemployment when the public's expected rate of inflation is unchanged

positive externalities activities creating benefits for others who don't pay for the benefits. Also termed "external economies."

positive relationship *X* and *Y* are positively related if when *X* goes up, *Y* goes up. And when *X* goes down, *Y* goes down.

precautionary demand for money money demand due to money holdings allowing people to meet unforeseen expenses

present value value of future dollars in terms of what they are worth today. The loan amount one could borrow today and pay back with the future dollars.

price ceiling law imposed by the government prohibiting the price from going above a certain level

price discrimination the selling of the same good at different prices. See also **perfect price discrimination.**

price elasticity of demand percent change in quantity demanded for every 1% change in price (both percent changes stated as absolute values)

price elasticity of supply percent change in quantity supplied for every 1% change in the price

price floor law imposed by the government prohibiting the price from falling below a certain level

price index cost of a market basket of goods in a given year expressed as a percent of its cost in some base year. When the index is 140, the basket costs 140% of its base-year cost.

price searchers buyers or sellers having large enough shares of a market such that when they buy or sell more, the market price changes

price takers buyers or sellers whose individual actions have no effect on market price (and thus they "take" the market price as given)

private cost cost borne by those producing a good

problem of the commons abuse of resource when no one owns it and thus no one has an incentive to keep it up

producer surplus what producers are paid less their marginal costs

production possibility curve graph showing combinations of goods an individual, firm, or an economy is capable of producing. Also termed "production possibility frontier."

progressive tax system tax system under which those with higher incomes are subject to higher marginal and average tax rates

public good good whose consumption by one person does not diminish its consumption by others (e.g., national defense)

purchasing power parity when exchange rates between nations change so that goods, both domestic and imported, sell for the same price. Also called the "law of one price" because different units of the same good tend to sell for the same price in any given market.

quantity demanded maximum quantity of a good buyers are willing and able to buy at a given price (during a fixed period of time)

quantity supplied maximum quantity of a good sellers are willing and able to supply at a given price (during a fixed period of time)

quantity theory of money theory that uses the equation of exchange to make predictions by assuming the annual change in velocity is small and predictable

quota a limit on the amount of an import

random error unpredictable error or mistake

rational expectations expectations that are unbiased and based upon the best available information

real business cycle theory theory that main causes of the business cycle are from real sources (such as changes in tax rates and technology) rather than shifts in aggregate demand

real *GNP* *GNP* valued at prices from a given year (currently, from 1972; also known as *GNP* in constant dollars)

real interest rate percent increase in purchasing power (i.e., in real goods and services) that borrowers pay back to lenders. Equals the nominal rate of interest minus the expected rate of inflation.

real shocks shocks affecting the relative price of goods and inputs, e.g., unanticipated changes in taste, technology, or factor supplies.

real value measure of value removing the effects of inflation. The value of a good (or goods) in terms of their price from some given year (called the "base year"). Also called "value in terms of constant dollars."

real wage hourly earnings of workers stated in real terms (equals money wage divided by price index)

real wealth effect increase in aggregate demand due to lower price level (the lower price level increasing the real value of nominal assets, especially money, causing people to spend more). Also called the "real balance effect."

recession when output falls for two consecutive quarters

recognition lag time it takes for the government to recognize that something is wrong with the economy

relative price Good A's relative price tells how much of Good B must be given to get one more unit of Good A.

rent see **economic rent**.

rent-seeking activity costing resources and time with the object of obtaining resources or laws having economic rents; considered socially wasteful as this activity adds nothing to total output.

required reserve ratio fraction of their deposits banks must keep at the Federal Reserve Bank

savings unconsumed portion of disposable income

scarcity condition that exists when current resources are inadequate to provide for all of people's wants

self-correcting mechanism means by which an economy gets to full employment without government intervention

shift in autonomous spending initial shift in spending that occurs at a given level of income

shift in demand change in demand curve such that a different quantity is demanded at each price. Curves shift only when some variable *other than price* changes. Also called "change in demand."

shock an unanticipated event. See also **real shocks**.

shortage quantity demanded exceeds quantity supplied (caused by price being below market equilibrium price).

short run period when the firm can change (either increasing or decreasing) some but *not all* of its inputs

shutdown price price below which firm shuts down

slope how much the variable on the vertical (or side) axis changes when the variable on the horizontal (or bottom) axis increases by one unit

social benefit benefit all persons get from a good

social cost cost all persons pay for a good

speculative demand for money money demand due to money holdings being safer than many other assets

spending multiplier number by which an initial increase in spending must be multiplied to get the resulting change in total spending

spill-over effect higher union wages causing those losing their jobs in union plants to seek jobs in nonunion plants, forcing nonunion wages down

stagflation inflation and recession occurring at the same time

structural unemployment unemployment caused by changes in demand or technology seriously affecting certain industries, occupations, or areas of the country so that only with very high costs can workers relocate and/or retrain for new careers

substitute inputs two inputs that to some degree can replace one another. When price of one goes up, the firm uses more of the other input per unit of output.

substitute products two alternative goods that could be produced with the same (or very similar) set of inputs. (Examples are gasoline and heating oil.)

substitutes two goods that compete with each other (such as butter and margarine). When the price of one good goes up, the quantity demanded of the other also goes up

substitution effect of a price change a lower relative price means a lower opportunity cost of buying the good, which encourages buyers to buy more of the good (holding real income constant)

sunk costs costs that can't be avoided

supply curve curve showing relationship between price and quantity of a good that suppliers are willing to supply. Usually upward sloping; the exception is in a decreasing-cost industry.

supply-side economics theory emphasizing the negative effect of government taxation on aggregate supply

surplus quantity supplied exceeds quantity demanded (caused by price exceeding market equilibrium price)

tariff tax on imports

tax-based income policy (TIP) policy calling for the government to increase taxes on firms and workers who raise prices too much and reduce taxes for those who keep their prices within guidelines

tax incidence who actually pays a tax

tax multiplier number that a tax change must be multiplied by to get resulting change in *GNP.* A tax multiplier of -5 implies that a $200 increase in taxes will reduce *GNP* by $1,000.

tax shifting shifting tax one pays onto others. For example, firm raising its price shifts tax onto consumers.

terms-of-trade relative price for goods offered in marketplace

theory of public choice economic theory of how governments act

tiebout hypothesis theory that smaller governments and greater mobility of citizens and firms between cities, states, and nations produce more efficient government

total revenue total sales (usually per year)

total surplus excess of the total value of a quantity of a good over its total cost; sum of the difference between demand price and supply price added across all units of a good being bought and produced. Equals the consumer surplus plus the producer surplus.

total utility total satisfaction derived from consuming goods and services

trade-off when satisfying *more* of one need means satisfying *less* of another

transaction demand for money money demand due to money holding's allowing people to buy and sell goods more easily

transfer payment payment for which no goods or services are received in return. Examples include gifts and food stamps

unbiased forecast forecast that is neither wrong on average nor systematically wrong

undervalued currency currency whose exchange rate is below its free market equilibrium rate

unemployment rate percent of the labor force that is unemployed. One is unemployed if actively seeking work or waiting to be recalled or to report to a job.

unitary demand when a given percent increase in price causes the exact same percent decrease in the quantity demanded, leaving total revenue unchanged

value added value of a business's output minus its purchases from other businesses

value-added tax (VAT) tax on a company's value added

variable cost cost of all inputs the firm increases in the short run to produce more

velocity number of times an average dollar is used in a year to buy final goods and services (also called "income velocity")

voting paradox how a majority will vote on a set of issues can be changed by altering the order issues are presented in.

wage-threat effect higher union wages causing nonunion employers to also pay higher wages to reduce threat of being unionized

wealth net value of all the assets a person owns (including the value of his or her skills, i.e., the value of all future earnings)

ELEMENTS OF ACCOUNTING

Every business is interested in two things:

1. *How much is the firm currently worth?* The answer to this question is given in its balance sheet.

2. *How much did the firm make last year?* The answer to this question is given in its income statement.

THE BALANCE SHEET

A company's worth is:

$$\text{Net Worth} = \text{Total Assets} - \text{Total Liabilities}.$$

A company's **total assets** is the value of all it owns. This includes its holdings of cash, its current inventory of goods and materials, as well as its land, plant, and equipment.

Total liabilities is everything the firm owes others. Most firms borrow to buy their assets; the amount a firm still owes its creditors is part of its liabilities. Another common liability is what a firm owes its workers when the workers retire and start drawing on their pensions.

Net worth is the answer to the question "How much is the firm currently worth;" net worth equals the excess of what the firm owns over what it owes.

THE INCOME STATEMENT

A company's net income is:

$$\text{Net Income} = \text{Total Revenues} - \text{Total Cost}.$$

Total revenues equal total sales. Unlike national income accounting, most firms do not count unsold output as part of its revenues (the exception is when the firm takes several years to build a good, such as a ship; in this case, future revenues from the yet-to-be-sold and uncompleted ship may be allocated over the years it takes to build).

Total cost includes all material and labor cost used to produce the current period's sales. In addition, the firm's machinery and plant has been worn down; the cost of this wear and tear is depreciation.

Net income after taxes is the amount "the firm made last year." Net income after taxes represents an addition to the firm's net worth.

HOW TO OVERSTATE PROFIT

Firms sometimes try to overstate their profits in several ways:

1. *Understate Depreciation:* By overstating how long a machine will last or by understating how much its value has depreciated, firms increase their reported profits. For example, some computer leasing firms once pretended that their computers would last ten years while in fact technological progress was making them obsolete within three years.

   Inflation increases the value of wear and tear, so by ignoring inflation (and instead valuing depreciation on the basis of the equipment's original cost), the firm overstates its profits.

2. *Overstate the Value of Increased Inventory:* Suppose a firm can't sell all its output. That may indicate that its output may never be sold. In this case, the firm should add the cost of producing this unsold output to the current period's costs. But a firm might "pretend" this excess output will eventually be sold and wait to record the cost of producing it to the time when it will be sold. This increases the firm's current reported profits.

3. *Ignore New Liabilities:* When certain liabilities are incurred, some part of them should be reported and/or recorded as a cost in the income statement. But some firms have ignored such liabilities (examples are potential lawsuits and increases in pension liabilities).

4. *Overstate Sales:* A firm sometimes gets new sales by lending buyers money to buy the firm's goods. The firm then records these as sales without taking into account that some of its buyers will likely not be able to pay back what they borrowed. A manufacturer of bowling alley equipment pulled this trick and nearly went bankrupt when bowling alley after bowling alley folded. But it had a wonderful income statement up to that point.

It should be noted that for income tax purposes, firms try to *understate* profits, using the opposites of these techniques.

SOURCES OF ECONOMIC DATA

Some of the major sources of economic data are listed below. Some you can get free; some are available at most libraries. You are encouraged to at least get the money supply data from the St. Louis Federal Reserve Bank (see below).

1. *Barron's*
National Business and Financial Weekly
World Financial Center
200 Liberty Street
New York, NY 10281

weekly, $82 per year

If you are or intend to be a business professional, you should be reading this and the *Wall Street Journal* (see below).

2. *Economic Trends*
Federal Reserve Bank of Cleveland
P.O. Box 6387
Cleveland, OH 44101

monthly, free

Supplies charts on most major economic variables, along with helpful commentary.

3. *Federal Reserve Chart Book*
Publication Services
Room MP-510, Mail Stop 138
Board of Governors of the Federal
    Reserve
Washington, D.C. 20551

quarterly, $7 per year

This publication presents nine-year charts of the major financial and economic series (including *GNP*, prices, durable goods, debt, and foreign exchange rates). This allows a longer-term perspective of where the economy is and has been.

4. *National Economic Trends*
The Federal Reserve Bank of St. Louis
P.O. Box 442
St. Louis, MO 63166

monthly, free

National Economic Trends supplies charts and data on *GNP*, prices, costs, spending, and inventories.

5. *Statistical Abstract of the United States*
Superintendent of Documents
U.S. Publishing Office
Washington, D.C. 20402

yearly, $28 per year

This has over 1,500 tables on subjects ranging from population, to finance, to foreign commerce, and data on almost every aspect of our economy that is collected by our government. It is a good place to begin any research project, as it tells you where to go for more information.

6. *Survey of Current Business*
Superintendent of Documents
U.S. Publishing Office
Washington, D.C. 20402

monthly, $30 per year

This has too much detail for most persons, but is perfect for anyone who must keep up with the details of our economy.

7. *U.S. Financial Data*
The Federal Reserve Bank of St. Louis
P.O. Box 442
St. Louis, MO 63166

weekly, free

U.S. Financial Data is one of the best sources of monetary statistics reported in both chart and percent change form. Interest rates and other financial data are also presented.

8. *The Wall Street Journal*
200 Burnett Road
Chicopee, MA 01021

daily

No list would be complete without mentioning *The Wall Street Journal*. The editorial page is an on-going lesson in economics.

BUSINESS CYCLE INDICATORS

Each month, the U.S. Department of Commerce publishes a series of economic indicators, including the widely followed leading, coincident, and lagging indicators. These are designed, respectively, to lead, coincide, and lag the business cycle. The components of each indicator are given in Table A-1. These components can be thought of as describing the business cycle.

Table A-1. Components of Business Cycle Indicators

Leading Index Components

1. Average weekly hours of production of nonsupervisory workers, manufacturing
2. Average weekly initial claims for unemployment insurance, State programs
3. Manufacturers' new orders in 1972 dollars, consumer goods and materials industries
4. Vendor performance, percent of companies receiving slower deliveries
5. Index of new business formations
6. Contracts and orders for plant and equipment in 1972 dollars
7. Change in manufacturing and trade inventories on hand and on order in 1972 dollars
8. Change in sensitive materials prices, smoothed
9. Index of stock prices, 500 common stocks
10. Money supply M2 in 1972 dollars
11. Change in business and consumer credit outstanding

Coincident Index Components

1. Employees on nonagricultural payrolls
2. Personal income less transfer payments in 1972 dollars
3. Index of industrial production
4. Manufacturing and trade sales in 1972 dollars

Lagging Index Components

1. Average duration of unemployment in weeks
2. Ratio, manufacturing and trade inventories to sales, in 1972 dollars
3. Index of labor cost per unit of output, manufacturing; actual data as a percent of trend
4. Average prime rate charged by banks
5. Commercial and industrial loans outstanding in 1972 dollars
6. Ratio, consumer installment credit outstanding to personal income

Before a recession, stock prices and the real money supply almost always decline (both of these being the most reliable indicators of what is to come). New orders, new businesses being formed, and housing permits decrease: an indication that aggregate demand is falling. Businesses typically cut back on the hours of work of their employees.

During a recession, firms move to cut back on their number of employees. Real sales and production fall.

At the end of the recession, the lagging indicators fall, thus predicting the end is in sight. Unemployment usually peaks *after* output has hit bottom. This is because firms typically do not let go of valued employees until they must, so changes in employment lag after changes in output. Interest rates also hit bottom after the economy has.

The opposite process occurs during an expansion. One popular rule of thumb is that the economy will turn (going into recession or expansion) when the leading indicators change direction for two consecutive months.

REVIEW AND ADDITIONAL MATERIAL

THE GEOMETRY OF PROFIT-MAXIMIZING

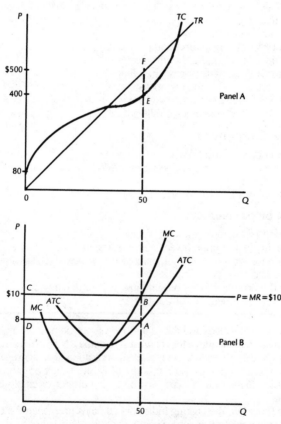

Figure A-1 Determining Profit Maximization

This material presents the graphical approach to analyzing the selection of the best output so as to maximize profits. It shows the relationship between total revenue and cost to marginal revenue and cost and how they should appear at the optimal level of output (where profits are maximized).

Figure A-1, Panel A, shows how total revenue and total costs increase with output for a competitive firm. As Q goes up 1 unit, TR increases by P; so TR is a straight line with a slope of P ($=MR$). TC starts out at TFC (of \$80) and increases by MC: The slope of the TC curve is MC.

The firm wants to select Q to maximize its profits, which is the vertical distance between TR and TC. When TR and TC are smooth lines curved in the manner shown, they will be furthest apart at the output level where both their slopes are the same: The firm will be maximizing profits at this output. In addition, since the slope of TR is MR and the slope of TC is MC, we have $MR = MC$ when the firm is maximizing profits. This occurs in Figure A-1 at an output of 50, where the vertical distance $TR - TC$ is biggest (and equal to \$100). F and E are \$100 apart. The firm's profit is \$100.

Panel B shows the same conditions in marginal terms. At 50 units of output, P ($=MR$) $= MC$ at \$10 and $Q = 50$. Area $ABCD$ equals \$100, the firm's profit. This area equals the base (output DA, or 50) times the height (AB or $P - ATC$ at $Q = 50$ is the average profit per unit of output, \$2).

$$\text{Output} \times \text{Average Profit} = \text{Total Profit.}$$

An increase in fixed costs shifts the TC curve up but leaves its slope at each Q unchanged. So the optimal Q stays the same. If fixed costs go up \$100 (to \$180), the TC curve will just touch the TR line at Point F. In Panel B, the ATC curve will intersect MC at Point B.
Some other points:

1. A straight line drawn from the origin to any point on the TC line (in Panel A) has a slope equal to the ATC of the corresponding level of output (Slope $=$ Rise/Run or $ATC = TC/Q$).

2. The straight line to TC with the smallest slope has a slope equal to the minimum ATC.

3. The area under the MC curve up to a given Q equals that Q's TVC (since $TVC =$ sum of MCs).

4. A review:
   Profit $= TR - TC = P \times Q - ATC \times Q$.
   Profit $= (P - ATC) \times Q$.
   Profit $= TR - TFC - TVC$.
   $TVC =$ Sum of MCs.
   $TC = TFC + TVC = TFC +$ Sum of MCs.
   $MC =$ Change in $TC =$ Change in TVC (when Q goes up 1).
   $MR =$ Change in TR (when Q goes up 1).
   $TR =$ Sum of MRs.
   Change in Profit (when Q goes up 1) $= MR - MC$.
   Profit $=$ Area between MR and MC curve $- TFC$.

THE ALGEBRA OF INCOME DETERMINATION IN THE KEYNESIAN MODEL

If you are called upon to solve for equilibrium income from algebraic (or numerical) formulas for the Keynesian model, use this procedure:

Key Procedure For Solving For Equilibrium Output

1. Write the consumption function (C) as a function of Q. Be sure to include the effect of taxes, if any.

2. Write the expression for total spending ($D = C + I + G$) using the consumption function from Step 1 and the expressions for I and G.

3. Write the income = spending equation, or Q = the equation from Step 2.

4. Collect terms. Solve for Q.

For example, suppose consumption spending has the following functional form:

$$C = 100 + .8Q.$$

This equation indicates that consumption equals $100 when output and income is 0, and that consumption spending increases $.80 for every $1 increase in Q. The $100 is called autonomous consumption spending, and 0.8 is the marginal propensity to consume (MPC). As it stands, this equation is in the form required by Step 1. But suppose we have:

$$C = 500 + .8(Q - T).$$

$Q - T$ is disposable income, where T is the tax revenue that the government collects. If $T = \$500$, we substitute this amount into this equation, and then rewrite the equation in the following manner:

$$C = 100 + .8Q.$$

The equation is now in the form required by Step 1.

Example: Income in a Simple Economy

PROBLEM   What is equilibrium income and output (Q), when $C = 100 + .8Q$ and $I = \$400$? ($G = T = NX = 0$).

SOLUTION   Following the steps in the key procedure, we have:
1. $C = 100 + 8Q$
2. $D = 100 + .8Q + 400$. (Recall that $D = C + I$.)
3. $Q = 100 + .8Q + 400$.
4. Collect terms: $Q = 500 + .8Q$
   Solve: $2Q = 500$
   $Q = 500/.2$
   $Q = 2,500$

Example: Equilibrium Income With Government Sector Added

PROBLEM What is Q, when $C = \overline{C} + b(Q - T), I = \overline{I} + iQ, G = \overline{G} + gQ$, and $T = \overline{T} + tQ$?

Note: The terms with bars over them are the autonomous, or fixed, components of the equation. For example, investment spending equals $\overline{I}$ when $Q = 0$; then, as Q increases by \$1, I increases by \$$i$. Government spending increases by \$$g$ for every \$1 increase in Q, and taxes increase by \$$t$ for every \$1 increase in Q.

SOLUTION Using the key procedure, we have:
1. $C = \overline{C} + b(Q - \overline{T} - tQ) = \overline{C} - b\overline{T} + b(1 - t)Q.$
2. $D = \overline{C} - b\overline{T} + b(1 - t)Q + \overline{I} + iQ + \overline{G} + gQ.$
3. $Q = \overline{C} + b\overline{T} + b(1 - t)Q + \overline{I} + iQ + \overline{G} + gQ.$
4. Combine terms: $Q = (\overline{C} - b\overline{T} + \overline{I} + \overline{G}) + [b(1 - t) + i + g]Q.$
   Solve: $\{1 - [b(1 - t) + i + g]\}Q = (\overline{C} - b\overline{T} + \overline{I} + \overline{G})$
   $$Q = \frac{\overline{C} - b\overline{T} + \overline{I} + \overline{G}}{1 - [b(1 - t) + i + g]}$$

In the first line of Step 4, the term in front of Q on the right-hand side of the equation is the Marginal Propensity to Spend *MP*Spend (the increase in total spending when national income increases by one dollar). A dollar added to spending is spent and respent according to the multiplier process formula:

$$1 + MPSpend + MPSpend^2 + MPSpend^3 + \ldots$$

which equals the spending multiplier: the spending multiplier is $1/(1 - MPSpend)$.

To get equilibrium Q, sum all the terms not multiplied by Q in Step 2 (this sum equals total spending when $Q = 0$) and then multiply this sum by the spending multiplier, $1/(1 - MPSpend)$. In effect, the spending at $Q = 0$ is multiplied by the spending multiplier to get equilibrium national income. This yields the equation in Step 4, with autonomous spending in the numerator and $(1 - MPSpend)$ in the denominator.

SUMMARY OF MACROECONOMIC MODELS

The following chart summarizes the results we've derived in Chapters 7 through 15. Each entry shows the effect of an increase in the fiscal or monetary variable mentioned; the effect of a decrease would be the opposite of the effects shown (for example, an increase in the money supply increases the price level, so a decrease in the money supply decreases the price level). Long-run results assume that the economy begins at full employment.

Table A-2. Summary of Macroeconomic Models

	Aggregate Demand	Effect on Aggregate Supply	Price Level	Output[1]
Keynesian Model (*Chapters 8, 10, 12*) Government Spending Up	+	0	+	+
Government Taxation Up	−	0	−	−
Autonomous Consumption, Investment, or Net Export Spending Up	+	0	+	+
Money Supply Up[2]	+	0	+	+
Monetarist Model (*Chapter 12*) Money Supply Up Short-run	+	0	+	+
Long-run	+	+	+	0
Government Borrowing[3]	+	0	+	+
Money Demand Up Short-run	−	0	−	−
Long-run	−	−	−	0

	Aggregate Demand	Effect on Aggregate Supply	Price Level	Output[1]
Rational Expectation Model (*Chapter 15*) Anticipated Increases in Aggregate Demand	+	+	+	0
Unanticipated Increases In Aggregate Demand	+	0	+	+
Government Borrowing Up "Deficits Don't Matter"	0	0	0	0
Constantly Changing Government Policies	?	−	?	−
Supply-Side Economics (*Chapter 10*) Marginal Tax Rates Up	0	−	+	−

[1]Once the economy reaches its capacity, output can longer be increased in any of these models. Also, in the long run, output will remain unchanged *unless* aggregate supply is affected. Because monetary policy has no effect on aggregate supply, it has no effect on output in the long run. On the other hand, fiscal policy (government spending and taxing) can change aggregate supply because taxes affect the incentive to work while government projects may enhance the productivity of the economy or, alternatively, waste the economy's resources.

[2]In the simple Keynesian model, an increase in the money supply only increases aggregate demand if it reduces interest rates, thereby stimulating investment spending and the economy.

[3]In the simple Monetarist model, more government borrowing only increases aggregate demand if it increases interest rates, thereby causing people to reduce their desired money holding (which in turn increases total spending).

INDEX